About the authors

DOUGLAS PAYNE was born in London, lived his early childhood in Northern Rhodesia and completed his secondary schooling in Norfolk - away from his family in Africa. During World War Two, he served as a Lieutenant in the King's African Rifles in Africa, Ceylon, Burma and Germany before completing a law degree at University College, London.

To his great delight, Oxford University offered him a position of distinction as Reader at All Souls College for some years, before he decided to migrate with his young family to Australia in 1963, to become Professor of Law at the University of Western Australia.

Douglas met Shobha at the university in 1983 when he was 62 and she was 36, and their tumultuous relationship blossomed over thirty-three years until he *slipped sideways* at the age of 94. Their 3,500 letters on which this book is based, enabled them to survive an otherwise impossible situation.

SHOBHA CAMERON carried out post-graduate research in anthropology on the influence of eastern mysticism in western countries until her five-year sojourn in the Indian ashram of Bhagwan Shree Rajneesh a.k.a Osho. Returning to Australia and the academic world, she shared her mystical poetry which had been written in India, with Douglas - and their rapport was instant and complete.

*This is the story of how they inspired each other
in a literary, musical and spiritual way
so that when Douglas slipped sideways
there was no farewell
but a continuation of the energy
which had animated them for so many years.*

*It is a book for those who have found their soulmate
and for those who wish to find theirs
but it is not for the faint-hearted.*

Kissing the Joy
as it Flies

*

Letters to the Beloved

*

Douglas Payne
Shobha Cameron

The love letters

of

Douglas Payne

and

Shobha Cameron

All rights reserved. No part of this book may be reproduced in any form or by any means, electronic or mechanical, including photocopying, recording or by any information storage and retrieval system, without written permission from the publisher.

Copyright 2017 © Shobha Cameron

www.shobhacameron.net
www.onthelipsoftheinfinite.com

Publisher : Angelicus : Australia 2022
angelicuspub@gmail.com

spirituality-biography-love-letters-BhagwanShreeRajneesh-Osho-beyond
slipping sideways-mysticism-dying

ISBN 978-0-9872746-6-3

9 780987 274663

for

all those

who have ever loved

He who binds to himself a joy

doth the wingéd life destroy

but he who kisses the joy as it flies

lives in eternity's sunrise

William Blake

I see no reason for our love
unless it be to lead us
towards some higher purpose

Unless it leads us
into realms hitherto unknown

Unless it unlocks
corners of our hearts
which have never yet been opened

With you my love, it is so

May it ever be

Wherever the winds take us
however fate deals with us
may the soul-enriching nature
of our love and friendship
continue
until we cease to be

Shobha - August 1983

*

I have never been sure what love means

but if it is measured by delight in your company
ecstasy and tenderness in making love
and longing for you when I am away from you

then I love you more deeply
than any woman I have known

Douglas - November 1983

Contents

About the authors

Kissing the Joy as it Flies

- The Meeting — 1
- The Letters — 7
- The Lovers — 9
- Where words fail - music speaks — 17
- Your body is the harp of your soul — 19

The Extracts
Comments on format
Chapters

1	You were born together	27
2	When love beckons to you	37
3	A song of praise upon your lips	53
4	A prayer for the beloved in your heart	63
5	And think not you can direct the course of love	69
6	To bleed willingly and joyfully	77
7	The pain of too much tenderness	103
8	The deeper sorrow carves into your being	119
9	Let there be spaces in your togetherness	137
10	Sing and dance together and be joyous	155
11	In the dew of little things	169
12	The heart knows not its own depth	191
13	You shall be free indeed	209
14	A moving sea between the shores of your souls	223
15	All things shall love do unto you	239
16	The wind bids me leave you	249
17	Sing to me a deeper song	255
18	Then shall you truly dance	261

Illustrations — 271
Publications and Media — 274

The Meeting

Soulmates

It sometimes happens that a man and a woman meet
and instantly recognise the other half of themselves
behind the eyes of each other.
Even their voices are familiar to each other's ears.

These are two who immediately sense the unalterable fact
that they have been – are – and must always be – one.

Almost from the first moment they meet and gaze upon each other,
their spirits rush together in joyful recognition,
ignoring all convention and custom, all social rules of behaviour,
driven by an inner knowing, too overwhelming to be denied.

Inexplicably, often without a word being spoken
they know that only through each other
can they hope to find wholeness;
only when they are together
can they both be complete in every way.

Linda Goodman**

Shobha's version

I was walking along a path through the bush on the way to the university, when I said aloud to the cosmos - in one of my everyday conversations - that I felt it was time for me to fall in love. I was feeling overburdened with well-being and wanted to share myself with a like-minded soul.

The next day I met Douglas – at least, the next day, events transpired which led to our loving each other for the next thirty-three years and beyond.

Prior to our meeting, we had individually reached the apogee of our lives and were ready for something new. I had explored my inner life in an Indian ashram (*meditation centre*)** for the past five years, and found many answers. Douglas was about to retire and leave academic life forever and this would have created a vacuum in his emotional and intellectual life - to which he was looking forward expectantly - and into which I unwittingly stepped.

At the age of thirty-six, I had returned from my years of living and working in the ashram community where I had become to some extent - institutionalised. Managing in the western world after such a long absence had its difficulties, so I returned to my alma mater university where I had graduated as an anthropologist and social worker some years before, and was happy to take any employment that was on offer - in order to reinvent myself.

Douglas was then sixty-two; a professor in the faculty of law at a university and an ardent reader of the English newspaper *The Times* - having been born in London, grown up in Africa, served in World War Two in many countries and ended up in Oxford, before his migration to Australia with his wife (N.**) and four children.

I first noticed Douglas when his beloved redsetter Ned died. As usual I arrived at the university early, and Douglas came in from his morning swim and told me about Ned's demise. He was laughing at the time, which given my years of studying and practising psychology, alerted me to the possibility that, because he was laughing - he was probably crying inside. I never looked at him in the same way again. It broke my heart.

Forever after, I have joked with others –

> *How do you know when an Englishman means 'yes' ?*
> *Answer : When he says 'no'.*
> *How do you know when an Englishman means 'no' ?*
> *Answer : When he says 'yes'.*

I swear it is true - at least it was so, in the early decades of my acquaintance with Douglas. It was a long time before I understood that, in the Gilbertian** sense, *things were seldom what they seemed,* as far as Douglas' behaviour was concerned.

By contrast, in Australia - what you see, tends to be what you get. Australians are forthright, straight as a die, in-your-face sort of people, though I have never identified as Australian, and prefer to consider myself 'of English heritage'. After living for five years in India – I also feel my soul has become indelibly 'eastern'.

I was working at the university when Ned *slipped sideways* as I put it, and Douglas was employed in the same department. I was about to attend a gathering of thousands of sannyasins** in America - after the ashram relocated from India. Douglas spied an article in *The Times* written by the celebrated British journalist, Bernard Levin - which he felt might be relevant to my impending holiday - and passed it on to me.

Meditation in the ashram

Levin had taken a year off to 'find himself' in the spiritual sense, and had ended up in the same ashram which I had just left in Poona - in the hills east of what was then known as Bombay (now Mumbai) - and he wrote a series of articles for *The Times* on the ashram activities. Douglas was impressed by the article, as I was also. Levin's words are still the only ones I have found which seem to accurately portray the philosophical orientation of the ashram at that time for the masses, and that of its guru Bhagwan Shree Rajneesh.**

Many other accounts by individuals or the media have been attempted, but none to my mind, are, from my perspective as a participant, true - even those written by the ashramites themselves.

My relationship with Bhagwan is covered in depth in my book *Journey of a Sannyasin* and my understanding of the 'path of love' is explored in the poetry written in my *Song of Love*. I regarded Bhagwan as my spiritual teacher, who could enable me to experience spiritual love - of which I had only had glimpses until that time. At first Douglas appeared to appreciate my attachment to Bhagwan, but when the global media became antagonistic and the ashram disintegrated for a while, he was less accepting. Nevertheless, Bhagwan was a powerful influence on our lives together, which underpinned our relationship.

Douglas' wife (who I euphemistically called N.), found it easier to think that I regarded Douglas as a substitute for Bhagwan i.e. a teacher - though this was far from the reality. Rather, I felt that 'I' was Douglas' spiritual teacher - since this was a field with which he was unfamiliar.

When we made love in the early years, Douglas would kiss my mala (the traditional sannyasin necklace given to me by Bhagwan, which I wore and never removed - unless I was under water. It became an unexpressed acknowledgement that it was Bhagwan (in a sense), who was responsible for our union.

It must have been a little galling for Douglas, when I so often prefaced our discussion with the words "Bhagwan says that...." but he bore this bravely for many years, since he himself had his own muse – the English author Samuel Johnson - whose writings were likewise inflicted upon me from time to time.

Before I left India, Bhagwan had suggested to me to "fall in love totally, and hold nothing back" and it transpired that I became in every way totally devoted to Douglas.

Bhagwan Shree Rajneesh

As mentioned, I was about to visit the transplanted ashram in Oregon (which had relocated to America from India). Douglas phoned me at home to say he would like me to read the Levin article before I departed. I was surprised that one of the professors would ring me out of hours, for such a reason. To express my gratitude - as I knew I would not see Douglas for a month - I gave him a copy of my book *Song of Love* - the devotional poems I had written while I was in India. When I returned from America, I discovered Douglas was 'in love' with my poetry - and had extended this love to the poet herself.

N. became aware that Douglas was behaving differently in my absence overseas (though he maintains he was not aware of this himself). He apparently gazed out over the river from his balcony at odd moments - as if in another world. N. knowingly remarked "It's that bloody girl at the university."

My first contact with N. had not been propitious. I was working late and received a call from her, which had inadvertently been diverted to my office. "Get my husband, girl" she commanded imperiously - whereupon I immediately put down the phone, as it was not usual for me to be addressed in such a peremptory manner. I remarked to one of my associates "that was the rudest person I have ever encountered in my life." From this you may surmise I have led a rather protected existence.

My first impression was confirmed, when another member of the academic staff (who heard N. calling out for Douglas' attention across a crowded courtyard at the university), stated that he would not allow anyone to speak to him in that way. From this limited information, I concluded that Douglas was probably not happily married. Perhaps the thought was sown in my mind - to rescue Douglas from his supposed unfortunate life. I have noticed that many women have an innate desire to rescue or fall in love with the afflicted - though it is not often in their best interests, to do so.

I recall Douglas coming into the university one morning having just returned from his early morning swim at the ocean. He said he had been listening to opera and felt "there ought to be someone with whom to share it." From this utterance, I gathered that he could not share his deepest enthusiasms with N. So after my return from America - having gifted my poetry to Douglas before my departure - I was not altogether overwhelmed when he asked me to have lunch with him in the park.

I acceded to his request, and once in the park, we shared a mandarin, while sitting on a blanket overlooking the river. I laughed incredulously when Douglas suggested we enter into a *pen* relationship. "Are you sure that is what you really want ?" I queried - but I don't recall there was an answer. I imagine he thought a pen relationship was relatively safe and would not cause any marital difficulties.

Douglas with his beloved redsetter Ned

The interlude in the park must have been satisfactory from Douglas' point of view, because he asked me to meet him again the following day. This time the arrangement was terminated, as N. called Douglas to request him to meet her in the city - at the same time as our proposed meeting, and he agreed. I erupted in fury - insisting he honour his commitment to me.

At some subterranean level of my being, I realised then - that if I was going to continue a friendship with Douglas - this might be an ongoing pattern - where he would embark upon a course of action - but be unable to follow it through. Upon reflection – at this critical moment - I should have shown him the door. Instead, in my naivete - I threw down the gauntlet to him shortly thereafter - asking "Can you not love two women ?"

However, as the French mathematician Pascal asserted (so many eons ago), *the heart has its reasons - that reason cannot know,* and within a week, we were lovers.

Apart from one or two half-hearted attempts by Douglas to effect a reconciliation with N. at her request (in the following year, when they were overseas), their relationship became platonic - from this point. I would not have accepted a situation where I was sharing the person I loved - at the physical level - and Douglas was aware of this.

The evening after we first made love, Douglas was admitted to hospital for an emergency operation. I was distraught as he had not turned up for work - and I did not know why. When I did discover his location - we acted like adolescent sweethearts - cuddling and kissing in hospital corridors and wherever we could find a space that was private. We were definitely head over heels in something.

Although there had been risks with his operation - within a week or so, we were lovers once again, *in the biblical sense*. I insisted Douglas apprise N. of the situation, and he gallantly did so. I had never for one moment - entertained the idea of operating in secret.

From that first day in the park, Douglas and I corresponded by letter, and some time later, I found there were also many letters Douglas had written, that were not sent (at this early stage in our relationship). These additional letters indicated he was smitten indeed - in a manner which he himself did not comprehend, and the content of which he did not reveal fully to me until much later.

Thus ensued thirty-three years of travail and anguish as we teetered between adoration and separation - unable to leave each other due to the intensity of our feelings and unable to be together in a satisfactory way. One evening when the sun was setting, I felt it was an opportune moment to beard the lioness in her den, so that N. would realise I was just an *ordinary woman,* and not a figment of her imagination - so I called at Douglas' home. N. said she wanted to make it quite clear that she did not believe in *sharing* - and I replied "neither do I" – and so the battle lines were drawn.

Shobha Cameron

**   Linda Goodman – Love Signs, 1979, Macmillan, London p.5

**   ashram : a spiritual community - usually with an Indian philosophical orientation

**   Bhagwan Shree Rajneesh (who is also known as Osho) was an Indian professor of philosophy who is considered by many, including myself, to be an *enlightened* master. His ashram attracted Indian and western sannyasins and was located in Pune, east of Mumbai (Bombay), which had been the British colonial centre of education.

**   W.S. Gilbert – librettist for the English comic operas of Gilbert and Sullivan

**   sannyasin – a student of the eastern concept of enlightenment, who has renounced attachment to the material world

**   N. was an abbreviation of the word *numbat* - a small furry marsupial, native to Western Australia, and an endangered species. At the time, I chose to believe that N. was endangered, but this did not prove to be so, at least in the legal marital sense.

The Letters

1

Douglas and Shobha decided to publish extracts from the 3,500 love letters they exchanged during the first sixteen years of their thirty-three years together, because they felt - like many lovers - that their experiences were unique - as were the circumstances surrounding them - and the mode of expression of their love *in writing* - even more so.

After sixteen years of writing however - no more letters were exchanged, and Douglas and Shobha themselves, wondered why. The cessation of correspondence coincided with Shobha moving into her own home, and it was not so convenient for Douglas, whose health was ailing - to deliver his missives early in the morning on his bicycle - as was his custom.

Despite the absence of correspondence in their later years together, Shobha had always written down the sayings of Douglas which she found particularly moving - and this practice continued for another eighteen years. A sample of Douglas' *sayings* are reproduced in *Chapter 17 : Wellsprings of Joy.*

It can be assumed there were perpetual declarations of love and devotion from Shobha on a regular basis - though these were sadly - or perhaps fortunately - not recorded.

The many thousands of hours spent talking to each other on the phone and in person at Shobha's home, are not of course available, so the letters and sayings are the only evidence of their thoughts and feelings. They debated whether to record an occasional conversation, as they felt the ideas they expressed were perhaps radical and worthy of sharing with others. But this was not done. The only sound recording of any quality is that of both of them singing operatic and other arias in the local hall (where the acoustics were superb) - and the laughter that followed, when the songs came to an end.

Given their wish that their words would not be lost forever after they slipped sideways, Douglas and Shobha agreed they would one day publish extracts from their letters, so their ideas would endure. Shobha hoped the letters might encourage those who had similar experiences - to follow the path of love to the very end, whatever the cost.

In the two years following Douglas' departure from his body at the age of ninety-four years - Shobha completed the selection of extracts from their letters which are contained herein. They speak for themselves and give an accurate picture of the kaleidoscope of their feelings over time and the development of a deep and spiritual understanding - which sustained Shobha - in Douglas' physical absence, as he did not leave the marital home.

The content of the letters is not always lofty, and deals with the difficulties of sustaining love in an often hostile environment - and therefore may be of some value to those who are similarly placed - during their earthly sojourn. Douglas and Shobha corresponded in a way which bordered on being literary and was reminiscent of an earlier time - as if they had known each other before - and were simply reverting back to their familiar mode of discourse.

When they wrote and spoke to each other, they used a mode of speech which is not likely to be heard in the street in general conversation. Although they did not search for the better word in their utterances, the better word would always arise by magic when they conversed (unless they were in heated argument).

Nevertheless - on many occasions, they would rush to a dictionary if they came upon some word of which their understanding was not complete. Sometimes it was Shobha who would say to Douglas "What is the precise meaning of this word", and he would tell her if he knew.

His mastery of the English lexicon was greater than hers, but on a number of occasions, he himself would not know, and they would then take care to search out its meaning and common or uncommon usage.

Their use of language (in speech and letters) became the vehicle by which they exchanged their deepest thoughts. Poetry - both original (in the case of Shobha) and the works of the poets of years gone by - became a heightened way of alluding to feelings which were otherwise difficult to convey. Douglas in particular, felt it was not unknown - but rare - for lovers to exchange thoughts and feelings in letters, and in the case of Shobha and himself - not by choice, but through force of circumstances.

It was always assumed by Douglas and Shobha

during their thirty-plus years together,

that their letters would be preserved in some form,

and would one day be made available for others to read,

though it was by no means clear how this would be effected.

The Lovers

Taj Mahal – Agra, India

It is probable in these times - where email is a favourite mode of communication - that few people write letters to their sweethearts. During wartime, this was of course one of the primary, if not the only, means of contact for many - but the habit has fallen, not into disrepute, but is sorely neglected - due to the rapidity of other ways of maintaining contact.

It is possible that a lover who has been rejected might put his or her feelings onto paper, in the hope the other might re-consider - upon reflection - once a letter is received. It is also possible, but not likely, that lovers may write poems to each other, if they are overwhelmed in the first glow of their meeting.

Let us hope so - for poetry is an attempt to capture what is transient, in a way which is ennobling and transcendental. How many of us quote well-known lines again and again in our lives – both to ourselves and others - which have emanated from the pen of those who have been in love ? For this reason, this book is dedicated to *all those who have ever loved*. It is Shobha and Douglas' *Taj Mahal.*

The Taj was created by *Shah Jahan* - the fifth emperor of the Mughal empire in India in 1631 - to celebrate his wife *Mumtaz Mahal*, to whom he was betrothed at the age of thirteen and married at nineteen. He fell totally in love with Mumtaz, who died in childbirth at the age of thirty-seven - after bearing fourteen children.

The Taj was Shah Jahan's way of expressing to the world, the depth of his love, and it was twenty-one years before its completion. It is easier and less time-consuming to write a book - but there can be the same motivation.

The celebrated twelfth-century French philosopher *Peter Abelard* corresponded for many years with his wife, *Heloise of Argenteuil*, and maintained that -

If I am remembered, it will be for this: that I was loved by Heloise.

These words were often echoed by Douglas in a similar vein, as he believed the letters between himself and Shobha, might be the only way they would be honoured after their death.

Several years before Douglas left his body at the age of ninety-four - Shobha and Douglas agreed they had explored all that was possible together at the spiritual, psychological, intellectual, physical and emotional levels; had resolved the differences between them that were at first apparent, and had shared as much of their souls as they felt was humanly possible.

So - they were both ready when the time came for Douglas to depart physically - and almost looked forward to it - as the next stage of the adventure. For Douglas, there would be a release from physical suffering (because he had been in extreme pain for many years with neuralgia and other medical conditions). From Shobha's standpoint, it would be the culmination of fifty years of her spiritual journey - which accepted the continuity of consciousness after so-called death. In recent times, she has called the process of dying - 'slipping sideways'.

As a student of mysticism, she had been preparing in many ways with Douglas for this experience, even though he was by no means sure there was a next stage and kept an open mind on the subject. Yet Douglas had a brief near-death experience a year before his departure - and commented to Shobha that he had not realised before how pleasant it would be to die. He described it as transformative and a revelation. After that day, they both felt it was now only a matter of time.

The characteristics of their union which they felt were unique and therefore of possible interest to others, were:

1. *The length of the relationship* (thirty-three years), given that they were unable to sleep or spend nights together, go away together, or indulge in many of the activities a couple with freedom might enjoy.

2. The physical-sexual-affectionate relationship between them had a *spiritual quality*, while the relationship between Douglas and N. was *platonic* (after Douglas and Shobha met), though Douglas and N. continued to live together - for reasons which are outlined in Chapter 8.

3. *Their diverse backgrounds*

   Douglas was born in London; spent his childhood in Northern Rhodesia and was educated in Norfolk in England from the age of eleven to seventeen in boarding school (while his parents remained in Rhodesia). He enlisted at the age of nineteen in the King's African Rifles as a Lieutenant in World War Two, and served in several African countries, Ceylon, Burma and Germany.

   Douglas graduated in law from the University of London, married N., became the father of four children and was appointed as Reader at All Souls' College, Oxford before he migrated with N. and his family to take up a professorship at The University of Western Australia.

   After twenty years of academia (in Australia) he retired - shortly after meeting Shobha. Until then, his personal life had centred around running, swimming, sailing, climbing in Europe with N. - and his love of classical music and literature.

   Shobha was born in Western Australia and forced to leave school at fourteen, due to her parents' financial situation. She worked in a bank for five years, while studying at night to obtain a scholarship to university, where she completed post-graduate degrees in anthropology and social work. From twelve to twenty, her life was underpinned by a deep devotion to Christ and she contemplated becoming a minister in the Congregational church. Instead - as a political folksinger - focusing upon social justice issues, Shobha hawked her guitar around the city playing in concert venues and churches. Singing and writing poetry and prose were the two features of Shobha's life from an early age.

Shobha married a fellow-student (a lawyer) while at university, but after receiving a vision - two years later, she left the marriage, gave up her social work career and commenced a doctorate in anthropology on *the influence of eastern mysticism in western countries.*

As a participant in what was then termed the *new age spiritual movement*, Shobha sold her few possessions and went to India – whereupon she gave up her doctoral studies and became a sannyasin of the Indian spiritual teacher – Bhagwan Shree Rajneesh. She came back to Western Australia briefly to help establish a meditation centre and commune in the bush – where she lived alone for the first few months.

When the commune was thriving – she returned to India and remained there for five years – only choosing to come back to Australia, when her father was dying and the ashram was relocating to Oregon in America. Within a year after her return home, she fell in love with Douglas (when she was thirty-six and he was sixty-two) at the university where they were both working.

Douglas retired soon after he met Shobha, but she continued to study and work at the university for another twenty-eight years - in public relations, publications, marketing, heritage and conservation until she retired in order to sing, dance, write and *smell the roses* - which gave Douglas and Shobha the opportunity to be together in a more relaxed way.

4. *The realisation of Douglas* that, although he would like to be with Shobha in freedom, he felt duty-bound and indebted to N. - for all that she had contributed during their lives - especially his four children.

He was also *afraid* if he left N., she might take her own life - as she had said this on a number of occasions - and he could not live with that possibility. He was also *afraid* that if he left his home, it might not work out with Shobha because of their age difference, and he felt their love would become routine and domesticated and lose its beauty – due to close proximity.

Douglas and N. were lawyers; walked and climbed in Britain and Europe and swam together at the ocean every day in the early morning in all weathers - which formed a strong bond until their later years. But Douglas was unable to discuss 'ideas' in any depth with N. or any of his children. Despite their twin son and daughter also becoming lawyers, Douglas was not able to relate closely to his children, which saddened him deeply. He felt they had no love of ideas, but he also found it difficult to relate closely with others generally - except on a one-to-one basis. His eldest son however, also loved classical music which allowed them to share some precious moments.

6. *No attempt was ever made by Douglas or Shobha to hide their relationship.*

They walked, talked, visited cafes, sang together or listened to music, made love and occasionally swam out to sea together - but little else. They were almost never in the company of others. Douglas met Shobha's brother on several occasions, and her mother - only once.

Shobha officially met two of Douglas' children in hospital as he lay dying. There was one son she did not meet at all - though all four children were aware of her role in Douglas' life.

Though for Shobha, encountering N. in passing, was an almost daily occurrence - either at her house or at the beach, it could be said, that almost every moment they were together – *they were alone.*

7. Shobha and Douglas *did not engage in planned or social activities.* Attempts to do so were usually disastrous and not repeated. Douglas rarely ate during the day and was not interested in food. When he became unwell, they stopped meeting at night - which further reduced the time they were able to spend together - as Shobha was still at work during the day.

8. The way in which Douglas and Shobha spent their time together, can be summarised as *touching and talking.* Due to their limited access to each other - often only an hour or less - time was critical - and for Shobha especially - affection was vital. Whenever they talked, they were physically touching. Whenever they talked, they held each other's hands - in coffee shops - when walking in the park, or simply sitting beside each other on the sofa.

> At times they sat or lay for hours talking or making love - after which they again talked deeply for hours on end - without separating. It was not possible for Shobha to be close to Douglas without touching - except of course on the phone or in a letter.

For Douglas, touch was not so critical - but he never had the opportunity to experience 'not' being in touch, because of Shobha's constant delight in affection.

There is a saying of the Indian mystic Kabir that *the fish in the water is not thirsty*, and so it was with Douglas. If he had been deprived of Shobha's affection, he would not have been content, but this did not occur.

9. Shobha was aware, almost immediately, that they *had known each other before,* in past lives. She accepted reincarnation as a fact, acknowledged that they were soulmates, and that there was a spiritual purpose for their being together.

   Douglas however, had no spiritual framework by which to understand the immensity of their attraction to each other. The lyrics of Shobha's song *The Wheel of Karma*, written three years after they met (when Douglas was in Europe with N.) - express her early realisation (refer to Chapter 18 for full lyrics).

10. Their *inability to separate* - despite many attempts to do so, in an attempt to reduce their distress. The maximum period spent apart - not counting overseas travel - was two weeks.

    Douglas commented that when they eventually met by chance in the street during one of their separations, it was *like taking off tight shoes after a marathon*, and the relief was immense. It became obvious that it was not possible to separate, so they eventually gave up the attempt.

11. Their *love of language* has been discussed at length in the section on *The Letters*.

12. They were able to say - that if there was a purpose that their love was to serve – as Shobha expressed it only days after their first meeting - *then that purpose had been fulfilled*. Their love blossomed - despite the immense difficulties of access to each other; misunderstandings which frequently occurred, because they were often apart, and the difficulties of communication. They had reached a degree of empathy and understanding which was complete.

    Before they met, Douglas and Shobha accepted they had (individually) experienced all they could have wished for in life - though in hindsight they were yet to experience an all-encompassing spiritual love.

    After thirty-three years together (however fraught with difficulty), they came to a moment where they were finally content, and ready to embrace the unknown, because they had in so many ways, already embraced the known – and were ready for the next phase of the *journey* (as it is euphemistically expressed these days – in the spiritual jargon of the times).

13. *The twenty-six year age-difference* and its effect if any, upon the nature of their love.

    For the last twenty years of Douglas' life, Shobha was deeply and continuously involved with Douglas' medical care. She visited and interceded with his doctors and specialists to ensure he received appropriate professional attention and medication, as this was not an area in which N. was experienced.

    In his final two years in the body, Douglas became too ill to visit Shobha in her home, so she visited him at his house every other day - with N.'s unwilling assent. They continued as always - to speak on the phone each day for lengthy periods.

    Lack of privacy made it difficult to communicate as freely as in the past, but by this time, they had reached such an intimacy and understanding - they were able to be together in harmony, despite the extreme limitations of time and place.

    Douglas continued to swim, run and cycle until his eighties, but in his last five years, was no longer able to swim in the mornings, which seriously affected the quality of his life. During this time, he had little, if any, social contact with anyone except Shobha, N., the occasional visit from his family and his reluctant and very occasional acceptance of visits from his doctor.

Douglas left his body at the age of ninety-four when Shobha was sixty-eight, and her long-held wish to be with him at this time, was met.

For the last six days of his life, N. was in hospital and Shobha was therefore able to be with him during the day and fall asleep with him on his last night – a state for which they had always longed.

2

14. *Continuity of the spirit*

Not surprisingly, given her understanding - Shobha remained in contact with Douglas following his departure, and was able to communicate with his spirit in many beautiful ways - so that she was continually aware of his presence, and initially, felt little grief at his passing.

Her deepest wishes - following Douglas' exit, were :

- to improve her communication with those who had already slipped sideways

- to remind those still in their bodies, that there is no such phenomenon as death: simply a movement into a disembodied parallel universe which exists side by side with our material world - with the possibility of being recycled back to a planetary life at some point in the future to 'have another go'

- to make her own journey into this parallel universe, when it was time for her to slip sideways

These matters had in any event been her primary preoccupation for over forty years as part of her acceptance of and involvement in the life of the spirit, and Douglas' physical disappearance simply validated her existing understanding.

15. A significant aspect of Shobha's current relationship with Douglas, is that she is now able to more fully empathise and *contribute a little understanding*, to those friends who have said farewell to someone they deeply loved.

It is no longer an occasion for sadness – but for celebration, for the only factor preventing communication with those who have left their bodies, is a lack of the will to do so. According to Shobha, they are listening and aware of us, and waiting for us to attempt to bridge the gap and make contact. It seems to be up to us to make the first move. Shobha searched the web at one point with the question (tongue in cheek) *How to communicate with the dead,* and was delighted with the answer which was "first of all - speak - and secondly – listen." How simple.

The first photo of Douglas by Shobha

The first and only photo of Shobha by Douglas (in his garden)

Where words fail music speaks

(Hans Christian Andersen)

3

How sweet the moonlight sleeps upon this bank
Here will we sit and let the sounds of music creep in our ears
Soft stillness and the night
become the touches of sweet harmony

Shakespeare – Merchant of Venice

*

If music be the food of love – play on

Shakespeare – Twelfth Night

It is apparent from the letters, that Douglas and Shobha shared a great love of opera. Though possessed of a mediocre voice, Shobha attempted - often with the support of her teachers - the most difficult arias in the repertoire – her favourite being *Casta Diva* from Bellini's opera *Norma.*

Although at first Douglas encouraged Shobha's performance as a folksinger, playing with her guitar, he did not actively encourage her singing of opera. He was a connoisseur of the art and a perfectionist - but not a performer, and found it easier to criticise, than to sing himself.

Once he began to sing with Shobha (after fifty years of never raising his voice in song), his criticism diminished - because he realised the enormity of the task, and the extreme joy he experienced by 'doing' rather than simply 'listening'. Music gave wings to their souls as they sang together and shared their massive library of operatic recordings.

Douglas had not sung since his school choir in Norfolk, England - yet discovered - with the encouragement of Shobha, and to her piano accompaniment - that he had a magnificent voice, which he applied to some of the most difficult arias in opera - to full effect.

From the age of twelve, Shobha sang and performed solo in churches and concerts, as an organist, pianist, folksinger with guitar, in choirs, oratorios including the Verdi *Requiem,* Gilbert and Sullivan operas and Verdi's opera *La Traviata*. Music transported her to a higher level of fulfilment, and her enthusiasm was transmitted to Douglas.

Shortly after they met, Douglas literally begged to be able to buy Shobha a guitar, and the one that was chosen was a beautiful instrument which enabled her to sing in festivals and concerts for many years - both alone and as a member of the folk duos *Heart and Soul* and in recent times – *Angelicus.*

Following his near-death-experience a year before slipping sideways, Douglas became enamoured once again of the hymns of his youth - their lyrics being of sublime beauty. He was also deeply affected by the language of the King James version of the New Testament and the Anglican Book of Common Prayer.

In the latter years of his life, Douglas became interested in rock musicals such as *Jesus Christ Superstar* and other areas of music he had hitherto not explored. His musical soul was definitely on the wing. Douglas always loved classical instrumental music for violin and piano, and now extended his appreciation to cantatas, blues and a variety of other genres. He was incredulous that he was able to appreciate new forms of music at his 'advanced' age.

In one of her many writings, Shobha referred to the interrelation of love, death and music. "When all these three are present, there is the possibility for enlightenment to happen. My soul comes closer to understanding, when great music inspires me. Because of the love for my beloved, and through the inspiration of music, I momentarily touch death in all its ecstasy and beauty. I only wish that from these great moments, I did not return."

Music gives a soul to the universe
wings to the mind
flight to the imagination
and life to everything

Plato

Your body is the harp of your soul

*Sacred (tantric) lovers – temple of Khajaraho
(Madhya Pradesh – India, circa 1000)*

**The giving and receiving of pleasure
is a need and an ecstasy**

Kahlil Gibran

> Had we but world enough and time,
> this coyness, lady, were no crime.
>
> We would sit down
> and think which way to walk
> and pass our long love's day.
>
> *Andrew Marvell*

As there are so many references in their correspondence to making love, the reader could assume that this was a regular happening, but it was not always so. During their attempts to separate from each other permanently, there was often little actual contact, and on one occasion, it was six months before they were able to curl up again in each other's arms.

Yet when they finally made love, it became a celebration – a sacrament – and they both felt transformed, as if an alchemical process was at work. In eastern mysticism, in the school of 'tantra' - making love is a path to the divine – a way to experience a heightened state of consciousness.

Although this certainly was not Douglas' intention, Shobha was aware of this tradition and practice through the teachings of Bhagwan, and there were many times when making love became an act of prayer.

Chapter 17 includes many of the sayings of Douglas from both the letter-writing period of sixteen years and the seventeen years thereafter - until he slipped sideways. His sayings were often recorded by Shobha after making love, because she was aware that Douglas would not recall what he had said when he had recovered from what was an altered state of consciousness.

Douglas often quoted to Shobha the saying of William Wordsworth that *poetry is emotion recollected in tranquility*. In this sense, the effect of some of their letters and Shobha's reflections upon Douglas' sayings - was poetic. But not all their letters were tranquil. *Au contraire*. Some were vitriolic, complaining, beseeching, critical and difficult to digest.

From time to time, in periods of conflict, Shobha dared not open letters from Douglas in case they were heavily inclined towards criticism, rather than expressions of endearment.

Her own letters for several years - expressed a continual longing for them to be together - and make for tedious and exhausting reading.

Shobha's all-too-frequent declarations of love must also have been heavy-going for Douglas, who was less inclined to be expressive with his pen, though many verbal sayings have been included in Chapter 17 (Wellsprings of Joy), which reveal he was as deeply committed as Shobha - just more reticent in sending letters to her - in which his soul was totally bared.

Douglas occasionally chastised Shobha for the degree of her devotion, embodied in her oft-uttered phrase *Je t'adore avec tout mon coeur* (I adore you with all my heart). The bronze sculpture commissioned by Shobha, of a man raising a woman to the heavens, which was erected in 2017, by the ocean where they used to swim – is not surprisingly, entitled *Je t'adore.*

Their love-making or *being made by love*, almost always took place in daylight hours at Shobha's home - often during Shobha's midday break, for she continued working at the university for almost thirty years after Douglas retired. In the early years, Douglas managed to spend evenings regularly with Shobha, but due to his early morning routine of swimming and running at the beach, this did not continue as he grew older, for he was often weary from his morning exertions. Thus they moved between heaven and earth on a regular basis. Coping with the contrast between the two worlds verged, at times - on the impossible.

Douglas became frequently unwell around the time he was seventy-four when he was diagnosed with multiple medical conditions following his enforced withdrawal from one of his medications which was no longer available (because of its deleterious side-effects). He had no faith in the medical profession, but was unable to live (literally) without it. His health was never again fully under control, and made his life extremely uncomfortable. Against his advice and often his knowledge, Shobha began liaising with his doctors and specialists - negotiating for variations in his medication and administration of tests to monitor his health; ensuring he was taken to hospital on two occasions when he almost died (for insertion of a Pacemaker and urgent blood transfusions) and generally making a nuisance of herself. After one nearly fatal episode, their behaviour towards each other changed somewhat, and they found they were not as desperate in their love, but more at ease and trusting of one another. Peace descended - where once there had been anguish and a longing for something more.

Acceptance of the new regime enabled Shobha to minimise her expectations of Douglas, which was met with gratitude on his part (for both her medical intervention, and her reduced need for his ministrations). There was a shift from personal desire to loving each other *more than oneself*.

Affection continued to play a vital part in their life. From the beginning, kissing has been a staple part of their diet, and this assumed greater significance as the years progressed. They often joked about their inability to stop kissing - especially after making love, and Douglas felt this was something quite unique to themselves.

The phrase 'joined at the lips' would not have been inappropriate. It is a wonder Douglas ever made it out of the door. Hence the title of this book.

Not only did the joy fly each time Douglas exited Shobha's portals - but so did the kisses – in abundance. In the sixties, there was a saying of Kahlil Gibran which was much-quoted amongst the hippie population – *If you love someone, let them go, for if they return, they were always yours. If they do not, they never were.* Douglas and Shobha were given an opportunity to test this exercise in surrender, each time they met and parted.

4

Let me not to the marriage of true minds
admit impediments

Love is not love
which alters when it alteration finds

O no - it is an ever-fixed mark
that looks on tempests and is never shaken

Love alters not with his brief hours and weeks
but bears it out even to the edge of doom

If this be error and upon me proved
I never writ, nor no man ever loved

Shakespeare - Sonnets

JE T'ADORE

I adore you

Artist : Ayad Alqaragholli

Bronze sculpture commissioned by Shobha in 2016
to honour the beach community
of which Douglas and Shobha were members
for fifty and thirty-five years respectively

5

The Extracts

This book is in no way a serious attempt to analyse a relationship which - by any standard - is unusual. It is primarily a record of letters given and received (which include a considerable wealth of poetry), with occasional annotations to make their context clear to the reader.

However, a few minimal observations have been made in the introductory sections - to clarify why this extensive body of correspondence might be of interest to others. They are merely reflections of one of the authors, after the event - not the contribution of an independent witness to all that transpired.

A variety of illustrations and photos have been included by Shobha (which evoke some of the feelings associated with being with Douglas), in an attempt to convey the spiritual, literary and totally absorbing nature of their union.

Apart from the opening section on Shobha's version of *The Meeting*, the book is written in the third person – as it can become extremely tedious for the reader to hear that "we did this" and "we did that" ad infinitum.

It was also an excellent exercise for Shobha in developing objectivity, after Douglas slipped sideways, to re-read the 3,500 missives (a considerable time after the events contained therein), and to view them in a different but often heartening way - as so much can be lost to our memories due to the passage of time.

As Douglas held all of Shobha's letters in his possession and she did not have copies and did not re-read Douglas' letters after receiving them, it was quite a shock to recall events and feelings almost twenty years after they had occurred. Douglas by contrast, had regularly re-read Shobha's letters, and referred to them in their conversation.

By reading Douglas' letters, Shobha *fell in love all over again,* in an even deeper way - recalling their moments of grandeur and peace, and inevitably - the torment and distress, due to the physical limitations placed on their love.

It is a risky exercise to make your thoughts and emotions available to others - for their scrutiny, and perhaps delight - and at a stretch – even their possible edification - but Douglas and Shobha felt they had something to share - in the journey of their hearts - in search of understanding.

The artists responsible for the various classical paintings are given in the list of illustrations at the end. Sadly, there are several paintings for which the artist could not be discovered.

Such is the nature of the web. *Pinterest* performs a valuable service - but has a lot to answer for - in that it includes a dazzling array of artworks – but does not always give due credit to their source.

Throughout the publication process, Shobha was aware of Douglas working with her to ensure the letters saw the light of day. Douglas might not have agreed with the choice of illustrations at every point, as he preferred the Impressionists to the Pre-Raphaelites, but the story had to be told in a way which truly reflected the emotions experienced, and he would certainly be delighted to find that after all - as he intended – all their ideas and feelings were not lost.

Comments on format

All sections which do not contain extracts from the letters were written by Shobha.

Each chapter - from 1 to 18 - is comprised of extracts from *one year of correspondence - which appear in chronological order.* The letters encompass sixteen years of letter-writing. Letters were not exchanged in the following seventeen years.

The *headings* given to the chapters, are shortened versions of quotations from *The Prophet* by the poet Kahlil Gibran.

The opening *words of address* in the letters from Douglas to Shobha are in *green*.

The opening *words of address* in the letters from Shobha to Douglas are in *red.*

Two asterisks at the beginning of a letter imply the subsequent letter is *from the same person* as the one preceding e.g. Douglas – in order to reduce annoyance to the reader from incessant repetition of similar forms of address.

Two asterisks after a word, indicate that an *explanation* will follow *in blue text.* Elsewhere, blue text or words italicised in brackets, indicate an explanation of what has gone before.

It can be assumed that all letters without *opening forms of address* began with *Dear Shobha* or *Dear Douglas* and ended with *Love–Shobha* or *Love-Douglas.* Any deviations from these simple forms of address are included in full e.g. *My dearest darling* or *Loveliest of all possible men.*

Items of significance, including those which relate to the anticipated use of the letters in a future publication, are highlighted in red. Significant statements about the spiritual framework in which their relationship could be understood, have been highlighted in blue.

For those who are of pedantic persuasion, please note that a comma has often intentionally been placed *before* 'and' - principally because many sentences are very long indeed, and the meaning might otherwise be lost, if this great taboo had not been broken.

Likewise, *the dash* (-) has been used prolifically, as it helps to convey the idea that the letters are being read aloud – and makes for easier understanding.

Hundreds of the letters from Shobha concluded with *a cartoon* of a cat (Puss, Minette etc.) in various states of ecstasy or distress. A few samples are given in Chapter 7. Hundreds of greeting cards were also exchanged by Douglas and Shobha during their sojourn together, which indicated the type of humour enjoyed by the protagonists in this plot.

Chapter 1

You were born together and together you shall be for evermore

Whenever two persons meet
a new world is created
and through that new phenomenon
both persons are changed and transformed.
Love is an alchemical phenomenon

When two centres meet
the thirst of many lives is satisfied.
Suddenly you become content
as if you have achieved everything
You have reached the goal
The destiny is fulfilled
It is as if the whole existence has stopped

Even death does not mean anything
to the one who is in love

For the first time
you will feel that existence is divine
that everything is a blessing

Bhagwan Shree Rajneesh

Carol

Would you be offended, or very surprised, to learn that the unaccountable sense of well-being I mentioned this morning (at the ocean) is attributable to you - in large part at least ? It was compounded by the upset you have (unwittingly) brought about in me, the afterglow of running along the beach and surfing, and the strains of fine music while driving back from town along the edge of the river. It's quite physical, in the sense that I consciously tingle.

And yet at the same time, I ache, almost drowsily – though for what I do not know. I find it difficult to believe, if choice came into the matter, that anyone would wish to escape such a high, simply because reason tells us that highs of necessity are ephemeral.

I thought I detected a trace of disillusion in your advocacy of quietism**. It is surely both escapist and a confession of defeat. One should strive for intensity of living, in which colours are brighter, when music moves you to the point of physical trembling and when, most of all in this cold world, we begin to feel the warmth and gentleness that comes from exchanging one's deeper and private thoughts with another person. In my experience at least, we live mostly behind masks - fearful of uncovering ourselves.

All this comes from showing me your *Song of Love*** to Bhagwan. Parts of it are good, by any standard. But I found myself putting your words into your own lips, and it was this that moved me in a way I simply do not understand. (3 August)

**   Carol was the birth name of Shobha
**   Quietism – calm acceptance of things as they are without any attempt to resist or change.
**   *Song of Love* – a book of devotional poems written by Shobha in the ashram garden by moonlight

Shobha

I find it increasingly frustrating that we can never talk except in almost accidental exchanges in your office at the university. And I am also becoming conscious that some of our exchanges may appear odd to people in the vicinity.

As I said yesterday (2 August), I'd like to meet you and talk to you away from the university. I realise that there may be dangers in this for me. Is this one of those situations where Bhagwan would urge me not to be governed by the conscious mind? (3 August)

Douglas

What I am trying to say is that the poetry was from the deeper part of myself - that is in fact the universal source of everything - therefore what you love is that – and not necessarily the less subtle manifestation of it - which is me. Nevertheless, if everyone thought of love in this way, no-one would ever act on their feelings and society would cease to function.

But in this case, because you are in a difficult social situation, it may be helpful for you to think of it in this way - that it is not so much the person that is important, but the state of consciousness that is brought about because of that person, or activity or poem. It may be, as you suggest, that in this particular case, it is sufficient to share simply through writing to each other. If that is your wish, then at least while the interest is there, I am happy to reciprocate (3 August).

Douglas' Journal Notes (to Shobha) – 3 August

I am by nature an analyst. But there are obvious limits on how I can analyse myself. I felt a sense of mind-enhancing liberation when I decided in March of this year, to resign from the university. In some way, this may have made me more open and susceptible to be influenced by you.

For reasons probably rooted deeply in me, it seems to me that the kind of love – but not the only kind of love – of a man for a woman that moves most deeply - is hopeless or unrequited love - as so often expressed in opera and poetry. I think it's clear that I still haven't explained adequately to you – or to myself – why I was so moved by your *Song of Love* to Bhagwan.

I can think of no better way of putting it than what I've said already, that I read your words, not as disembodied sentiments, but as emotions being spoken, by you (Carol/Shobha). Poems do not utter from any source, as you suggest. They're yours, no matter how much you felt they simply well out of you - and that your own individuality is unimportant.

I am so confused. Only last night, while listening to the Verdi opera *Pagliacci*, I said to N. that I felt on the edge of an emotional precipice', "It's obviously the effect 'that girl' is having on you" she replied. I had told her while we were having dinner, that I talked to you in the park today.

7

*Here with a loaf of bread
beneath the bough.
A book of verse, a flask of wine and thou
beside me singing in the wilderness,
and wilderness is paradise enow* **

But this is where an element of deceit comes in, because I have not tried to explain to her what is happening to me. Partly because, being the robust person she is, she wouldn't understand - though she would be hurt by our intimacy.

I have pondered on what you say about the sensations which are set in process, as you say, by sharing things, and the relation of those sensations to love. I have also thought of what you say about wanting something from a person who triggers these feelings.

But I'm not sure that you can share what you have - with someone of the other sex – without wanting something of him or her. It is true that I am cautious - though not I hope in a mean, selfish way. If we are seen together, the usual conclusion will be drawn. In view of my age and our present relative positions, wouldn't that be unpleasant - for you in particular?

In the world of practical affairs and administration, I have often argued that it is foolish to plan further ahead than is necessary, in order to deal sensibly with the decisions which need to be taken now. Could we adopt, or adapt, this ? In some way, your *Song of Love* and its commentary, make me feel humble and inadequate. I cannot find the words to respond properly. You must give me time – to allow this approach to life to work its way into me.

I cannot now, after encouraging you, fail to respond to your trust. It would be silly and artificial to go on just exchanging letters, however intimate - when we can meet and warm each other. What is it that we can offer each other, that would justify the distress it might cause to others, and ultimately to ourselves ? What is more to the point, what can I offer you ? Am I not perhaps putting a spiritual and poetic gloss on an all too human infatuation ?

Of course, that's not fair – to me and even less to you. I never thought of you other than as a member of the university staff, until I read your *Song of Love*. Nor has any hole suddenly opened in my life, which could make me responsive. I was not consciously hungry for something missing in my life (when I met you). On the contrary, and perhaps this is significant, I felt, before you even came into view, that I was then living more intensely than I had done, since my subaltern (second lieutenant in the British army) days in Ceylon during the war - eons ago.

Though this 'thing' for me, has exploded suddenly from a light, bantering relationship, perhaps we should now pause and take emotional stock, so to speak. You seem to me to be a gentle as well as a sensitive person. You have already told me you have been hurt too often in the aftermath of 'highs' - to seek them too readily.

In matters of the heart, it's difficult and unnatural to stay on an agreed level of feeling and communication. This morning in my room, shows how instinctive and almost involuntary it was for me to touch you and kiss you.

And what of desire, which at its best, grows from such beginnings ? I have not (yet) left desire behind me. The chief delight of making love is surely to give pleasure, rather than take it. And how can this be, unless tenderness is present. I'm still no nearer knowing what to do or suggest. If what you call my *whole social edifice,* is at risk, in this fish-bowl we live in - then it gives me pause.

Shobha

Though I love talking, I've found only five people in quite a varied life with whom I've been able to discuss the kinds of matters which we have begun to talk about. You dragged me out of prose into poetry. We seem to have discovered an affinity at some warm and vibrating level.

The teachings of Bhagwan do not take sufficient account of the ennobling effect of hopeless and unrequited love. However, if love is an appetite, then it is only to be expected that satiety should kill the muse. I also believe that all intense (heightened) feelings are necessarily cyclical. You told me you had grown to be wary of highs, because you had so often been hurt. But is not suffering part of the experience of love ?

8

9

Aimer c'est suffrir, mai aussi c'est vivre,
Et depuis si longtemps je ne vivais pas.

Benjamin Constant to Mde. Recamier

To love is to suffer, but it is also to live,
and for so long – I did not live !

and also

Mon ami, je vous aime, comme if faut aimer,
avec exces, avec folie, transport, et desespoir.

Julie de Lespinasse - to Guibert

My friend, I love you - and if we must love,
let it be with excess - with madness, transport and despair.

Douglas

Whenever I find someone with whom I can share things that are very important for me - this immediately sets in process a whole series of ideas, longings, sensations etc, which I have come to associate with what people generally call love.

In the past, I have often 'wanted' something from the person who triggered these feelings, and inevitably there has been distress, when the other person was unable to come up with the goods. I think this has happened because of my misinterpretation of the original feelings.

What initially starts off as a great need to share – a feeling of joy at having found someone with whom to communicate at a deep level, often gets confused along the way and becomes an attempt to 'get something' – to form a relationship and so forth, rather than simply accepting that it is a rare and beautiful experience to be able to share beauty with someone, and that it is sufficient to share without asking anything in return.

It is my understanding that when expectation creeps into a friendship, love disappears out the door. It is also my feeling that when there is any element of deception at any level, about the friendship - love cannot grow in such an environment. So then - what possibility is there for this friendship? As far as I can see, you are a little embarrassed by your feelings for me, in case someone should find out - and your whole social edifice would come crumbling down, as I have suggested.

On the other hand, what to do with these unexpected feelings which have arisen in you, towards me? You are sufficiently in touch with your heart to know that it is not possible to disregard your feelings and pretend they don't exist. But how to express them in a way which will not threaten your existing way of life ?

It is my observation that feelings of love definitely do threaten your way of life, and threaten it totally. At the same time I feel they are the only feelings worth living and dying for. Love is what makes life worthwhile. But it is crucial to decide just what these feelings are that have moved you so deeply. I feel in your case – many things could trigger a state of ecstasy or love - whatever you wish to call it.

You say that in some way the poems I sent to you triggered something in you – but I myself - in the book of poetry, said that when I wrote them, I felt as if it was not 'I' that was writing them and that they came from some other source, and it is so. There are many moments also when I feel that I am in touch with that *other source*, whatever it might be, and love especially, brings about such a state of consciousness.

10
The evening after Douglas and Shobha became lovers,
Douglas was admitted to hospital for an urgent operation.
Shobha discovered his condition by ringing his home
as he had not appeared at the university the next day,
and his cleaner advised that he was in hospital.

Douglas

What you said about the pre-med experience before your operation, is similar to what I was saying to you about meditation. In many ways and varying degrees, meditation brings about a similar state of euphoria - not always immediately, but from time to time - and without any chemical inducement. For me, love also brings the same state of euphoria. Perhaps now you can understand what I feel, when I close my eyes when I am with you.

The night we sat beside each other before the operation by your bed, was so perfect for me – such a gift. It is one of the most treasured moments of my life. The next few days will no doubt be more clinical and there will be more people around, so there may not be the opportunity for much intimacy. If so, I will write letters to you and soon you will be out of hospital and roaming about again. All my love, and all the hugs and kisses I cannot give to you right now, but wish to, with all my heart.

Shobha

I can still feel the trembling of your body as I held you. If it were not for the memory and promise of love making, I would be inclined to say that the tenderness I feel for you has in it something of the character of the gentleness one feels for a child. It seems so natural that you are lightly built and almost frail.

What can I say to you to explain my apparent perversity in saying I shall not leave N. or indeed hurt her to the point where we cease to be companions? My relationship with N. is very different from (mine) with you. You and I are closer and more in tune in many ways. You stir me as N. does not, and the explanation for this is not simply that you are a younger and more attractive woman. I think it has more to do with your abandon and relish in making love.

- *The Rubaiyat of Omar Khayyam* – a selection of poems attributed to Omar Khayyám, a Persian poet, astronomer and mathematician of the 12th century.

From the outset, N. has never treated our association as a cheap or casual one. She too has regarded it as an all or nothing matter. Despite occasional storms, she has been very forbearing in the hope that it will end. Not to hurt her, but almost by compulsion, I often talk to her about you. For some reason, this openness has made the breach between us less serious than it would otherwise have been.

But Shobha - I could not leave her - any more than you would consider abandoning your mother. Your injunction to 'follow the heart' without qualification, is simply not good enough. The heart, though the most important, is only one consideration. And because of the strange fluctuations in my need for you, for me even the heart alone is not a clear guide.

Shobha my darling

I miss you so much, and the ache has been made worse by the fine and generous letter you left for me. If it were simply a matter of the heart's inclination, there would be no problem at all. You mean everything to me. So why - you may ask – the agony of indecision ? Why do I not simply follow my heart and be true to our love ? The reasons are all mundane and prudential.

The teachings of Bhagwan do not take sufficient account of the ennobling effect of hopeless and unrequited love. However, if love is an appetite, then it is only to be expected that satiety should kill the muse. I also believe that all intense (heightened) feelings are necessarily cyclical. You told me you had grown to be wary of highs, because you had so often been hurt. But is not suffering part of the experience of love ?

Since we have never spent more than a few hours together, there must be aspects of my being sixty-two which are not apparent to you. The tempo and irregularity of a style of life natural to a person of your age and disposition would soon tire me. For some reason, I persist in taking risks. I get a childish pleasure from being known down at the beach as a person who does not flinch from taking waves that men half my age would not attempt.

My darling - leaving aside all other problems, both of us would have to face the prospect of my accelerating physical decline. The time soon will come when I shall not be able to run in the way that I do (as fast as I can), from my home to the ocean. You may say, as I sometimes tell myself, that we should live for the day, and be grateful for whatever time the future allows us.

Douglas

I feel very hurt and deflated. I am afraid I have misinterpreted you yet again. Somehow I picked up the message that you had fallen in love with me, and I responded in a similar fashion, much to my own surprise.

Once I actually acknowledge the depth of my feelings, I act upon them, without inhibition. In this, we are so different in that I am unable to wait. I respond immediately and totally, whatever the cost. Perhaps it is foolish – I don't know - and I'm not sure that I care. That is the way I am. I was going to say I am sorry I jumped in so quickly, and yet I always make the same mistake of feeling that the one I love also loves me in the same depth and totality, and it seems, I am always wrong. Forgive me.

11

There is so much longing in me when I find someone with whom to share, and I almost always experience resistance and fear and guilt in the other person. I am a little tired of constantly being the second person and not the primary relationship (with you), and for this reason you will probably understand when I say it is better if we do not see each other any more. I am not interested in things that are hidden - where a lot of energy goes into concealing the fact of the love that has arisen. I would prefer to be in love with someone who is open in the expression of his feelings and not afraid about who will be watching and what is at stake.

You have a wife at home to share many things and with whom (you say) you are happy. I do not have someone at home to share with – instead I have many friends, but not one in particular. I thought I heard you say that you would not like me to have another lover - and yet you have a wife.

Shobha

I find you a strange person. I was moved by your *Song of Love* to Bhagwan (for reasons I still don't understand). Whatever the reason, I did seem to hear you.

Last night I read your article *The Mystery of Love*. You say the possible combinations of body, mind, heart and spirit are many and "If there is incompatibility at some levels, it is important to acknowledge this, and not to expect your friends or lovers to be compatible with you in every way."

You then suggest that if you cannot be fulfilled entirely at all levels with one person, you must ensure you fulfil yourself from whatever other sources are available to you. If I urge you to take a lover, it is because I can see no happiness for you in continuing to meet me. I do not relish the thought of you in bed with another man. It would put an end, initially at least, to any form of relationship between us. If we switched to being mere close friends, I suspect this would intensify our love and not cause it to wither away. Love grows more strongly on deprivation than on consummation.

Douglas' journal during the first agreed-upon trial separation of three weeks

So far, it has been a strange mixture of elation and torment (since our compact not to see each other unless I am prepared to leave my home for you). The fullness of your love has often humbled me. I have been enriched by it and will continue to be enriched by it, whatever the outcome of our compact. I am tempted to tell N. (as I have told you) that at the end of the three weeks, I may lose my nerve and stay with her even though I am still in love with you. At the moment, this seems to me to be the most likely outcome. If I am so cowardly and unadventurous, I hope you will have the strength to reject any attempt by me to return to our earlier relationship, which we all three agreed was intolerable.

Douglas' journal - shortly before his retirement from the university

The farewell note from one of my colleagues, warms my heart, and it was quick and clever of you to say that it is because of my eccentricity (which he mentioned in his note) that I find you so lovable. I am genuinely surprised at suggestions of my eccentricity. But the surprise is perhaps only to be expected, whatever the truth of the matter. An eccentric - almost by definition - does not recognise himself as such.

Douglas' journal

Perhaps unwisely, I suggested to N. that she should acquiesce in my going away with you for a week or two. My reasoning was that by leaving her and living with you, even for such a short time, I might come to realise, more than I do now, how much she means to me, and also bring home more clearly to me, what leaving her would entail. But she was absolutely opposed to this alternative. I have to admit that I am stirred in an extraordinary way simply by exchanging glances with you, as I did once this morning and several times yesterday in the office. I think we may both be exceptional in this respect - in conveying so much and responding so much to each other's eyes. Your eyes are so much the most vital part of your face. We do in fact caress each other with our eyes.

Shobha my darling

I have just finished reading *Jude the Obscure* (the novel by Thomas Hardy). It has been a searing experience. You were constantly in my mind as I read it. I have the strange feeling - almost conviction - that Jude has some special significance for me and for you; that providence and not mere chance, dictated that I should read it at this point in my life, and that there is a lesson for me in this marvellously-moving and thought-provoking book. My mind and emotions are in a tumult. I long for you as I have never longed for you before. I suppose you believe that I, like Sue (the heroine in the novel), am acting under a perverted sense of obligation - instead of following my heart.

My darling

I miss you so much. Your letter moves me profoundly. The photo of you, in front of me on my desk, makes me long to touch you. I have never before attached any importance to a photograph, but this one brings you alive in front of me. In some strange way it also brings home to me how much I love you, and how simply ridiculous it is that I should even contemplate not seeing you any more. Yet I can see no way of resolving our problems.

Carol - a rare use by Douglas of Shobha's birth name

You do me an injustice in supposing I am not in love with you because I cannot (now) bring myself to abandon my wife, my home, my children, a lot of my friends, my music and much more, so I can see you whenever we wish. When I first asked to meet you in the park, I simply wanted to talk to you and had no thought of anything more. I was quite open about what I was doing with N. It was by no means inevitable that we would become lovers, though you might think differently. Can't we continue to meet from time to time - if only to walk and talk ?

My darling

I would so much like to talk to you, but am wondering nevertheless whether it would not be better for you and perhaps even for me, if we try to manage without each other (Christmas).

O never say that I was false of heart
though absence seem'd my flame to qualify.
As easy might I from myself depart
as from my soul, which in thy breast doth lie.

Shakespeare – Sonnets

Chapter 2

When love beckons to you

12

When love beckons to you - follow him
though his ways are hard and steep

and when his wings enfold you - yield to him
though the sword hidden among his pinions
may wound you

and when he speaks to you - believe in him
though his voice may shatter your dreams

for even as love crowns you
so shall he crucify you

even as he is for your growth
so is he for your pruning

Gibran

Shobha
I miss you very much, and was half hoping yesterday that you would ring. It is only when I am away from you and haven't seen you for some time, that I realise how much I love you and how important

you have become in my life. In the unnatural way we spend our time when we are together, we act as lovers might, if one was to be executed on the morrow. Not as we would act if we were living together.

It would be silly to try to explain what it is in you that pleases me so much. Your complete lack of affectation. Your voice and conversation and readiness to laugh. The crinkles at the sides of your eyes when you smile. The smell of your hair. The touch of your hand as we walk. Lying in the dappled shade of a tree in the park or by the lake - trying to obey your injunction to be silent.

Shobha my darling

I miss you so much. Life is quite barren without you. I mean to try to keep to our agreement that we should not meet again except on your terms. Perhaps therefore it was wrong and unfair of me yesterday to ring you. But I had just finished reading again your account of your spiritual development in Pune, (*Journey of a Sannyasin*), which is a commentary on your *Song of Love* for Bhagwan.

It filled me with such a rush of love for you that I couldn't resist ringing you then and there. I had also been worried about you since I left you on Sunday and was hoping for some assurance, which you gave me, that you are getting about and are something like your normal happy self.

Shobha

I am both glad and sorry to hear you are going to share a house with your friends. Glad - because you will be with people who love you, and also glad because it will force me to find a place of my own - away from N. - if we are ever to meet again as lovers.

At the same time, I'm sorry that you will lose some of your independence. Reading your book about your relationship with Bhagwan, brought home to me even more sharply than before, how much you need privacy. Solitude, in mind at least, seems to have been the most important feature of your life in the ashram in India.

Reading your book on India has also made me wonder whether you may not in fact be capable of casting me aside as someone who has served some purpose in your emotional and spiritual life. I am reminded that you said once or twice, with a touch almost of defiance, that you could manage quite well without me. If I find life intolerable without you, I don't want to leave my home - only to find you have flown.

My darling

I love you more now than at any time and I have no illusions about the anguish in store for me (if we part). We have talked so much that it would be pointless to try to explain the apparent contradiction in what I say and do. Over and above the more obvious problems of starting a new life, I am, I think, more deterred by the consciousness of my age than I have freely admitted to you. It's not so much that I'm a reasonably fit sixty-two, as that I will be physically decrepit in a few years' time.

Shobha

If I have the strength of will, I shall not get in touch with you any more. This is what I meant to say to you last evening. But you were so sweet and lovable that I could not say it to your face. This attempt to end things is not, as you seem to suppose, because I am losing interest in you. But I am causing you a great deal of distress in failing to offer you what you reasonably expect and in doing so, I'm occupying your life most unfairly.

It is of course full moon tonight, and I am wondering what strange rites you are marking it with. I miss you.

Douglas

Above all - I want you to do what makes you happy, and helps you to feel free - even if you prefer N. to me.

If we are meant to be together
nothing on heaven or earth
will keep us apart

Only time will reveal
the truth of our love

Douglas

It seems there is a source from which poetry springs which is activated whenever I am in love. Yesterday I sat by the river and was overwhelmed for quite a long while, with a feeling of love for everything without exception. I could have stayed there in that blissful state for hours.

Last night at the orange** centre, I was dancing so wildly and then we had a singing meditation for one of the women whose little son is in a coma, and I again went into a very beautiful state - *completely 'gone*, and during that time, I felt so much love for N. and her pain.

It was a beautiful moment, as if love has to transcend all boundaries between persons, and none of us are (actually) separate from each other.

- ** The orange centre, was where the sannyasins of Bhagwan Shree Rajneesh would gather occasionally for meditation and dancing. They were called the *orange people*, because initially - they wore orange robes.

Beloved

The only way to resolve our dilemma is for me to love you and let you go; to love you but ask nothing of you, or at least, not to expect anything from you. The French philosopher Voltaire has said that the only remedy for impossible love, is to love more. I would agree with him.

I am not sure whether I am capable of such love, but I would like to see if it is possible. When I truly love you, I feel so grateful that you are here, and I am glad you are alive. The only problem comes when I want more. If we could live day by day, perhaps we could be happy.

O bell'alma innamorata (beautiful beloved soul)

Though you love Bhagwan in a way which I don't comprehend, and are regarded as one of the 'orange' elite in Perth - to me you are a rare and beautiful individual woman. I won't try to explain, even if I could, what makes you lovable. I'm not alone in this view of you, though I occupy a special niche in your affections.

I love you for what you are, and what you were before you threw in your lot with Bhagwan. You are delightfully, and in modern times, exceptionally unmaterialistic. Yet when you left your husband and your homes shortly after your marriage, you were equally unmaterialistic at that time. It was your *Song of Love* for Bhagwan, which first attracted me to you, yet we live and feel, to some extent, in different worlds. I hold you and kiss you and you sob – but as a form of ecstasy. What manner of creature is this that will not let me talk?

The kind of talk I have in mind is rooted in history, literature, biography and philosophy and is as important to me, as Bhagwan is to you. If I had to deify someone, I would nominate Samuel Johnson. You have chided me for my incapacity to cry, yet some of the things Johnson said or wrote and some of the incidents in his life, have made me cry.

We certainly are a strange pair: dissimilar in many ways, and yet so much in harmony, as if we were made for each other. Perhaps the harmony comes from our being complementary to each other - rather than being in accord. It is true I yearn for you if I don't see you - and take delight in your company when we meet.

Instinct and convention tell us that greater happiness and fulfilment will come from living together in the traditional comprehensive and exclusive way. Does it sound cynical to suggest that cohabitation tends, through familiarity and routine, to destroy the love that inspires poetry ? We owe most of our greatest love poetry to unrequited love.

P.S. Mr. Tickle - the soft toy you gave to me, is sitting on my desk, and he asks me to tell you that the outflow of his love puts him in need of a refill. I shall try to nourish him with passages from your *Song of Love* to Bhagwan and other poems you have given me. Today, I have had some difficulty explaining Mr. Tickle's presence in my study, to my grown children. Only my grand-daughter accepts it as entirely natural.

Shobha my darling

Your standards and expectations are not of this world. No wonder that I sometimes lose you (don't understand you) and so disappoint you. As I have said before, you are a rare and beautiful person. We met at a time when I was receptive to change (leaving the academic world on retirement). Our strange and loving relationship has affected me profoundly, so that I now accept many ideas that six months ago were anathema to me. You must get back to living your life with the gaiety and zest your friends associate with you. Smiles, not red eyes - are your natural radiance.

Nothing will wipe out what has happened between us. I, at least, am richer and more alive for it. I love you and don't know how I shall manage without you. I can still feel the trembling of your body this morning, like the pulse of a small captive bird held in the hand.

Beloved Douglas

I don't know whether you realise it or not. I feel sure you do: that something is happening to us because of our love. It is as if we are touching heights we have never touched before; seeing things in a new way. It feels very full and rewarding. The problem comes for me when I want more; when I am not simply grateful for the beauty that we are sharing which seems so impossibly rare – and when I try to fix on our love, and mould it into some traditional pattern of how things 'should' be.

It is true there is not a lot of freedom from your side, but it is precisely your so-called bondage, which is bringing about our present dilemma and our present joy. Ultimately you will become free and then you may not need me any more. Who knows, but while we are alive and loving and knowing each other in more intimate ways each day - then we are very blessed.

13
' Dr Johnson arguing '
(Samuel Johnson by Sir Joshua Reynolds - circa 1770)

In our most sacred moments, it is also true there is no element of sex or passion. There is just an immense, overwhelming feeling of understanding and fulfilment – as if these are the moments for which we were born and have longed all our lives. Such is the grace that has fallen upon us: two children floating through the universe. I am so glad to share these moments with you. It is so uplifting to be treasured by you - for whatever reasons.

Both of us have a destiny to fulfil, of which we are probably only partially aware, and I am sure we are helping each other in a very deep way, along that path that leads to joy and peace. Your love has made me whole.

Shobha

I love to be with you and I feel very tender towards you. As I've said before, no-one has ever moved me in the way that you do. Merely to exchange glances (with you) is to play with fire - for me at least. Your little note to me this morning – so generous in tone – makes me feel mean and petty. Yours is so clearly a finer nature than mine.

Last night I sat and thought of you, though conscious all the time that N. was watching me – knowing I was thinking of you. I talked to her about you in a more sensible and moderate way than ever before. Seeing us together yesterday, and finding I was inclined to side with and protect you, seems to have made her more conscious of what you mean to me. I told her that I had found moments of happiness with you which I had never experienced with her. She made the point that there could be no real future for you and me, because of our relative ages and many other differences between us. I could not dispute this, but questioned whether this was sufficient reason to reject what little happiness I might expect to enjoy.

My darling

Last night was indeed magical.

Douglas

> You fill a place in my life
> where no-one else can ever be
> Just remembering you
> brings tears to my eyes
> I love you with all my heart

My love

I am sitting here listening to *Tristan and Isolde* (opera of Richard Wagner) which made me feel like writing to you. Douglas and Wagner seem to go together. I feel as if you are in the room.

You asked me yesterday what love was, and I called it "a quiet surge of ecstasy when you remember the one you love." Sometimes the ecstasy and the tears become one. To be with you is for me, to be in god. I feel utterly at home. As you said only a few days ago, we seem to 'fit'. Even when we are not physically together, we are still aware of each other. For me - you are a constant presence. **Often I wonder why it seems so painful to be in love. In the words of Gibran –**

> The deeper that sorrow carves into your being
> the more joy you can contain

And he also says elsewhere –

> love has no other desire
> but to fulfil itself
>
> but if you love
> and must needs have desires
> let these be your desires
>
> to melt
> and be like a running brook
> that sings its melody
> to the night
>
> to know the pain
> of too much tenderness
>
> to be wounded
> by your own understanding of love
>
> and to bleed
> willingly and joyfully

I have just been to the little park at the top of your hill. There is a little glade there which felt very magical in the rain. Since I again began living alone, I feel that magic returning for us. Being alone naturally throws me back into that world of mystery, but to be alone and then to share it with you, is absolutely magnificent.

Shobha

It was only yesterday I found myself questioning why I should not walk out of my own house, where I spend most of my time, but N. spends little of hers, in order that we are able to meet freely, without N. hanging over us like a dark cloud.

Why not simply say to N. that I propose to regard myself as completely free and leave her to do whatever she thinks fit about it. So last night I put this to N, and suggested that the practical alternatives for her would be to start moving in the direction of a divorce, or try to ride it out in the expectation that our affair will not last.

Though I am fond of talking, I prefer in general to be alone, as indeed I am now for practical purposes most of the time. I would not have resigned from my professorship, if I had been faced with the prospect of N. at home.

Douglas

I am glad that you say you would like to live alone and even to die alone. In my deepest heart, I long for you to be free – even from me – so that you can fall in love with yourself. That is the utmost and ultimate love affair. I am just a stepping-stone on the way to that beautiful state – as you are also for me. Until we are both ready to be utterly alone, my love - linger with me a little longer. It occurred to me last night during the orange celebration (while singing and dancing), that I have always craved the purity of love – uncluttered by other domestic arrangements and trivial things.

This is what we share together. Although we don't go 'out' or share lots of activities - when we do come together, it is almost always simply to share our love, so in an odd way, what you give me is what I want i.e. total attention and affection and devotion while we are together.

It is true that we don't share the warm delights of having a home together and my soul craves also for this at times, but we do share all the delights of pure love. If only there was a way to share simple homely comforts occasionally, my heart would be satisfied.

Shobha

You have always tended to talk of loving and being in love as if it were a condition like measles. Yet what you have said to me so often about the importance of love in your life has brought home to me, that we all differ, according to our natures, in our capacity to be overwhelmed by love.

You stand at one extreme, consistent with your openness, spontaneity and lack of materialism. As for me, I am beginning to think I must be near the other end of the spectrum. I say this, even though I have been closer to you and felt more tenderness for you, than for any other woman I have known.

Your letters make me feel humbled and even in awe. The intensity of your love frightens me. You do not live in my pedestrian world and I do not live in yours. Not forgetting my age, I cannot believe your level of intensity would survive an everyday, exclusive relationship. My flame does not burn very brightly, compared with yours.

This is why I prefer to stay in my comfortable, even though loveless, home situation. It has been enriching to know you so closely and to love you so far as my nature allows. I shall never forget the radiance of your face in moments of intimacy. To my surprise I found myself thinking repeatedly of our making love. This has never happened before. Perhaps I delude myself about the principally spiritual character of our relationship, which is more acceptable to my ego.

Beloved

I wish we could be all things to each other, but it seems that is not the way it is, right now. I wish we could hug and kiss and make love and share music and nature together, but it seems you only want to share matters of the mind and soul, rather than those of heart and body. We have been all things to each other, but it is a very consuming way to love – a bit like dying. If you do not wish to die in me, that is your right and your choice. But I am ready to die in you. But if it is too much right now (for you), then let us at least be together in mind and spirit and perhaps the heart and body will return. You are very dear to me.

Dear Douglas

My feelings about you keep changing. This afternoon in a moment of 'insight', I felt it would be possible to have a pen relationship with you for a while and not to see each other. However tonight, as the sun is setting, I am aware of wanting to see you – in the flesh. What to say - except that in the course of one day, there are many moods – all of them true.

Beloved Douglas

I have just finished listening to Mozart's opera *The Magic Flute* and I want with all my heart to ring you. Do you realise how difficult it is, not to be able to contact you when I wish ?

The hardest thing in the world for me is *waiting,* or feeling impotent in a situation because I am unable to contact you. This takes away all feeling of power and self-respect for me. I am dependent upon your inclination and mood and not my own.

Perhaps in bygone times when women were not liberated, love could still survive, but in these times, love can only exist in freedom.

> I am full with longing for my love
> waiting every evening by my window
> Listening for his footsteps - yet he does not come
>
> My heart weeps for him without ceasing
> My tears flow into the ocean of my sorrow
> Yet a moment with him is delight
>
> Once he came and knocked so gently on the pane
> I found him standing silently
> as if in fear of his discovery
> Our love has been through hell and heaven many times
> yet still the thread endures
>
> I have blamed him sorely for my wounding
> for he has another woman in his bed
> though they do not touch
>
> Yet in stronger moments
> I can see it is my doing
> that the love has lost its magic
> though it never ends
>
> He would turn the hands of time back to those days
> when we entwined ourselves together
> on the river bank
>
> But I would say - my friend and my beloved
> there are many thorns and roses on this path
> Stay true a little longer
>
> Do not waste the precious time we share
> by moving far away
>
> We are injured by our words and deeds
> but still the power of love can heal
>
> O my love
> I wait for you each evening by my window
> listening for your footsteps 'til you come

Douglas, my love

I am slowly beginning to realise, that everything has a way of happening in its right season, and to attempt to hasten or influence the ways things are naturally going, is utterly futile.

The basic reason for my unhappiness in recent months has been my lack of trust – a spiritual crisis as much as anything – not trusting that whatever is needed for me and for you, will happen despite ourselves. We are part of a greater whole, that is caring for both of us, in its own way.

The love that happened to us early on, came as a gift, and no doubt will evaporate as easily as it came, if there is no substance to it. I have a quote in front of me which comes from Corinthians in the New Testament –

> Love bears all things
> believes all things
> hopes all things
> endures all things
> Love never ends

I offer our love to something beyond ourselves. We have a song in orange-land whose lyrics are apt and biblically-based. It concerns the principle of surrender, and is beautiful when sung as a round –

> Into your hands I lay my spirit
> Into your hands I lay my life
> Thy kingdom come
> Thy will be done

If our love is true, then nothing will keep us from being together. Such are the ways of the divine. Until our paths meet again.

My darling

Bhagwan has just delivered his latest bombshell. He has asked his sannyasins to become celibate if possible, and if not, to stay with one partner and deepen their love, rather than shifting from one person to another. The reason for this is that AIDS, which is a sexually transmitted disease, is now spreading rapidly, and it is thought it may wipe out two thirds of the world's population in the next ten years. Bhagwan wants his orange people to survive - so their love continues on the planet.

Shobha

I can't really see that Bhagwan's latest edict has any bearing on our relationship, since it is obviously aimed at promiscuity. You seem to think I have some kind of hang-up about making love which inclines me towards celibacy. This is not so. Because of my age, and perhaps because I tend to idealise women, I regard making love as important and precious – an occasion not for simply seeking gratification, but for bringing someone you love to a peak of delight.

My darling, we have been lovers in the fullest sense. When I told you last week to be proud, I was urging you to hold yourself apart until I agree to treat you as I should - by finding somewhere to live which would allow us to meet freely - without forever watching the clock.

I am inclined to think that it would be better for us not to meet (at present) except perhaps in my car - where the separate bucket seats and the handbrake would help us to keep a proper distance from each other.

Ours is an extraordinary love affair. Our meeting this morning left me with a feeling of relief and simple happiness. I was again surprised at my pleasure in unexpectedly seeing you. I wonder whether we may not be near to discovering, largely by chance, a novel but rewarding kind of loving relationship between a man and a woman.

We seem to stimulate each other, so that I, at least, come away from seeing you refreshed and almost uplifted. I believe the inspiration (or love) will be enhanced, if we continue to lead our separate and different lives.

You said today, that when dancing last night at the orange centre – your happiness was not dimmed by the thought that I was not there. If we were to live together I wonder whether our relationship would not immediately lose some of its stimulation. The edge, eagerness and freshness would not survive – the deadening effect of familiarity.

I do not talk to N. at all - though I occasionally express my ideas by *talking 'at' her.* Would you and I talk as we did this morning – and have done so often before – if we were living together ?

When we first met, I got the impression that you were a woman with a number of interests and many friends. I was attracted to you by your poetry - in the first place. Very soon we found happiness in simply being together - sometimes talking - sometimes silent. And then in time, our love-making added a magic of its own.

N. knows we are lovers. She too, accepts that our relationship is not a casual one. To her it has seemed an all-or-nothing affair, the extreme of which will be, that I shall either leave her or leave you.

Dear Douglas

You are caught (so I believe) in the classical situation, where - having failed to make an emotional break from your real mother, which is a prerequisite for psychological maturity, and which you could not do - because your mother was not physically with you from the age of eleven (but in Rhodesia), you idealised her and then married your mother – or at least a mother-figure (not a lover, a free spirit or a soulmate). How is that for a theory ?

Now that we have met, you are aware that your choice then was a very limited one. It gave you security and stability as a mother does, though your own mother did not, as she was not there - but no ecstasy.

It is a sign of emotional development that we can choose a path of freedom and insecurity rather than cling to the patterns of the past. This is the real issue for you (in my humble opinion). As you know, I also married a man who was not - as you are – my soulmate - so we are all affected by our past. The issue for me now is to find my spiritual counterpart, for whom I have been searching my entire life (albeit often unconsciously). I feel it is you - and therefore want to share life totally and intimately with you.

It would not be a relationship of this world. Far from it ! There would be an underlying spiritual purpose that would sustain us.

I know you are afraid of love and intimacy and surrender and love-making and loss of control and the tears and anger and all that I represent. My life is fluid and dynamic and spontaneous. I ask you to share it with me. Somewhere along the line, you have acquired the belief that (true) love is not possible and does not endure.

Remember your early love for your mother. It 'is' possible. I - on the other hand, believe spiritual love deepens with propinquity, since our initial attraction was not of the mundane world. Deep down, I feel we belong together.

My love

Even though your body will soon be far away from mine (in Europe) - know that the sweet joy we share continues deep inside our hearts. You are as close to me as my own heartbeat. Neither space nor time has any impact on our love. I rejoice in you, my darling, and in all the precious moments that we are together – and now will know the depth of love through being apart for a little while, as Gibran says

> And ever has it been
> that love knows not its own depth
> until the hour of separation

and he continues -

> When you part from friend
> you grieve not
> for that which you love most in him
> may be clearer in his absence
>
> Your friend is your needs answered,
> for you come to him with your hunger
> and you seek him for peace
>
> When your friend speaks his mind,
> you fear not the *nay* in your own mind
> nor do you withhold the *ay*
>
> And when he is silent
> your heart πceases not to listen

Though you are far away, my love will always be with you. Whatever mountain you stand upon, in whatever country, if you ever want me, just close your eyes and whisper my name, again and again, and I will be there. Love cannot be confined – it is so vast.

> Until our fingers touch
> our arms entwine
> our lips caress
> our bodies melt as one
>
> the coming and the going
> have no meaning
> for the heart
> that is aflame with love
>
> *Shobha*

•

> A single moment of intense, ecstatic living
> is more valuable than the whole of eternity
>
> *Bhagwan*

To Shobha – from Douglas in Europe

I promised to write to you from Europe if N. and I became reconciled while we were away. To a degree, it has in fact happened - though only in the last two days. Quite how or why, I don't know. In part, strangely, through my being able to persuade N. to talk about my relationship to you without bitterness - though she realises you are often in my thoughts.

I don't yet know what the implications of this are for you and me. I say this because my feelings for you do not seem to have changed - almost as if you and N. are not really in competition. My relationship with you is quite unlike any other I've experienced. You move me more deeply than I have ever been moved before. N. knows you fulfil a need in my nature that she does not.

But you and I looked upon this enforced five weeks parting from each other to resolve a situation which you have said is intolerable. This being so, I think we should not meet again, except as friends, if this is possible. We must of course meet. In any event, the thought of not seeing you again is simply ridiculous, almost as silly as cutting off a limb.

> When love becomes friendliness
> no possessiveness, no jealousy
> no desire to dominate
>
> When love gives unconditional freedom to the other
> then it becomes friendliness
> and that is the highest human consciousness can reach
>
> The moment you have reached to the state of friendliness
> you have arrived home
>
> *Bhagwan*

Shobha my darling

I hope I shall not offend you by saying how surprised I always am at the pleasure I get from meeting you unexpectedly, as I did yesterday when I caught sight of you on the foreshore. It is only two weeks ago that I was standing at the end of the Cobb in Lyme Regis in Dorset** and thinking of you.

**   The Cobb was immortalised in the novel *Persuasion* by Jane Austen, and also in the film *The French Lieutenant's Woman*, which was based on the novel of John Fowles.

Dear, dear Shobha - having returned from Europe

The cold and smoothness of the sea under the moon was sheer ecstasy. I do not have to tell you how pleased I was to see you this morning. Coincidence seems to smile upon us. Do I need to say I miss you.

Dear Shobha

I don't think I deceive myself in believing the physical aspect of our association has always been less important than the spiritual one, though I realise that the one contributes to the other. I also admire and respect you – chiefly for qualities I lack in myself. And if I have not been able to bring myself to leave N. and my home - many people, knowing my age and circumstances, would not take my behaviour as showing that I do not love you.

My darling

I am afraid to listen to opera (at the moment) lest I long for you even more. I now have your watch on my wrist *(a gift from Douglas' trip to Europe),* so I can never forget you - even for a 'minute'. The days are so beautiful - the sun so glorious. Love makes everything so much more alive – magical - as was our walk last Sunday.

Shobha

When you said recently on the foreshore that my marriage is dead, I said that when I met you, I was not conscious of anything seriously lacking in my marriage or life generally. Because of advancing age and familiarity, my love life had become dull.

But I did not realise this until you and I entered into our love affair of poetry and passion. Perhaps what you give me is not really to be expected in ordinary married life.

in my arms, I thee entwine
thou my love, and I am thine
encircled in your loving loins
as our hearts and souls conjoin

rare the hours when we commune
and let our bodies fall in tune
yet my love, i long to be
surrounded by you lovingly

tenderly we touch each part
of our bodies and our hearts
beloved douglas, don't presume
that the flesh should be taboo
i can feel that you are true
when you love my body too

to separate the heart and soul
from the body, is not whole
we are one my love, when we
embrace as fully as can be

hold me not so far away
learn to love in every way
body, heart and mind and soul
only then can we be whole

if you leave out any part
you will never know my heart
come beloved, lie with me
come, and love me totally

when you kiss and call my name
in my heart there burns a flame
in my body also grows
a longing, when you hold me close

enter in my deepest core
love me, leave me nevermore
commingling by the waterside
i, my love, with thee abide
forever in your loving heart
nevermore to be apart

Douglas

I can see how difficult it is for you to contemplate a change in your life of the magnitude that would be necessary if you were with me - or even to be on your own, and I know how difficult it is to leave someone you have been with for a long time, and how much guilt arises, and the fear of what they will do to themselves when you are gone.

Given all this, I realise that if you decide to stay with N., it is not simply out of weakness, but because of the immense upheaval it would cause in both your lives. The only thing that would enable you to take such a step would be a tremendous love in you for me, or a great desire to be free and on your own.

As times goes on, I see you more as you really are, and you are now beginning to criticise me to my face, which although it hurts - feels better than receiving painful letters from you and suffering in silence for days - in consequence.

You are now seeing me in all my colours, and obviously you find me wanting in some ways and I disappoint you in others. It is good that this should happen now. I have never wanted you to worship me - unless that worship was based on knowing both sides of my nature – the dark and the light – and yet you did once worship me. Now you can see that I am just an ordinary woman – capable of great love, and also capable of wounding you at times.

It is not possible for us to love deeply without also experiencing much anguish now and then. They go together. It is easy to settle for a relationship that is comfortable and placid, but then there will never be the delights we have known. I do not advocate a life of anguish and misery Far from it. I would love to be happy and contented, but I do not expect this to come easily. Bhagwan - in one of his provocative moments, used to say "If you *don't* fight at least once a day with the one you love – then it is not love."

Shobha

I angered N. only a week ago by saying that for the past year, you had been my whole life. This is true. To love you and to be loved by you has been a profoundly disturbing experience, which has made me a different person. I suspect that only a woman of your extraordinary openness and emotional honesty is capable of the kind of love I seem in some strange manner to have aroused in you. It has often humbled me and, to my discredit, sometimes even frightened me.

Music, especially opera, pierces me more deeply - because of you. Colours are more vivid. Reading your *Song of Love* to Bhagwan made me more responsive to poetry and the beauty of language. In some way, I think you are even responsible for my taking risks down at the ocean in the mornings, which I would not otherwise take.

My love

Your idea of 'having a child' together is beautiful to imagine - but I do not need a child to bring me close to you.

If you wish to see me and not leave your home, you must be prepared for my fits of rage and frustration now and then. You cannot expect to have me in the way you want, and to have peace and quiet as well. That is how I show you that all is not as it should be, and nor can it ever be, while you are divided in your loyalties. So accept it, and suffer my anger and my tears as part of what I am - given this messy dilemma.

I would love to sleep with you in my bed, and hold you in my arms at night, yet there is something in our love which is not sexual. There are such deep moments like today (when we are simply lying together and I feel at peace with you), that the thought of love-making does not even arise. With you my darling, I will never pretend to be the same woman from one hour to the next - let alone from one day to the next.

Dear Douglas

I am so sorry I was angry with you yesterday. I wish I could have been more understanding. It hurts so much after we have a row – the ache seems to last for days, and I sense you feel the same. When we have a real fight though, as happened last week, somehow it brings us even closer together. A half-hearted fight seems to be a thousand times worse than a total one.

Douglas

The essence of a love that is true, is the capacity of both lovers to state their feelings (and if known - their causes) to each other, at the time – rather than after the event – though even the latter is better than nothing. The closer lovers come to being able to express at the precise moment, their feelings as they arise – the greater the possibility that understanding can occur.

I am sad you are disappointed in me, and do not find me a source of constant merriment. When our love is 'good' you take me for granted, and when there is misunderstanding, you discard me.

Douglas

I feel you may be in love with some sort of fantasy and not with the real woman that is Shobha. However much I give to you, you seem to find me wanting - as if I should embody all you have ever wanted in a friend, a lover, a wife or a mother. I obviously cannot be all things to you.

Surely you cannot expect our part-time relationship to fulfil you in every respect, when you are not prepared to make any sort of commitment towards that end. We are fortunate to share many ideas and interests, and you are blind if you do not see that.

I suggest you find someone at university with whom to discourse in the areas we do not share. I do not feel I am lacking in any way. On the contrary, I feel I have much to share with you, and find it extremely frustrating that you do not make sufficient time to engage in anything other than cuddles, walks in the park, a little music and much talking.

I feel you want me to fulfil your every whim and fancy, without giving the necessary time and attention this requires. I think you should be grateful for what we already share, and not ask for more unless you yourself are prepared to give.

My dear love

My heart has softened at last. Now the tears flow, the anger abates, and I feel warmth arising for you again. Sometimes the hurt feels so great, I have to retreat to heal the wounds.

As I have said to you before, 'greed' seems to be my major problem. I am always asking for 'more'. You seem to be content with me (provided I don't ask for more). You never ask me for anything at all. When I 'get in touch' with my devotional nature, I am glad we are in love at all - and to want more, seems almost a violent concept.

When I move into my masculine, assertive, demanding self – I want more, and probably nothing would satisfy. The feminine, devotional approach feels more beautiful in this moment.

There is much about my life that I cherish as it is. At times I am not discontented with my lot. I went to the Gilbert and Sullivan opera *Princess Ida* last night, and it made me wonder whether our love has flourished because it is forbidden - and romantic love needs such conditions in order to arise. Once things become formalised - love is lost. So says Bhagwan and many of 'the greats'. My ideal would be a state where both partners were free to meet when they wished - without any third party - but did not live together.

I came down to watch you running and swimming this morning. I also watched you through binoculars at the ocean as you waded out to sea. I was also able to watch N. for once, which I have not been able to do before, as she is either angry with me or engaged in conversation, which does not allow for observation.

Bhagwan 'used to say' if you are jealous, go and watch your beloved with the 'other woman' and see what you can learn from the experience. In other words – face the fear that is possessing you, and feel the attendant emotions.

I was surprised and glad to find I can't help agreeing with you - that I am not at all in competition with N. Two more unlike women I cannot imagine. I can see what I offer you is something quite different from what she offers, and I did not feel particularly jealous.

However, you have formed a pattern over the years, and deep-rooted patterns are hard to break, so I understand these ties are reassuring and supportive to you. But I feel the joy we share is not 'of this world', and that is the level at which I wish to live. If domesticity tends to eliminate a spiritual dimension in love, then I do not want it. I like to think both are possible, but I have rarely seen it in others.

Dear Shobha

For some time, I have felt more concern about N. that I did before. In part, this is because it is only recently that I have realised my continuing to see you will bring about her breakdown - even if I don't leave her.

I am simply not prepared to do this to her. It would be a dreadful thing to do to a woman who has devoted the whole of her adult life to me, while at the same time being an example to other women of what a married woman with four children can achieve on her own in legal practice. Despite having had four children, she has never at any time been away from her office for more than six weeks. For the most part, her life has been one long rush. But not an unhappy one - until I met you and turned away from her. Can you seriously wonder that I feel compunction about causing her misery at a point in her life when she was beginning to look forward to a more leisurely lifestyle - with me ?

There has been no amatory reconciliation between us, and it may be that, because of you, it will never occur. So far as I'm concerned, I'm prepared to retire from the sexual race and live on 'the recollection of emotion in tranquility' - as expressed by the poet Wordsworth.

Douglas

Do you not consider that to tell me what is in your heart, could heal differences that arise between us? I wish you could tell me if I offend you at the time - rather than after much reflection, and then with bitterness. Is it my ardour that quells your own ?

Am I to play the part of the aloof heroine Bathsheba in Thomas Hardy's novel *The Madding Crowd* - to win your favours ? Is it the challenge of pursuing me that you wish for ? When I offer myself too freely, you take me for granted.

Shobha

As you know, I was shaken when I discovered recently, that N. thought our relationship had been platonic since I came back from England. How she came to believe this, I don't know.

Reading the English novelist *Thomas Hardy* may have reinforced my belief that marriage or exclusive cohabitation is not the natural circumstance of romantic love. Hardy thought 'true' love was inseparable from heartache. I left a note for you when I left for England, to be delivered to you in the event of my not coming back (i.e. dying). It said –

> Ours has been a strange affair by any standard,
> with moments of great joy and tenderness and spiritual uplift.
> You are a rare and beautiful person
> and I consider myself favoured by fortune in having known you
> and in having been loved by you.
> Goodbye, my love. Do not shed tears. I have lived a good life.

My darling

I hope our separation 'will' cause you anguish of spirit - so you may find out if your love for me is worthwhile. Only through such suffering a soul is born, and for your sake and mine, I wish you could pass through this fire, which burns away the old and paves the way for the new. By now you must realise my love does not waver – only my moods.

I wish you courage and trust in the days to come and hope you discover what it is you really want in life. I wish it was me, but the issue is deeper than that. I suspect you wish for freedom from all constraint - even that of a wife or lover.

I know your house alone is sufficient reason for you to stay where you are. It is so convenient and comfortable. As I have moved so many times, it is easier for me to negate the importance of physical luxury such as you enjoy. And I have few possessions, by choice, so it is easy to suggest that you leave yours - though you could take them with you.

The spiritual dimension which you seem to call 'affinity' can only really flourish in freedom, and that is the dimension I most covet. You are indeed my soulmate. Perhaps life will see fit to bring us together when the time is right. All my love – Shobha

My dear one

It is true, as you have often stated, that romantic love survives because there is no guarantee of tomorrow. It is inherently insecure.

Far from seeing you as a 'way out' of my position as 'social misfit number one' - when I first came to you, I felt I was offering 'you' an alternative way of life, and sensed that at rare moments, you were on the brink of jumping over into my world. As things evolved, I regarded our being together as arriving at a completely new lifestyle, which combined the best of both our lives.

Shobha my darling

I miss you so much. My longing for you seems to follow cycles, which I cannot fathom. Last week I found my desire for you grew steadily as I read Hardy's novel *Jude the Obscure,* and when I finished it, my aching for you was almost unbearable. I long for you as I have never longed for you before. There are points of resemblance between you and (the heroine) Sue, as both of you are rebels against the mores of your times.

I thought that this, coupled with the sensuality of Hardy's depiction of her, may have accounted for the surge of longing for you. But yesterday, after an interval of several days, my longing was even greater, without any stimulus from Hardy.

Douglas, my love

Now it is clear me, in the words of our poet Kahlil Gibran, that 'there is no purpose in our friendship - lest it be for the deepening of the spirit'. This is where we began. This is also where we have failed - or lost the path.

For myself, I have now returned to that state where I am aware that above all else, there is no possibility for me to live in any way - save the way of the spirit. This involves a reversal of the values of the 'world' as you know them, and a conscious decision to 'let heaven move my heart'.

My attraction for you lay simply in that you 'seemed' to be thirsty for a spiritual dimension in your life. Whenever that thirst abates, and whenever I lose contact with my spiritual nature, there is no point in our being together.

It is my prayer that you will at some time before you die, discover that you have a soul - a spiritual side to your nature - and if this ever happens, then perhaps we will have something to share. Until then, all my love is with you.

I have read Samuel Johnson's epic poem *Rasselas* and found it very moving, but Johnson seems to have missed the point that true 'happiness' is not found by any external search, but by entering the inner realms of one's own being. It is a tremendous revolution in consciousness – almost impossible - yet not quite.

Chapter 3

A song of praise upon your lips

The guitar was Douglas' first gift to Shobha

Shobha

A couple of days ago, I put your letters and notes to me together - and your poems in another pile. As far as I could, I arranged them in chronological order. But without dates, this was no easy matter. I found it was only rarely I had pencilled a date on a letter or poem.

It is possible to fix an order in your early letters, but where the later ones had no internal clues, I fell back on the order in which I had put them in the file. The task was made more difficult, because at one time I collected together all your letters in which you said the situation was intolerable, and you wanted to see no more of me.

In another pile, I put the letters and notes from you - which you returned after one of our differences. I also found seventy pages of letters, mostly unfinished, which I wrote but never gave you. Also many quotations of Bhagwan which you gave to me, and copies of your own articles on *The Mystery of Love*, *The Death Experience in Love*, *The Ultimate Fit* and *When It's Time to Say Goodbye*.

It was moving, but very distressing, to read at one sitting all you have written to me over the past months. Many of your letters are beautiful, with a fluency and urgency which comes from the heart. But the fluctuations of mood are quite bewildering - almost as if governed by some law of alternation.

It was only when I was near the end of sorting your letters and poems into different piles, that I realised I was making a mistake by separating them. Your poetry is the natural expression of your joy, while letters can be the vehicle of your despair - so your letters divorced from your poems convey too gloomy a picture of our relations. This is not invariably true, for some of your letters are quite lyrical, but it is near enough the rule, to make my separation a mistake.

Dear Douglas

Your letter was full of condemnation. Your pen is mightier than my sword, and if you have anything unpleasant to say to me, it would be better if you said it to my face, so I have an opportunity to respond – rather than by letter – which I find a very cruel medium to express negative emotions.

I was very hurt by many of your comments which are resounding through my mind with surprising frequency. You are painting a picture of me as a moral degenerate, whereas I would say my devotion to you has been total and undeviating since I met you, and my respect for your body – likewise. Our love, despite the pain, has been the only love I have experienced that was mutual and totally fulfilling, and our love-making has for me, always had the same quality. I sensed the possibility of a very nurturing and even spiritual, life with you. But that would require trust and commitment to love.

Above all, you should do what makes you happy. If it is enough for you to be with N., I can re-create a life for myself that does not include you and restore old friendships and find new ones, if need be. I wish it could have been with you. You seemed to be the other half of my soul. Love needs to be nurtured and given infinite care - for it to flower.

It is so good to be in love with a man with whom I can have intelligent discussions and exchange different points of view. Our love is a growing thing – learning from each other every day, trying out new ideas and arriving at new remedies for difficulties we are experiencing. It is so exciting and demanding at times - yet always fruitful in the end.

How I love you for being able to test possibilities, find them wanting and then revising our approach to a situation. How I wish we might evolve day by day and experiment day by day, so our love grows from a small seedling into a beautiful tree.

Douglas

Lying with my head in your lap was so perfect. I felt I could stay there forever. I lose myself, when we talk in this way. I find such intimacy with you, that it is almost overwhelming.

My love

Nothing else in life matters save to be in your arms. You are a kind of opium to me. You raise me above all others things** and only in you, do I find peace. Your beloved Shobha

> When I am down, and O my soul, so weary
> When troubles come, and my heart burdened me
> Then I am still, and wait here in the silence
> until you come and sit awhile with me

> You raise me up, so I can stand on mountains
> You raise me up, to walk on stormy seas
> I am strong when I am on your shoulders
> You raise me up – to more than I can be

These words echo the song *'You raise me up'* which Shobha now associates with the sculpture *Je t'adore* which she installed on the oceanfront in 2017 to celebrate Douglas and the beach community. The words of the song came to her unbidden just before the installation occurred. The lyrics are by Brendan Graham and Rolf Løvland.

Douglas

When we are constantly concerned about the 'fate' of our love, it is difficult to keep the flame burning brightly. Meeting at night as we do, brings with it a magic that is not possible during the day, though meeting early in the morning at the ocean, has a different kind of freshness and exaltation.

I want to fly with you, my love. I feel we have become a little earth-bound in recent weeks. If love becomes a serious matter between us, all is lost. I want to laugh and dance and sing with you, and treat each other playfully. I am learning a lot from being with you, and it is not an easy education - but despite the trauma, occasionally I see the light and feel we are moving towards something which neither of us has ever dreamt.

It is full moon. I love you with all my heart and soul and will never leave you unless you cease to love me. I ask you to be with me until one or other of us encounters death, and give you my being - body, heart, soul and mind, while at the same time remaining true to my inner light and following my own destiny. Our love is not a transient phenomenon, but of the beyond. I ask you to trust the power of a love which is borne of the spirit and will never die.

My dearest love

I have been sitting by the river meditating - feeling overwhelmed with love and gratitude that you are here, and I am absolutely content. Perhaps you are right, and we have already arrived at the peak, and there is nothing more to be done. The miracle has already happened !

When I meditate, I understand there is nothing more to desire. All is perfect as it is. We are already so blessed to have each other. In recent weeks, I realise that only through meditation can peace arise and I can only truly love when I no longer need you (the paradox). May that day come soon. It is such a delight to appreciate you without wanting more.

My darling Shobha

I have often said that romantic love is likely to be killed by an everyday, domestic relationship. The last eighteen months have been the most exhilarating and disturbing period of my life. You have lifted me from the mundane to the edge at least, of the spiritual. I have loved you very deeply. But I do not want to share my everyday life with you. I want to treat you like champagne, not common everyday table wine. There have been times when you seem to agree with me.

You wrote in one of your letters that we were touching heights we have never touched before and see things in a new way, and share a beauty which is impossibly rare, but when you try to fix on our love and mould it into some traditional pattern of how things should be, the problems arise. In one of your early poems, you have also written 'If I could accept the highs and lows of love without attachment, I could die fulfilled'. But (typically) this is only one of your voices. Your next poem runs :

> dear one
> with all my heart I love you
>
> yet bitterness and rage are also true
>
> if you can understand
> then you may love me still
>
> if you cannot
> then you have never loved
> nor ever will

Though I did not covet your body when I was first drawn towards you - looking back it was inevitable and natural, that we became lovers. Our talk has been the chief glory of our love (for me) - not so much the ideas themselves, as the wonderfully relaxed and 'in tune' manner of our talking. Without being lovers, we could never have achieved such intimacy. At times I have felt the fusing of our bodies has generated true freshness of thinking.

You may say that for a person like me, it is only through making love that I manage to slough off for a while the conditioned layers, which ordinarily make it difficult for me to form close relationships with others. When we are together, I find myself fondling you, even when we are engaged in serious talk. We touch each other almost as if we 'charge' each other in an electrical sense, by doing so.

Despite the offensiveness of my note to you, half of me is hoping you will overlook and ignore it. You have been so good to me, while I have so often been grudging and my lack of consistency worries me more and more.

I keep looking in the post-box in the hope of finding something from you. Last night I drove past your home. Why I did so, I can't explain. Your car was gone and there were no lights, so I drove past your mother's house, thinking you may have stayed with her. What is the explanation of behaviour of this kind ? It seems that I cannot keep away from you. Is this the test of love ? Why is it that the simple passage of time since I saw you last, progressively strengthens my need for you, as if seeing you assuages a thirst ?

You gave me the impression a few days ago, that you had come to the conclusion that your best strategy (as far as our being together was concerned) was simply to wait for your 'elderly plum' (Douglas' words) to fall into your lap. Events may prove you right.

Who ever loved
that loved not - at first sight

Christopher Marlowe

My darling Douglas

I have realised in the past week, how important the 'law of alternation' is for us. It is the crux of the matter. Yes, I love you dearly, so dearly that I almost feel like saying "Because I love you, I will not live with you" (in a similar vein to the French scholar Heloise, who wrote to her ill-fated lover Peter Abelard in her letters - "make me anything, other than wife (excerpt below)."

On the other hand, I would never reject the opportunity to live with you - if you wished. I am prepared to 'try and see'. Yet, given our different backgrounds and lifestyles, it may be better for us to retain independent households and be together 'when the spirit moves us'. You are as important to me spiritually, as you are physically - but both are best.

> The name of mistress instead of wife
> would be dearer and more honourable for me.
>
> Only love given freely,
> rather than the constriction of the marriage tie,
> is of significance to an ideal relationship.

And on the importance of letters - on which their relationship in later years was based, and for which she and Abelard are renowned – Heloise adds :

> What cannot letters inspire?
> They have souls
>
> They can speak
> They have in them all that force
> which expresses the transports of the heart.

Abelard was equally eloquent when, despite his reputation throughout Europe as a philosopher - he penned the following lines, which as has been mentioned earlier, were echoed by Douglas in a slightly different way, when he stated that the letters between himself and Shobha would be their only memorial.

If I am to be remembered – it will be for this : that I was loved by Heloise

Abelard with his pupil Heloise - 14

My love

I realised tonight how careful I must be, not to allow you to consume me: to be consumed by love, but not by you (if that is possible) - for your values are, as yet, still vastly materialistic, and you are still predominantly governed by the expectations of others.

I cannot allow you therefore to influence me while this is the case. In time, perhaps you too will come to understand the depths to which love can go - the extent to which it can risk - and how finally, it transcends death itself.

Would that I could be with you until your death - and would that you could accompany me to mine. I desire above all, never to be separated from you in spirit.

From Shobha to her friends to be read before or after her death (1983 and updated 2017)

Beloved friends

- I have done all that I wanted in this life

- I have loved many people and been loved by them

- I have lived with Bhagwan, an enlightened master, which fulfilled all my spiritual dreams

- I have sung, danced, written poetry and cried and laughed to abandon

- I have moved amongst many different people

- I have meditated for many years - and in that time been blessed with beautiful moments of ecstasy and understanding

- I have spent many years discovering all there is to know about myself, without which this note could not be written

- All that remained for me – was to love and be loved by my soulmate - my beloved

- I found him - and he found me

- We were together on earth for thirty-three years and shared countless spiritual moments together, as well as much agony due to his personal circumstances

- Having shared such a love, I knew I would be happy to leave this body and not return again to a physical existence

- Douglas has now left his body - yet we are in constant communication - between his world and mine

- I did not want children as I always knew that I was waiting for a guide, who would lead me on a spiritual path

- Bhagwan's last words to me before I left India were "fall in love totally and hold nothing back" and one year later, I met Douglas

- Bhagwan knew that without this ultimate experience of total love, I would not be complete

- Now the journey is over – at least the earthly stage – and I look forward to reuniting with Douglas at a different level. He has let me know on a daily basis – that he is with me.

- In one of my letters to Douglas, I wrote "I cannot conceive of life without you. You have become my very soul." And this awareness has not altered, since his physical departure.

- I do not expect ALL my friends to comprehend these words, but fifty years of meditation, five of them lived in India - have contributed to this understanding - which is based upon my experience - not knowledge from any other source.

- I thank them for their love for me and all that we have shared and ask them to remember me with joy, for I am happy to go on the next stage of the journey.

My darling

Whenever I find myself feeling creative – about to explode with something unknown - there are two urges. One is to escape; to pretend that the urge is not there; to divert myself by some other activity, for there is fear I may not be able to make it happen; that what I may produce will be mediocre; that I may not be the perfect medium for its expression.

Secondly, there is the fear that I will be interrupted in the course of my endeavour, and that the thread may be lost and may never come again. There may never be another moment like this one. There may never be another chance. I may never again be so receptive - so open to the divine.

Can you understand? It is not that I consider that anything I create is worthy - but still the fear is there. Fear that *nothing* of worth may come, and fear that *something of worth* may come, and I may not be able to allow it to come in all its fullness - through my own incapacity or through some external diversion.

If we were ever to be together, I ask you - if such moments arise, that you allow me the freedom to be alone until they have passed - however long that may be. I love you with all my heart.

Dear Douglas

I was hurt when you said you felt I was blackmailing you by talking of wanting to die, but surely that is what N. has been doing for a very long time? There was a time when she constantly talked of drowning herself if you left her. Please allow me a little latitude also - to consider disposing of myself.

Dearest

Do not lose heart. I am today reading the Persian love epic of *Layla and Majnu* from the seventh century – a true story of thwarted lovers whose families would not allow them to be together. In their own ways, they go mad with longing for each other.

I do not want 'only' to support the notion of romantic love. On the contrary, I support the idea of 'mystical union', which this Persian epic extols. Our love has not been ordinary in any sense. There are many lines in the epic poem which imply that 'contemplation' of the beloved is a greater joy than possession. I am not yet at this lofty stage, but there have certainly been times when this has been so.

Dear Douglas

Tonight I wandered by the river and there was a blue mist over the water and everything was covered with dew. I thought of you and felt tears in my eyes. There was a sweet happiness in remembering you. I don't understand it. I don't pretend to have any control over it. I don't know what will happen to us, but I do know that when I am in nature, I am overcome with a sweet delight which reminds me of you.

Perhaps it is the same for you in the early morning when you are swimming in the moonlight. It is as if the world stops for a moment and there is peace and tranquillity.

Shobha

My life is in a terrible tangle. As I've found so often in the past, my need for you grows as the days pass without seeing you - or at least speaking to you. If I haven't heard from you for more than two or three days, I sometimes find myself beginning to wonder if you may not be finding solace with someone else and the most ridiculous suspicions enter my mind.

This happened last night. I am too ashamed to tell you the form of my latest bout of jealousy. You would laugh, if you knew. But it was strong enough to send me out in the car just before midnight. I hoped N. would not notice my absence, but I found her sitting waiting for me when I returned home.

Why should I be so unreasonably jealous ? Despite your occasional (deliberate ?) mention of other suitors, you have given me absolutely no grounds at all to doubt your love and fidelity. What frightens me is this sudden flaring jealousy, which comes over me out of the blue, and I imagine you and some other man making love as we make love. A green-eyed monster indeed.

I simply can't understand the fluctuations in my feelings for you. Whereas your love for me is constant - there is an almost drug-like need in me - for you.

> As when with downcast eyes we muse and brood
> and ebb into a former life, or seem to lapse
> far back in some confused dream
> to states of mystical similitude
>
> If one but speaks of him or stirs his chair
> ever the wonder waxeth more and more
> so that we say "all this hath been before"
>
> "all this hath been"
> I know not when or where
> So friend, when first I looked upon your face
> our thought gave answer each to each, so true

> Opposed mirrors each reflecting each
> that, though I knew not in what time or place
> methought that I had often met with you,
> and either lived in either's heart and speech
>
> *Alfred Lord Tennyson : A sonnet on Friendship*

Dear Douglas

I feel that both N. and myself are sitting on a volcano of jealousy and anger and resentment most of the time. Although there are quiescent phases, it is always a potentially explosive situation, and you as the man in the middle, can never know when it will blow up. A wrong word or look or allusion might trigger a reaction in either N. or me. It is inevitable. It is part of the dynamic of a triangular arrangement, where neither woman accepts the other's presence.

> Today the sun shone
> but I did not
>
> I lay upon a carpet of the greenest grass
> that grows upon the hill
> above your house
> and gazed into the arching boughs
> of gums that towered overhead
>
> Beyond the sky so blue and still
> as was my heart
> I saw the parakeets in pairs
> chasing one another through the air
> and my heart so cold and lonely
>
> Such beauty - yet no beauty I beheld
>
> However green the grass
> However blue the sky
> However sweet the song of any bird
>
> I cannot hear and cannot see
> and cannot feel
> unless I sense you
> stirring softly deep within
> and know that we are one

In the last week or so, especially when your first grandchild was stillborn, I felt a strange sweetness with you that seemed to herald a new phase. I felt your eyes had - to some extent - been opened. I will visit her plot at the cemetery often - until I hear from you again.

Sunday was the first day of Spring. How strange it was to see you at her grave. I sang the song I wrote for her (from the mother to her child) at the folk club and it was well received. I will also be singing it at the folk festival very soon, so she will be immortalised in music.

Dear darling

Today left me feeling happy inside. It was so beautiful lying with you - kissing you. A very sweet moment in our troubled existence. When I leave you and go back to work, it is so difficult to retain the sense of your presence. I am assaulted by so many different influences. Today, it was quiet and tranquil, and I was able to feel you with me a little longer. Dear love, thank you for your tenderness. I wish there could always be gentleness between us. Please tell me if I hurt or upset you at any time. Only then can I become more caring. Much love

My darling Douglas

I have just come from your grand-daughter's grave. It is sunset. I wish I could have been there for the funeral, but of course - that could not be. I wanted so much to kiss the earth and commune in some

way with the spirit of the child. To me - she is not gone. Even though some like to think there is no spirit that continues, in my deepest heart I know it is not so.

Tonight I am thinking of death also, as my mother is not well and there is always the possibility she too may leave us. Sometimes I feel she wishes to go - so she can be with my father. I am enclosing some earth from your grand-daughter's grave, in case you wish to keep it.

Dear love

I am full of ideas and this is a very creative time. Lately, you and I have been sharing so much wonderful music: the songs of Alfred Deller, of Purcell and the *Songs of the Auvergne.* These are the moments that make mystics out of mere mortals such as we are.

Plans for my workshop at the folk festival are proceeding. It is to be called *Songs of Love, Lust and Longing* and we have nine singers participating, including an Irish harpist. We must now weave the whole pattern together in a coherent and interesting fashion. There will be much fun and laughter and the audience will join in the choruses. The songs of longing - which I sing - are balanced by the hearty, lusty, joyful love songs of the other performers.

Beloved

The workshop was absolutely perfect. It could not have been better, except that M. forgot to press the recording button, so we have no record of the occasion. I prepared the workshop for you my love - and because of you. Our love inspired it and I wanted you so much to hear it and share with me - after the event. The laughter was tremendous and there is such joy in singing together. I wish with my whole soul you could have been there.

Although folk is not your type of music, I am sure you would have been infected with the enthusiasm we shared during those hours. If you ever see something soft and cuddly which I could hug, to remind me of you, please buy it for me as a Douglas-substitute.

It seems my mother's recent attack of anxiety began when your granddaughter was stillborn. It may be connected with her grief for my father, which was never expressed. She never mentioned him again, after his death - which is pretty catastrophic. Her first child died at birth, and the association with your granddaughter's death, seems to have aroused some deep feelings in her. I was a fool not to realise this might happen. Since then, she has not been able to hear your name. Sweet dreams and all my softest kisses upon your eyes and lips.

Dear Douglas

I have just read the article you gave me by the English author *John Fowles* on 'writers', and it seems so apt. One of the difficulties of writing, is or are the popular misconceptions about writers. If only it was possible to ignore completely what others thought; to be unconcerned with the outcome of a piece of writing i.e. whether it is published or not - or even appreciated. But most of all - to be free of the wish to make a career out of it.

When Shobha worked at the university, she was known as the 'wordsmith' and was often given the task of either writing a document or article in the 'best possible' language or correcting language that was not well-written. She loved the description.

Writing is a strange gift. I have always felt that to sing for money was wrong - for no logical reason that I could discern. I sang for weddings, but only accepted small gifts in return. Yesterday, a local tradesman said to me "I heard you singing. Are you professional ?", and I replied that I did not like to sing for money - and it is quite true.

Art or beauty in its purest form cannot be bought or sold or produced at will or on command. It arises spontaneously at sometimes awkward moments. And then it must be obeyed - almost like a god, or a call to love. To feel great love arising and not to pursue it, only destroys the energy that has arisen. To deny the impulse to create, is also to go against one own's nature.

My darling, today was delightful. To sing is delightful. To hear you sing - is also. To sing with you is fun. I follow two genres, the classical and folk. They give me an insight into both ends of the spectrum – the disciplined and the spontaneous. You follow the classical line primarily, but it would be beautiful if you could include both in your 'repertoire'. It gives a wholeness that is otherwise absent. To be able to relax and sing folk songs easily and effortlessly is quite different to producing a prescribed sound, as is required in the classical tradition.

Dear heart, bless you. Today you were, in your own word – sweet. Perhaps that is the only word that adequately describes it. Much lovingness – Shobha

My sweet bed-mate

Because of the loveliness of this morning's coming together, I am feeling rather mellow, after the traumas of the past few days and weeks. I dream of such quiet contentment. I am feeling warm and nourished by our morning sojourn. I am glad you have initiated my new abode with your presence. I pray for peace above all. All my love and care – Shobha

Chapter 4

A prayer for the beloved in your heart

15

To wake at dawn with a wingéd heart
and give thanks for another day of loving

To rest at the noon hour
and meditate love's ecstasy

To return home at eventide
with gratitude

And then to sleep
with a prayer for the beloved in your heart
and a song of praise
upon your lips

Gibran

My dear friend

You may doubt my words, but as I have often said "If we are meant to be together - nothing on heaven or earth will keep us apart." Remember me always.

My dear love

I have been reading and enquiring of late into the post-death dimension, which you do not believe exists. But 'even if you do not believe in it, that does not mean that it is not so', *(This is an adaptation of the saying of Rousseau – French philosopher of the 18th century.)* Voltaire *(his French contemporary - and also a philosopher)* said that to accept the idea of being born 'twice' was no more difficult than to accept the idea of being born 'once'.

I am now absolutely convinced that we slip quite easily upon death - from one physical reality into a non-physical one, and that preparation for this state, which is similar to a dream state (which often seems more real than earthly reality) is highly desirable, even though we may return to another physical body at a later stage (if you accept the idea of reincarnation).

It is even possible to communicate between realities, so that if you – for instance - left your body - I could contact you and vice versa. Because of this new awareness on my part, about which you no doubt vehemently disagree, I am not in one sense, worried about us - because I know we cannot ultimately be separated.

My own position is also that of Bhagwan viz :

> I would like all my sannyasins (friends) to die so deeply
> that they are never born again
>
> so that they can disappear into the cosmos
> and become part of the whole

Shobha

Looking back now, you may agree it is a pity we have no record of the ideas we exchanged in our years of talking. The interplay of our minds and characters brought us occasionally to the brink of valuable insights. Still, even if memory has dimmed, the detritus is probably still there, so that ideas will surface again. Deep down - nothing is ever lost completely.

My dear, dear love

I have just returned from a sannyas orange celebration. Such ecstasy ! We meditated for an hour - after which I felt I was floating in a world where my senses, intellect and emotions were intensified. I felt awakened in a tangible way, and experienced a reaffirmation of all those values I know to be true and absolute for me – the presence of love and the continuation of the spirit.

I realised how much we differ, and how deeply we meet in other ways. Apart from my days in India with Bhagwan, our love has been the deepest experience of my life. You are a mirror to myself (as I am for you) and a dearly beloved with whom I want with all my heart and soul - to impart what I have learnt in my short life.

You have of course, also imparted much of your soul to me. We have balanced each other - but there is much more to be done. We have been so tender with each other, and praised each other through poetry and opera and song. We have also been exceedingly unkind to each other in our judgment of the other's behaviour, because we are both trying to bring the other around to our viewpoint. Nevertheless - ours is a very powerful union.

You often look at me wonderingly as if I was a strange creature, and in a way - I am. There is another state, of which we can barely conceive. We have touched upon that joy. You are a co-celebrant in that magnificent experience. I feel I can pour my whole soul to you, even if it is not always fully understood. You have also opened your heart to me, and received my outpourings of love and devotion, and for that - I can never thank you enough. It is as if the cup is overflowing.

I know I am not yet 'home'. I am still struggling in the dark some of the time, but when I am not struggling, I am flooded with joy. Part of the reason I love you so, is that you allow me to enter your soul, just as I allow you to enter mine, and in so doing, the magic happens, and we are no more the same.

Although our paths are different, I sense we are heading in the same direction. We are to each other – an inspiration. Even death will not destroy my love for you. I feel we are part of the same fabric, albeit with different dyes. Until we merge again, be true to your inner light and follow your heart to the ends of the earth and beyond.

Dear Douglas

On one hand I am delighted to talk to you about the many ideas that are passing through both our minds. On the other, I feel my heart must first be engaged, otherwise there is a feeling of intellectual enquiry for its own sake - without the underpinning of emotion - which I cannot accept.

It may be true that in order to engage the body, say in love-making, it is necessary to engage the heart of a woman first, or the soul. It may be true for you, as a special variety of the male species, that in order to engage the body or heart or soul, it is necessary to engage your mind. Once engaged, you move quite naturally from a profound intellectual idea into your heart.

A variation on this issue is expressed in the words of an unknown author (not myself) :

> With women
> love usually proceeds from the soul to the senses
> and sometimes does not reach so far.
>
> With a man
> it usually proceeds from the senses to the soul
> and sometimes never completes the journey.

Until we embrace again, in the heart, as well as in the mind – my love is with you.

Douglas

You view life as ending with physical death, and while alive, you give high priority to the materialistic lifestyle viz. family, children, house, possessions, education, intellectual knowledge, cultural achievement, physical prowess etc. Love, tenderness, affection, meditation, prayer and spiritual awareness come at the end of the list – if at all. It is the reverse for me.

I am primarily 'eastern' in my consciousness now. This is the subtle difference between us. You are constantly trying to get me to function in western, rational terms. I am no longer western - nor rational. I respond intuitively and emotionally and spiritually to impulses and messages I feel - from within my own psyche.

I am in touch (but unfortunately, not constantly) with another level of reality which I long to share with you - but which you seem unable to grasp. It is therefore left to those rare moments of 'exaltation' - during extreme intimacy between us or after making love, or sharing a deep and profound insight, that you may 'have a taste' of it.

The basic premise from which I operate (on a good day) is that 'when the time is right, it will happen'. Just as I have said to you recently "If we are meant to be together, nothing on heaven or earth will keep us apart". Again, on a good day, I have a fundamental trust in the universe - and our part in it.

My dear friend – I do not know what your life purpose is. Perhaps it is to live each day as it comes - accepting each moment. Being 'reborn' each day – as you yourself put it - and dying each night. That is very sound, and of course, the core of eastern mysticism i.e. living in the present. Perhaps you are more eastern than me ?

I know that 'love' has become for me, not only something for which I am willing to live and die, but also in a strange way, a 'vocation'. My proposed doctorate on the *Sociology of Love* is a step towards this - if only because it gives me a *raison d'être* for discussing my favourite topic with a wide range of people.

My dear one - full moon

I started listening tonight to a tape of a woman by the name of Jean Houston**. Her entire discourse was related to the topic of my thesis, and more specifically to questions of 'spiritual' love, which you and I have discussed in depth over the years. She was speaking of the difference between loving 'god' or the 'beloved' as she (and the Sufis**) call it - and loving a human lover.

The fatal mistake - Houston believes - is to direct all one's love and energy towards the human beloved, rather than to the divine, as the sheer intensity of the love given - burns out the recipient (in our case – yourself).

- **Jean Houston - American author involved in the 'self-development' movement**
- **Sufis are the mystics of Islam. Their practices are centred around adoration of god as the beloved, who is celebrated through song, music, dance, poetry and devotion.**

Is it possible I may have been giving you all the devotion and adoration I previously gave to the divine beloved? If so, this might explain in part, why you find me so intense and withdraw from me from time to time, and feel suffocated and uncomfortable at being 'worshipped'.

In some eastern traditions, the human lover is worshipped as the divine, but only when both partners willingly enter into a spiritual union and are aware of the divine principle, which forms the basis for their evolution in a spiritual way. In the west, many people enter marriage or relationship with no conscious intention of spiritual growth.

Houston states that if a lover pours gifts on the other in a cornucopian fashion, it is inappropriate. There should be a reciprocity of giving. You have often said "I love too much" and that is my downfall.

The difficulty lies in the fact that you may not recognise a divine element in our love, and thus do not see it as a way of contacting an even deeper dimension. Many people, Houston continues, who add creatively to the world, are those who are in a spiritual relationship with each other. I'm not sure what our contribution to the world will be. I hope there is one.

Dear Douglas

It occurred to me today that perhaps what attracted you to me in the beginning, was the quality of 'worship' which was evident in my poems to Bhagwan - which you admired. If this is so, you also, to some extent, worship your muse Samuel Johnson, and may have recognised this quality in me.

The Russian sociologist Pitirim Sorokin *(whose ideas Shobha incorporated into her doctoral thesis which was not completed),* distinguished between western and eastern cultures which he called 'sensate' versus 'ideational'. This division may no longer be so easy to sustain in the present, where technology has made the exchange of ideas between eastern and western cultures - an instant phenomenon.

Whereas in the West - romantic love is predominant, and familial love and spiritual love or love of 'god' are not: in the east (because romantic love is less common and marriages are often arranged) spiritual love of 'god' and familial love may be the cultural ideal.

Although 'self-development' is becoming popular in the west, spiritual practices of meditation and yoga for example, were not common in the west, until the sixties. Until then, they had been traditional eastern methods of attaining spiritual understanding or enlightenment.

As the cultures collide, so romantic love will become more prevalent in the east, and spiritual love more prevalent in the west (as was demonstrated in the 'new age movement' of the sixties and seventies in western countries).

Dear Duggles – I am going to bed. I have zillions of ideas which I wish to discuss with you. There are lots of lovely dichotomies, just waiting to be explored - apart from east and west, romantic and spiritual etc. Love, love, love

My dearest love

I am a person who is not overly oppressed by guilt, largely because - for the last ten years, I have been consciously attempting, in every manner possible, to understand the sources of my guilt, and to eradicate them. Your life by contrast, is plagued by this emotion - which is not surprising, in the circumstances, and the destructive effects of this are enormous. They account for your many changes of mood and attitude and inconsistencies in your behaviour which cannot be otherwise explained. I understand you have tried to come to terms with it, but without success.

Whatever you do - you feel guilty. If you love me - you feel guilty that N. is unhappy. If you stay with N. you will feel sad because you have abandoned me. As far as I can see, the only possibility is for you to delve deep within your soul to discover what it is that 'you' truly seek.

In one version of your favourite archetypal legend of *Parsifal*, your hero was required to ask the wounded fisher-king (who is the guardian of the Holy Grail) "What ails thee and what is it that can heal you?" In every man or woman's life there comes such a point, where without answering this question - no resolution can be found and no peace achieved.

The Consecration of Parsifal by Gurnemanz (a knight of the Holy Grail)
Artist unknown

My particular dilemma is how to value myself enough, in order to trust that the universe will sustain me, even if I withhold myself from you, in the hope of a deeper union at a later date. I have never had that necessary courage, just as I imagine you have not had the courage to penetrate your own internal boundaries of understanding.

It is my innermost feeling that our love has not been for any small or paltry purpose. It has taxed me beyond my limits of endurance and pain, and there has been a reason. It seems to me that if I truly love, as I profess to do and feel I do, there must come a time when it is put to the test. As in the *Judgment of Solomon* from the Hebrew Bible.

The king was called upon to arbitrate between two women who claimed the same child as their own. To resolve the dispute, he suggested the child be split in two and one half given to each woman. The true mother immediately responded by relinquishing her right to the child - that it might be saved.

Dear Douglas - full moon

What seems to happen in love, is that initially there is a great sense of release and all fear is gone. Great risks are taken, and it seems as if 'paradise is here now'. In our case, because of the lack of freedom, either due to possessiveness or external restraints, this initial beauty is lost. Whereas I try to hold on to love to deepen the pleasure, you tend to let go - and then the magic returns.

I have been wondering what is the answer, and it is obvious – to let nature take its course, without attempting unduly to influence the outcome. The truth will assert itself, if we do nothing. Given time, I hope you can find what it is that moves you to the core of your being, and trust it can bring you out of darkness. This struggle of the soul (called, in the literature of mysticism 'the dark night'), is very much what your muse - Samuel Johnson, must have passed through. Perhaps that is why you identify so closely with him, because you are also struggling to find your path.

You were born together
and together you shall be
for evermore

But let there be spaces in your togetherness
and let the winds of heaven
dance between you

> Love one another
> but make not a bond of love
> Let it rather be a moving sea
> between the shores of your souls
>
> Fill each other's cup
> but drink not from one cup
> Give one another of your bread
> but eat not from the same loaf
>
> Sing and dance together and be joyous
> but let each of you be alone
> even as the strings of a lute are alone
> though they quiver with the same music
>
> Give your hearts
> but not into each other's keeping
> for only the hand of Life
> can contain your hearts
>
> And stand together
> yet not too near together
> for the pillars of the temple stand apart
> and the oak tree and the cypress
> grow not in each other's shadow
>
> *Gibran*

Dear Shobha

Bearing in mind all the complications of separating from N., I suspect that age and inertia will keep me where I am, though I may misjudge the real strength of my need for you and how empty life will be without you.

My love

I have never seen you more beautiful than you were today – tender, soft and vulnerable. You were all I could ever desire in a lover. When we lie side by side and our eyes meet – listening to gentle music, I feel a serene kind of 'knowing' that fills me with great joy. There is a tremendous sense of peace and delight.

Love, for me, is the greatest force in existence. When tenderness and passion come together as they so often do for us, it is as if a fire is lit inside – whose flames can never be quenched. I give you my heart.

My dear one

While meditating a few moments ago, I felt that we truly share together what can only be seen as a spiritual relationship. We see each other rarely, yet you are an inspiration for me, if only because of the longing you engender in me to be with you again; to make good any misgivings and redress any perceived wrongs. It seems to me at least, that ours is to be a love where we come and go. We become very close and then move apart, to create a space to bring us even closer - when we come together again.

Dear Douglas

Keep singing. It is the key to the wellsprings of joy.

Chapter 5

And think not you can direct the course of love

16

Shobha

Yesterday was the first time I managed to resist your siren call. It was a very difficult and distressing thing to do. Ours has in many ways been a beautiful relationship. Its essence has been a kind of communion; a state of ease and peace and warmth and gentleness, which has not been quiescent, but in some strange way, has fostered the easy exchange of ideas.

I believe, paradoxically, that this communion exists *because*, and not in spite of, our frustrations. It is often said that marriage is the death of love. Perhaps the greater truth is that anguish is the seedbed of that form of exaltation which people call love - and that satiety is fatal.

Dear Douglas

Consider that in three and a half years, we have never slept together (in the sense of going to sleep together). It is so horrific as to appear brutal - even to a casual observer.

Jiminy**

You seemed to be on the brink of something, while you were engrossed in your reading in recent times. Because you were also feeling somewhat fragile (while you attempted to give up your medication), you were more open and receptive to new ideas. But there are some glimpses in life that are permanent, and I feel that you have in some tiny way stepped over the boundary between the old and the new.

> ** Jimmy was the name by which Douglas was known as a child and a young man – as his second name was James.

I have found you tremendously confiding and warm during the past week and I love to share with you the intricacies of language, but sometimes I simply want to lapse into a very human condition, where I enjoy you simply as a heart and spirit and body – without the machinations of the mind.

I sit here at my writing desk with my beloved dictionary at my right hand. I feel as if I am relearning the English language because of our conversations - but my darling - my treasure - I am still primarily a creature of the heart, and the languages of touch and feelings are mine - beyond all words. I hope you can understand.

My love

Love is not determined by such mean and limited factors as duty, pity, compassion or obligation. It has a life of its own, that sweeps such considerations aside. While you are governed by such things - know truly that love is not there. In those moments of abandonment, when you are ready to risk all - know that love is alive and well. Nature asserts itself. The consequences of going against her are vast and subtle.

To deny love is to destroy your own soul. No amount of profound reading or inspired music or even the sensual delights of the flesh, are a sufficient substitute for the sweetness and intimacy of love.

You know my heart. Trust in my anger and in my tears. Trust in my audacity. It is the greatest gift that I can give.

I have been touched by Bhagwan again. Tonight - during one of his videos, he talked about love and the law that operates between lovers – of attraction and repulsion, and of course I thought of you, and how much we have hurt each other and how much joy we have also given.

According to Bhagwan, when two lovers are really intimate – so close that they almost feel they are one - at that very moment, there is an opposite movement that pushes them away from each other. They start to find fault with each other - to fight.

The closeness is too much and they cannot bear it. They fear some loss of themselves, and then after being apart for a while, there is a longing to be together again.

You have often said, the degree of the joy we experience is in direct proportion to the degree of pain, and I don't want to agree with you, though it is possible. I would prefer to think it is possible to *always* be in love. But then I am a romantic.

Bhagwan was also talking about physical love and said there can't be any real union at the level of the body and the level of the heart. There are only *moments* when there is union - and then those moments are gone.

The *real* union happens when individually - you and I become whole in ourselves and only then, can we be wholly together.

For lovers, when they feel as one - they give each other a taste of what can be, and hate each other because it is only a taste which does not continue. Even so, *he says*, we should be grateful for the taste.

My love

I sometimes feel as if your body is my own. It is so dear to me. I feel as if you are inside my own flesh and can actually feel what I feel. How is that possible? It is uncanny - to say the least. Our caressing of each other in deep relaxation is so enriching. It is entirely different to the more torrid form of lovemaking which has its place and is a great catharsis of body and emotions, but which lacks the extreme delicacy which we shared today. May you also feel blessed.

how to tell the world
about our love

how immortalise in some way yet unknown
this tremor running through our hearts

how to say what can't be said
the joy so inexpressible

I had not thought of love becoming *even deeper* after physical death. What a wonderful possibility to experience. My heart yearns for yours.

Being with you, gives me such glimpses of beauty, that it is almost too much to bear, and at the same time, there is such a fear that we may some day be parted - if only by death. Yet my love for you is such that I feel we will not be parted - even in death. It is probably quite irrational and illogical, but then, most truly great things are. How I wish you could experience this immensity. That is my dearest wish.

It occurs to me that we spend more time *talking about* love, than actually loving. At the entrance to Bhagwan's house in India, where we went for his discourses in the morning, there was a sign which read LEAVE YOUR MIND AND YOUR SHOES AT THE GATE. Could that be our sign when we meet - so it is like a sanctuary where we can commune? Perhaps you could take off your shoes, as a sign of your willingness to put aside reason - at least while we are together?

Today you said that ninety percent of the time you are in your rational mind. I seem to live one hundred percent of my life in the heart. It is only in rare moments that you slip out of the mind and we become really close.

I do not subscribe as totally as you, to the idea of love as an experience of excess, madness, ecstasy and despair. For me, it is primarily one of tenderness, caring, warmth and sharing beauty, and only secondarily one of sadness etc. I believe trust is possible.

I agree with some of the suggestions you made today about engagement, occupation, absorption etc. Until I met you, I was content to live simply – walking, meditating, singing, dancing and writing. Because of our difficult situation, I am more restless and require company so much more, so that I do not dwell unduly upon our lot.

How did you like the line from Oscar Wilde's play *Lady Windermere's Fan*? *The greatest tragedy in life is to get what you want.*

In the last few days, due to accumulating pressure of company at work and tasks to be done, I have learnt so much about the need for solitude and peace. It seems as if for some people viz. ourselves, this is often an urgent and consuming need, without which we suffer a subtle yet excruciating tension and find all else burdensome and tedious, unless our *need to be alone* (for a time) has first been satisfied.

Today I left you with a curious mixture of satisfaction - combined with a feeling that we had not *plumbed each other's depths* – as if I still wanted to connect with you at the soul level. Yet I was very glad we made love - though I had not considered the possibility beforehand.

You mentioned that you thought I had *courage* several days ago, and surprisingly - two of my friends have said the same in the last few days, and even more surprisingly, for a very long time I have woken in the morning and gone to sleep at night with my last thought being a prayer to the universe for 'courage' to endure our situation.

It occurred to me a day or so ago, that making love (for me) is somewhat akin to listening to opera for you. You are so keen to obtain the best possible sound, using the most finely-tuned equipment.

So too, I feel making love is a little like creating or listening to a beautiful piece of music, and just as you are not interested in one aria from an opera, so I also prefer to indulge in the entire opera - if at all possible. Perhaps you can understand?

Yesterday I talked to you of meeting you *soul to soul* and you were a little cynical. Although you may never have had any experience of the soul and are skeptical, that does not mean it does not exist, and since I have had countless experiences of that nature, I would prefer you allow me to use the term, as it has meaning for me.

17

I am amazed at times at how perceptive you have become. I am often insensitive to the mood of the moment, whereas you seem to have an inbuilt acceptance of what 'is' and do not ask or desire more. I am often seeking a *deep* harmony between us. You are content to let the harmony descend as it wills. When I let go and relax with you, I find this comes so much more easily, than when I seek it consciously.

Today was beautiful. I love to hold you in my lap. I love to stroke your face and hold it in my palms. I love to kiss your warm forehead in the sun. As you have often said, I give the word *afterthought* new meaning.

I would like to reiterate that tears that have a definite focus to them are easy for another to understand e.g. loss of a parent or child, but tears that imply blame or neglect by the other are difficult to comfort. Perhaps that is why you find it difficult to accept my weeping at times.

When I mentioned to you today that I was feeling tired and a little ill, I was hurt by your retort that women with families are happier than single women. For a start, I don't feel that I am single. I felt your response was surprisingly lacking in warmth and understanding. You often tell me of your tiredness and aches and pains and I am sympathetic. Your response to me was unthinking and tactless. If you want me to be married and happy, then perhaps you should come and live with me. I am aware that although you may extol the virtues of family life, and fancifully think I should partake of them to alleviate my fluctuations of temperament and disposition, I do not feel you respect the family and the domestic life any more than I do - quite the contrary.

To simply reproduce the species and live in a permanent liaison with a man, simply because this is the prescribed social pattern and earns respect and acceptance, is to me the most degrading unforgiveable human spectacle. That most people choose to engage in such a liaison is their affair, but I would never (again) become a party to such an arrangement.

That I have chosen to live alone for forty years, is a decision closely associated with my desire to follow a mystical lifestyle, which I doubt many members of the population would find attractive. In this sense, I am rare. And I wish to be respected for that (by you), not condemned for not participating in the mass mentality of inevitable procreation and conjugal responsibilities.

I do not consider myself 'single' in any sense. That I live alone is without question. That I am not legally married (to you) is obvious, but I do not consider myself emotionally *single,* since I have a very close and intimate emotional life with you - though we have no legal contract to *sanctify* it - nor are we socially acknowledged as a marital pair.

Nevertheless, in every sense I consider that I am not *alone,* and I prefer to have the intimacy we enjoy, a thousand times more than the so-called *happiness* of the married couple. I prefer my lifestyle to the absence of intimacy tolerated by so many couples who face the television together night after night and read their separate books and newspapers for hours on end, without exchanging anything that could be termed intimate. If this is happiness - then I am glad to be without it. If the constant routine of domestic life is joy - then I forsake joy.

I choose in this life to forsake all that is repetitious, boring, lacking in energy or interest, that dulls the heart and the body and mind and soul. I choose only that which energises and enlivens and enchants and promotes love and warmth and understanding.

You say I am *different* from you, yet your tone of voice carries both condemnation and admiration. I said to you tonight that I *need* you to believe in me, but it is not so. I don't need you. If you don't believe in me, I am not reliant upon your faith in me. I am strong enough on my own.

But it would be easier and more beautiful if you trust in me and gave me encouragement. I do not need parental figures in my life any more. I choose to be guided by those who encourage and inspire. I have no time to waste with those who analyse and dissect. I am only interested in friends who create and enjoy.

Never try to place me in a box that is already too full with so many unconscious souls who have never questioned their lot - let alone taken steps to change it.

**

I am beginning to understand that your *soul* is literally in your *hands* – just as mine appears to lodge in my breast. I used to feel so content to lie with you by the river with my head in your lap - holding hands. In the words of the mystic Kabir – *Why should we two ever want to part ?* Can't you see that what we have is precious ?

The peak of mysticism is *to be* - not going anywhere - not asking or seeking for more. I simply want to *be* with you. Sometimes I think I want a conventional relationship, but I detect an immense sense of claustrophobia at the thought of ever again being in a situation where I am forced to compromise my own soul - in order to co-exist with another. At least with you, I voluntarily choose you - despite the difficulties. You do not bind me to you. If you tried, I would escape.

My love

At times when I am away from you, I am more at ease. I feel a sense of freedom (as you once expressed it) like "taking off tight shoes after a marathon". And yet there is also a vague feeling of disquiet that surfaces when I am physically alone or unoccupied – an ache – a sense of emptiness, of futility, of meaninglessness - that something deep inside is *missing* viz. you.

When you return my love, I feel utterly fulfilled as a woman, as a person, as a spiritual seeker. I feel as if I have found my god – that for which I have sought so long. If you then withhold your love, for whatever reason, I feel that I shall die.

To taste the beauty of perfect intimacy may be known to few, but I have tasted it so often with you. Perhaps it is my greed for such communion that is my downfall, for when it is not there, I am distraught – bereft.

My wish is that even when we leave these bodies far behind, we shall meet again, just as we have been together, long before this little life began. We are old souls, you and I. Our meeting in this life is not accidental. We belong to each other, throughout space and time. I give you my heart. Love such as ours can never end.

Dear darling

Tonight was the gathering where my singing duo *Heart and Soul* were the guest artists, and we were magnificent ! We sang for a very mixed audience of university friends and family, and taught a number of songs to those gathered – some with harmonies.

The highlight came at the end of evening when we dimmed the lights, asked for requests (which is a risky proposition) and for hours sang calypso, folk songs of the sixties, Australian folk songs, pop songs etc. It was unbelievable. Suddenly the whole evening became an integrated, intimate, cosy affair.

When I arrived home, I remembered that I had spent my adolescent years from fifteen to twenty, going from one gathering to another, singing along with the guests and feeling as if this was my mission in life. Tonight I felt the same way - though the sing-a-long at the end was totally unplanned. But with a singing partner, the experience is so much more rewarding   I feel I was born to sing and to love.

My love

When I returned home from my friend's wedding, I caught the final scenes of Shakespeare's *King Lear* with Laurence Olivier as Lear - and wept profoundly. It was so brilliant. The father and daughter (in the play) were acting for all intents and purposes almost as lovers - with such adoration for the other.

I thought of us, and how innocently I loved you when we first met – without fear, and I felt how I wish I could love you so again – so trustingly.   Tonight I feel swept away by a love that encompasses all. I kiss your lips. I kiss your heart.

**

I think you are right in observing that after love-making, your dark mood descends – for a variety of reasons. As you know, I keep a journal of sorts, and I went through it last night to see if there was any cycle in our moods. I expected to find some correlation in my case, with the moon or menstrual cycle, but this was not so apparent. What was quite obvious, was that after making love – on many, but not all, occasions, you withdraw emotionally. I therefore feel threatened and start to cling and this exacerbates the situation.

I am beginning to see my own shortcomings, a little belatedly. I am quick to attack (if I feel hurt) and suspect I often injure you, without knowing I have done so, unless you tell me - and you do not.

I wonder if the word *delight* means *of the light.* I have just thought of it. I could hardly move for an hour after you left – you were so *delightful.* I was in a kind of stupor – rather pleasant but very strange.

I agree with you that love-making often precipitates a crisis for us and brings things to a head. I feel we were swept away by a current today, as so often happens, but despite its intermittent intensity, I want to believe that our *kind of loving* is as precious as any other and to be greatly cherished.

Dear Jiminy

If paper be the fuel of love – type on ! I treasure our letters as if they have almost a sacred quality (some of them, at least). I have been immersed lately in my search for songs to sing, and am suffused with melodies that make the heart lighter and the day brighter.

Douglas

The verse I wished to quote to you as I left today - was from Shakespeare's *Hamlet* :

> Doubt thou the stars are fire
>
> Doubt that the sun doth move
>
> Doubt truth to be a liar
>
> but never doubt I love

Beloved Petrarch (Italian scholar and poet c.1300)

As you know, my folk duo *Heart and Soul* performed at two gatherings this week, one of which was a three-hour singalong in a very laid-back fashion. Last night however, it was an exercise in opulence (i.e. the setting). It was a little daunting as everyone continued to talk at maximum volume when we were about to start singing, so we sang with much gusto.

Every few moments the whole crowd would burst into song as a phrase caught their attention and jogged their memories. It became a very happy occasion, but an exhausting experience nonetheless. We were not used to such an atmosphere.

Two singers joined us for most of the evening, and another encouraged everyone to participate. Several people remarked that the world war one songs were a "bit before their time", which I found rather amusing, as they were mostly in their sixties. They wondered how two such young women could possibly know them.

It was an amazing experience to have under our belts. We have also been asked to sing carols at another street party in December, so the work continues to come in. We have been asked to sing at the Casino which is not our scene, and at a well-known restaurant in the city - which is very cosmopolitan. I doubt we will take up either offer.

I am becoming more aware lately of the *performer* personality - the excitement of preparation, costuming, makeup, the nerves and high expectations; the almost gruelling nature of the performance itself; the relief and ecstasy when it is over, and the inevitable *lying-in* the next morning to recuperate. We have both been doing this since we were children, and it is *in our blood* so to speak. I wish you had been there, but felt you nearby. I would love to share with you the excitement before and afterwards.   Signed Laura (*the love of Petrarch's life).*

Douglas

I watched a video tonight, which stated Bhagwan has been unwell for the past two months, from poisoning (when he was imprisoned briefly in the United States awaiting deportation), but he has now recovered a little. The poison (which was later identified as Thallium) leaves no trace in the body, but has a long-term effect, and was administered to him in his food.

Bhagwan said he had been struggling with death for some time, had lost his immunity to infection, lost weight and his hair has turned prematurely white. These are apparently symptoms of poisoning. He said only the love of his friends *kept him here (on earth) - otherwise there was no longer any reason to stay.*

I had felt instinctively that something was wrong, hence my desire to go India soon to see him, and this has strengthened that wish. Now I have a reason to work, and to work with love. I wish I had gone to him earlier, but the time was not right. Life is very sweet right now. I feel suspended between two worlds – the east and the west – as I will soon be returning to India.

Chapter 6

To bleed willingly and joyfully

18
Hero awaiting the return of Leander
to swim across the Hellespont,
holds her beacon to light the way - in vain

Evelyn de Morgan 1885

Douglas

Tonight is full moon. Would that you were in my bed beside me. The night is still. I stood outside your castle in its darkness and felt again how wrong it is that we cannot spend even a night in each other's arms. When will that day come?

A short poem by Anon :

> Gladly I'll live in a poor mountain hut
> spin, sew, and till the soil
> in any weather,
> and wash in the cold mountain stream
> if we but dwell together

and another from the English poet Percy Bysshe Shelley :

> The fountains mingle with the river
> and the rivers with the ocean.
> The winds of heaven mix forever
> with a sweet emotion.
>
> Nothing in the world is single.
> All things by a law divine
> in one another's being mingle.
> Why not I with thine?
>
> See the mountains kiss high heaven
> and the waves clasp one another.
> No sister flower would be forgiven
> if it disdained its brother.
>
> And the sunlight clasps the earth
> and the moonbeams kiss the sea.
> What are all these kissings worth
> if thou kiss not me?

Shobha's notes after arriving in India

Traumatic trip in light aircraft from Bombay (now Mumbai) to Poona. Felt the plane would explode. The noise was tremendous. Wondering why we are here. *(Shobha was travelling with a friend from Perth.)* We already have all that we seek. We are already buddhas *(enlightened persons)*. Have we been called ? I hope it will become apparent.

Sannyasins regularly felt the 'call' to come to Poona to be with Bhagwan - often for reasons which became very obvious - once they arrived. Thousands would flood into the ashram at these times - like homing pigeons.

The next day I began to feel more at ease and at home. When Bhagwan spoke later in the day - after an absence of seven weeks, due to illness. I felt he was speaking just for me and I was totally consumed by love. My whole body was weeping and shaking uncontrollably, as if my heart would break with joy.

In my first *individual session* which was called *Voice Dialogue*, one of my inner voices said "I don't know, and I don't need to know". The whole session was light and full of laughter. I felt such a sweet release.

In the West, I am surrounded by people who *need to know*, in order to make decisions and to have control - but that is not my way. There is no decision to make. Krishna, who was conducting the session, said he had trouble finding any problem in me.

It didn't seem that the problem was Douglas, but it was my mind which kept interfering and saying I must make a decision about him. That was the difficulty. Krishna said the energy in my session was very beautiful and mentioned my ambitious streak – to save the world, write a great book etc. but added there was no need for such a purpose.

Musicians at the ashram came from many countries

The following day, Bhagwan said our task was to create as many buddhas as possible, for the world could not last for many more years. I realised that I wanted so much for Douglas to be a buddha (as if he was not one already) - and this was the basis of my love for him. I was stunned after the discourse and could not speak. It seems as if this is why we were all called to the ashram at this time, and why Bhagwan had come out of silence. Tonight he said again that the only message to spread, is that we are already '*god*'. If we can at least remind people - it may catch on and the seed will sprout.

Strangely or perhaps not – *remembrance* has been my deepest understanding, and this is what Bhagwan said to me when I first become a sannyasin, when I was kneeling at his feet and looking into his eyes wonderingly. He said "It is only a question of remembrance".

The words of the Persian poet *Hakim Sanai* have since become most precious to me, and will be my epitaph –

> Remember - this is work entrusted
> Remember beloved - we shall meet again

Letter sent by Shobha to Douglas from India

I am sitting in the most beautiful tropical ashram garden surrounded by bamboos that tower into the sky, and trees and palms that intertwine to create a paradise of colour and cool tranquility. I am surrounded by marble buildings which have a certain sanctity, and everywhere there are fairy lights giving splendour and fantasy to the nights.

Since I was last here, the entire six acres have been literally covered in green - with waterfalls, rocks and paths and wooden benches in nooks and crannies for meditation. The atmosphere is relaxed and peaceful, despite the thousands who are here. The mornings are cool and crisp – very conducive to falling in tune with nature. It feels so friendly. Gone is the heavy bureaucratic feeling of the 'old days'. There is an easiness that is very pleasant. I find I am not at all restless – wondering why life should be a problem at all, and why we don't simply relax.

As I have mentioned, Bhagwan is speaking again, after a long absence, but whatever he says, does not seem to matter. It is quite apparent to me that I don't *need* to be here – it is just a refreshment. Yesterday I sang and danced and the music was very moving. Peace is the only way to describe this setting - despite Indian traffic, the dirt, the queues and of course - mosquitoes. Our trip to the ashram was quite traumatic in little ways. It was not at all certain the hotel could find us a room (despite our receipts for the booking), my luggage tore open on the tarmac and our plane was delayed.

We now have an air-conditioned room with refrigerator and television (none of which we use), but no hot water. It is lukewarm in the middle of the day, but we boil the water in any event, swallow lots of vitamins and buy fruit in the street to take home. Everything is utterly contaminated. The air is thick with dust. The rickshaws speed into the path of oncoming trucks. Beauty and ugliness together.

It seems as if half the 'orange' population of Perth is here at present. Just like being at home. Much of the time I am here, I feel you with me. It doesn't really feel that we are apart. Perhaps it is because I am so used to writing to you, that it bridges the distance of space and time. The first four days here were transformative and I was floating high above the clouds.

Now that I have begun to work in the office for a short period, I am temporarily on the earth again and I miss my wings. But being here has made me more aware and grateful for what we both have. You have given me such a gift in yourself. I have just been treated to a fireworks display outside my window. Very impressive. Indians love crackers.

By the river near the ashram

When I stop long enough to relax and imbibe the beauty of the gardens, I am uplifted. I just heard a few strains of opera as I sat by the pond, surrounded on all sides by leafy green fronds – and my heart leapt. Opera and nature and Bhagwan and my love for you, are enough to convince me that I am already home. Bhagwan has me in the palm of his hand. I have wept copious tears. How I love him. I wish you were here. There is so much overflowing energy. It is delight-ful. All my love – Shobha the Buddha

Beloved darling – second letter from Shobha to Douglas from the ashram

I was amazed that, from the moment I arrived at the ashram, I felt you with me so closely - as if you were actually there inside my body. Yet still I wished you could at least taste the atmosphere of the ashram, but more importantly - Bhagwan himself – in the flesh.

I have learnt so much in such a little time. I have realised I can be there or here, and it makes little difference. except that in Australia I am comfortable and my love for you *binds*' me there. In India I am extremely uncomfortable physically, though this might settle if I were here for a longer period. Yet in my deepest heart, I feel I am one of those who wishes to be free and apart from the *central organization*.

When I arrived at the ashram a few days ago, Bhagwan had been ill for seven weeks and had not given any lectures in that time. He was poisoned as I mentioned to you - in America, and has been battling the after-effects for three years.

They day after I arrived, it was announced that Bhagwan would appear again. I felt as if he had been waiting for me. Naturally, the atmosphere in the ashram was ecstatic.

Bhagwan has said in the past, that he wants his lovers (a.k.a. friends) to *set the world on fire with meditation* and that *the most creative act in the universe is to remind each individual that he or she is already a Buddha (i.e. enlightened), and that when we relax and trust ourselves completely, without concern for the dictates of others, we realise that we are already home* (i.e. that we are divine). This is the change I perceive, however subtly - in myself.

Although theoretically, I have accepted for about eight years that I am already *whole,* and have experienced many times what that state might be like, it is only now that I feel it to be an *almost* ever-present state, even though I sometimes forget who I am.

Many times, in great stress, of course the *remembrance* is lost completely for a time, but Bhagwan is working in such a way these days, that it is not possible to forget for long. It naturally follows that if I am, in my natural state, a buddha - then of course, you also, in your natural state, are a buddha as well.

Voice Dialogue

When I arrived, I signed up for two sessions - one called Voice Dialogue - which isolates the conflicting inner voices which pull a person in one direction - then the other. Of the many voices in my mind, I identifed four, viz.

- the heart - which longs to be with you
- the mind - which tolerates the situation resignedly, but understands why you have not been able to be with me fully
- concern for the future - which makes me feel a decision needs to be made about what we will do together, and finally
- the not knowing space in the present moment - which surrenders and simply trusts, in innocence - that life will take care of the outcome (for us)

Most of the session I spent laughing, as I realised I had no real problems, and that my attempt to resolve our dilemma was the problem. I felt a great weight had been lifted from me. To remain in the *not knowing* space is not that easy, however. It requires an exceptional openness and vulnerability. The tendency of the heart is to 'long' and for the mind to 'try to resolve'. Letting go - is the most difficult process of all.

Sufi dancing

While in the ashram, I joined in Sufi dancing, i.e. the singing of devotional love songs (Christian, Muslim, Hindu, Buddhist and original) while moving in circular dance formations. You might remember that at a folk festival in Australia, I ran a workshop that included Sufi dancing. I have mentioned to you before that the Sufis are the mystics of Islam - who worship through love, music, dance, poetry, nature and beauty.

In the ashram previously, I worked with a Sufi dance leader, who used to be a Jungian psychoanalyst in England. At the time, she said she had been inspired by my enthusiasm to put together a computerised edition of Sufi songs, and she gave me a copy shortly after I arrived on this occasion. She would like to work with me to issue a complete book of songs with music and dance instructions.

De-Hypnotherapy

In the De-Hypnotherapy session, I asked to *work on* my relationship with Bhagwan. In a guided meditation exercise, I found myself on a mountain beside a gushing stream and out of that stream – came Bhagwan.

He came towards me and we embraced like old friends. There was such warmth and I could feel his heart beating with a deep and overwhelming love. When I looked into his eyes, there were no questions any more. This was the answer - simply love. We walked, arms around each other, to the edge of the mountain and sat there together. I asked what I should do (but not in words) and he replied "The world is very dark. It needs more light." Then I asked again, but not in words, what I should do *about you* (i.e. Douglas), and he said "Be a buddha."

Sufi dancing in the ashram

In the same session, I recalled incidents in my past which had given me the same warmth as the episode I have just mentioned viz.

- making love with you - with your hand upon my heart while I was looking at you
- sitting at the back of Bhagwan's garden long into the night - under the stars - writing my S*ong of Love*
- the experience or vision I had - just before I decided to leave my marriage

At the close of the session, I was asked to visualise what my heart most wished for in terms of love, and I felt Bhagwan holding both yourself and myself in a very warm embrace. You may remember, I once drew a picture of this same moment.

As a further extension of this, I was asked by the person guiding the session, to go even further and see what more was possible, and I felt the three *of us (Bhagwan, you and me) sitting side by side, all as buddhas, - each one having arrived home.* It was a marvellous moment for me. The de-hypnotherapy technique - of which I have had many sessions in the past - taps the deepest layers of the unconscious and even points to events that will take place in the future.

Past Lives

Later, I signed up for a Past Lives session and Bhagwan discoursed on this topic a day or so afterwards. This always seems to happen. It is as if he knows one's most intimate thoughts. Whenever I was wrestling with an issue in the past, he would mention it in his lecture that night.

The Past Lives session was illuminating. In order to recall past events, it is absolutely necessary not to force memories, but let them come, as if out of nowhere, of their own accord. I asked "Why have I not realised I am a buddha in previous lives?" In other words - why did I not find understanding - at that time?

Recalling childhood moments and my not very comfortable feelings about my current mother's womb, I remembered a life as a monk in Tibet, meditating on the side of a mountain – with beautiful scenery. Mountains seem to figure prominently in my unconscious remembrances.

I died in Tibet in a peaceful state, yet that peace lacked joy and laughter. Bhagwan's last life was seven hundred years ago - in Tibet. Perhaps I was with him then? I then recalled a life, where as a female Hindu devotee with a spiritual teacher, I engaged in all forms of devotional ritual and worship. There were flowers and incense everywhere but it felt very musty and confined.

Sannyasins celebrating in the ashram

My final recollection was of a life as a gypsy - singing and dancing in the presence of many people who were laughing, making love with their beloveds, swimming and generally enjoying life. I felt very at home in this setting.

Coming back to the present, I acknowledged a conflict in myself between my Zorba (gypsy) and my Buddha-nature (monk, meditator). Whenever I wish to let Zorba reign, my buddha stops me. Yet the art lies in pursuing both paths at the same time – quite a tricky endeavour.

As you know, Bhagwan states his philosophy is that of *Zorba the Buddha* – a blend of spirituality and materialism. There seems to be a certain frustration in my life about singing. For me - *cantare è vivere* (to sing, is to live). Otherwise I die inside. I must find a way.

What's in a name ?

Bhagwan informed us that Gautama the Buddha (i.e. the original buddha) had asked Bhagwan if he could use him as a vehicle for his work - thus fulfilling Buddha's prophecy that after two thousand five hundred years, he would return as *Maitreya* (the friend).

Bhagwan said he had accepted and would now be known as Maitreya the Buddha, and he and Buddha would work together. He would no longer be known as Bhagwan (which means 'the blessed one') - which was a name rooted in Hindu tradition, and which he now totally rejected.

Several days later, Bhagwan stated that Buddha was also so grounded in archaic traditions, that Bhagwan could not co-operate with him either, and would henceforth expose Buddhism for its repressive philosophies.

Having disposed of the Hindus and Buddhists, he said he would now be called Zorba the Buddha - as this was his unique way. Soon afterwards, he said he had received criticism from Buddhists about his use of the word 'buddha' - therefore he would now be called simply Rajneesh, and his disciples could call him 'Beloved'.

Some time later, Bhagwan decided he would call himself *Osho* – meaning *oceanic* - though I believe there are several other meanings. This name has remained. I felt it was hilarious at the time, but some people were taking him seriously. It was all a game, but I felt I had arrived at an auspicious time.

Bhagwan has decided to mount an all-out attack on the world's religions and to expose their hypocrisy e.g. the chauvinism of Christianity, Islam and Buddhism, where women are relegated to the status of lesser beings e.g. four wives in Islam, no souls in Buddhism and the male Trinity of Christianity. It is a fire and brimstone approach.

Coming home

I write all this to give you the context in which I was placed while in Poona. Because I was an *old* sannyasin, I was given a seat right at the front close to Bhagwan, which made me feel incredibly at home. It felt like *old times* to be there, as it was often my lot in days gone by, to sit in the front row, eyeball-to-eyeball from a distance of only several feet.

I was also given a pass which enabled me to sit for one week with the *workers* - so again I sat in front of him and could see his eyes while he spoke. This meant so much to me. Many times I felt he was looking and talking to me. Yet as I have said, I felt no urge to stay.

The difficulties of the climate, food, dirt etc., plus the crowds and queues in the ashram (Christmas is the busiest time) combined to make me grateful for my visit and grateful to return *home* – especially to you, my love.

My darling

I feel bemused today, because of some special magic in our love-making. Your taking the house and moving into your new position at the university have drawn me further into your life, so that your concerns become increasingly my own. Quite simple things, such as free access to your house, may have something to do with this.

Third letter from Shobha to Douglas from India - after speaking to him on the phone

I was so happy speaking to you on the phone. I had not realised how much I missed you. Talking to you is like talking to the deepest part of myself. I have enjoyed it here, but it is a strain – this way of life. I long to be in your arms again. Nothing can substitute for the intimacy between two lovers. After I spoke with you on the phone, I felt so elated and cried copious tears. A woman standing beside me, said I looked as if "I was in love."

My love for Bhagwan is deeper than ever, or perhaps I should say it is unchanged. I have always loved him utterly. I always will. Being here or there - makes no difference. In fact, being in love with you has kept the flame of love burning brightly, despite my physical absence from him of five years.

As I mentioned, I have been spoilt while I am here, and I have been able to sit close to him. For this, I am grateful. Yet now, I no longer feel any distance. I only feel love and a kind of familiarity - as if he is my 'friend'.

Darshan is a meeting of the teacher or guru with his or her disciple or sannyasin, wherein an exchange of spiritual energy takes place – in this instance – the transmission of the insight of Bhagwan to Shobha in a non-verbal way. There is an assumption that unless the disciple is receptive to the teacher, the transmission cannot occur.

Darling

Since I have returned to Australia, I feel moved to write again – a rebellious, controversial book challenging many of the established religions, in the same vein as Bhagwan, yet incognito - as many people will not read Bhagwan because of who he is. The more people who write independently with the same ideas, the better. I am utterly at one with his philosophy. I can still anticipate the words he is about to utter, as I was able to do when I lived in the ashram. This letter my love, is my only record of my recent Pune experience, so it is precious.

I am extremely glad we did not meet this afternoon, as I have had time to assimilate my experiences and refresh myself, yet I am even more glad that you called this morning. I felt so at home with you and you have been *with me* all day. Until tomorrow, my love.

Shobha the Buddha

My interest in Bhagwan - like Bernard Levin's interest (in the ashram) - is as a social and psychological phenomenon - the viewpoint of a student observer, whereas you are a member of the flock - on the inside. I have a basic aversion to groups. I don't claim it is a healthy aversion, but it is certainly fundamental.

Darshan

Following her sojourn in India, Douglas – in jest – jokingly addressed several letters to Shobha as *Your Grace - Shobha the Buddha'*. One of the meanings of Shobha's Sanskrit name is *grace*. Her full name is Ma Deva Shobha – mother of divine grace, splendour, elegance and grandeur. Sannyasins used to laugh at the beauty of the names they were given – and wonder at their import.

Douglas

I cannot abide friendships that are not deep and intimate. Hence I prefer my own company to that of the amorphous crowd. I am staggered sometimes by your capacity to engage in meaningless social engagements, rather than seeking out those with whom you could form a deeper connection. Also, I do not want to know anything about what you do with N. It tortures me to think of all the things you do with her that we cannot share.

Tonight there is a stillness in the air as the sun sets and such a refreshing coolness after such a sweltering day. I have just been walking around the river, before all light faded from the sky. Such moments are for lovers. The waves were lapping roughly on the foreshore and I felt there were so many things we have not yet shared – to walk in the rain and in the wind, to sit on the rocks by the ocean as the sun disappears - and to see a simple sunset.

Life is passing us by and these moments are precious. Yet the night is beautiful for us - because we can embrace outside *in the open* and be surrounded by nature. I want to share the best parts of the day with you – when all the earth is quiet. It is *our* time – the time for love.

Perhaps your scepticism about cohabitation is because you have not been truly happy (in your marriage). I have just finished reading *Mister God, This is Anna* and have been trying to find a copy to give to you.

It is an irreligious five-year-old child's perspective on *god* and one of the most moving books I have read. It is based on a true story - but you have to embrace London's East End English totally in order to appreciate it. A tall order for you, perhaps?

I was leafing through your letters last night and found your oft-quoted lines from Lord Byron. Could you add these to your list of poetry *not to be quoted* to Shobha in future, as they offend my sensibilities. I found a line from the film *Shadowlands* about the life of the English author C.S. Lewis last night which is relevant for us –

It's always easier for the one who goes (dies) first.

It will be interesting to say the least - to see which one of us *goes first*, and the effect this will have on the other. It could be the making of us – the ultimate test of love.

**

I have never been closer to you than I am now and I feel this is also true for you. We are beginning to understand each other; to speak our minds more freely, and to tolerate each other's foibles - if not to actually accept them.

Sweetheart, you are so precious to me. Last week I told you I only wanted two things from life – to be enlightened and to love you. You said you were frightened by the latter, but you did not perhaps acknowledge sufficiently the importance of the former - which has been, and always will be, a twenty-four hour preoccupation of mine. It is not a mission lightly undertaken. When I first accepted this as a life goal - fifteen years ago - I left everything in its pursuit. It is not to be easily dismissed, even though it is a path not at all visible, to those who are not similarly engaged.

Have you asked yourself - what is your purpose in life? What is it you desire most from existence – believing that all things are possible? You have seen the biblical quotation *All things that ye ask, believing, ye shall receive*. This is not only a Christian idea, though there are ample references to it in the bible e.g. to have faith enough to move mountains.

It is also a central tenet of mysticism and of most current psychological schools of thought. But it requires a revolution in consciousness – a refusal to allow fear and doubt to dominate over trust, though they are of course, natural obstacles which must be overcome - before the *tide can be taken at the flood,* as Shakespeare expressed it in *Julius Caesar* -

> There is a tide in the affairs of men (and women)
> which - taken at the flood
> leads on to fortune
>
> Omitted
> all the voyage of their life
> is bound in shallows and in miseries
>
> On such a full sea are we now afloat
> and we must take the current
> when it serves
> or lose our ventures

Darling - cherish me in your heart. If fear and doubt arise - let them be there, but do not become their victim. Remember Gibran's words -

> And think not
> that you can direct the course of love
> for love
> if it finds you worthy
> directs your course

Remember me – until you come.

Dear Douglas

You hurt me a little today when you said the Bhagwan part of me was a stranger to you. And yet it was the Bhagwan part of me that attracted you in the first instance - through my poetry. Perhaps it is the stranger part that attracts you. That which is known is not necessarily appreciated.

There is no need to feel threatened - because the Bhagwan part of me is the innocent, trusting, childlike, loving, natural, friendly self that you say endears me to you. If you find difficulty with the word Bhagwan - replace it with the word love.

Bhagwan is merely a symbol for these qualities. You certainly never need fear the influence over me of any group. I am not at all group material, and survived the rise and fall of the *orange people* (as depicted in the world press) – unscathed - unlike many others.

You have said you want me to become "more my own woman", as if I was not already that - but when I am in touch with my loving side, I am my own woman totally. In your most vulnerable moments, you have also shown your tears and your tenderness. It is simply a matter of degree.

You know that Bhagwan is not the real issue – it is love. When I am truly in touch with myself - I am less reliant upon you. You should welcome such a shift, when it occurs - since it frees you to be 'more your own man'.

There is no gulf, no gap, no strangeness, no difference, that cannot be bridged by love. It is the ultimate alchemy.

If you were to ask me what are the finest moments in life, I would say – when I am deep in meditation – when you touch me with great tenderness – when we kiss each other deeply and totally and I feel the earth move beneath me – when I am suddenly overcome by the urge to sing – when I am lost in dance – and when I feel such an aching in my heart to write to you, and another letter - however great or insignificant, is born - and in the very writing, I feel released.

Dear love, treasure me as I treasure you. Ours is a strange union, yet no less, because of it. I long for you in this moment and am overwhelmed with the longing. I have been reading the *Oxford Book of Quotations* yet again, and it has touched my heart. In the words of the Irish novelist Laurence Sterne.

> 'Tis sweet to feel by what fine-spun threads
> our affections are drawn together
>
> Laurence Stern
>
> •
>
> I feel
> that our letters
> because of what we have said
> will be our only monument
>
> and perhaps
> that is more than enough
>
> *Shobha*

Douglas

I suspect that you are afraid it might work being with me. As the journalist *Bernard Levin* says - *The English seem to deny all possibility of real joy.* If it feels good, it must be wrong etc. Be kind to yourself. Trust your feelings.

Dear friend

Today was a day of magic. Poetry exalts the spirit, and the day began with a poem. Things can only improve. My yearnings are not well-defined. They are not specifically for love-making - rather for union, which tends to imply love-making, but is not necessarily so.

An hour is not enough (during the day), for the alchemy to work, though the English poet Blake says otherwise. The forty-minute effect of being together, which we have discussed, produces a state from which I am loathe to emerge. Let us commune again on the morrow.

> Like as the waves make towards the pebbled shore,
> so do our minutes hasten to their end
>
> *Shakespeare – Sonnets*

•

> To see the world in a grain of sand
> and a heaven in a wildflower
> Hold infinity in the palm of your hand
> and eternity in an hour
>
> *William Blake*

•

> When I died last,
> and dear, I die - as often as from thee I go,
> though it be but an hour ago
> and lovers' hours be full eternity
>
> *John Donne*

Beloved friend

Weekends are strange for us. As you once said - they are times for refreshing ourselves for each other. On the subject of *mornings* - it is certainly true that many of our early encounters have taken place after the hour of six and before the hour of nine. This must have an effect upon our moods and thus the quality of our love.

During weekends, I feel an urge to create something great and wonderful – as if my sojourn upon this planet will not be complete until I have contributed something magnificent. I wonder what it will be ? Perhaps our love is enough ?

Why are we here at all ? To become buddhas – to realise we *are* buddhas? If the latter, then simply to enjoy (and share) poetry, music, theatre, walks and making love.

This afternoon I became stranded on a rock in the river. The sand was under water and I could either take the risk of falling or turn back. I thought of you and went forward.

Dear Douglas

In case you are interested in applying for the position of my *mat*e, the qualities I am looking for are as follows :

- jollity – sense of humour, fun
- warmth – affection, sensuality, love
- spirituality – interested in meditation and our purpose for being here
- devotion – commitment (implies availability)
- aesthetics – love of beauty, music, dance, poetry, art, nature
- athletic – running, dancing, swimming etc.
- intelligence – to see
- wisdom – understanding born of experience
- free spirit – explorer of the soul, unattached to the past or to anyone or anything (except me)
-

Where would you rate yourself on these criteria?

Darling

Our moments of intimacy are the joy of my life. I only wish they could abide. I remember how we laughed together today, and I am amazed and delighted at our simple, childlike innocence. Would that I could remember all those times when we have looked into each other – and *seen*. Darling, I can still feel you here, in my room and my heart.

Ah my beloved
fill the cup - that clears today
of past regrets - and future fears

The Rubaiyat of Omar Khayyam

Dear love

I strolled along the bay at dusk. The grass was covered in dew and the air heavy with it, and the leaves were falling. It reminded me of our misty morning meetings, when we were at university – so pregnant with promise !

I was singing in my weak, insipid fashion on the foreshore - the song *I don't know how to love him,* and I meant the words for you. When Mary sings to her lord, in the rock opera *Jesus Christ Superstar*, I imagine myself singing her songs to you – especially *Try not to get worried, try not to turn on to, problems that upset you..... Sleep and I shall soothe you.......etc* - to which we have listened, on so many occasions.

Have you noticed how you and I are capable of moving from a state of frequent love-making to a state of suspension of the same - without an undue sense of deprivation? I wonder if you realise that for many people, this would not be easy.

Perhaps it simply reveals, as we both know - that physical love is the cherry on the top of the pudding for us - though I must admit that life without any cherries, would be inconceivable.

My darling

I am so excited. I have just arranged for an audition with the director and founder of our state opera company. Occasionally he takes private students - when his other commitments allow. Of course, he may say - as you have done, that my voice is too thin and unsuitable for opera, but he may not - and I am delighted to at least be heard – since as far as I know, he is the only Italian teacher of opera in Perth, and for opera (in my opinion) - one must have an 'Italian'. At the very least, it will be a worthwhile experiment. By the way, you were wonderful today – almost radiant.

Douglas - midnight

This evening at dusk, I meditated at our trysting place at Point Resolution or perhaps I should call it Point Irresolution, in view of our past behaviour at that site. The stillness of the river enveloped me and I felt exultant. If only it was possible to live in a constant state of joyful equanimity. Be gentle with yourself.

Dearest love

Perhaps you and I will always differ in our ideas? Perhaps this is the very basis of our conversation i.e. sanctioned disagreement?

My love of opera has again put me in touch with my ardour and passion. Just as for you, to run and swim is to be alive - for me, to love and to sing are the very essence of life.

Yesterday, you reminded me yet again, that love begets love. It is one of the most profound truths of all. This morning at the beach, I almost felt beneficent towards N. – as if I could take her hand and call her *friend,* but such a gesture could only arise out of a feeling of abundance, not deprivation – as when one feels loved, as I have felt this week - because of our deep communion.

Sometimes it is so transparent that you do not fully understand me, and yet in another way, you are the only one who does. Meditating this morning, I again realised that I do want to add some colour yet more beautiful to the world, as I wrote in one of my poems. It is a pity that when I sing at concerts, festivals and workshops, you are not there to hear me.

When I write to you and am able to express myself freely to you in language that we both enjoy - I feel a little taste of greatness, as if I have touched another dimension. It is not my lot to be tethered to the earth. Some of us are meant to fly. Are you one of those? We are two of a kind – eccentric, full of ideas and yearnings - yet your training is in pragmatism, though I do not feel that that is your nature. Perhaps you see in me, your desire to break free, and that both annoys and attracts you.

You seem to be concerned that I should fail, but the fear is for yourself – lest you follow me - and fall. Life is a risk. For you, the risks are largely physical (e.g. swimming out to sea). Since you have known me, you have entered the world of emotional insecurity. It requires courage in a different way. Please allow me my freedom to explore and experiment (even when you don't understand), as I also give you yours.

I do not believe our lives here are accidental. When I became a sannyasin, Bhagwan said to me "You belong to the stars. That is your destiny. You only need to remember." If I was to take you to the stars, this could mean I might lose you to god *itself* - if you discovered your true nature.

Perhaps I am not ready for you to be that enlightened (full with light). My love, I can hear the birds singing outside my window. It is as if the whole existence is happy today – because I am happy. May it ever be so.

Douglas

Tonight, after many tears and much despair, I realised my primary purpose in life (at present), is to be loved by you. That may sound strange. Your love for me is intermittent, sporadic, uneven, inconsistent, fluctuating in depth and intensity and interspersed with periods of active disavowal.

My work in this life will be complete when you are able to say - without fear or hesitation and with your whole heart, that you love me and will continue to do so – god willing.

I have seen glimpses of your inner glory. When we met, your heart was open like the heart of a child. You were innocent. And many times since. When you were trying to give up your medication, your tenderness and vulnerability were revealed.

My pain seems to have been watching you open like a flower, only to close once again. My heart cannot bear to see such beauty disappear. My work will be finished, when your flower stays open. I only ask for the strength to love you when your petals close. It is a painful process. The only gift I can give you is my patience. How I wish there was more that I could do.

Darling - full moon

Last night's folk music gathering reminded me of my solitary state, as everyone brought their partners with them. At least orange celebrations are not couple affairs. We are all independent souls. I am beginning to wish I was not living alone. I live like a hermit. Your loving moon-mate.

Duggles the Great

Giuseppe, the Italian opera singer, has accepted me as his pupil. He said (for the record) "You have a beautiful voice." Even while rehearsing with him today, the improvement in the quality of my voice production was apparent.

His studio is covered wall-to-wall with photos, including those of himself with *Placido Domingo* (the foremost international tenor), who is a family friend of his, and whose life he once saved from the sea - when Placido went into dangerous waters.

There were also photos of himself with Joan Sutherland. It gave me a shock to realise I had inadvertently stumbled upon a man who is in every sense an inspiration - because he has *been there* and *done it*. I was amazed he would want to take me on, but I was greatly stirred by his encouragement. He played me a video of his daughter singing *Lucia di Lammermoor* at age twenty-two - for the Pope - inside the Vatican - to an immense audience. She became a nun and used to play harp with the Sydney Symphony Orchestra and is now at La Scala. She has long blonde hair almost down to the floor – quite angelic.

We also talked about Bhagwan and the orange people at length and I was flattered by his obvious enthusiasm and understanding. His home is full of scores, opera videos and memorabilia of his career in Europe. He said to me "You need passion to sing" and I told him I had come to him because I sought a teacher with passion.

Mio caro

I have just finished your video recording of Maria Callas and have not blinked from beginning to end. I was riveted - transfixed – as you predicted. For me, as for all those with passion – love is all. Byron be damned ! Can he be compared to what I have just seen? He pales into insignificance - as does all desire to be balanced. Balanced one may be – but almost certainly, dead. The world of opera, and especially Italian opera, is so vivid for me – where emotion reigns supreme.

It is not enough to live in poetry. Love requires real expression – real intimacy. You must find the courage to live in truth, so your heart and soul are not suffocated under the weight of reason. Life without enthusiasm is not worth living. With love and passion – Shobha

Shobha

I felt such pleasure at suddenly seeing you on my front lawn this morning. It is so good to see you happy and excited about your lessons with your singing teacher. Whenever we part in a friendly way, it soon seems ridiculous to have cut myself off from you, when you are as much a part of me as my right arm. Mia cara - you were very sweet yesterday. I never cease to be surprised at the radiance of your delight at such moments.

Darling

Last night was a wonderful experience. The world leader of the Sufis (*Pir Vilayat Khan*) spoke to a group of about eight hundred, and there were so many people I knew - from many different walks of life. It seemed as if the entire *alternative* population of Perth was present.

Pir Vilayat Khan is a beautiful man of seventy-two with a long white beard and masses of white hair. He is a scientist and much of his talk was laced with scientific analogies and references to the discoveries of contemporary physics. A very bubbly, laughing fellow, wearing a long woollen cloak and hood in traditional Sufi fashion. It was a very loving evening.

Duggles

This has been an eventful weekend; one which has produced or created a discontinuity with what has gone before. The Sufi master was so eloquent – so English, though of Indian heritage. He was born in London, and educated in England and France. He spoke of developments in modern physics, and with such enthusiasm that I feel encouraged to find out more. They parallel the insights of eastern mysticism - viz. that each cell contains within itself, the potential of the whole universe.

Are you familiar with these notions? I used some of these ideas in my doctorate before I went to India, but the Anthropology department at my university was not receptive to them, and actively discouraged doctoral theses which drew upon several disciplines viz. sociology and science, which is incredibly narrow for a university, is it not?

Vilayat Khan cited two incidents in his life which affected him deeply. His sister Princess Noor Vilayat Khan GC MBE was the last link between the English War Office and the French resistance when the Nazis occupied France and she was imprisoned in chains for a year, before she was beaten to death. Somehow it made our (yours and mine) difficulties seem insignificant by comparison.

Pir also spoke of when he was young and in Oxford, and his fiancée was killed on a motorcycle he was driving - due to a fault in the machine. He was so distraught he went to India (with the British Navy) to recuperate, and said that the only way he became healed, was to listen to the entire Bach Mass in B minor every night. With your love of Bach, I am sure this is something you will fully understand.

Sufism, he says, is concerned not so much with the ecstasy of the heart, as the ecstasy of the soul - and Bach touches that depth. You may remember I sang the Bach Mass in B minor when I was in the ashram in India. It was quite a feat.

Darling, you would have appreciated the grace of the man – the elegance - the play on meaning - the exceptional use of language. It was a banquet - a feast of words, amongst other things. Keep the faith, whatever it is. Your Puss

Shobha

An important day in our lives. There seems to be a new firmness and confidence in our agreement to put our relationship to the test of separation, though I realise the separation is not wholly voluntary, but forced upon us by the work at the university which you start tomorrow, and my going to France shortly.

Darling

I have just come from a dancing meditation and in my more surrendered moments, feel we must trust in existence, and the course of nature, because my feeble efforts to understand and control and manipulate come to naught in the end. Full moon is tonight, and I wish I had a dictaphone in the car, because I fear some of my thoughts will be lost forever. Suffice to say, I am feeling that you and I are so deeply connected *in spirit,* that I don't feel we can ever part. We are united, despite ourselves.

Pir Vilayat Khan

All the way home, I sang the song I wrote for you when you went on your last trip to Europe – *The Wheel of Karma* :

*Do you ever get the feeling
that we've met somewhere before,
in the dim and distant corners of your mind ?*

*Do you ever wonder why it is
our hearts are in rapport
and the love we feel inside us seems to bind
and melt our hearts together
as if we were as one
through the ever-changing scenes before our eyes ?*

*Do you think we've been this way
some time ago - my friend?
Can you see it written clearly in the skies ?*

My dearest love, I feel like a misfit in this world. Every now and then, I desire a home with you - a log fire, a redsetter, a piano, and a warm, homestead atmosphere where we invite friends to talk and wine and dine and sing and laugh together. Then there is a tiny voice that says "Be content with things as they are. It is not so bad. Be grateful you are able to love Douglas at all. Many people are not blessed with this experience."

Then there is yet another voice reminding me that my salvation, as it were, resides not in you, but solely in discovering my own 'god within' and until that happens, I will never be satisfied; that love indicates the direction, but is not the entire answer; that there is a higher form of love which is not possessive, exclusive or attached.

Dear, dear Douglas, all these voices have an element of truth in them. The latter is the most grandiose and therefore the most difficult to understand. Yet I know it to be so. But I am so in love with you, that I want to linger awhile in the fond illusion that you can satisfy my soul - at least in part. Today I said to you that you are my 'soul', and in a way, it is so. When I feel removed from you; when I cannot contact or write to you, I feel as if I have lost, not an arm or a leg - but my very heart. In the last week, I realised that I am only truly happy when I am in your arms or when I am in meditation. All else seems mundane – tolerable, even pleasant, but does not satisfy the deepest reaches of my being.

I felt during meditation tonight, that I am in many ways, a fortunate women. I have found Bhagwan, who is to me, enlightened, and capable of inspiring great love and devotion in me - and I have found you - and in a similar way, I am inspired by, and devoted to you. Yet surely it is only natural that I should want to bring all my dreams to fruition by being with you in freedom.

Dear Shobha

I have your rhapsodic letter, and as I re-read it, I am filled again with mixed feelings of wonder and guilt. Wonder - that you should write me such a fine, happy and elevated letter – a minor work of art - dashed off in a state of excitement and at great speed. Guilty - because it brought home to me so vividly how different – and finer – a creature you are.

I am still not well, but have missed only one morning at the ocean this week. I'm forever wavering between the timidity of rest and a long-standing belief that most aches and ills can be shaken off by carrying on - regardless.

After re-reading your letter, which is so evocative of the English novelist Thomas Hardy's ideal that I drape you in, I was half-wishing that your resolution would weaken and that you would call. But my wiser and more cautious self will not allow me to take the initiative and get in touch with you. Although the outcome of our separation may be uncertain, I have little doubt that inertia, and possibly failing health, will prevail (and I will not leave N.).

Dear Douglas

Pride, prestige, security, inertia, comfort, public opinion, habit and history, the fear of death - how do these compare with love?

My dear Shobha

Apropos what you were saying about love and volition, Byron, in a letter to one of his many lovers - Caroline Lamb - said *Our affections are not our own*, and in his last poem, *Love dwells not in our will*. He also wrote - in a letter to his friend - the Irish poet Thomas Moore - that *There is no such thing as a life of passion, any more than a continual earthquake or an eternal fever.* With my involuntary love – Douglas.

Shobha's attempt at writing to Douglas in Italian

Innamorato mio

La sola cosa in vita che desidero e che non ho
è essere con te in libertà
in qualunque momento che noi vogliamo
Ma forse noi dobbiamo imparare amare
l'un l'altro nonostante le nostre catene
Io t'amo con tutto il mio cuore ed mia anima
Spero che la nostra assenza da
l'un l'altro generarà frutto
Bell'alma inamorata
Possiamo sempre deliziare 'esistenza

Translation

My love

The only thing in life I want and I do not have
is to be with you in freedom
anytime we want
But maybe we must learn to love one another

> in spite of our chains
> I love you with all my heart and my soul
> I hope our absence from one another
> will bear fruit
> Lovely sweetheart
> We can always delight in existence

My dear Shobha

I was very moved by your letter to me in Italian, though puzzled by the '*Ma forse noi dobbiamo...*' God be with you.

My darling Shobha

I've been strangely happy since you rang after such a long interval. All this, despite the fact that we haven't seen each other - let alone exchange caresses. Or is it possibly in some way because we haven't met. I do so ache for you.

You asked me recently and ambiguously - whether I think of you in bed. Last night, while in bed, I thought of you being in bed with me in that week, when N. was in France, and of the sweetness of lying beside you.

Isn't it possible that in matters sexual, at least, the greatest and most inspiring highs, are the memories – and anticipation – of such moments. Our minds embellish and enrich the actuality of experience, which is raw material for the imagination.

This is what separates us from the rest of animal creation. It also explains the element of trepidation I believe we both often feel, when we actually make love. It also brings me closer to your view of love-making as a spiritual experience, something I have hitherto refused to accept. I accept however, that if you combine physical union with the imaginative *highs* which arise from it, it becomes spiritual.

The last five years have been the most stirring period of my life. Music, colour and even the experience of running and swimming – all have become more vivid - because of you. Sweetheart, I seem at last to have written you a true love-letter.

My dear Shobha

I'm so glad to feel your excitement about singing again. ***Con amore***

Douglas

I don't want you to even imagine that a pen and phone relationship could satisfy me. Yet you have not made any move towards doing anything about our plight. Nor do I want you to idealise me in my absence. I am a flesh and blood woman as well as a spiritual being, just as you are yourself (except that you are not a woman of course), and I could never be content solely with a romanticised, sentimental form of love.

Kissing you has stirred up such a passion in me – or is it a longing? I will not be at peace again until I see you. I would like so much this very moment, to fall asleep in your arms. Be gentle, my love. Forgive me if I have hurt you.

My dear Shobha

Because I am not alone, I find it difficult to write to you on the weekend. It is also the time when my children might float in at any time. Oscar Wilde has stated that 'Nothing succeeds like excess'. So far as it encourages 'highs', Wilde's *bon mot*s are not without a vein of truth.

If you don't mind, I'll save Bernard Levin's book *Enthusiasms* which you gave me, to read on the plane to France. Levin represents a kind of bond between us, since it was his article on Bhagwan's ashram in India, that caused us to become acquainted more deeply.

I still have not exhausted my current 'enthusiasm' for Mozart's opera *Don Giovanni*. Could your bursting into song with our duet *La ci darem la mano* (you lay your hand in mine, dear*)* have something to do with it? The aria *Dalla sua pace* is also quite wonderful and the words, though simple - are beautiful and relevant for us.

> Dalla sua pace
> la mia dipende
> Quel che a lei piace
> vita mi rende

> Quel che le incresce
> morte mi dà

*

> On her peace, mine depends
> That which gives her pleasure
> gives me life
> That which grieves her
> gives me death

My time at Rottnest Island with the family was pleasant and interesting, despite the poor weather. One evening, we talked for several hours while my son-in-law and I worked our way through two bottles of wine. It was mostly about the upbringing of children, the role of sensible parents and other conditioning factors - in modern times. I found there was more *ad idem* (meeting of the minds) with my ideas, than I expected. I get the impression my daughter and her husband feel like a pair of ducks who have hatched a swan. The swan is a delightful child. You can gauge what a fool she is making of me, by the pleasure it gave me when my name emerged distinctly from a babble of words.

Just as you have taught me so much that had withered in me or never grown, so she is reviving in me the sense of fun and the joy one can get from stirring the intelligence of a young human being. *Con amore anche*

Dear one

Tonight I came across an extract from the novella *The Little Prince* by Antoine de Saint-Exupery, that I sent you some time ago. It was about a wild fox who asked what it meant to be *tamed,* and was told by the little boy who was trying to communicate with him, that it meant to *sit a little closer every day*.

Most of the poetry I have given you is probably still *sealed up* from your last European trip. Will you do the same this time (i.e. put all my letters and paraphernalia in a sealed box - in case of adversity) ? Much love – Shobha.

My dear Shobha

I still feel shaken from my battering this morning in the ocean. Not physically - though I have a few grazes and bruises, but rather the thought of nearly being cut off suddenly at this particular time in my life, with so many loose ends - if you know what I mean?

After our long and happy telephone conversation this afternoon, while I was writing this letter, it seems unnatural to continue writing now. It's strange how we often manage a unique rapport when we talk on the phone. The explanation may be that we can be intimate and spontaneous, and indulge in every kind of word-play and word-caressing, without the opportunity (or risk) of progressing into physical love-play.

You, I suppose, think it proper that, being endowed with only one pair of lips - kissing should put an end to talking. I don't disagree with this. But a talk such as we had today had a special quality and should not be regarded as a poor substitute for a face-to-face meeting.

An analysis would show that our manner of talking to each other face-to-face, is different from our conversations on the phone, just as we also do not write to each other in the way that we speak. It may be that, as in the confessional box, the fact that we do not directly confront each other - encourages greater freedom.

Because of your vetoes on a range of topics (e.g. N. and my fond feelings for my new grand-daughter), I have to be constantly on guard when talking to you. I certainly cannot *bubble*. I don't complain - though I am conscious that your conversation is not subject to any constraints at all. Don't take this amiss. I'm teasing you, for the most part. *Con amore*

Darling

I seem to get into a complete *tizz* when I see you out with N. - and today was no exception. It hurts so much.

> how many times have I watched him
> come and go with her
> and yearned to be in her place beside him
>
> how many times have I watched their light at night

> behind the heavy curtains of their home
> and wondered what they do together when I am gone
>
> how many times have I seen him
> take her to her office in the morning
> and wished I sat beside him in his car
>
> how many times have I watched them
> in the waves
> and swimming out to sea
> and wished that I could join him there
>
> so many years spent waiting for him
> longing for the place that is not mine
> and she - in turn - wishing she was me

My love

Because of the bond that exists between us when we listen to opera, I find it impossible to understand when I am listening to this wonderful awe-inspiring music, how you cannot be as totally in love with me as I am with you. Opera seems to me to be my life, just as you are my life. How is it that I am not also your love, your life, your soul?

Our life together is so much like an opera – so full of passion and tragedy and longing. How can you not know the glory of love – the sweetness of dying inside, from the sheer immensity of the feelings. How can you not know? Love is all there is. Nothing else matters !

When I lie with you and listen to opera, as today - my entire being is healed, and I feel it is also so for you. Likewise, when we make love, it is as if, for moments, we touch 'god'. Do you remember saying once "There ought to be a god - so that we can thank him"?

How I wish we could unite at some deepest level of our being and you could acknowledge that I am for you, as you are for me - the inspiration for my life. Why must we hurt each other when there is so much possibility of joy?   All my love – come soon

Dear Shobha

I can't get out of my mind the unhappiness of your face as you lay beside me yesterday. Though I know myself to be a heartless person, the chink in my armour is that I respond to naked grief, such as I saw in your face then. My daughter, at her child's graveside and N. (once or twice - because of you), have also shown the same kind of *dissolving* grief – a form of collapse, to which the only possible response is to offer comfort and tenderness - however little this help may be.

It may be that in my cold, undeveloped soul and stunted emotional life, my response to grief is a sign of attachment. This means that I – and perhaps others too – may not be aware of my attachments - until I am faced with grief. I am not simply playing with words. I am genuinely puzzled by the confident way in which people (such as yourself) declare or deny their love for others.

Darling – anniversary

Seeing you today was so perfect. In my lesser moments, I want so much more – to share with you every corner of my soul. In my greater ones, I feel so blessed that we two can love so totally when we are together - as if there was no time - as if there were no other souls upon this earth, save us - and our love. Dearest love – I adore you – please treasure what we have.

Duggles

This has been a weekend full of opera. Yesterday I taped Puccini's opera *Madam Butterfly* from La Scala in Milan, and today I sang two arias in the hall from Bellini's operas *Norma* and *La Sonnambula* viz. *Casta diva* and *Tutto è gioia* - my first airing.

This morning by chance, I met my singing teacher of twenty-years ago. I have not seen her since I was fourteen, when I learnt every aria she sang because I was so inspired. She sang lead roles with the opera company and is currently on their Board. It was wonderful to see her again, and to let her know I was still singing - which in some small way, is a tribute to her.

Shobha's attempt at Italian

Oggi, caro mio, sono piena con una gioia
che non posso spieghare
Sono in amore
Sono piena con te
benché non hai entrato il mio corpo
hai entrato la mia anima
Mio amoroso
Ch'è questa gioia che ha alzarsi da qual tempo
quando si abbiamo distenduto insieme
In quel momento il mio cuora ha esploduto

Sono sedendo alla cima della collina a mezzogiorno
ed è cosi bella
Sento come se sono alla cima del mondo
Dio è qui
Tutto è pace
Forse è a causa della sofferenza
che posso sentire tale bellezza
Non so
Resti nel tuo cuore, innamorato – Shobha

Translation

Today, my dear, I am full of joy
that I cannot explain
I'm in love
I'm full of you
even though you did not enter my body
you have entered my soul
My love
There is this joy that rises from time to time
when we relax together
In that moment my heart explodes
I'm sitting at the top of the hill at noon
and it is so beautiful
I feel like I'm at the top of the world
God is here
Everything is peace
Maybe it is because of the suffering
that I can feel the beauty
I do not know
Remain in your heart
In love – Shobha

Shobha's attempt to communicate with Douglas in French

Mon cheri

Merci pour aujourdhui
Mon coeur est ouvert a tu encore, à une fois quand j'avais
Presque ferme pour toujours
Je t'adore, mon bien-aimé
Il y a ne plus rien dire
Je cheris votre le corps
Et votre âme, le même que mon propre
Aujourdhui, bien que ne soyez pas entré dans mon corps
j'ai senti que nous étions pour un instant une âme
Les votre yeux sont très profound quand
te es dans mon les bras
Avec tout mon amour. Shobha
Il est trente années depuis
j'ai écrit le français
J'ai beaucoup appris

Translation

My darling

> Thank you for today
> My heart is open to you again
> when I had almost closed it forever
> I love you, my beloved
> There is no longer anything to say
> I was looking for your body
> and your soul, the same as my own
> Today, I felt that we (were) for a moment one soul
> Your eyes are very profound when
> you are in my arms
> With all my love - Shobha
> It has been thirty years since
> I wrote in French
> I have learnt a lot

I skimmed through *Portrait of a Marriage*** today. As yet, I cannot find any evidence of what you call a spiritual relationship between Vita Sackville-West and her lover Violet. There seems to be nothing to distinguish their relationship from that of any other lovers who are possessive, jealous etc.

**   The marriage to which the book refers is that of Vita-Sackville West and Harold Nicholson. They were both part of the celebrated literary and revolutionary London-based Bloomsbury group, who experimented with lovers of both sexes and were considered to be ahead of their time.

I have also obtained a copy of *The English* by writer David Frost, who has since been knighted. His book is a caustic comment on the English upper-class personality with quite potent comments on the legal system. It gave me further insights into why you are as you are; why you are unable to leave your castle, and why you and I are in some ways so in opposition to each other.

I am everything you are not, because I am not a product of your system, yet in the field of aesthetics – love, beauty, nature, music, poetry – we are one (at times). In terms of culture, background, values, habits – we come from opposite ends of the earth. I loved one of Frost's epithets viz. *The English know only one unit of erotic currency – the full clinch.* Remind you of anyone? I look forward to singing with you soon.

Darling

Spring is here. Last night was full moon and also a lunar eclipse. It was lovely to see you twice on the battlements of your 'castle' – surveying your domain.

I have finished *Portrait of a Marriage.* It certainly has a lingering effect. But your situation in no way parallels that of Vita. Her marriage to Harold Nicholson was based upon trust and honesty - despite her sexual dalliances with both men and women.

> Marriage is a wonderful institution
> but I'm not ready for an institution yet
>
> *Mae West*

Your so-called accelerating decline has no doubt been arrested by the breath of Spring. Age is a quality of mind. If you ever feel old, I suspect it is simply that you are not happy. One can be radiantly youthful to the grave. So speaks one who is young and probably naive. As you informed me, the Scottish philosopher David Hume smiled - on his deathbed. That is more than enough testimony to his life. Perhaps we will too. God be with you - since I am not.

Dear Shobha

Herewith the complete Savoy operas of Gilbert and Sullivan. I see one of the operas - *Ruddigore* - received good reviews in the press. Should I expect you to attend, and break into song from the auditorium ? I am rather disappointed with what I've read of David Frost: no real insights and much of the humour is feeble. So I'm mainly reading the passages you thought worthy of marking, which tell me something about you and how you see my situation. There's a programme on *The Second Sex* (perhaps based on the book by the French intellectual and writer Simone de Beauvoir), which I shall record for you tonight.

Yesterday I ran fast yet again and I see from my running book that August was also a good month last year, so Spring may indeed have something to do with it, as you suggest. We tend to forget in modern times how heart-lifting Spring must at one time have been, especially in the cold-temperate and mainly deciduous countries of Europe, after a cold, dark and leafless winter, with candles as the only source of artificial light.

Your mention of David Hume was very apt. As you know, I have always admired him - both for his thought and for the way he lived and died. A truly inspiring man. I was once moved to tears in reading a biography of him. Your letter is a ray of sunshine.

Douglas

Guess what? My singing teacher has asked me to help him start an opera school in Perth to teach others to love that art form. It would be a wonderful opportunity to learn his techniques, with a view to perhaps teaching myself in a few years' time - and also a means of learning many more arias.

I only wish I had been aware twenty years ago of his presence in Perth. I could have learnt so much, and yet perhaps it is only now, after being with you, that I can truly sing with passion. My teacher says that I always sing better, when my heart is broken (by you).

After I left you yesterday, I practised singing for a while in the hall, which has fabulous acoustics - and managed to emulate the singing style my teacher had explained to me. I found myself singing top C's without effort and was so pleased that I wanted to phone you to say "I've done it". I want to see you – to hold you – to whisper sweet nothings in your ear. Life is so rich. I want to share it all with you.

I admit that I probably do not consider your age and hence your needs, sufficiently. I am ignorant of them to some extent because I rarely see you, and then in an artificial environment. As Shakespeare expresses it, in his sonnet :

> To me fair friend, you never can be old
> for as you were
> when first your eye I eyed -
> such seems your beauty still.

I have never considered there was any difference in age between us, and find it difficult to do so now. Perhaps you need to educate me a little more in the changes that are taking place in your body, mind, heart and lifestyle, so I can understand. It pains me that we should not make allowances for each other and be intolerant of our differences and limitations.

**

I have just finished watching the film *The Devil's Disciple* based on the play by Bernard Shaw, and it has moved me immensely, because it tells of two men whose true natures are revealed only in a time of crisis. Perhaps that is the only time we ever really know of what stuff we are made?

I have often wondered how you would act or react if I died, or fell in love with another, or simply went away. Likewise, I often imagine how I would behave if you left me – though the truth may be otherwise.

How would you behave if N. was to leave you? Neither of us can be sure of our responses, and although in one sense, each day is the proof, we are such complex creatures, it may be that it is only when we are really challenged, that a deeper truth emerges.

What seems to matter most (to me) is to be true to oneself, at any cost - even the loss of one's life. It may be that in the realm of love, it is vital to love where one's heart is - even if that love is not returned, though I find the prospect of unrequited love, terribly sad and probably not healthy. I'm sure you would not agree.

Today, while meditating at Point Resolution, I began to wonder whether I have in fact chosen you, *because* you are not available fully, so that when we are together, we are really together ,without the complex network of domestic ties that tends to suffocate love.

Last night, while watching a video of Bhagwan, I realised yet again, that my calling is to be a mystic, and for that, it is easier to be alone. Being with you paradoxically, forces me to be alone in a way that I do not always enjoy, but may be absolutely necessary to enable me to relinquish my notions of love and attachment – at least in the physical sense.

Darling - in order to become enlightened, one must depend only on oneself, and although I find it excruciating at times, perhaps this is the only way I can learn to love, and be free. God be with you - dearest love.

I have looked into the question of astrology over many years, and the astrologer Linda Goodman - who is recognised widely as the last word in this area - has written thus :

> Even when the soulmate is at last discovered, there are often many complications and tests of worthiness which cause temporary pain. Only in continually and consistently practicing tolerance and forgiveness, can the hurt be alleviated.

You may not be receptive to the foregoing, but it is my understanding also, and when we first met, I knew that you were my soulmate.

Dear Shobha

You were sweet yesterday. For a few moments, we lay still, simply looking at each other, in a way which I cannot remember happening before. I think it was when we both realised that the point of no return had been crossed - bringing a feeling almost of peace. Which reminds me of our *double-helix* discussion, by which I meant the reciprocal and heightening interplay of both mind and emotion.

We need a concept of people being literary mates, such as we are – though of course, not only this. Talk, too, is also important. But can you imagine the last five years (between us), without any exchange of writing?

Dearest love

I realised today that many of your virtues, I take for granted. We are so used to each other, it is easy to forget how much we 'fit'. It is so easy to talk to you. That in itself is a miracle. I wrote you a note earlier today which said "the beauty of love above all, seems to me, to be its capacity for forgiveness, even after terrible injury. If this is not present, it is not love." Goodnight darling

Darling

Although we often joke about your level of being *peeled* (like an onion), you are probably far more peeled than we often assume. Your healthy outdoor life, in itself guarantees a level of fitness and enjoyment of life, which many do not experience.

Although there are many areas where we disagree, it still remains true that you are not afraid of the truth, if you divine something to be so, and probably because of your legal and academic training, you enjoy its pursuit, as of course – do I.

Hence, even though you do not profess any form of spirituality; are skeptical of anything paranormal or psychic; have no obvious experience of meditation in an ongoing way and are not highly demonstrative or extroverted socially; you nevertheless, exhibit a healthy enquiry and an ability to listen and learn, that I simply take for granted.

You are not in any sense petty or trivial, and considering our amazing differences, it has been a minor miracle that you have been able to tolerate and absorb to some extent - a few of my values, as I have also done with you. With you, I have grown in ways which would not otherwise have been possible.

Dear Douglas

The video of the composer *Andrew Lloyd Webber* has disturbed me deeply. It has made me aware once again of my own great love of music, but more than that, my desire to perform.

It is now almost a year since I sang in my folk duo *Heart and Soul*, and I feel frustration at not having an audience and a companion with whom to sing.

There is definitely a performing type of personality, and I become unfulfilled when I am not in some way creative. Live theatre - especially musical theatre and opera - are superb ways to express the vitality of one's being. I am only truly happy when I am able to sing with my whole heart.

We must all realise the dreams of our youth to feel fulfilled, even if only in some small way. My entire childhood and adolescence was music. I long to sing into the night or whenever the mood takes me. In order to truly sing, one must be in love, or have been in love.

Chapter 7

The pain of too much tenderness

19

Douglas

The sad fact is that because you remain in your present environment, it is not possible for your heart to open any further. Often I leave you in a vulnerable and tender state, only to find that when I see you again, you have returned to your former self – cool, aloof and rational, and it requires many hours of being together, before you again soften and melt.

Because of your alternating moods, I have placed myself in a most destructive pattern. To love someone who does not return the love is possible to accept. But to be loved on Monday and not on Tuesday and to be loved on Wednesday but not on Thursday, is enough to drive any sane person completely mad.

This has always been the cause of my distress, yet you seem to be almost completely unaware of the effect of your behaviour. After seeing me, you return to your abode and find an ever-consistent, if dull, companion waiting for you. She does not reject or abandon you, as she is so dependent upon you. I also am consistent and loving, but the conflict between your dual lifestyle, creates such a division in you, that when you return to me, you are another creature.

Our situation reminds me of *Sisyphus* (from Greek mythology) rolling the stone uphill, only to find that when he reaches the top, the stone rolls down, so he starts the upward trudge, yet again.

My dear Shobha

You were very sweet today. I spoke of innocence and abandon, but not of your sheer joy - so untrammelled, as if you reach a truly higher state of being. This fills me with a sense almost of awe. We are well matched, in a complementary, not an equivalent, way. You are much that I am not – gentle and physically timid, spiritual and mystical beyond my comprehension: completely open and honest emotionally and intellectually.

It is only recently that I have come to realise how full a part you play in my life.

For me, life is compounded of parts of many different kinds, varying in importance, but each contributing something to the whole that I am. Music, running and swimming; the almost painful climax, leading to serenity, of making love; the excitement of ideas; the joy of coming across a thought beautifully expressed; the rich, sad wisdom of Johnson; even the light banter of the beach.

In a sense, I suppose I am talking of beauty in its many forms. I seem to be more responsive to beauty than I was, say, ten years ago, which is perhaps to say that I live more intensely. Much of this I clearly owe to you.

Douglas

I wept bitter tears after speaking to you today. You said "undying love - inevitably dies". Do you realise these words contain your whole philosophy that love does not work – does not last. Your belief that love does not endure, is the very reason why you are still in your marital home. You think it is preferable to accept the disappointment of love that has died, than try again with someone else. Yet staying put, is what prevents love from happening for you - with another.

From the moment we met, you implied love could not last – a self-defeating, self-perpetuating belief. What you believe, has come true - at least for you. And the corollary is that you believe if you live with a woman you truly care for - love will disappear. O ye, of little faith. Can you not see that your lack of trust is what is causing it not to work? It is self-fulfilling.

Where did you develop this negative attitude to life? From your marriage? Or when your parents left you in boarding-school in England and you did not see them for years? It is so insidious. It pervades all that you do, and explains why you are unwilling to enter into real intimacy, except for an hour or so. I am horrified when reminded that I am in love with a man who does not have confidence in love – only doubt. You are missing so much.

Cynicism, according to the Oxford Dictionary, is the attitude of *one who has little faith in human sincerity or goodness,* and this definition is derived from the Greek school, which had a contempt for ease, wealth and enjoyment. Byron** who is one of your heroes - certainly enjoyed himself. You have wealth – relative to mine - yet you are against ease and enjoyment and the higher pleasures of the lovers' bed.

Perhaps one of the main differences between us is that I am a total romantic and you tend towards cynicism? You have said that you are at your best, when you are pulling things apart (debunking) - whereas I focus upon love, truth, beauty, joy, peace, freedom etc. You seem to be preoccupied with condemning sloth, gluttony, avarice and the evils of wealth - and joyful experiences as well.

The question for us is can a cynic and a romantic commune? This may account for our endless discussions in which neither of us shift ground, and why there is a constant desire on both our parts to influence the other. Maybe we are poles apart and we are not on the same wavelength at all? It frightens me.

** *Lord George Byron* – English poet and peer, notable for his scandalous lifestyle

Darling

The workshop on *Public Speaking* was terrific. The co-ordinator was an English actor/director who has coached two United Kingdom prime ministers. We each had to present a topic for five minutes, and the leader remarked that he wondered why I had come to such a course, because I obviously did not have any difficulty making a presentation. Rather surprising. Did you know that when surveyed, many people rate public speaking as that which they fear the most - even more than dying !

It made me realise that perhaps we are unusual in our ability to communicate so well together - even though we mostly disagree with each other. The leader of the workshop said it is very unusual to find a good conversationalist – that they are as rare as hen's teeth. Treasure me therefore – as I do, you. Shobha the Buddha

My love

The film last evening on television, featured a discussion between French philosophers *Simone de Beauvoir* and *Jean Paul Sartre*, who were of course, lovers. Neither of them were very heart-warming people, but they both had brilliant minds and have been forerunners of modern thought.

I remembered last night the source of the quote *Do not go gently into that goodnight. Rage, rage, against the dying of the light* – which as you know, comes from the pen of Welsh poet *Dylan Thomas*.

Having just completed a writers' workshop, I am aware that for me, the real purpose of writing is for the sheer pleasure of creating. One of the joys of writing to you by letter, is that it is so immediate i.e. my pleasure, and sometimes your response - without waiting years for the approval of a publisher, and then a possible audience.

We are fortunate to have this way of sharing. A friend of mine told me last week she cannot speak at all to her special friend on the phone - in part because he is French, and in part because he is not terribly verbal. How lucky we are to talk face-to-face and on the phone for hours at a time, and also through our letters - as well as through touch. Yet we almost take these for granted. I hold you dear to my heart.

It is full moon, and I am wrestling with my heart this evening, as I was not clear today about whether or not we should have made love. I felt we had insufficient time, and that to make love would make of it a regular practice - rather than a spontaneous expression of feeling.

Yet I now feel such disquiet. I wonder if we should have entered the holiest of holies, and whether my inhibition was caused by not wishing to overindulge in what is to me - the foremost pleasure of my life.

And yet, having held you at arm's length, figuratively speaking, I desired you more. Perhaps when the time is right - there is no hesitation. Darling, when we make love, it is your excitement and abandon that serves as a catalyst for my own response. There is a sense of fusion - if only briefly. It is such a mystery and such a glory. It moves me greatly. Such a tremendous blessing is in our hands. How much I care. I love you so very much.

Douglas

You looked so very caring, when we were entwined today. Thank you for loving me as you do. Sometimes I almost adore you. I know you are not fond of that word. Please realise that my letters are not intended to be literary, and accept them as the simple expressions of my heart. I would not like you to see them just as words upon a page, which are to be examined and judged, when every word has probably cost a tear or two in the process of being written. Only if my words stir your heart, do they have any value.

Dear friend

I have given birth – well, at least, the labour pains have well and truly begun (of putting together the ideas for my thesis). There is an excruciating sense of something missing, and yet not knowing the cause. It seems to happen thus - just before a new idea is to be born. Surely you must have felt something akin to this when writing articles, or giving lectures.

I remember once at the folk club, running outside when someone was in the middle of their song, and a friend - who was a singer-songwriter of some repute, asked what was the matter. I replied I had to go immediately, because there was a song coming (waiting to be written down) and I had to leave before it disappeared. It was as if a child was about to be born, and he said "I know what you mean" and "that's how it is for me, as well."

Tonight I watched the film based on the novel *Name of the Rose* which is about the Spanish Inquisition investigating heresy in an Italian monastic order in 1327. The heretical book they wished to suppress was one supposedly written by Aristotle - stating that laughter, if allowed, would destroy fear, and if fear was destroyed, so would belief in god.

Hence the church had to ensure the book, and therefore laughter, was hidden away so that it could not be read. It seems to me, that when we laugh, we are even closer to god - or ourselves. It is the greatest weapon and the best medicine. Sweet dreams

Douglas

It has been suggested (but I am not sure of the source) that intimacy is only possible when one has reached a certain stage of spiritual evolution. If that is so, then we must be getting close. We are certainly intimate in many ways.

I feel so frustrated at present because I am not singing. Someone should write a programme or workout for artists/writers/musicians, to maximise our energy and potential. After working all week, especially on a computer screen, it is difficult to psych oneself up (do you know the expression?) to a regime or discipline on the weekend, but that is the only real time available for creation - while I am working at the university.

Watched a good film called *Maurice* tonight - based on the life of the English novelist E.M. Forster and his gay propensities. Forster insisted his biography not be published until after he died - in the seventies.

You were so good to hold yesterday. *Mfg thope swyxubr staoie*** - your soulmate. Do you remember that you sent me a card, to the effect that soulmates are often lost for words?

The Verdi incident i.e. when you went to the opera with N. without telling me, has thrown me completely off kilter. It was as if our sacred ground had been trespassed upon. Opera for me, is the vital thread that binds us closely and I could not bear to think of you sharing it, even though I am arranging with other opera buffs to set up various operatic groups. I am so jealous of our love. The ecstasy I feel when I am in your arms listening to opera, is incredible. I could not bear to think you shared such joy with anyone else.

Everyone I know intimately, weeps for me - because they know how much I love you, but they wish to see the end of my degradation. I am so weary, my dear, of the struggle. It is tearing me apart. How I wish we could go to sleep together at night. I am too tired to continue. I often want to die - simply because I wish the matter might be resolved.

Dear, dearer, dearest to me than all others

I feel that you and I are part of a tremendous emotional plot between men and women, which reduces us both to simply being pawns in some universal game. It is not a role I relish, though you said today, even though we prefer to think we have free will, to some degree, we are victims of the way things are.

We are trapped in a labyrinth and there is no easy way out, yet to stay in the labyrinth is not acceptable. We fit together so well in many ways. I am, like yourself, afraid of the claustrophobia of being together in a more extended way, but I am, unlike you, not so afraid, that I would avoid the experience.

It seems to be a case of damned if you do, and damned if you don't. What on earth does N. imagine our relationship to be? I am aware that the last thing I would want is to make you less free, just as I would not allow you to reduce my freedom. There must be a middle way.

It seems that many women worship men as being superior and feel themselves of course, to be inferior. There is a long cultural tradition to this effect, as you know. You stated today that if I was with you, I would have to fit in, and tolerate your idiosyncrasies, which bore testimony to this cultural truth.

But I would not simply fit in - and there would need to be compromise. If one partner subjugates the other to his or her own interests, there can't be love - even if the submission appears to be willingly given. I would never allow you to dominate me, nor would I wish to dominate you.

You have become part of me. It is as if only half the conversation is there, when you are absent. I don't mean that we are always in harmony, but that our thoughts are intermingled. Darling, cherish me as I cherish you. I am so glad we met today. You were very tender.

Dear Shobha

Your cards for my birthday are delightful. The bathers (swimsuits) are also very welcome, and I am especially grateful for the letter from the radio presenter Michael Harrison and his photograph.

Whatever was it you said to him to induce him to respond in such a thoughtful way to our interest in his opera programmes? I have listened with moist eyes, many times in the past week, to his session on Verdi's *Othello*, which is really superb. My respect for Harrison grows with each new episode.

On another matter, I believe people such as ourselves can be nobler – uplifted, and feel more keenly - after separation. In some strange way, I suspect the very nature of our association, with its extraordinary blend of affinities and disparities, rules out the possibility of the everyday happiness that you seem to wish for.

What you call love, involves a large element of idealism, which is a form of make-believe. This idealism is simply not compatible with everyday cohabitation. Love, like opera, is at the same time, an escape from ordinary life, and a refreshment for it. Doesn't this make sense of my moods? If you cherish something, take care not to embrace too much of it.

Douglas

Love between two soulmates is impossible, unless both consider the other before themselves. I cannot conceive or concede, despite your words, that I am not the most important person in your life. Being in love automatically confers that value on the other, and I perceive that your life without me would lack joy and meaning and would be a spiritual, emotional, intellectual and physical desert.

Dear Friend

On Monday, when we listened to the *Four Last Songs* of Richard Strauss, we reached quite a peak of spiritual and emotional pleasure - despite your difficulties with attempting to give up your medication. I have become very aware of the difference between *Douglas plus* medication and *Douglas without* - which was not so apparent before.

I wonder what a completely *medication-free Douglas* would be like. You seem incredibly alive and full of laughter, and terribly responsive to me at those times. You look at me more and take the initiative in caresses etc. *Douglas plus his medication* is much more cool and passive and less sensitive. But you must know this yourself. It frightens me a little to see the two sides – so different from each other. Who is the real Douglas ?

For example, if ever I feel ill, you do not seem to notice or understand, but those with whom I work are aware of the difference in my behaviour. My friend Helen, who you admire, will readily attest that I am the type to soldier on until the last moment, but you do not seem to know this side of me. You see it as being sorry for myself, and deride me, but it is not so. What is so, is that you rarely have the capacity to care for another person when they are not at the peak of their energy. I would not like you to think that only N.'s pains are authentic (to you) and not mine – which seems to me to be the case.

Dear-ling

Today was very special, because the absence of words made it so. For a short while, our minds were laid to rest, and we simply enjoyed each other. How sweet it was. I felt such a peace with you – and when you fell asleep for a few moments, I was glad.

For me, that indicates trust. If ever I fall asleep in your arms - know that I have abandoned myself to you completely. It feels so strange to return to work after such a sacrament.

After a day like today, my love, I can only pray that we may always be gentle with each other, and if we cannot, that we find the grace in ourselves to heal any hurt we may cause. I can still feel you all about me.

Dear Shobha

Having watched the Verdi opera *Aida* today, I am confirmed in the view that imagination is better than visual spectacle in opera, as also in Shakespeare - though for somewhat different reasons. Much of Shakespeare is too profound or wonderfully expressed to be put into the mouth of a player.

I am nearing the end of your biography of Simone de Beauvoir *(who wrote The Second Sex - which has achieved notoriety),* and have found it increasingly interesting. To my shame, it has made me much more conscious of the problems women face. It seems *de Beauvoir* thought there can be no harmony between a woman and her biology. In comparison, the male seems infinitely favoured: his sexual life is not in opposition to his existence as a person, and biologically it runs an even course - without crises and generally without mishap.

Please be forbearing my darling, as I feel a strange lowness, related in some way to N.'s retirement yesterday. As one of the world's do-ers, she hasn't given a moment's thought to what effect it is going to have upon her ordinary daily life. She is in an expectant state, without any clear idea of what she is expecting. And I haven't helped by quoting Sam Johnson to her, on filling the vacuities of life.

I enclose a review from *The Economist* magazine, on the relationship of creativity and genius to attacks of depression. This could be what made Sam Johnson a profound thinker by the age of twenty or so. The point is that despair and depression encourage reflection. Depression is a form of introspective solitude. As I have said to you - a child should experience solitude, either by force of circumstance (as happened to me), or by external discipline. Am I saying that I also have a Black Dog (i.e. I am subject to depression)?

Cartoons appended to Shobha's letters to Douglas

Dear Shobha

Having read the novel *84 Charing Cross Road* by Helen Hanff, I was led to the poetry of John Donne in the *Oxford Book of Quotations,* and discovered the following lines which I found relevant for us :

>A naked thinking heart that makes no show,
>is to a woman, but a kind of ghost

and also

>So if I dream I have you, I have you,
>for all of joys are but fantastical

and further

>Whoever loves, if he do not propose
>the right true end of love,
>he's one that goes to sea
>for nothing but to make him sick.

and on another tack completely :

>Tread softly - for you tread on my dreams - *William Butler Yeats*

I had no idea that Donne was not only a man of such genius, but was recognised as being so, by his contemporaries, even though none of his love poetry was published in his lifetime. Many of the poems circulated in manuscript form - within a small London circle. He admits in one of his lines that *It cannot be love, till I love her, that loves me* (with which, I am sure you will agree).

You will find him congenial to your own way of thinking, in what he says about physical and spiritual love. *"Only through two bodies coming together, can love's mystery reveal itself in the union of two soul Even true lovers must descend to affections and to faculties, only through the body, can weak men actually see love manifested."*

You may also be inclined to echo the astonishing opening line of another of his poems viz. *for God's sake hold your tongue, and let me love* as you have said, so many times. So many of his single lines are jewels. It is strange that I, as a Johnsonian and thus of a more analytical and cynical temperament, should find Donne so delightful. Perhaps I am affected by you – or by love.

My dear Shobha

I am (still) deep in Donne. What think you of :

>I wonder by my troth,
>what thou and I did, til we lov'd ?

My friend

Your quotes from Donne are very apt. Would it surprise you to know that almost all your quotations I had already highlighted some time ago in my *Oxford Book of Quotations.* The last one you quoted (above) however, is my favourite.

Since we are not meeting at present by agreement, I will not, and must not, meet with you as yet. Have courage. When you are ready for me, I will most certainly come. In the meantime, as Jesus said to his disciples in Gethsemane – *"Watch and pray."*

Darling

I have found a few tenor arias for you to experiment with, when we next sing together viz :

- *Celeste Aida* – (heavenly Aida) from Verdi's opera *Aida*
- *La donna è mobile* – (women are fickle) from Verdi's opera *Rigoletto*
- *E lucevan la stelle* (the stars are brightly shining) from Puccini's opera *Tosca*

Dear Douglas

Sometimes I have moments of insight and realise that you are an unusual man, and living a domestic life with you would not be a bed of roses. Your *limited tolerance for me* theory, would place severe strains upon us, but has it ever occurred to you that I might also have limited tolerance for you ? How I wish I knew how to heal you when you are out of sorts. There seem to me to be only two states i.e. love and gratitude or complaint. Oh - to be in a state of love all the time. It is possible that your alternating moods, and mine, may be simply cyclical, and a product of the intense nature of our interaction, which may not be evident in more prosaic relationships.

There are many ways to work on emotional problems with which I am familiar, but of which you may not have heard. Some therapists use breathing patterns to contact unconscious feelings. Some work analytically with the mind. Others concentrate on contacting feelings by ascertaining what is happening in the body in terms of sensations, pain etc. - then encouraging expression of those feelings, with a view to evoking old childhood traumas, and by doing so in a safe environment, enabling the subject to experience old wounds, so they are no longer fearful.

20

Catharsis is one of the words for this process, i.e. a cleansing through expression of feelings. The deepest form of catharsis is known as *primal,* where very early childhood experiences are accessed. Some people even relive their birth trauma - which is now accepted in professional circles as being responsible for damage to body and mind in later life. Stillbirth and spontaneous miscarriages are also known or thought to be nature's way of preventing the birth of a child, who is in some way - not whole.

In the early days of the orange movement, catharsis was extolled as the supreme method of healing. There was a virtual cult of catharsis, and emotions were freely expressed - but within a structured situation. This process was later frowned upon, and quieter forms of therapy involving meditation, were employed. Tears and anger were driven underground again. It was not in fashion. I passed through both phases - at one stage, participating in a primal therapy group - underground - for two weeks.

I am assuming that when you went to boarding school in England and left behind your family in Rhodesia - many feelings were also pushed underground. You mentioned for instance, that you learnt not to cry. You told me it was agony to say goodbye to your mother at the station when she left you to return to Africa, as the other boys were watching. You could not express the love you felt for her, because of the embarrassment of being seen to be affectionate by your peers.

Darling

You state you have never focussed on the past with regard to your family, and suggest this is a futile exercise. Is not the mention of your early influence upon your offspring also a reference to the past? Where is the cut-off point? Is there only life after marriage - or only death after marriage – perhaps? I recall you once said "love ends at the altar" and your "intellectual and aesthetic life ended with your marriage".

Is the procreative cycle the beginning of one's life? In which case, I have not had a life. Since you bathe yourself in Johnsonian principles, which stem from an era long since gone, and since we both immerse ourselves in the literature and music of bygone times, surely the past is always with us ?

In my not so humble opinion, those who do not look even cursorily at their personal past, are simply afraid of what they may discover. *Knowing thyself* also implies knowing one's personal history intimately. The inability to remember one's childhood has often been found to be a defence system against recalling traumatic experiences, which would be too painful for the psyche to recall. However, their influence is still there. Knowing the source of one's attitudes and feelings, can actually release much of the original pain and enable healing to take place.

You criticised me vehemently yesterday for my psychological bent, and you also condemn the discipline of psychology as being of no value. Do you not realise that my whole training and experience is psychologically-oriented? It would be like my insisting that you *not* think in legal or rational, theoretical concepts: in other words - expect you to change your spots.

If I do not labour psychological interpretations of behaviour with you, it is not because I don't make them, but because it seems futile to discuss such things with you, if you are not skilled in their application, or are skeptical, cynical and not receptive, because of your lack of knowledge in this area. Yesterday, I tried to cross the barrier with you, but failed. It is like talking a different language. The same would be true if I tried to discuss the intricacies of meditation or spiritualism.

In the past, you have been very critical of my ideas initially, but as time progresses and media coverage widens, you have conceded a little. The phenomenon of pre-menstrual tension (which you had not heard of before); the effects of stillbirth on the mother and her ensuing grief; the early effects of bonding on children and the spiritual nature of love-making - for example. Yet at first, you became irate when discussing these matters.

We belong to different generations, and it is more difficult with age to accept new ideas. For thirty years or more (since the sixties), the world has been enveloped in the *psychological movement*. All my adult life, I have been exposed to the ideas of Transactional Analysis, Gestalt, Primal and Encounter therapies, rebirthing, Jungian, Rogerian and Adlerian psychoanalysis, the work of Wilhelm Reich, John Bowlby etc., which are widely read amongst those with a tertiary education, especially in the Arts. They are almost old hat, and taken for granted.

Yet you have probably not read about any of these. That you are not familiar with this body of theory and practice, simply indicates a degree of isolation on your part. But do not condemn me, because occasionally I attempt to bridge the gap and explain matters in psychological terms.

We have both talked at length about your children, and made observations which have been valuable. Just as I am interested in my family history, I am also interested in yours (and have spent ten years researching your genealogy, to the greater benefit and understanding of us both). Yesterday, you mentioned you had been apart from your mother in boarding school for two and a half years at a stretch. I awoke this morning and was filled with horror at this revelation, as you were only eleven when this period of separation began.

It occurred to me that you might unconsciously wish to punish me by making me wait to see you, because you yourself had to wait so long to see the woman you loved - as a child. I am not your mother. Please don't punish me any more.

Sometimes I feel such a wave of tenderness for you, and want to hold you in my arms, and say that I will love you and never leave you - but you do not often let me get that close. Yet both of us need to know that we are there for each other.

You might be content with a letter a week, as you are used to deprivation i.e. long intervals between letters in boarding school and later in the army during the war. I am not so skilled.

My issue is that my parents were always there, but did not consistently give the quality of love that a child needs. Childhood feelings don't die. You have an aversion to over-demonstrative affection. You have learnt to close off your heart.

Your reaction causes me sadness, for I want to rush towards you and feel your response, but you are often cool. What has happened to that spontaneity which causes you to run joyfully to greet me? Have you noticed that what we condemn, we are attracted to also? You have said to me that you criticise people for what you do not have yourself. That you hate people because you envy them. Perhaps you despise what might be your hope of salvation.

Bhagwan used to say "If people hate me, that is good, because hate can always be converted to love. But nothing can be done with indifference". The degree of revulsion often equals the degree of attraction.

On a video at the orange centre last evening, Bhagwan spoke of the importance of working (with love). The Dutch painter *Vincent Van Gogh* was penniless, but continued to paint until he achieved what he felt was perfection - and then committed suicide. He worked solely for love - despite hardship - and was not recognised in his lifetime.

French philosopher *Jean Paul Sartre* was awarded the Nobel Prize for Literature, but refused it, because he said it was such a joy to create - he wanted no further recognition.

Bhagwan also contrasted trust with love. Love is a struggle - but trust is not. It became apparent to me that I have not trusted you since N. retired, because of my terror of being left - despite your assurances. Your welfare is dear to my heart. I care about the spirit inside you, that longs to be free. Balancing the sacred and the mundane is quite an art. To be able to love another truly, when one is caught up in one's own needs and frustrations - is the ultimate.

Shobha

I have been listening entranced to the whole of Mozart's opera *The Magic Flute* since coming back from the beach. My run along the ocean this morning was pure delight, and in some way made me particularly vulnerable to Mozart's music. Did I tell you what the Irish playwright *Bernard Shaw* said of the Flute?

> "I am highly susceptible to the force of all truly religious music, no matter to what church it belongs; but the music of my own church for which I may be allowed, like other people, to have a partiality – is to be found in *Die Zauberflöte* (The Magic Flute) and the ninth symphony of Beethoven."

This is in line with the composer *Richard Wagner's* comment (on the Flute) that a god-like magic breathes through the score. Musing – as I do – on the possible causes of things – I wondered whether my exposure to choral music as a ten-year-old member of a fine church choir, could have something to do with my geriatric discovery of Mozart's magic.

I was, of course, exposed throughout my childhood, in school and church at least, also to the language of the Common Prayer Book and the Bible, which may have had some effect on the person I am now.

Dear Shobha

It took me some time to track down the passage from Donne, which you asked me to find. It comes from his *Devotions* published in 1624, and was written while he was ill in the later part of his life - when aged around fifty.

> No man is an island
> entire of itself
> Every man is a piece of the continent
> a part of the main
> If a clod be washed away by the sea
> Europe is the less
> as well as if a promontory were
> as well as if a manor of thy friend's or of thine own, were
> Any man's death diminishes me
> because I am involved in mankind
> And therefore
> never send to know for whom the bell tolls
> It tolls for thee

Some further snippets of Donne - culled at random :

> I am two fools, I know
> For loving
> and for saying so
> in whining poetry

> •

> Licence my roving hands
> and let them go
> before, behind, between, above, below
>
> O my America
> my new-found land
> My kingdom
> when with one man manned
>
> My mine of precious stones
> my empire be
> How blest am I
> in thus discovering thee

Incidentally, in one of my books about Donne, I came across an interesting definition by A.N. Whitehead of religion: *What the individual does with his own solitariness*. Perhaps Bernard Shaw listening to the *Magic Flute* - or being in meditation?

Dear Douglas

I wandered at Point Resolution at mid-day, and there was a letter to you flowing through my mind with such eloquence, that I wished I had a computer there and then, as the beauty of the words had evaporated by the time I was back at the office.

Have you not noticed that there are times when you almost feel possessed by what you wish to say. Even seconds later, the sentiment can be lost forever.

Last night I had not thought of making love with you, but after lying with you for a time, I could feel myself wanting you. You are content to talk without any particular display of affection. It is not so for me. The talk is a prelude to a deeper degree of intimacy, which can only be expressed through touch.

I have belatedly realised that your language is talk and mine is touch. Perhaps there is a male-female difference here, though I would doubt most men wish to talk - before making love.

Douglas

A poet who only tugs at the mind and not the heart, is not a poet.

Shobha

My enthusiasm for Donne's prose is beginning to flag. I have little stomach for his sermons, and find his obsession with death, distasteful. I prefer the outlook of the Scottish philosopher David Hume, who cheerfully accepted that all ends at death.

For some people - belief in some form of afterlife seems to make for melancholy - instead of being a comfort. It militates against being lost in the present, which is the secret, not of happiness, but of minimising unhappiness. Unhappiness, like ill-health, is a state of consciousness: happiness, like good health, is not.

Dear Douglas

It gladdened the cockles (snail-shaped ventricles) of my heart to find your letter waiting for me when I returned from watching the film *Dead Poets' Society***. I judge the worth of a film by how many buckets of tears I weep, when it is over. I wish you had been standing by - to catch them all.

** Dead Poets' Society : the film centres around an inspired teacher of poetry who wishes to transfer his enthusiasm to his students. One student in particular is greatly affected, as he wishes to be an actor, but feels trapped by his father's expectations of him. He takes his own life – rather than compromise.

With reference to discussing G-O-D, I was simply going to state that in the East, enlightenment is understood to be remembrance of one's own true nature – which is a state of innocence, freedom and recollection of one's divinity. In mundane life, we rarely touch those heights, but when we do, it is as if we have come home.

You said if *god* simply meant feeling exalted, then it was meaningless, but I say, that only in those moments of remembrance, do we catch a glimpse of the greater reality. Paradoxically, it is (only) as you say, when we are immersed in the present, that we are able to experience such exaltation.

Life is rich, because of you. Yesterday, you said to me "I feel so alive, I could burst". What a magnificent utterance. Dear Douglas, come and kiss me into sleep. It would be so beautiful to curl up with you and disappear.

My gyana yogi (gyana means wisdom in Sanskrit)*

We talked of generosity today. Perhaps I can only be generous where I have insight. Until I fully understand my jealousy with regard to your sudden overwhelming love for your new grand-daughter, I cannot be generous. Jealousy comes from a perceived or actual deficit, in this case, of your affection. Only when the deficit is rectified or understood, can the overflowing abundant energy return. Your bhakta (devotional) yogini.

Dear Shobha

Donne has described *love* as the richest mantle, as in the words from the Gospel of John that *God is love, and he that dwelleth in love, dwelleth in god, and god in him.* This hovers nicely on the brink of meaning.

My dear Shobha

This morning at the beach was a blend of after-glow and painful back. Could it be that *missionaries* tend to have back troubles (based on the notion of the *missionary position* when making love) ? I found myself humming and almost singing, some of our arias from the *Flute*, while showering this morning, which is very out of character for me. *The Magic Flute* has for the time being, become my *musical bible*.

As so often on Mondays, I feel languorous – the delayed effect of my five-kilometre run from the house to the beach - yesterday. It's certainly not unpleasant, though it involves some loss of alertness. Perhaps that is the very reason for it being pleasant. An alert mind is no certain way to contentment. Singing with you yesterday was really very satisfying, yet I have no illusions about my voice**.

Dear songbird

You will be delighted to know that your singing turned out well on the tape. The early scales were really very good. Scales are difficult to sing at first. The aria *E lucevan le stelle* from *Tosca*, was also well-produced. The scales took their toll however, as they do when I am singing for my teacher, so from the beginning of *Di Provenza* from *La Traviata* (opera of Verdi), it is evident that your voice is tired - as you felt it to be.

But you will be amazed at how big your voice is – compared to mine for instance. I think you will be pleasantly surprised to know this. I was. You can learn so much by taping the lessons. I am quite excited. Darling - I am quite proud of us. If you listen to the tape, it will inspire you to greater heights.

Yesterday I remember looking at you, when you were touching me in my costume for *La Traviata*** which is so very beautiful. I felt such a tenderness in you and for you. Opera is life.

> As has been mentioned, after fifty years of not singing at all, apart from in his school choir, Shobha encouraged Douglas to sing in the local hall where she practised her own songs - and was surprised to discover that Douglas possessed a strong baritone voice and was able to sing a number of operatic arias quite well, as they were so familiar to him (after years of exposure to opera - through attendance at the theatre and his own recordings).
>
> Shobha participated in the chorus of a full-scale production of the opera *La Traviata*, having previously only performed in Gilbert and Sullivan operettas.

La Traviata

Darling

I am beginning to wonder at the complexity of the human mind - or mine, at least. Sometimes all seems in order, everything is tranquil, all is peace and even happiness, dare I say it - and then, it changes unexpectedly, and the anguish and pain return, and I am disturbed and discontented once again. Is it so for you?

Singing with you is the greatest joy – almost as great as making love – what an admission. It is so delightful to be *doing* something with you, which is a first – for us.

My love

You have taught me so much and I am glad. It is rare for lovers to be each other's teachers, or perhaps that is the true test of love, that we both impart all that we know, so that the *melding* deepens. There is a programme on television tonight entitled *Rajneesh (i.e. Bhagwan) – Spiritual Terrorist*. How apt – he is certainly wishing to do away with the existing institutions in society and the hypocrisy they engender.

Dear Douglas

I have just purchased a book called *Soprano on her Head,* which has been written as a guide to singers, musicians and performers - using a kind of reverse psychology - as when I say to you *When you sing a high note - think down.* This appears at first, to be contradictory, but is the key, as far as I am concerned - to overcoming barriers to singing easily. At least, that is my experience. In a similar vein, Bhagwan used to say "Out of chaos, stars are born", which was supposedly first uttered by the German philosopher Friedrich Nietzsche, and this has since become my own *mantra* (guide to live by).

My dear Shobha

I am using my computer for this letter, so that if N. comes into my study, she is less likely to assume I am writing to you. She knows, of course, that we write, but it adds to the hurt, to catch me *in flagrante* – as the lawyers put it.

Dear Douglas

I wonder how much ability to sing lies hidden in your unconscious. You certainly show an amazing propensity for picking up an aria and singing it with relative ease - on first airing. That pre-supposes you have skills of which you are probably unaware. I hope you enjoyed the tape. The laughter especially - fills me with joy.

Darling

Life feels very rich at present. I can sense all sorts of currents flowing through me. Tonight as I left the university club, I almost felt, dare I say it – happy. Bacchus reigns supreme. As you know, alcohol rarely touches my lips. I felt there was a reason for being. I talked to one of the professors about education and the function of inspiration, and asked him how many teachers had inspired him, and he said '*none*'.

I believe we are moulded by our mentors, even if we don't see them as such, at the time. One of my colleagues told me today that in his village in England, the parson used to show coloured lantern slides of John Bunyan's Christian allegory *The Pilgrim's Progress,* which held the whole village spellbound. He said it changed his life. Surely this is what we must be for others - an inspiration, at whatever level? Even if it is only to ask provocative questions, so that we enable others to question the status quo (which is very much the role I wish to play).

My darling

Wouldn't it be intelligent to go back on your medication for a day, then take a day off, as is usually advised when embarking on drug withdrawal? You know rationally, that is the wise course of action, yet you persist in what can only be a damaging venture. Giving up completely can place a strain on your body and heart and puts you at risk – to what end? Far better to alternate or further halve your dosage, than go *cold turkey*. I appreciate your intention, but you are playing with fire.

Douglas

I meant what I said - that a woman (like me) wishes to be adored and to be seen as a goddess, and she wishes to regard her beloved as a *god* - and to adore him.

10

Dear Douglas

Met the dean of the Education faculty to discuss my doctoral proposal. A provocative, subversive, eccentric, stimulating woman. We hit it off immediately. I mentioned my topic of *aesthetic hedonism* and she responded *"Ah, my field exactly"* and plied me with books and article. We swapped life stories and skated over eastern philosophy, *Wittgenstein***, *Dead Poets Society* etc. It felt like *coming home* or rather putting on my rucksack to climb Everest with the best Sherpa guide that god could provide. So I am enthused, to say the least.

** *Ludwig Wittgenstein* was the pre-eminent European philosopher of the modern era.

I'm amazed you have not drowned yourself in the philosophy of education, aesthetics etc before now. Many of the topics you and I have touched upon are relevant here. The whole creative, educative process is fascinating. I said to her that "I have no philosophical training" and she said "Maturity makes a philosopher."

All in all - very reassuring. The main problem is convincing the doctoral committee I can work full-time and complete a doctorate. They are very much against it. Divine intervention is required.

You are my heart's delight is the song we were trying to recall yesterday (from the Franz Lehar operetta *Land of Smiles*).

Dear Douglas

You looked very enticing this morning in your new swimsuit. How dare you be so attractive. When you were running along the beach I noticed belatedly perhaps, how good you looked as you ran, and how fast you seemed to be.

Dear Shobha

My visitors from England - who have also been swimming out to sea in the early morning - seem genuinely surprised that almost everyone they met, was greeted - in one way or another. And all in carefree mood.

It is clearly no trivial thing to start each day in this way. It is in clear contrast to getting up at the last moment, gobbling down breakfast and going straight off to work. All the more important therefore, for you to improve your swimming and gain more confidence *(having learnt to swim only recently),* so you become one of the 'truly elect'.

Dear Douglas

While I agree with you about the beneficial effects of the early morning adventure at the beach, I have only recently encountered smiles and joviality. Bear in in mind that I have not been introduced to anyone at any point. This certainly greases the wheels of social intercourse. A woman who 'fronts up' to a man on the beach may be thought to be forward and arouse suspicion.

Certainly you have never seemed particularly pleased to see me, and I can't ever recall you smiling at me or making a joke. I presume you feel you are being watched.

**

Christmas produces such subtle tensions. Everyone wants so much to be happy, that this in itself, produces the opposite. There are more deaths, suicides and engagements during this period than is usual - and many broken engagements and applications for divorce, after the festive season is over.

One of my friends slept under her Christmas tree a night or so ago, after a Christmas-inspired argument with her new husband. The wife of one of my colleagues, of perfect marriage fame, told me today she hates Christmas and wants to become a Muslim. I warned her that her husband may have four wives.

You may recall that we typically have a major rift just before the peak of the season, and then you refuse to see me during the holiday season until New Year is well and truly over.

On our first Christmas Eve together, you swore you would not leave your matrimonial home, made love to me, and then left me to cope with the after-effects - so it is traditional for us to fall out about now.

Chapter 8

The deeper sorrow carves into your being

Bhagwan

On 19 January 1990, Bhagwan Shree Rajneesh (Shobha's spiritual teacher) left his body after a long illness. While driving down to the sea, Douglas heard the news on his car radio.

As Douglas came out of the sea after his swim – he met Shobha coming into the water. From his expression, she guessed immediately what had happened. It was a poignant moment for them both.

Dear heart

The celebration for Bhagwan last night was magnificent. Just like old times. Flowers everywhere – overlooking the river at sunset, and everyone in white except a couple of sannyasins - including myself.

Felt Bhagwan's presence very much. So many tears - but tears of tremendous love. We are all so bound to him – as if he is our very life. I suspect that in his physical absence, there may be more cohesion now between those who love him. Impossible to say at this stage. It felt so good to see my friends again.

Dear one – sometimes I wish I could share some of these times with you, but it is not your way. I can only say how miraculous it was for me, that you were the one to let me know (when he left planet earth). From anyone else's lips – I might have felt bereft. From yours – I did not. I am very blessed.

Dear Douglas

This evening - perhaps because of our meeting, I have a renewed sense of Bhagwan's presence, though there are still tears that well up quite often. But they are tears of tremendous longing, my love - to meet, to dissolve, to disappear, to find peace ... and with you this afternoon, the longing was also there - for us to surrender to each other.

No wonder you fear my intensity sometimes. It is the longing for god itself.

Bhagwan once told me that only when the longing was total, would I find that union. You are a provocation to me, because when I am with you, the longing arises. It is so deep. My darling, you are my heart's delight.

Dear Shobha

While I was showering last evening, I heard someone say on the radio that Bhagwan was by no means a fraud, as he is often portrayed in the media, but was original, in that he tried to blend the mysticism of the East with Western psychology. Is this a novel slant? (Shobha's comment : that was the whole point of Bhagwan's work and hardly novel.)

It was wild down at the beach this morning. The wind was blowing so strongly that I turned back at the buoy. But, as ever, it was exhilarating.

**

Please don't misconstrue my reasons for being lukewarm about your doctoral ambitions. I think you seriously underestimate how much of your time and energy it would take. As it is, you lead a pretty full life at the moment - with your singing, meditation and swimming.

Dear Douglas

I was dismayed to realise you are lukewarm re my thesis, though it does not alter my resolve. My supervisor was greatly enthused by my ideas. I would prefer if you have doubts about this project that you share them with N. and not with me. I would like your encouragement and support – nothing less.

My dear Shobha

Yesterday was strange indeed. Our singing session was great fun. If - as you said several times, I seemed very different from my normal self - so too, did you to me. But this was not solely because of changes in my body chemistry. I felt then - before we went to the hall to sing – as I do now – that you were looking at me in a speculative and almost detached way – which was quite new.

Saying this makes me wonder whether your strangeness may not have been attributable in part to the effect on you of Bhagwan's death. In some curious way, it seems to have given you a new confidence.

**

Herewith Michael Harrison's** recording of excerpts from Puccini's opera *Turandot* with Maria Callas, Jussi Bjorling, Birgit Nilsson, Luciano Pavarotti and Joan Sutherland. It has been said that *Turandot* is a wrecker of soprano voices.

**   Michael Harrison, was a broadcaster with the Australian Broadcasting Commission, who featured comparative excerpts from hundreds of operas in his programme, over several years.

Note from Shobha to Douglas

After watching the film on the composer (Giacomo) *Puccini's* life, I weep for the stupidity of the human condition. How easy it is for Puccini to say he 'loves' his wife, yet his every action betrays that love. Puccini simply loved himself. That his wife remained - in view of his many lovers - was equally distasteful.

A man with Puccini's disposition should not marry unless the wife condones his licentiousness or is herself engaging in the same behaviour. I do not agree with you that no-one is at fault. Puccini should have left his wife and indulged himself, or the wife should have left Puccini.

Tales of this kind leave a bad taste in my mouth. I am reminded of our own situation, where we are unable to fully share our love, because of your domestic attachments. It is so wrong that love between us is not able to have its full expression. I detest hypocrisy. People should be with the ones they love. I cannot abide mediocrity in love. It goes hand- in-hand with mediocrity in other areas of one's life.

Dear Shobha

Herewith your video of the Austrian-British philosopher *Wittgenstein*, together with a copy of my legal article on *Definition* which I wrote about twenty years ago, but never tried to get published - though it was once used as the base text for a course in Jurisprudence at an American law school.

Do you realise how close Wittgenstein's thought and attitudes are to mine, in some respects? For example, I think he would have agreed that love - like ethics and religion, is not for talk - but for being and action. The moment the mystical is expressed in words - corruption begins to set in. Don't hesitate to ring me if you are in distress. I am your friend - so that your problems are also mine – as mine I think, are yours.

22

My dear Shobha

Yesterday was quite extraordinary and delightful. We have never, I think - caressed each other before in quite the same relaxed and serene way. And this was primarily your doing. There's a lesson somewhere in what happened, and how we behaved - though what it is, I do not know.

Sweetheart

Your little note made my homecoming. One word can mean so much. *Steppenwolf* (by the German-Swiss novelist Hermann Hesse) is on television tonight, so I shall video the programme and we can watch at leisure. Much of Hesse's material is semi-spiritual, but it sounds as if this film explores the more seamy side of one's nature.

Douglas plus *Tannhauser* (opera by German composer Richard Wagner) today, were a heady mix. Yes, I have also noticed I don't go to the beach after we have been close - but not after love-making - strangely. Then - I seem to wish for continued reassurance of your elevated mood.

Today when I spoke of wanting you to be happy, it was no trivial comment. I suspect that this is the true test of whether one loves or not. Anything less is probably only concern for oneself. I avoid the word selfish, which I do not recognise - as such words are greatly tainted by the past i.e. the Christian concept of sin, which has always been simply a way for the church to control its people.

Dear love, how rich it would be to live for love and art and nature and ideas and beauty and language. I wish I could make them my total existence.

Dear Shobha

Herewith Harrison's recording of *Tristan and Isolde* (Wagner's opera). Almost against my will, I felt my enthusiasm for his opera *Tannhauser* yield place so easily - and found myself completely swept away. Since you say you do not know it well, and are, I suspect, in the throes of conversion to Wagner's spell, your reaction will be very interesting.

**

Singing was fun yesterday. I think I enjoyed bellowing (which is *la mot juste* - the right word) the aria *To an Evening Star*** even more than *Di Provenza***. I seem to find more satisfaction trying to sing baritone arias than the tenor ones. Perhaps for the crude reason, that the deeper one is more powerful than the other - emotionally.

It was exhilarating at the beach this morning. Only ten degrees, but very little wind and a firm, flat beach for running. The nip in the air seemed to make running easier and more natural. It was too rough to swim out, but I must have spent twenty minutes in the surf and caught some good waves.

**   To an Evening Star from the opera *Tannhauser* by Wagner
**   Di Provenza from the opera *La Traviata* by Verdi

Darling

Have just been watching a programme on the Swiss psychoanalyst *Carl Jung*, and wish I had seen the previous episodes. Jung says, as you know, that each man carries a woman within – the *anima*, and each woman carries a man – the *animus*, and when two persons fall in love - it is because the inner archetypes of a man and woman are met by the outer persons - to some degree.

But from where do we develop these archetypes – from our parents? Am I simply your mother – warbling away at opera as she did, in the kitchen? Are you my father – tinkering in the workshop for hours on end as you do?

We must both admit that there is - like your redsetter Ned gnawing on a bone - an element of childhood remembrance and comfort in these images of sound and sight from the past. *(Douglas was terribly moved by the memory of his beloved dog gnawing on a bone - which he felt, had a primeval significance for him.)*

Jung was apparently one of the first Western thinkers, dare I say it, who gave great attention to eastern philosophy - especially Zen Buddhism.

This programme reawakened my interest in his work. Jungians describe all addictive behaviour – alcoholism, drugs, love, gambling, the stockmarket etc, as a search for a high - and thus for god, and that given this definition, it is at one level at least, an attempt to surpass oneself.

Being tossed by the waves and swimming out to sea in winter, is also seeking an experience of ecstasy - whether during or after the event. For me, love-making is a way to god – how I wish it was so for you, or perhaps it is - on occasion? Singing yesterday - likewise. Laughter – fun – also ! Running – Wagner – poetry – is there no end to it? Life is simply an opportunity to experience one high after another. Writing to you is another high. Receiving your letters is even more so. Kissing you is the best of all.

Dearest

Perhaps that little section of the river by our tree** where we used to meet - is magical? We always end up doing strange things there, such as lying wrapped around each other under an umbrella - and singing in the rain. Shobha

Dear Shobha

With a mild wind, the water was quite rough today and it was hard work getting out to the buoy. Even so, it was pleasant - the swimming that is. It's strange what a difference the presence of other people makes - even if you don't talk to them. An empty beach is like an empty church.

Dear Douglas

It is difficult to say exactly what transpired while listening to Bhagwan on tape last night. Suffice it to say, that I felt that after a confusing time in the last few weeks, I had come home, and remembered what it is I am truly *about*. It is a relief occasionally to realise that I am not alone in my understanding - for in my daily life, I am surrounded by those who do not hold any of my deeper values.

*The magic of the river***

And yet I would not like to cluster together too closely with like-minded souls. It can create insularity and egocentricity. It is good to dip in and out of both worlds. Especially between us - we often need to be apart for a while - and then after a little absence, the desire to share returns in some measure.

**

When you are off your medication, you seem to be warm and responsive – what I consider normal. When you are *on it*, you are withdrawn and emotionally aloof. You appear to be cut off from any deep or sensitive feelings – absolutely invulnerable. The greatest pity is that you are not even aware that you are different.

Douglas had great difficulty giving up a medication to help him sleep, which was prescribed by a doctor some time after his arrival in Australia in the sixties. He continued with the drug for many years, which had serious consequences for his behaviour in the long-term, and the withdrawal process was very debilitating.

At first he would give up the pills totally, which was quite dangerous, and then go back on them when he could not manage, despite Shobha's insistence that a gradual reduction was the only recommended way to withdraw.

Eventually, when the drug was removed from the market, he embarked upon a successful gradual and painful withdrawal over a year or so, but when this was achieved, he began to develop multiple serious medical conditions which affected his health from then onwards.

The relationship between Shobha and Douglas suffered greatly during the withdrawal process, but was followed by a stabilisation of Douglas' moods in consequence, and a greater harmony was then possible between them.

**

I was hurt by you saying that the ocean is *your stamping ground* and not mine. Surely after eight years of patronising the beach (since we first met), you should concede that it is as much mine as yours. My ashes are going into the ocean and hopefully you will be taking them (if I go first), so I insist you take back your statement.

Dear Shobha

I am still very influenced by the British historian Jeremy Wilson's book on *Lawrence of Arabia* which deals with his last, mainly literary, years. Lawrence was a complex, gifted and dedicated man. No-one seems to have understood him and Wilson himself does not seriously profess to do so - despite the length and detail of his book.

It may well be that aesthetic experience and some forms of loving a person, have the common features of surrender and losing oneself in a pleasurable way. Lawrence did not come to love anyone, but became very fond of music. It is not uncommon for people whose lives are transformed by dreadful injuries, as his was - to discover new sources of aesthetic pleasure.

After weeks of weltering in *Tannhauser* and *Tristan and Isolde*, Harrison's treatment of the *Mastersingers* (another Wagnerian opera) strikes me as thin – almost trivial. Progress is important in listening to opera. In some ways – as Harrison himself says – '*Tristan* is the ultimate - beyond which there is nowhere to go'.

Dear Douglas

The word 'love' is misleading. There are so many kinds of love - for a man or woman, a child, parent, dog, nature, music, a cappuccino, god, Bhagwan and even for oneself. There is a hierarchy of love from primeval lust towards prayerful, spiritual love. Even Hitler was capable of feeling love for Eva Braun and for music. What differentiates one person from another may be the degree to which they love, and the variety of ways in which they love. Even the most abject of creatures probably has moments of exaltation, when there is a temporary release from the abject state.

What is also important is that love is not limited to persons. One can love almost anything. Some people swear they love trees, and when hugging one, feel a sense of affinity and attunement. You love dogs – hence your deep attachment to your redsetter, Ned. I would tend to argue that aesthetic experience is synonymous with love. It all depends on definition (your favourite topic). Perhaps I will conclude that love, aesthetic experience and mystical experience are manifestations of the same phenomenon.

As far as I am concerned, the love of a man (you), who goes to the other side of the world without giving the woman he professes to care for (me) some form of contact with him, should an emergency arise - is bogus. Nothing could be more unkind. It is not as if you are going to war – or perhaps you are?

Dear Shobha

The reason why children are not conscious of being happy is that happiness is - even for adults - not a conscious state. Distinguish pain and unhappiness, which are conscious states. Compare also being well-fed and being hungry. Your recent unhappiness comes from looking ahead and comparing your own lot with the (imagined) lot of others.

Dear Douglas

Remember, you used to say to me that you were not unhappy because you were absorbed – hence my decision to write a thesis on creativity and absorption (because this seems to the secret of creativity - that all else fades away from consciousness in such moments). How influential you are for me, my love - though of course, Bhagwan has always said totality is the essence of the mystical experience. Goodnight – sweet dreams.

**

On the first day we met, you suggested we meet again for lunch the next day, and the following day you said you could not meet me, because you had to go into the city to see N. At the time I screamed at you in protest, yet continued to see you on what became your terms. I should not have done so. I should have realised you set a pattern then, that would not change.

If we have an arrangement to meet, I expect you to keep to it, unless there is a very good reason which you divulge - not act as if you can do as you wish, without even feeling the need to offer an explanation. If you want to live without claims or demands on you, then you should go and live on an island, where you will never be called to task, for your conduct.

Your arrogance amazes me. You always assume you are right and your behaviour is perfectly justifiable. You look at life with blinkers on – you are only concerned with yourself. You cannot put yourself out for anyone. But if you wish to go somewhere, you assume the other will follow.

**

I have just come from an evening talking with my friends. We have been plotting the course of human history in the space of a few short hours. They are so enlivening. We would like to form a subversive group to promulgate ideas through the media and also for our own refreshment.

We feel this could be done by writing freelance provocative articles for the press. I wish you could participate in my social life. I would love to bring together combinations of people for different purposes. I am sure you would be excited by the conversation today.

Dear Shobha

I was so pleased your letter this morning was a happy one. You are a creature of mercurial moods.

My dear Shobha

I have just been talking to an old university friend, who rang from San Francisco on the eve of my leaving for Europe. I never cease to be astonished when I pick up the receiver - expecting a routine local call - to find a voice speaking strongly and clearly from the other side of the world.

I can't raise any enthusiasm for going away. I wonder why? I tend to question whether all the disruption and preparation is worthwhile. What I object to is living out of a suitcase, rather than spending a month in a house in another place.

The cutting from *The Economist* may interest you. It illustrates the extraordinary range of matters the magazine covers. Because of its title, most people assume it's a staid, dull journal - whereas in truth, it's probably the most stimulating journal in the world.

Dear Douglas

Have just attended the most marvellous seminar in the Education faculty at the university. Eleven lecturers were present. I found myself unable to resist throwing in my contribution - at regular intervals. I was amazed at how at home I felt - despite my lack of teaching experience.

Perhaps teachers are naturally fairly responsive and extroverted. They certainly have a high verbal facility and quick intellectual response. I found many of the philosophical issues of our lives seemed to emerge. It is as if there was an innate philosophical awareness amongst those present.

I am beginning to wish I had studied either philosophy or education in the past. I can honestly say I have never experienced a tutorial before, which I came from - with fire in the belly. With you I cannot argue purely philosophically, because we are lovers. It would be too cold. It must be tempered with consideration. In a seminar, there is consideration, but of a different kind - especially when all the others are strangers. A delightful pursuit. How I would love to teach such a game of words – or rather, facilitate its occurrence.

As far as travel goes, I agree with you that it is better to go to one place as a base, settle in and then make forays each day or so, to other places within a small radius. Travel for its own sake seems pointless. One cannot appreciate anything in depth.

Notes of Shobha for Douglas - during his absence in Europe

In your absence, as is always the case - I enter a new dimension of myself. It has not been traumatic while you have been away, though I have many moments when I am wistful and cling to my little Wimsey** teddy bear, at night. When you return, you will find I have learnt to live without you - although you have of course, been in my heart. But I have come to realise in your absence, that I am basically a delightful, happy person for most of the time; that I have a lot of wit and humour to share, and I am genuinely interested in a large range of people.

I have also rediscovered some of the finer elements of my nature - in particular the longing for the ultimate; and for self-understanding of a complete and final kind. My reading in philosophy has led to the interrogatory methods of Socrates, and I have found a new thirst arising in me to share what I know, and what I have learnt from others - including yourself.

I find myself a natural philosopher, though not in the traditional or textbook sense or how it is taught in universities, but in the original form in which Socrates carried on his dialogues with his students, and his provocative and catalytic discussions with all he met.

I now see life as a philosophical exercise. I would like to think that your life was also a philosophical endeavour. Indeed, it is because of you in part, that I have discovered my own leanings e.g. the love of meaning and language, if not the love of wisdom itself - which I also gleaned from Bhagwan.

Your own search for understanding is more moderate than mine. It is there, but you camouflage it beneath a veneer of analysis that threatens at times to destroy. How I wish you would come and join your life with mine, so we can pursue this remarkable journey of self-discovery together.

At times I wonder how I would have time for all this marvellous diet of philosophy, aesthetics and art, if I was sharing my life with someone from day to day. At other times, I wonder how I can bear to be alone, when there are so many new ideas to share with you.

I have come across the most exciting book, which has put all my intellectual yearnings into perspective. It is by an American professor of philosophy with an exhaustive background in eastern philosophy. He brings everything back to its Socratic roots and in so doing, has helped me to realise that what I have always wished to do, and in a way have always done, even with you - is to provoke and question, and to ask the obvious e.g. are you happy – a question which you struggle to answer, and always end up avoiding - just as you cannot bring yourself to reach a conclusion about 'what is love'.

There is much to say. Why are you not here? It is not right that you should be on the other side of the world with someone who is not at all sympathetic or even capable of understanding your ideas. You are meant to be with me. We are two spirits of the same kind.

Do you remember asking N. whether she had been changed by your marriage, and she said "no"? That is an indictment in itself. Do you also remember saying you had "talked to me more in one week, than you had talked to N. in thirty years."

I have regained a sense of integrity since you have been away. I have rediscovered my innocence, if you like – as I was when first we met. I am no longer interested in debating our situation. There are so many more wonderful ideas to explore. Life is one great exercise in enjoying beauty, art, love, music and ideas. There is so much joy in the world.

> ** Wimsey is the teddy bear given to Shobha by Douglas and named after *Lord Peter Wimsey*: a fictional character from the novels of English author Dorothy Sayers. Wimsey was, in recent times, voted the ideal man, by English women.

My dear, dear love

This missive comes with no purpose other than to remind you of my presence. Your phone call (from abroad) has gladdened my heart. I can't wait to see you. There are many things to share, especially your own reactions to being away.

At this moment I am ensconced in *The Last Days of Socrates* by Plato, and his discussion of immortality. Love yourself, as I love you. Until we meet again in the flesh as well as in spirit.

My dear Shobha

I do not want to write at length about making love, but wish simply to say that we would, I'm sure, make love naturally and spontaneously if we slept together, and also that knowing each other as we do, there is something unnatural and almost unhealthy, in this not happening (i.e. not sleeping together).

This is not an oblique declaration of love – nor a denial of it. You are very dear to me and I look forward very much to seeing you.

Dear love - my creature

I would, as you well know, have met you at the airport if you had been alone, but I did not wish to share my meeting with you in any way. Ours is a precious love and must be treasured. Seeing you again will be wonderful. I am so glad you are home again. Your creature – Shobha

My dear Shobha

I trust you did not suffer any ill-effect from your over-indulgence yesterday. You were really quite delightful. Many thanks for the poetry from *Rossetti, Wordsworth, Tennyson, Arnold* and *Goethe*. How did you find them?

Dearest

I rushed home today thinking you might be waiting – and was so glad you had written. Yesterday was quite literally intoxicating. I felt as if we merged while lying in the sun – our words flowed so easily. Quite perfect.

But I did not realise you had to go early and wish I had known. I too, listened to Joan Sutherland in *Lucia di Lammermoor* (*opera of Giuseppe Verdi*) and she is absolutely faultless – stupendous as they say - but there is no soul – no guts. She is without passion - in my opinion.

You have been so loving since you returned, that I don't wish to enter into a deep analysis of our situation (at present).

My dear Shobha

Herewith a copy of Harrison's programme on José Carreras (*Douglas' favourite opera singer*). For some reason, it moved me to the edge of tears at one point. It was so heart-warming to find Harrison sharing my high regard for Carreras - for I thought I was out of step with the general current of opinion.

Speaking of being moved - which is of course, a rare experience for me - walking around the London house in which Samuel Johnson was born and grew up, has also affected me very much – as if walking on hallowed ground. I am going to have my print of Johnson reframed and am annoyed to find that the original, which was painted by the celebrated painter Joshua Reynolds in 1778, was in the Tate Gallery in London (and I did not know, when I was there several weeks ago). My love – Douglas

Shobha

I have thought of you many times as the rain has been falling so heavily since I returned. I am not yet ready to respond to your letter - written while I was overseas - only to say that I treat it as probably the most important and critical, that you have ever written to me.

My love

I am surrounded by your letters and tapes – a feast of words and music ! Your reverence for Sam Johnson is vital. It matters not who or what triggers the emotion of adoration - be it Bhagwan or Sam Johnson. What matters is that we are moved.

I thought we had agreed we should not meet unless you saw the light and we could be more fully together. We did not mention phone contact or letters. I would like to try being out of touch (literally), to see if it crystallises your attitude in some way. It is like damming up the floodgates not to be in touch, as we both know. There is no other way to bring you to me, dearest soulmate. You are right. That letter was the most important one I have ever written to you.

Dear love

I liken our current ordeal to that of Tamino and Pamina in Mozart's opera *The Magic Flute* – to be apart and unable to acknowledge each other for a time – so that a 'spiritual' purification might take place. I enclose an extract from Socrates on spiritual love.

Dear Douglas

I am missing you terribly tonight. It would be good to spend these winter nights with you. I hope you enjoy your birth-day, even though I am not with you in the body. Your note seemed devoid of feeling. I presume it was because of our pact.

You said you had not read my books. That hurt – not because I expect you to read them, but I wish you would at least open the covers. Is there no point in passing any reading matter on to you? You seem to expect that I will read what you pass on to me. I miss you very much. Hurry up and come !

My dear Shobha

It can hardly be a breach of the rules you have imposed on us, for me to thank you for your *potpourri* of birthday gifts, which took me back to childhood days of exploring a Christmas stocking.

Our behaviour, and yours particularly, has not been consistent since I came back from Europe. I am not complaining, but I think we should acknowledge it exists. How can it be wrong for us to write to each other, and yet acceptable to exchange caresses, as happened last night when I met you by chance outside your home. Of course, it was not in truth a chance encounter.

Dearest

Your letter gladdened my heart! Last night was beautiful and tender. There is no inconsistency. When I see you, I cannot and will not - *not* touch you. I am one flood of feeling when I am near you. I will not be otherwise. Hence, it is essential not to see you.

For you - it is difficult *not* to write. For me - it is difficult *not* to touch. Truth, according to Bhagwan, is what works. It does not work to continue physical contact. Only absence of contact for you, will move you to act. Until there are no *buts* - you are not ready for my love. As you know, you are my heart – Shobha

Dear Douglas

In view of the importance of these last few days for both for us, I would again request that you only contact me to discuss practicalities. I realise that vacillation is a natural part of your present predicament, and turmoil is - as you stated - inevitable.

For this reason, the struggle - if there is one - must, for the time being, be yours alone. Only then, may I be of any nourishment for you. I have never seen you looking so happy as the other night.

My love

I had to write – not because there is anything to say – quite the opposite. Our sweet coming together last night has left me with a happy heart. It feels as if we have truly begun. Peace my love – peace

Dear Douglas

As we mentioned yesterday, now that you have poured your heart and mind regarding the reasons against living together *(refer to final page of this chapter),* perhaps as a psychological exercise you should also consider the reasons *for*.

Obviously this is a game for the imagination, since one cannot know what is possible or in store. This is the case of course when people marry or undertake any vast enterprise. There is no way to know in advance. It requires courage and a capacity for taking risks. When one loses this capacity, one is 'old'. Remember the words of Sam (Johnson) that one should never cease to learn. When one is no longer capable of change, that is the end – spiritually, psychologically and intellectually.

What is amazing is that you say you are capable of change of an internal kind, but seem not to be, at the external level. Perhaps you have simply not had enough practice? At one point in my life, after I returned from India, I moved twelve times in one year. I enjoyed the experience and looked forward each time to packing up and moving on. It is a wonderful way of assessing one's priorities in a material sense and in other ways also.

You have asked - what would we DO - if we were together and free.

Taking this week as an example, the Verdi *Requiem* is being performed in Winthrop Hall on Thursday. *Placido Domingo (the Spanish opera singer)* is performing on Saturday and there is a gala opera concert in Winthrop on Sunday – all of which I would like to attend with or without you. As Spring is here, I will be returning to the beach in a day or so.

As your son and his partner are arriving from Canberra on Wednesday, I would assume that if we were together or you had your own dwelling, you would ask them over for dinner, or alternatively you would visit N. and have dinner there in the evening.

I do not usually go to films regularly, but there are several on at present that are worthwhile. Tonight I am going to the theatre with my sister-in-law to see a play. I have not been out with her before. So this week at least, would be rather interesting.

As far as other weeks are concerned, I simply do not know. Beach in the morning – possible swim at lunch for myself in the pool – maintenance on house for yourself – evening (in winter) could be spent by a log fire reading or listening to music. By the way, I have never had a dinner party in my life.

There is no reason why the odd person could not call in for a cup of tea or breakfast, which is far less onerous for the chef and you might appreciate intellectual company. Soirées are something I dream about, but do not know whether it would be possible to make them happen.

My dear Shobha

After Sunday (when I read my long letter to you under the trees overlooking the river – giving sixty reasons why I could not leave my home) - you may think it is strange for me to write to you. The emotions and the body work against the mind. (A summary of the reasons is given at the end of this chapter.)

My present state may owe something to having listened last night, not once, but twice, to the whole of Act Two of *Tristan and Isolde.*

My son and his partner have just left for the country in my four-wheel drive vehicle, with their two racing cycles. He is taking part in a three-day one thousand kilometre race, starting tomorrow in the early hours, while his companion is taking part in a one-day three hundred kilometre race the following day. I shall follow their progress for a couple of hours.

It is good to have someone in the house who really loves opera. Witness last evening with *Tristan*. My son has a fine mind - as yet not directed to the best employment. But he shows signs of being responsive. You are much in my thoughts – and veins.

Dear Douglas

There were moments during the Verdi *Requiem* last night, when I wondered why I was there, and moments when I was transported. Some deeply moving passages. It was a wonderful venue, and we were given the best seats in the house – front row gallery.

The effect of your Sunday letter has been to make me wonder how much you truly consider others - and how much yourself. Even with your son, you seemed to want him to admit your tape of *Tristan* was better.

While he is here, listen to him, without trying to influence him or impose on him. He probably has a lot to teach you. I suspect you may try to bring others into your realm of ideas, without penetrating yourself - into their worlds. In this way, no growth can happen. If you are only interested in 'your' friends, operas, activities, books - there is no relationship.

It is also necessary to involve yourself in the world of the ones you love. You have not even seen me swim. Yet you go to the country to see your son cycle, and have not been to the folk festival, which is nearby - to hear me sing, though I perform there every year. This is unforgivable.

I realise after listening to your Sunday letter - how impossible it would be to live with you in the same house, because you do not in fact wish to share anything. Love means considering the other and finding a balance between each other's needs. It does not mean imposing one's will on the other – that is the antithesis of love. There is much to say, but the pillow beckons. Goodnight, my love

Dearest

Lord Peter Wimsey (my little teddy bear) and I - are thinking of you. He is cuddled against my left breast for comfort.

Shall we go to England together? It might crystallise for us what is possible. Placido Domingo and José Carreras are singing in *Tosca* at Covent Garden in May. All I wish to do is walk and talk and visit opera houses and make love of course, now and then. It would be wonderful. Wondering if we could effect a compromise. Go to Europe, then find a home for us here and spend weekends together? Who will make the first move?

My darling

I drove past your office window (at university) about ten minutes ago on my way to the bookshop. I could see you, though only dimly, standing by your desk, apparently sorting papers. I paused for a few moments in case you looked out, but you didn't, and so I drove on.

Written by Shobha to Douglas from folk festival in the country

My dearest love

I am sitting by the river. It is early morning and there is dew on the car – on the ground and in my eyes. Your landcruiser is my home and I am glad. Birds are everywhere – crows cawing - so peaceful – no-one else is awake – all abed after the night's frivolities. Slept so well – surrounded by soft doonas and pillows.

Dear Douglas

There have been some excellent songs at the festival e.g. a folk musical on the life of Rear-Admiral Sir John Franklin, who tried to find the North-West passage linking the Atlantic and Pacific oceans across the Arctic and died in the attempt, around 1847.

His wife sent expeditions for fourteen years to find him, and finally - evidence of the crew and Franklin was found. They had died from various causes viz. hypothermia, tuberculosis, starvation, scurvy and lead poisoning (from the cans of food they had eaten). Dearest – wish you were here. Shobha the blessed

Dear Douglas

Have been reading *Anthony Storr* (eminent British psychiatrist). Some of his thoughts are excellent. I am particularly delighted by his statements that all good ideas arise at times when the usual mental processes are in abeyance, as in meditation etc. I love you, and even miss you a trifle.

My dear Shobha

You were very sweet – and also slightly surprising – last night. Eccentricity is a view of oneself that others may take. It is not an assessment one can make of oneself.

N. is often in tears and speaks of the Sword of Damocles hanging over her head, as she is aware we are considering what to do together in the future.

My dear, dear love - full moon

Last evening was a feast for me and rather special. I don't pretend to understand love-making. I only know that it seems to open doors to the heart and soul and to let in some new breeze.

Douglas

I have been thinking of you very much since yesterday. I am glad we arrived at some semblance of peace after a stormy beginning.

I agree with your general attitude that it is better to declare one's state of being, and request rather than demand, but sometimes the emotions are too strong. I also agree in general that complaining is counter-productive, and action is a better strategy.

This morning on my way to the university, carrying my various hats or should I say bags (viz. one for swimming, one for opera, one for studies, one full of work for the weekend, and my bag crammed with lunch and personal paraphernalia) - I stopped to sit in one of the university gardens - as is my custom - to inhale some of its sweetness.

It is always lovely early in the morning, and there was a heron near the pond, looking for fish. So white and elegant and such graceful neck and body movements. I sat there for fully twenty minutes - taken aback by its presence. I have not seen one before. It reminded me of a Japanese setting – bird plus water lilies.

Apparently it has been systematically devouring the small fish in the university ponds - despite its beauty. It sits on the very tops of the trees and when it takes to the air, is really magnificent. Literally breathtaking. I wonder what happened to its mate - if it had one?

Darling

You warmed my heart by ringing today – you are a ray of sunshine in my rather busy day (at the university). Please bring your music again on Sunday if you wish. We seem to sing much better 'afterwards'.

I am listening to the *Agnus Dei* from Verdi's *Requiem* and know in my heart that love is the only answer. Writing to you puts my heart at rest. Today was sweet to lie with you – so welcome after the disasters at work. It was also fun singing yesterday. This very moment I would like to snuggle into you and sleep for a little while – it has been a taxing day at the university - though not unbearably so.

Shobha

I hope the transition to your new house goes smoothly, despite my qualms about your deciding so quickly on such an important move. Let me know if I can help to load and unload your hi-fi, television, tapes, books and suchlike. You are bound to have a few unforeseen problems and I may be able to help you with some of them.

The university gardens

Shobha

I hope the transition to your new house goes smoothly, despite my qualms about your deciding so quickly on such an important move. Let me know if I can help to load and unload your hi-fi, television, tapes, books and suchlike. You are bound to have a few unforeseen problems and I may be able to help you with some of them.

Last evening (with you) was rather strange. Perhaps we were both affected in some way by the events of the day. Touch is an important factor. Perhaps the most important - in intimacy. But it is not the measure of intimacy and at times, may militate against it. With humans, touch is surely best regarded – and indulged in – as one of the roads to a shared state of mind.

Dear Shobha

Am writing this letter on my computer because it attracts less curiosity than if I sit at my desk with a pad in front of me. The events of the last week have left me feeling uneasy and rather out of sorts.

Since coming back from Europe you seem to have become cooler and more calculating. I am not against coolness and calculation as such and have often urged them upon you.

It may be that this new coolness comes from reflecting - while I was away - on the frustrations of the previous seven years. Ironically, as I write this, I look across to the scales you gave me some years ago, which enjoin me not to allow the mind to prevail over the heart.

The coolness seems also to have led to some uncharacteristic lack of candour and openness, as in withholding from me two letters written some time earlier. In each case, the reason for doing so could only have been that you thought the contents might cause me to bolt.

Though I may not love N., this is not to say that our life is barren and totally without reward. We tend to get on tolerably well when we are engaged in doing active things together, such as swimming, gardening, climbing – or managing young children.

Douglas and Shobha had arranged to spend a mock honeymoon in the country

Douglas

I cannot see how you can live with yourself after what you have done. After all, it was not my idea to go away - as a first step. The idea came solely from you. My suggestions were for a house (of my own), weekends together, a visit to Europe etc. but in order to cooperate with you, I agreed to the idea of going away - since it had obvious merit, in that it would reveal to N. that we were not just friends, and it would have given us an opportunity to be together for a longer time, to see how we managed.

The fact that you left it to the last few days before our honeymoon, to renege - is despicable. You obviously do not know yourself at all well. But you have no idea of the amount of hurt you have inflicted by your decision.

Have you no honour at all? How can anything you say ever be trusted again? You are totally unreliable and probably deceptive as well, since you knew you would probably not go through with it - before I arranged to rent the new house.

My decision to take the house was probably in part due to my deep gut feeling that you would not honour your suggestion, and my own wish to do something 'I' wanted, for a change, since I was never likely to be given anything I wanted - by you.

Your statement that you only go overseas to give N. a holiday, was laughable. Do you not think I need a holiday? I have accrued more than two years leave at work because I have not taken a holiday. I have never been on holiday with someone I loved. I was excited like a small child. I trusted you, despite your bad behaviour in the past and the fact that you have let me down on countless occasions. What a fool I have been.

I find there are elements in your character that are very poorly developed. You seem to be incapable of commitment, unable to love in any consistent way, unable to be relied upon or trusted, deceitful with N. and probably therefore also with me.

I hardly think you are the one to exhort me to tell the truth, or be candid. Your life is one continuous sequence of deceptions and untruths.

Consider for a moment that you might tell N. that you love me, that we are lovers (as we always have been), that we are going away together, that we will spend weekends together, that we will go to Europe next year. This would be honesty. You fall so far short of this, that it is ridiculous. How can you expect others to be open with you, if you are so riddled with lies?

Not going away with me is the equivalent of leaving a bride standing at the altar - with the social embarrassment this entails. Consider my having to tell everyone at work that my holiday is off. I have arranged leave with the other staff and distributed my work to others, so they can function in my absence.

You do not consider these matters. You think only of keeping your so-called marriage intact. Your feelings for me are obviously of no consequence.

Dear Douglas

This is a lovely house to wake up in. A home certainly gives a sense of dignity that is lacking in a flat – also a kind of peace and serenity - and a sense of potential. It is not necessary to 'own' a house to have these feelings. In many ways I prefer to rent, because of the caravanserai nature of our existence.

It is a reminder that our bodies and our homes are indeed temporary. Remember the biblical verse about putting your treasure where moth and dust do *not* corrupt and thieves do *not* break in and steal, *for where your treasure is, there will your heart be also.*

In a brief moment today, I surrendered my own will with regard to our situation and asked IT (or god) to intervene so that ITS will might become apparent - rather than my own. Although you do not 'believe' in the same sense, you might nevertheless understand, when I say I felt an immense sense of relief - as if for a short time at least, a burden had been lifted.

I think and feel that I shall resort once again to the law of affinity. If we are to be together, then it will be so. If not - then not. Must go – a little weary. Seeing you this afternoon was so 'necessary'. Reflect and pray if you can - as I will also.

The house is very pleasant and bright at this time of the day. It's so open and yet so private. Thank you for all you have done to help make it comfortable for me.

Dear Douglas

Tonight was quite moving at moments (at the orange celebration). Everyone in white except me (dressed in black). Seeing Bhagwan on a video was marvellous. I feel so in tune with him, but even to say that is far from the truth. I feel I AM him. To dance - after a long absence was thrilling. I was amazed to find that I am more fit than when I last engaged in this form of exercise.

Your former girl-friend was also there, and we spoke at length. She thinks I am eccentric, and says she feels sannyas is alive and well when she meets me, because I express my feelings - or so she thinks. Flattery will get her far. Still, it is nice to have the odd compliment here and there in life.

Your roses have hung their heads yet again – after one day. I can't imagine why. Yet when you gave me a bunch of pink roses last year, they lasted for weeks and I photographed them in various stages of bloom. It saddens me to see your beautiful love offering in such a condition.

Watching Bhagwan this evening on video reminded me of *your being there*, when he shuffled off his mortal coil. That moment, more than any other - when you came out of the sea to tell me he had gone - bound us to each other in a way I will never fully understand. Love you – may see you at the beach tomorrow – Shobha the blessed

Dear Douglas

I wonder about your tiredness etc. I find for myself, these things develop or become apparent when there is some underlying discontent or malaise.

Susceptibility to bugs is often heightened by some emotional unease, for example. Conversely, it may be purely physical and you overdid it with the running plus swimming (on the weekend).

I hardly think that to make love with me is to overextend yourself. It hurts me a little when you phrase it this way. Please don't try to make me feel guilty for our pleasure, nor condemn yourself for what brings you joy. It is an insult to god or whoever or whatever else runs the show. Miss you – think of me - wish you were here.

Dear one

The roses look a little promising today. I will pray for them and talk to them in a loving fashion.

Dearest love – Christmas Eve

In view of the overwhelming unhappiness which I have been feeling due to the Christmas break, and the feelings of loneliness and abandonment which this occasions, I feel this might be the time to reiterate the sentiments (which I have) expressed in the past. My wish is to sleep and wake with you, which is the natural end of love. Please do not ever think that you are mean. You may be taxed beyond your resources, and may have too many people to look after, but you are certainly not mean. One has only so much to give.

One of the many bouquets given by Douglas to Shobha

Although you often alternate in mood, and go back on things you have promised, this does not come into the category of meanness, simply an inability to find any other way out of a stressful situation. You have for the most part been uncommonly giving - in all manner of ways. It's surprising sometimes how we run into each other in the street. The neighbours must be agog with delight (viewing our meetings). Love and hugs and kisses and many things besides.

My dear Shobha – Christmas Day

What exactly I mean when I say I am mean (pun unavoidable), I do not know. Analysing oneself is not an easy exercise. Though I sometimes think of others (when others do not), I do seem to have a cold streak in my make-up, which can get colder, when I am under attack.

My present to you *(The Concise Oxford Dictionary)*, is modest, useful, appropriate to the highly verbal nature of our relationship, and far from being ephemeral - in the way of chocolates – and roses. Though it is a new edition and more pleasant to handle than the earlier one I gave you, it is not meant to be a replacement, for you need a dictionary with preferably the same publisher - both at home and at the university. I once had four Concise Oxford Dictionaries in different locations.

I was touched to find your candlestick on the step this morning. I thought I heard your car and opened the front door, but saw nothing. Perhaps I simply failed to see it in the half-darkness. As you have said to me *"Not all the darkness in the world can put out the light of one small candle."* But the wind is another matter !

Dear Douglas

Enjoyed my visit to the hills and my friend's family - but I am always glad to leave. The conversation is intensely political, intellectual and philosophical and one can only take so much of this. It is in no way like our style (i.e. yours and mine) of conversation, which is more aesthetic. We play with words, but our conversation is gentle, for the most part, and sweetly sensitive, although we are both so involved in it, we probably don't realise it at the time. Have thought of you most lovingly since we last met.

Would love to watch Carreras with you some time - on the screen. I have been surprisingly impressed by him. He is certainly boyish and pure in a way that *Placido Domingo* and *Luciano Pavarotti* are not. There was a simple charm in the way he described the Christmas customs with which he is familiar. If Placido is a cherub, then Carreras is an angel. He is unearthly. He seems to be largely untouched by the real world – what we called in India, a *deva* (one touched by the spirit), of which, by the way - I am one. Note my name – Deva Shobha - given to me by Bhagwan ! Placido, by contrast, is rooted deeply in the earth, as is Pavarotti.

This is a very interesting moment in our relationship. We are rich in what we share and yet now and again, I am still wanting to share in a deeper way. I yearn, as I said today, for you to be 'around'. I hope that doesn't sound as if I would take you for granted. It is rather a feeling of your presence, even though we may not be in the same room – but knowing you are there – somewhere.

Dear love – making love with you evokes a longing in me at times for continuance of that sweetness. I hope to see you on the morrow – perhaps at the ocean.

Dearest

My orange friends have just left. We discussed all the problems of the world - agreed that we still have no solution to the existential crisis which is the human condition, and postulated that a war might bring people closer together through a common bond !

Whenever we meet, it is as if we long for a time when we can be on fire once again, as we were, when we first became sannyasins in the heady seventies. I don't know whether such an experience can be repeated. Perhaps it is a once-in-a-lifetime occurrence. But we knew what it was to be totally carried away with emotion and a kind of ecstasy that is difficult to define.

When you and I make love, there is the same feeling of abandonment at the peak? It is certainly better to live on the brink - than simply to be. Life ought *not* to be measured in duration - but intensity.

Dear Douglas

Have been reading the Hungarian-British author *Arthur Koestler*, and feel quite excited to find he supports my ideas or vice versa. Your idea that developments in one field can be transposed to another, is at the heart of his philosophy. A synthesis of two dissimilar areas of thought - according to Koestler - is the basis of all creativity. We must discuss this further. Just as you and I come from different worlds - so too perhaps, in other areas of life. Bring together two opposites and there is a new fusion. The two are no longer the same. The transformation has taken place. Until we meet.

Dear love

After keeping vigil at your doorstep with my candle this evening, I was feeling a little sad. Lying with you today was so tender. In many ways, I am happy with the way we are, and the time we share together, but - and there is the *'but'* raising its ugly head - I am also aware of the longing for you to stay, to relax with me into something deeper.

Who knows whether it is fantasy or simply the natural yearning to come closer? It is possible we have both come to accept what we share and to *not* seek for anything more. It is also possible there is a greater degree of closeness that might only be possible, if we were to melt and meld by being 'around' each other.

Your experience of marriage seems to have convinced you that this is not possible, but I am not N. The type of union you have with her is not the type that we share. We are a new phenomenon. Cynicism about cohabitation probably comes from those who have not achieved communion.

Who knows what depths we might plumb if we were to be more fully together? I agree with you that it is impossible to know in advance, but it also seems impossible to stay still, when I can feel a gnawing inside to reach beyond.

> A man's reach must exceed his grasp - or what's a heaven for ?
>
> *Robert Browning*

I'm not sure about a woman's reach? Know that my only intention is for our intimacy to deepen in whatever way is possible. I have no other desire. Everything reminds me of you – music, poetry, my thesis, my work at the university and my proposed travels to England. It is all part of my love for you.

I will be on your doorstep at midnight on New Year's Eve. God bless - my dearest

Dear Douglas – New Year's Eve

You were very kind this evening ! My heart was breaking, yet I left you feeling whole. I pray for our new year together and that we will see the resolution of our dilemma. All my love

Reasons given by Douglas for not leaving his home and N. for Shobha

which were revealed over time in discussion,
referred to in Douglas' letters,
or specified in the thirty-page letter
Douglas read to Shobha under a tree in the park
in the eighth year of their relationship.

Concern for Shobha
It was not a question of the heart – he felt Shobha was the most important person in the world to him

Concern for how they would be if they were together
He thought Shobha might abandon him
He felt he might not be able to keep up with Shobha due to age
He was concerned about the effect of age upon their physical intimacy
He thought they might find it hard to live together, because of his age and personality

Concern for himself

He felt would be too lonely living on his own if he moved out of his house
He knew he would feel too guilty if he left N.

Concern for the opinion of others
He thought his children would condemn him
He felt he would be a hypocrite because he condemned his two brothers who left their wives
He thought he would be shamed by others who would condemn him for leaving N.

Concern for N.
He was worried N. would kill herself if he left

Attachment to the house
He was very attached to his house and workshop which were designed for him
He thought he was the only one who could look after the house and garden

Concern for management of affairs
He felt his finances were too complicated, and N. would not be able to manage them

Chapter 9

Let there be spaces in your togetherness

23

Dearest Wimsey

These hot nights make me long for you. I imagine you wandering up and down the stairs, looking for some relief from the heat. Sometimes on nights such as this, I have met you by chance, at your mail box.

My darling

I feel bemused today, because of some special magic in our love-making. Your taking the house and moving into your new position at the university have drawn me further into your life, so that your concerns become increasingly my own. Quite simple things, such as free access to your house, may have something to do with this.

It is not really a paradox for me to say that you are particularly precious to me when I come into your house at times when you are not there. Your books, tapes, notes and clothes conjure up a vivid picture of you, as suggestive as a fragrance.

This evokes a feeling of warmth and tenderness towards you (Douglas-speak for *love*) which takes me almost by surprise, Am I so peculiar in saying this? One possible partial explanation is that these moments are not clouded by having in mind all that you think wrong in our situation.

Dear Shobha

No significance should be read into this note being typed rather than handwritten. When N. is drifting around, I am less conscious of her suspicious presence when I am sitting in front of my computer. I fully understand your wanting to go to England, especially as some of this wanting has been fostered by me.

Douglas

After you left, I was so annoyed by your attempts to dissuade me yet again, from my doctorate (in education), that I worked on it late into the night. There are some wonderful ideas to be explored, but the main difficulty is couching them in an educational context. The writers upon whom I am now drawing, including *Anthony Storr*, are not educationists, so I will have to search further.

Dividedness of any kind is deleterious to love. I watch you day by day, sometimes supporting my endeavours, and at other times, hell bent on stopping me from following through on my latest project.

Has it not occurred to you, that it is you who is divided in your loyalties, and you are projecting your feelings of frustration onto me? Since you are unable to act, you seem to wish to also reduce my level of activity so that I too, am unable to take risks and embark on dangerous enterprises.

I have also observed that whenever we become particularly close, you become afraid, and shortly thereafter find some cause of complaint against me, which ruins the intimacy we have developed. It is as if you do not want love to succeed. I am sure that more than anything else, you are afraid there is a small possibility it might work.

The fireworks tonight were for a few moments, very moving and almost meditative. The final burst was like a bomb in the sky, which lasted and lasted and turned from gold to purple in a spellbinding way. There were times when I felt stirred, which surprised me. I felt quite grateful to be in a relatively beautiful, untroubled country.

Although you criticise Australia continually and long for home *(England)*, there is much here that is to be treasured, although you only realise it by going away.

I am sorry you feel our relationship is one-sided. There are many ways to give. Material giving is only one of them. I realise you come bearing gifts very often : books, tapes, cuttings, letters etc. but I have never felt remiss in not delivering the same quantity of goods. It bothers me that when I lend or give you books or tapes, you do not read or listen to them. There has to be a two-way reciprocity of interest.

I wish you could find your true heart - so you could allow me to follow mine.

Douglas – full moon

Sitting meditating this morning, I feel that perhaps separations might be a good idea now and then so we don't take each other for granted. How I wish I could fall asleep with you and feel you all around me. Why are we denied even such simple pleasures? To sink into oblivion and peace with you even for a few moments – would be all I could ask. In those moments, the transformation happens.

Dear Shobha

In his book *Footsteps of a Romantic Biographer*, Richard Holmes is really quite fascinating e.g. 'fresh thought needs to be given to the different ways in which a man and a woman may fulfil each other, some of which exclude the numbing effects of cohabitation. A relationship may be kept alive and rewarding by keeping apart most of the time.'

Dear Douglas

I wish you were coming with me (to England). The roundabouts on the motorways sound terrible.

> *This royal throne of kings*
> *This sceptre'd isle.*
> *This precious stone set in the silver sea.*
> *This blessed plot*
> *This earth, this realm.*
> *This England.*
>
> *Shakespeare : King Richard II*

My dear Shobha

I enclose a cutting from the latest *Economist* on air travel and the fear of terrorism. I do this - not to deter you from going forward with your holiday plans, but because it occurs to me that if there are outbreaks of terrorism, British Airways will be one of the prime targets, in view of the heavy British involvement in the Gulf War in Iraq. The risk should be less if you travel on one of the Asian airlines.

Dear Puss

I suspect it is you who has changed a lot since your time in India - despite your constant love for Bhagwan. You no longer belong to a movement or group. So what do you say when someone asks you whether you are orange? Oddly enough, I have no idea at all what you would do or say, though I am (so) close to you. To me you are simply a lovable individual woman. If I respect Bhagwan, it is only because of the effect he has had on you - though I suspect that the essential *you*, antedates India and Bhagwan.

Dear Duggles

It may be better for us not to reflect (upon our situation). As reflection has not led either of us towards a proposition of one kind or another, it may be best to simply 'be'. Perhaps out of 'being' a solution will emerge. This is almost a kind of lateral thinking. Drop the problem and the answer will come. Until we meet again – much love – Puss – to sleep... perchance to dream.

Dear Douglas

You were particularly lovely today. Would you understand me if I said that the softer you are, the sweeter you are? Much love – Puss

Dear Wiggles a.k.a. Wim

Last evening when you came to my window, it was a fulfilment of that which every romantic woman, dreams. Witness *Cyrano de Bergerac* - the lover in the French comedy-drama - tapping softly on the window pane, whispering sweet words of love. I shall remember you holding me in the dark for a long while. The fact of the darkness was quite significant. Will ring you in the morning to share sweet nothings. Sweet 'somethings' are more than I can cope with right now. Your dearest Puss

Dearest soulmate

What an afternoon. We ranged from the opera singer Enrico Caruso to *The Lost Chord (composition of Sir Arthur Sullivan)* to life at Cambridge university to ageing, parenting and *The Holy City (well-known inspirational song)*. We are quite diverse you and I. I find myself dipping in and out of so many pursuits. Perhaps that is the trouble? To be focused on one - would make life easy.

With regard to power over followers which is exercised by those in authority in almost any group, the relief I felt when I left the commune in India was tremendous. I had not realised how institutionalised I had become. That is why many orange people now refuse to organise, in any way. What about the effect of boarding-school, the army, Oxford, academia - in your case? I wonder if you are not more affected by the war than you care to admit, or I care to recognise. Having been through a war, it must stir up memories and feelings which are not always pleasant.

How free are we? And yet to my mind, marriage and its associated roles is one of the most powerful of all conditioners. Once the knot is tied - how appropriate the metaphor - all is lost. Better to be a soulmate !

Dear Douglas

Come to me as soon as you can. It hurts to live without you. You are my creature and I am thine. May it ever be so. All my love

Dear love

You were kind today. How I wish that we had unlimited time. Would I ever tire of kissing and touching you? I doubt it. This evening I wondered whether the sole pleasures we enjoy are touching and talking. Anything else seems unnecessary. But talk without touch is impossible for me, unless we are on the phone. And touch without talk never happens, unless we are making love. I long to caress you and to feel you all about me. To love you is to be whole, and to be without you is death. Your loving Puss

Dear Shobha

I have a taped programme on Mozart which is truly delightful, as I'm sure you'll agree. Watch it before the film *Amadeus,* because it is a necessary corrective. Both the narrator and the conductor are excellent. It fills me with despair that a programme as fine as this, with limited audience appeal, was made by Grenada, one of the English commercial television companies. Is it any wonder that I sometimes feel homesick – almost a traitor in Australia? Could we watch it together soon?

Dear Douglas

Feeling exceedingly pensive after this afternoon's experience. Perhaps it's that weepy time again? I wish you could accept my tears - few as they are these days - without making me feel I should not cry. Dearest love, I wish you were here. The sky weeps and so do I. Only one who loves can weep and vice versa. See the truth of it. I love you so much – Puss

Dear Puss

Am sorry not to have comforted you sufficiently after seeing your friend leave for England. As for my response to your crying, I suppose it is as deep-rooted in me, as it is in your disposition to cry. I simply can't bring myself to accept crying as the natural measure of emotion. Why not simple silence?

How strange that you should expect me to be shy. No-one has ever thought this of me, and I have mixed in my time with all sorts of people. Social chatter is a kind of game, the rules of which depend on the type of person you are talking to.

Beloved Bottoms

Your letter was one of the loveliest I have received from you, even though there were no allusions to intimacy. It felt exceedingly friendly, for want of a better word, and quite light-hearted. I am willing to be corrected regarding your shy behaviour. It is simply that I have rarely seen you in social interaction with people I know, or who are my friends, and I tend to regard your beach encounters as a thing apart, and subject to laws of social behaviour of which I am not a participant.

An Indian student came into my office today and saw my picture of Bhagwan, and I could not stop him talking for half and hour about spirituality. It was like being home again. Much love until the morrow – Pussy

Dear one - full moon

Just a short note before I drift off into slumberland. This evening I went down to the orange centre to soothe my troubled soul, but there was nothing of consequence happening, so in disappointment I called in on a friend, and we discussed how to save the world. Both of us have always felt we were meant to do something of consequence, for humanity, but neither of us is sure what to do. So much for altruism. I am a *peacenik*, though I doubt that we would ever take to the streets again as a way of protesting, as we did against the Vietnam war - yet on several occasions recently – we did protest against the Iraqi wars.

Given the intensity of the years with Bhagwan, I yearn for a cause which will raise me out of the day-to-day world into something greater. Bhagwan used to say, that unless one had something to die for, one had nothing for which to live. That is also how I feel. Remember me.

Dear Bottoms

The film of *Hamlet* was good, but I did not want to go with you in case Mel Gibson was hopeless with his Australian accent, which I can't stand - but it was in true Zefferelli style and quite excellent. One should trust the great masters i.e. Zefferelli, Bertolucci and Fellini. Some of the lines from Hamlet have become virtual household words, *to be honoured in the breach, rather than the observance*, is one I used this week at work.

Dear Bottoms - please look at the *Oxford Book of Quotations* and see if there are any poignant phrases from Shakespeare that are dear to you. Surprisingly, I found that most of the moving moments in the film were not in the book. The actors gave new meaning to incredibly simple lines such *as 'sweets to the sweet',* for example, as Gertrude lays flowers on Ophelia's body. Ophelia was particularly good (the same actress Helena Bonham Carter was in the film *Room with a View*). Goodnight, sweet prince** – may flights of angels (guide) (sing) thee to thy rest (or rather, my door).

** From Horatio's speech in Shakespeare's *Hamlet*

Douglas

Perhaps you could come out over your depth a little way on Sunday in the ocean if we chance to meet : to get me over the fear of going beyond the waves, but not if they were of any size, of course? You do not realise how much of an achievement this would be (for me). So pray for a calm day.

Do not expect too much of me on the morrow at the sea. Bear in mind I have not yet been out of my depth in the ocean. And also remember that you have not yet fulfilled your part of the bargain i.e. that if I swam out to sea, you would spend a night with me. Pleasant dreams and awakenings

Dear Bottoms

Was shocked to see you riding along on your bike with N. this evening, so soon after being with you today, especially as I had mentioned earlier, the sweet ecstasies of riding at dusk along the river together. Sweet dreams – one tired pussycat.

The following day, Shobha swam out a long distance to the buoy for the first time - in a very turbulent sea (encouraged by N.) but there were no actual waves.

Always miss you terribly after making love. It feels so strange that you are not here. My whole body feels as if you are within touching distance. Heaven would be lying with you always. There is so much to say.

Today I started to read for my thesis on creativity, and discovered the Dutch theologian, Søren *Kierkegaard* - of whom I knew very little - but whose philosophy is akin to mine.

Books seem to fall into my hands which are not only relevant but central to my theme. I am quite amazed. Each book I have borrowed from the education section of the library before Christmas, has been a treasure.

I also discovered the psychologist Rollo May, whose thoughts reflect mine. His book is called the *Courage to Create* - a variation of the German theologian Paul Tillich's book *The Courage to Be,* which was acclaimed in the sixties.

Whenever I start work on my thesis, I become overwhelmed with the magnitude, not of the idea - but the task of expressing the idea well.

Dear Pussy

You were particularly sweet yesterday. Yet I am concerned that our making love disturbs you (adversely) so drastically. Perhaps it brings home to you the 'wrongness' of our situation. Whereas I then move into another world, in which my attention is engaged by other things and you do not.

I look forward to seeing you at the beach tomorrow for the next step in your round-the-buoy odyssey. Until then.

P.S. I don't like (being called) Bottoms. I have wondered about the initials J.C. (which my mother used to call me as a child – for Jesus Christ – as she felt I had a Messiah complex - but can't I just remain Douglas ?

Dear Puss – April Fool's Day

How strange that we should meet today. What better occasion to quote Shakespeare :

A divinity that shapes our ends,

rough-hew them how we will.

Shakespeare – Hamlet

I was pleased you swam (out to sea) this morning. You swim stylishly. I don't know whether I am breaking our rules, in writing to you. We came to no firm agreement on this, partly because we were paradoxically so much at peace, and you especially, were on such a high.

I suggest writing be permitted so long as what we say is happy or practical. This means all talk of missing each other is barred, whatever we may feel. Disentangling from each other, if it is to happen, will be no simple matter, for whatever the deficiencies of our relationship, each of us is very much a part of the other's life. Fond thoughts.

Dear Shobha

Am glad to learn that you are discovering new reserves of strength and tranquillity. In the space of three days you have moved from serenity to despair and then back to serenity again. Your Douglas

Dear one

Our kisses seemed so natural. Strangely, I had been thinking about our kisses earlier in the day. I would like to have lingered under the archway and become lost. You were very soft today. Softness, or at least, vulnerability, is I believe - a prerequisite for receiving.

My darling

Roses are on the kitchen table. I hope they last this time, and open properly. I began to write you a truly loving letter earlier today. But once I turned from the beauties of yesterday to questions of the future, it ground to a halt. Much love

Dear Douglas

I have been made aware of my deficiencies (by you) and the total idiocy of expecting you to help me, when I cannot help myself. Ideally I suppose, a lover simply holds the other, lets him or her weep to their heart's content, and listens patiently until all doubts and fears are dispelled - but this is the ideal, and not the actual.

How many of us can be there for the other in this way? You rarely bring me your worries. Do you have any - are you one of the blessed creatures who does not experience many ups and downs in life? Until recently, I felt I was also relatively free of immense problems, but the last week has been so severe, it has thrown my usual coping mechanisms out of order.

A friend said to me yesterday, that what I seek with you is in fact 'purple' experiences (i.e. those that are extraordinary), and it is not fair to expect you to provide this sort of experience, when you are not a 'purple' person. This gave me quite a shock. Must go – life calls.

Dear sweet knight

I have just returned from yet another charismatic Christian gathering with two friends. Quite an experience - unlike anything I have encountered before. I am familiar with fundamentalist churches and their emphasis upon sin and repentance etc, but this church had all the trimmings of fervour and fantastic music - without the negative associations.

The focus was rather upon spreading the love and the light. Quite healthy really - in a Christian sort of way. I have to translate some of the theology to suit my own purposes of course. It is certainly uplifting being in the presence of hundreds of happy, motivated, spiritually-oriented people, even though it is not my brand of religion.

During the service, my thoughts were often of you. I felt I could offer you a kindness which allows you to be utterly yourself and never ask anything of you except to be able to love you. I felt capable of such love, and even at times, that I was capable of extending my goodwill to N.

Perhaps in view of your children, grandchildren etc. you have made the only decision possible for you, which is to remain - because the alternative would produce disruption to so many other lives.

When Shobha and Douglas met, none of his five grand-children were yet born, and three of his children were unmarried. If Douglas and Shobha had decided to have children, the eldest would now be thirty-four.

Our talk and caresses of today left me feeling very much at peace. Being *en rapport* with you fills me with a sweet joy that is beyond words. It is our own personal tragedy that we cannot be free and able to sleep together and share more of life. Which is the higher love? That of a diluted nature for various family members or a more intense passion for one individual? There don't seem to be any rules any more. It is simply a case of doing what one is able to do.

Our lying together today and facing some of the more difficult issues between us has been a wonderful gift for me. I was so afraid I would have to leave you before I go to Europe, without our having commingled. I kiss you with great tenderness. Goodnight, my love

Dear sweet prince

This is a letter to keep you warm while I am away. I shall hold my little Wimsey (teddy bear) close to my heart if I miss you, and know that you are near. In the world of the esoteric - being spatially apart counts for nothing. The thought is the essential thing.

Think of me and I will be with you, and I shall receive your thoughts also. Perhaps we could keep a diary of moments when we feel particularly close. We might be pleasantly surprised if there was some synchronicity.

I hold dear all that we share. I cannot imagine how people survive without the presence of love in their lives. Perhaps If they have not known it - it is possible, but if one has known ? All my love and tenderest of caresses in all the right places - whenever you need them. Puss

Notes of Shobha - at Hammersmith, London - on first visit to England

Woke early on Saturday - full of beans. My cousin with whom I am staying, does not rise until much later. Walked miles through *Holland Park* and caught bus to *Harrods,* then on the tube (underground) to the *Embankment* and crossed the bridge to *Festival Hall* on the South Bank, to book tickets for the

Opera Gala. Will see *Montserrat Caballe (Spanish opera singer)* at the Hall the night before *Tosca* at Covent Garden. Crossed the Thames - in a bitter wind - and learnt how to catch the tube home.

Tomorrow I will venture into the city centre. Will walk *Hyde, Regent's and St James'* parks in the morning and head for galleries and museums in the afternoon. Must see *Covent Garden and Bloomsbury. St Paul's Cathedral and Westminster Abbey* also vital. Several operas are about to be staged in Holland Park – would enjoy to see them in the open. Sweet dreams – will soon be in the countryside. All my love

Douglas - Sunday

Wandered London alone from an early hour. What an experience. There was no-one in the streets except two American tourists. Walked *Bloomsbury, Russell Square, University of London, British Museum, Imperial Hotel* – all deserted at that time. Biting wind. Moved on to *Covent Garden* opera house and wept to see its portals at last. Chanced upon the *Covent Garden Market* which added a bit of human warmth to a chilly expedition.

On to *Lincoln's Inn* – everything closed of course, then to *Royal Courts of Justice* – the front entrance took my breath away. Discovered *Australia House* – quite impressive and a nearby *statue of your Sam(uel Johnson)*. Found Sam's house in a back alley but it was also closed. Only tourists out and about as London started to wake up.

Walked along the Embankment to see the *Temple Church* and statues *of Arthur Sullivan and Robert Burns*. Up to *Trafalgar Square and St Martin in the Fields church* where I sat for a while with some Dickensian characters who were in the other pews – homeless men. Could hardly move after five hours of walking without a break.

Entered the *National Gallery* for refreshments and to view the Italian masters, together with some of the French, Dutch and a few British. Wandered to *Leicester Square and Piccadilly* and then caught the tube home. Can't wait to see Rodin's '*Kiss*' in the *Tate gallery* .

Did I mention Hampstead - just north of London? I loved *Hampstead Heath and Kenwood House* - but most of all *Keats House,* where there were locks of hair of both Fanny Brawne and the poet John Keats, on display - along with their letters. The house exuded a vibe of tranquillity. I feel that I could - of all the places I have been - live in Hampstead for a time. Much love

Dear Douglas

Collected our Rover from Heathrow and managed to get onto the M4. I felt very proud of myself as I was driving and then found we were driving back into London as the signs said M4 in two directions. Also discovered the meaning of a roundabout. Had not seen one before. An oncoming bus came to a screeching halt when we entered one of the roundabouts and I did not know what to do next.

Life on the road is becoming very enjoyable. I have already charted a daily course around England. It is very educative - learning to negotiate with my friend Helen, concerning when and where we go and at what pace. The trouble with England is that everywhere you turn there is something of historic or other significance to take your attention, so it is hard to move on. For example, on the way to Salisbury, we unexpectedly detoured to *Jane Austen's house* in Chawton, where many original furnishings and letters were preserved – which you would have loved.

In the past three days, since leaving London, we have covered a lot of ground in terms of sites - but not so much in miles. We may have to seriously revise our itinerary as Helen likes to stop off here and there whenever an estate or church is available to visit. Her interest in history and architecture is quite deep and she wants to know the story behind each stained-glass window. I am happy to view a cathedral in twenty minutes.

Before we arrived in Salisbury we visited *Stonehenge* and kissed the earth. Dusk is a good time to visit – almost mystical. Salisbury Youth Hostel was quite beautiful – set in a large home on a hill overlooking the city. Spent a long time in the Cathedral. The spire is inspiring (joke). Did you know you can be hoisted up the spire in a cage? It is under renovation at present and evokes a feeling of fear and awe. One evening we were lost in Salisbury town for an hour and could not find our way out because of the one-way streets. I was not driving on this occasion !

On the way to Dorchester, which was not on our itinerary, we realised we were entering Hardy country and could not pass by. Ran with Helen at dusk, for miles around the river, farms, *Stinsford Church* (where Thomas Hardy's heart is buried), lakes, croquet courts and hedge gardens – all of which were magnificent. Did you know that when Hardy was born, he was thrown away because he was thought to be dead - but thankfully for the world - he revived !

Headed for the *Cerne Abbas Giant* on the hillside in white chalk and the *White Horse* (also in chalk) in Osmington. Then on to *Hardy's cottage* through *Black Heath* (magical wood with badgers) and later climbed *Maiden Castle* (old iron-age fort on top of hill). Breathtaking – my first introduction to heights, so coming down was a bit daunting. I think a taste for heights is acquired. I could sense the delight, but I am still too green to fully relax when coming down.

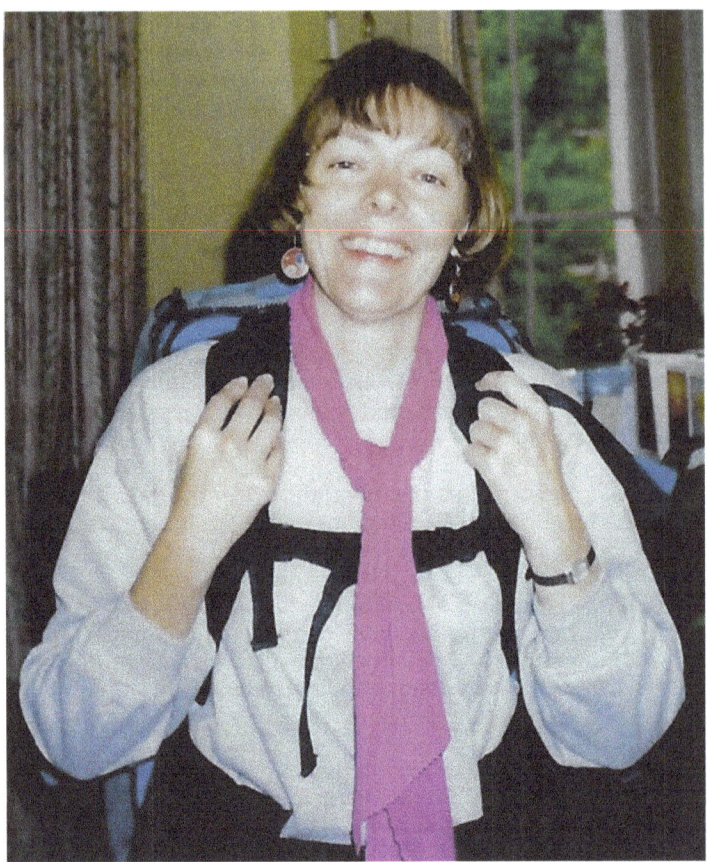

About to set off on a tour of England

We alternate a day about with the driving, and so far my days have been relatively quiet ! Realised *Lawrence of Arabia's grave* (T. E. Lawrence) was in Moreton through which we passed, and we paid our respects. The engraved windows of *Moreton church* were spectacular. I am developing a penchant for churches and graves - though my attention span is limited.

Moved on to *Lyme Regis* tonight - from where this letter is being written. We are overlooking the ocean, and we re-enacted the famous scene at the end of *the Cobb,* from the film *French Lieutenant's Woman*. We will hunt for fossils tomorrow (for which the area is famed). Helen just went for an hour-long run up the hill. I am content with fifteen minutes.

We alternate between youth hostels and bed and breakfast homes which is working well. Tomorrow we head for *Beer, Seaton, Exeter and Plymouth* and on to a youth hostel in Falmouth, which was formerly Pendennis Castle.

We are a day off schedule which makes me a little anxious as it means we may not get where we wish to be at the end of our time, but Helen wants to be more free - so I have to compromise. I am not used to giving in, as you probably know, but at least she is prepared to go along with my overall plan for our journey.

Darling - I think of you all the time (as this is your country). It is almost as if you are here in spirit. Wimsey (my tiny teddy bear which you gave me) keeps me warm at night.

All the literature we have shared together comes alive here e.g. Hardy's novels and Fowles' novel and Keat's letters. I would like to fill my house with prints of some of the paintings I have seen - it is such a feast.

We have been endeavouring to make our photos interesting for you by adopting ridiculous postures. I hope you appreciate our efforts. It is quite an art. It is now after midnight (yawn) and I must go to sleep. Helen is sitting writing to her family. We are both avid journal-keepers. I can't wait to see you and compare notes. I feel like a novice in a monastery or is it a nunnery, as Gilbert expresses it, in his operetta *The Pirates of Penzance.* Speaking of which, we will soon be near Penzance – how amazing it is that all my childhood knowledge of England is finally becoming alive and real.

My dearest Puss

If you are keeping to your itinerary, you will be climbing Mount *Snowdon* today in Wales. I have been following your planned progress from day to day including London temperatures for the previous day. You seem to have been tolerably lucky with the weather.

It's strange to sit in my study trying to recapture in my mind's eye the lovely sight of the early life (buds) of limes and horse chestnuts in an English spring - while the leaves wither and fall in indecent haste and with very little colour, from my neighbour's deciduous trees (in Australia).

I call at your house every two or three days and have driven your car around the block twice since I rang you.

Down at the beach, rough water has only prevented swimming once since you left. But the stingers (jellyfish) are hanging about much later this year, and in the last three days I was stung on the tongue and then on my right eye-ball. This leaves only one part of my anatomy unscathed. Both stings were in fact quite painful.

About a week ago, as I left the changing room wearing nothing but a towel about the loins, it started raining very lightly, so I opened my umbrella, whereupon one of the swimmers chased after me with his camera and took a photo of what he described as a typical example of my English madness, and meant no doubt, to be an adaptation of the saying *Mad dogs and Englishmen, go out in the noonday sun.* He then assured me the photo would appear in the next issue of the local newspaper (and it did).

As you know, I have been trying to give up my medication and it is now five days. It has been most disturbing, and I have the sense of being a different person each day. During the many sleepless hours, when I am almost frighteningly wide awake, my fantasies often turn to you.

Foolishly, I did not properly realise before you left, what a strange experience your going away would be for me, for in this instance, I am the one left in his ordinary environment and following my normal routine, while you are literally and figuratively transported to strange lands. It is a salutary experience for me. I am also expecting you to come back a different person.

You will be pleased to hear that after one-to-one swimming lessons, I have joined a more advanced group and my breaststroke and backstroke are good, but I have not made progress with freestyle, as I have trouble with my breathing.

I have been half-hoping to get a card or letter from you, and I just saw the postman and found your letters. They were written before you left London, and took ten days to arrive here, which is inexcusable. The delight I feel, takes me almost by surprise.

My darling, I am so, so pleased to hear you speak on the phone – it conjures up your presence so vividly that I can almost smell you, as when I kiss you where your neck meets your shoulder. I shall write again soon, in the hope you get my second letter before you leave for Oxford. Look after yourself.

Dear Puss

I have been tracing in one of my Snowdonia *(area surrounding Mount Snowdon)* guidebooks, the route you took in your climb - that is, via the Pig and Miners tracks.

I have never climbed Snowdon by that route, though I did have a shot last year at another route along the ridge to the north of the Pig track, but was forced to turn back by bad weather.

I hope I did not seem cold when you rang after climbing Snowdon. Though I was not being overheard, I still find it difficult to talk to you in a relaxed way when N. is fuming in the next room. I have been thinking about you a lot and very fondly.

The Lake District

**

I have just found several cards from you, and your letter from Lyme Regis.

You tell me you have been trying to make your photos more interesting for me by adopting ridiculous postures, which reminds me of the photos I took of you in academic dress before the university graduation ceremony.

I can't wait to see what foreground posture you and Helen adopt in front of the (very naked and naughty) *Cerne Abbas Giant*. He is supposed to be a fertility symbol, which implies our ancestors thought fertility was measured in inches !

Luciano Pavarotti is in Australia, for a series of concerts in Brisbane, Sydney and Melbourne. I've never been a tremendous admirer of Pavarotti, but he is a fine concert singer, and more than Carreras or Domingo, he exudes a kind of near-apoplectic animal power that goes well with strong arias. He is singing the whole of *Andrea Chenier* (opera by Giordano) on the weekend.

Since you leave London soon, I shall not be writing to you again, but shall be thinking of you tomorrow night at Covent Garden. Goodnight, sweet princess.

Dear Puss

Your little book of Sam Johnson's *Sayings* (which you brought back from his old house in London) is marvellous. Such a concentration of wonderful good sense - trenchantly expressed.

To my sharer of highs and occasional sighs – my darling

Forgive me if I have overstretched myself by trying to continue the 'high' I experienced, in being away, and also on my return.

So often you and I touch almost unknown heights and I try to hold onto them, and in so doing – they are lost. A friend said to me not long ago, that what I long for with you, and also experience from time to time, is the perfect union, that is only possible through spiritual understanding and meditation.

To expect to reach or more accurately remain, at those heights in our love, may be more than is humanly possible. Perhaps as you said today, the ideal I attempt to realise is not possible in the flesh. Yet so often we touch it - you and I - for a moment - and then it is gone. In love

Dear, dear love

As we left each other today, we spoke of how much there is both to learn and appreciate, and it does confuse me at times. We just have to go one step at a time, from one delight to the next. I feel incredibly privileged but also would like to give something back to the world, though I am by no means certain that this carries with it any real virtue. Perhaps it is simply enough to admire - to be enthused and to be transformed. My love, all my sweetest and fondest thoughts are with you. With deepest love.

> For the one who set my heart aflame
> and keeps it burning
> then tends the glowing coals

Dear light of my life

Yesterday you applied many of the criteria of creativity to yourself and I was pleased to hear you placing yourself firmly at the centre of creative endeavour, even though I have seen little that you have written, apart from our letters of love. Is it possible that deep within the breast of Douglas there are yet more creative works waiting to emerge, or have you already flowered? In terms of the inner spirit expressing itself, what is your current state? Is it enough for you to enjoy the creations of others? Much love – Pusskins – your princess - your swan

We come from very different families. I had no intellectual rapport with my parents, but there was affection - probably too much at times, and possibly sometimes for the wrong reasons, but it was built into the family ritual of greeting and leaving each other, and comforting each other in times of difficulty. Even now, if I see my brother, he reaches out and either kisses me or puts his arm around me.

From what you have said - you had a tender relationship with your mother, especially after the war, and I would therefore imagine she was affectionate when you were a child. Boarding school in England as you have often said, destroyed your natural emotional responses and since then, it seems you may have withheld your feelings and lived a detached and self-contained existence (until you met me). Is this so ?

Shobha and Helen visited Oxford and Cambridge – an essential component of the holiday for Shobha, for whom Oxford had an element of pilgrimage, as this was where Douglas had been a Reader at All Souls College before his migration to Australia.

Oxford served as a reference point for many of his discussions with Shobha. All Souls was closed to the public for examinations at the time of their visit, but Shobha offered to give the elderly porter a kiss if he would allow her to enter the college – and he did.

My darling

In haste. A few jonquils herewith to match your nightdress. Bicycle in laundry. Have oiled bearings in both wheel hubs. Am still slightly dazed from the splendour of last night.

Dear Puss

The beach was fine this morning. Firm sand for running, good surfing waves, but not too rough beyond, to rule out swimming. All this embellished by a clear sky with a full-ish moon directly overhead. When it's warmer, we should go for a picnic on a Sunday.

*The celebrated gates of New College, Oxford
where Douglas regularly dined in the evenings
when he was a Reader at All Souls' College*

Your early experience with your mother makes me feel that you are basically a warm person, even though you say you are not. What bothers me is the inconsistency. I am never detached from you, but circumstances can make me feel very insecure with you.

I may deceive myself, but I feel it is not so much the quantity of affection that is important, but the quality. A touch or look from you of intimacy would be worth a thousand kisses which are half-hearted.

Mon bien-aime amoreaux
>The rosy glow cast over us yesterday - as always - leaves its effect. You look so beautiful, literally, at such times. Much love

Shobha
>As I said when we spoke earlier today, you range across a gamut of attitudes and ideas, from wild anger to tenderness, from spiritual marriage to a platonic liaison. With N. exploding emotionally here at my elbow, I find all this confusing and upsetting - to put it mildly.

Dearest Duggles
>It is as if you need someone like N. as a mother, and someone like me - as a lover. Perhaps you did not get enough mothering as a child. I received too much. Just kissed the pillows where we lay at lunch – a sacred spot.

Dear one

I like to feel there is some naturalness in the landscape where weeds grow wild – so much more beautiful than the carefully-tended quarter acre, to which everyone seems to aspire. I love an unkempt garden full of leaves. Perhaps it is the *Edna Walling* in my ancestry.

** Edna was Shobha's second cousin and Australia's foremost landscape gardener (born in Devon and lived in Australia from 1895 until 1973).

Dear Douglas

Nothing brings me more pleasure than lying in your arms talking, when we are *en rapport*. It is for me, the supreme pleasure. Sometimes making love and the aftermath thereof also brings a sense of oneness with you, yet of course, we cannot remain in such a state forever. Bhagwan says there is no 'love' as such, only 'moments' of love.

> Whosoever shall be sore wounded by love
> will never become whole
> save he embrace the selfsame love - which wounded him
>
> *Mechthild of Magdeburg (Christian saint)*

It is always very energising to go dancing at the 'orange' centre. Last night I could feel myself coursing with delight. Bhagwan of course (on tape), was full of worldly wisdom and said 'marriage was a form of prostitution' and women should become independent and free. I agree there are many things to recommend a partnership such as ours, in that we are only together when we wish - but the problem is we cannot always be together when we want to be.

Dear Wimsey

Thank you for your love today – talking to you under the Buddha-tree returned me to some degree of normality. Listened lovingly this evening to the poetry of Shelley and Keats respectively (on tape) : *Ozymandius* and *La belle dame sans merci* (the beautiful lady without mercy). These were poems I recited to myself when I was thirteen and ever since. We were exposed to a great wealth of poetry through my English teacher, who was so inspirational, that under his tutelage, I was awarded the school poetry prize.

Did I show you the poem I wrote at Wasdale in the Lake District while Helen was climbing Scafell Pike (the highest mountain in England)? I felt I was touching god (in a different way).

Perhaps one should surrender academic struggles and simply love, enjoy poetry and music and the sun and surf and be content. When you first retired, you remarked you felt you were finally doing what you wished – reading poetry and critiques of the same. Why must we wait all our lives to do that which we most love?

'Bhagwan says' if one feels gratitude towards someone, the opposite emotion - which is latent - is anger or resentment - because we do not wish to be in debt to another. So I won't say I'm grateful to you, even if I am. Love – Shobha – the crestfallen academic but joyful mystic

Dear Douglas

Could we go through our letters and cards soon? They may be the only literary work of any merit that we produce. Much love until we commune tomorrow - Shobha

<u>*Note to Puss - On leaving a bouquet of yellow daffodils at Shobha's home*</u>

> I wandered lonely as a cloud
> that floats on high o'er vales and hills
> when all at once I saw a crowd –
> a host of golden daffodils
>
> Beside the lake -
> beneath the trees -
> fluttering and dancing in the breeze
>
> *William Wordsworth*

La belle dame sans merci - 24

Shobha

My daffodils for you are not a 'host' nor truly 'golden' – nor, at the moment, is there a 'breeze' to make them dance - but a small tribute nevertheless to a lover of Wordsworth – and also, strangely – a lover of me !

For some reason the beach was particularly exhilarating this morning. The waves were just right – large, but not brutal. Love – Wimsey (a.k.a. Douglas)

Beloved Wimsey

Had dinner with your daffodils this evening. I love the way you indulge me after making love. I would send you flowers, but you have said they are not your cup of tea, and they would probably be relegated to the bin by N.

Do you happen to have any books on Norfolk where you spent some of your early years? As I am helping to write a novel with a friend on *Boadicea (Boudicca)* - the Celtic queen of the Iceni - I feel it is imperative (one day) to walk the trail of Boadicea's army - from Colchester to London to St Albans, and also north-west to the island of Anglesey, where the Druid sanctuary was destroyed by the Romans.

When we climbed Snowdon, we were so close to Anglesey and could have seen it from a distance - if there had not been a mist on that day. I was so happy to have done it – having never even seen anything approximating a mountain before, so I just had to ring you to boast of my newly-acquired prowess.

Have been reading yet again, the legend of *Tristan and Isolde* according to Cornish folklore - which is one of your favourite operas. Helen and I have visited some of the sites which are sacred to King Arthur, but sadly we realised too late that Tintangel was one of those connected with Tristan and Isolde - after we had been there.   All my love – Puss

Boadicea (a.k.a. Boudicca) was the Celtic Queen of the Iceni tribe during the occupation of Britain by the Romans between (AD 43 to 410) and fought the Roman armies following the death of her husband Prasutagus, and the denigration of herself and her two daughters at their hands.

Boadicea with her two daughters
J. Havard Thomas (1916) – City Hall, Cardiff, Wales

Friend a.k.a. Wimsey - the disturber of my emotions

Now that I am no longer actively studying for my thesis, I am reading more widely and especially authors whose lives I touched when travelling in England and places with which I became acquainted viz. *Tintagel* (King Arthur), *Glastonbury Abbey* (again Arthur), Lewis Carroll (Alice in Wonderland), your alma mater (*Oxford University*) and *Dove Cottage* (the home of William Wordsworth in the Lake District).

Since retiring from my 'potential' academic life, I feel I can turn to one of my real loves for a while viz. literature - which is also your own.

I mentioned to a good friend the other day that you packed your hundred best books to take to war when you enlisted - and your general inclination at age eighteen towards classical texts. I'm sure that yours was not the usual kit for an officer to take into battle.

I am beginning to feel that the best way for some people to create is in twosomes, such as ourselves - so that one can motivate the other and test ideas against the other, and vice versa. I found a few lines from Lewis Carroll on 'Alice' for you - which I have come to appreciate :

> Still she haunts me, phantom-wise,
> Alice - moving under skies,
> never seen by waking eyes
>
> <u>Alice (to the caterpillar)</u>
> I can't explain myself, I'm afraid,
> because I'm not myself, you see.
> <u>Caterpillar</u>
> I don't see

Alice (while regarding the Cheshire-cat)
> It looked good-natured - she thought.
> Still - it had very long claws
> and a great many teeth,
> so she felt it ought to be treated
> with respect.

Alice (to her kitten)
> Now don't interrupt me.
> I'm going to tell you all your faults.

Remind you of anyone, Douglas?

There are many other Carroll quotes which are equally delightful e.g.

> You are old Father William, the young man said
> and your hair was become very white,
> and yet you incessantly stand on your head -
> do you think - at your age - it is right ?
> In my youth - Father William replied to his son,
> I feared it might injure the brain,
> but now that I'm perfectly sure I have none,
> why - I do it again and again.

This also reminds me of your yoga exercises every morning !

25

> *O frabjous day, callooh, callay,*
> *he chortled in his joy.*
>
> *Lewis Carroll - Jabberwocky*

and the final word from the Red Queen in Alice in Wonderland -

> *Why, sometimes*
> *I've believed as many as six impossible things*
> *before breakfast*

Love from your Alice

Dear Wimsey

There was a programme on television tonight on healing and alternative medicine. Doctors say pain is usually associated with feeling cold and healing is experienced as warmth or heat. National Health doctors in the United Kingdom are referring patients to eight thousand registered healers and working with some of them as a team - when other ways of relieving pain - have failed.

The programme suggested that if you believe it to be so - it will happen. I agree wholeheartedly. Doubt is to my mind, the greatest killer. Much love – Shobha the Buddha

Dearest Duggles

Wimsey (the little white teddy bear you gave me) and I are sitting here in bed, thinking of you.

There was a programme on Catholic moral issues this evening on television: the typical divorce/contraception/sexuality issues with ex-priests, new priests, old priests, ex-Catholic school children, journalists, politicians, lawyers etc.

I am so glad not to be part of any organised ideology. You and I may not always appreciate the incredible freedom we possess. So many people are guilt-ridden because of the church or some other authority.

With regard to our enthusiasms, I think both you and I are dilettantes, by which I mean that our interests can change quite drastically in a short space of time. Must toddle off as sleep is descending. Will dream about you tonight. Much love, my dearest – Puss

Dearest Wimsey

Having belonged to so many causes in my youth, I find it almost impossible now to commit myself to any group or idea. Having gone through several political parties, a number of churches, peace marches, green (conservation) groups, social work, psychiatric hospitals, children's homes, nursing homes and every possible 'alternative' new age spiritual group, I don't seem able to focus on one to the exclusion of others any more.

I care - but cannot apply this to any cause. Voluntary euthanasia is close to my heart, so that people have choice - though it seems a pity to focus on death. Celebration of life is equally important.

You seem to be rather of the same mind. You take an interest in many things, but don't become 'involved' in any causes. I am grateful for my years of outreach however, because I am such a different person now because of it.

The idea of actively 'helping others' doesn't occur to me any more - though I am glad to assist others individually and spontaneously - as their need arises.

What does occur is to be as lighthearted, playful, honest and provocative as is possible, in the hope that this will liven up the world a little. Will that do?

How I wish I knew how to live at the maximum all the time. Life is rich, but it would feel good to add something beautiful to the world.

Dearest love, do you ever aspire to something more - or have you accepted what is? Probably therein lies the answer, but I find it hard to accept my lot. I feel there is something I must do, but I don't know how to do it, or what it is . All I really wish for is to be able to love you always. There is so much to share. You are so precious to me. In love – Pusskins

Wimsey

Today - because Spring is in the air and perhaps due to chemistry, I felt very affectionate - and less like talking in depth. There are times when it is more important to be in tune physically and emotionally than mentally.

Full moon and Spring - when the chemistry is affected - are those times for me. I long to simply 'be' in your arms. All else is futile right now. Love - Puss

Dear Douglas

Somehow it seems appropriate that N.'s mother should die while I was away, so you and N. can share this time - without interference. I will certainly avoid N. for a while. I hope the service goes well and you find suitable words in the *Oxford Dictionary of Quotations*. The only ones that occur to me are -

> We are such stuff as dreams are made of....
> and our little lives are rounded with a sleep
>
> *Shakespeare – The Tempest*

though as you know - I don't think we do 'sleep'.

The folk festival was as usual heart-disturbing and uplifting. I did not feel really 'changed' by the experience until one of my friends sang this morning, and tears rolled down my cheeks – at last.

That is the way I define a good song – if it makes me cry - either from happiness or understanding. Otherwise it has no real value.

The standard of folk songs is improving and the 'folk opera' is becoming established as an art form, based upon historical and generally biographical material. Very satisfying. I must start writing songs again. Being out of town in the country is invigorating and essential for the soul. Much love - Shobha

The festival was certainly a family event. I can't imagine any social function more healthy than a folk festival. Such joy. Folkies tend to be people who are concerned and care about almost everything. There seems to be a definite set of 'core' values, and I rather suspect that many folkies are largely liberated from the debilitating effects of religion viz. guilt, fear, proscriptions for behaviour, rituals etc.

When I am at the festival, I rise before anyone else in the town is stirring, jog up the road, breakfast, shower, walk to the river and meditate on the rocks under the bridge until the mist disperses. By then, there are hundreds of campers rising from their tents, cooking on fires etc.

It's hard to describe the loveliness of being outside in the country when everyone else is waking up and eating breakfast in the open air. Makes one wonder why we have houses at all. Your army life must have left you with the same feeling. At this time of the year, the bush is splendid.

I will be thinking of you as you prepare for the funeral service for N.'s mother. One day I may do the same for my mother. There are many emotions intermingled when people die. Shock is one of them. Anger is also natural but most people feel guilty for what they did or could have done.

On the way to and from the country in your landcruiser, I play tapes of Welsh choral music and my heart explodes with joy. Hearing the massed voices of Wales is for me - a religious experience.   Must go – love - Puss

**

Do you remember recently saying that when making love, I was the 'centre of the solar system' (for you).   It was a very beautiful way of putting it.

Chapter 10

Sing and dance together and be joyous

26

Darling

A few quotes for your pleasure :

A man can be happy with any woman
as long as he does not love her

Oscar Wilde

The advantage of the emotions
is that they lead us astray

Oscar Wilde

Love slays what we have been
that we may be what we were not

Saint Augustine

If you wish to be loved
show more of your faults than your virtues

Baron Lytton

27

Douglas

There are so many unwept tears because of the nightmare that was Christmas. It felt like a crucifixion - and the resurrection has not yet come. Correction : I have come out of the tomb - but have not yet resurrected.

Do you remember once, for my folk festival workshop entitled *Songs of Love, Lust and Longing*, that I designed a banner which read 'Amo ergo sum' *(I love therefore I am).* On the banner - a knight knelt to kiss his lady's hand. This physical gesture to me embodies the ultimate form of love between a man and a woman, where a woman is in a standing posture, with her already loving heart open, and the man kneels - therefore surrendering to his heart (refer to *Leighton's* painting '*Accolade*' of the Lady Guinevere and Lancelot in Chapter 14 - though the sword has a rather different meaning.

Bhagwan says it is only possible for a man to love - if he becomes feminine.

> A man who is absolutely in love
> does not know
> whether he is more or less in love than others
> for anyone who knows this
> just on that account
> is not absolutely in love
>
> *Søren Kierkegaard (Danish philosopher)*

**

There are no little events with the heart.
It magnifies everything.

It places (on) the same scales
the fall of an empire of fourteen years
and the dropping of a woman' glove.

And almost always,
the glove weighs more
than the empire.

Honoré de Balzac – French novelist and playwright

Dear Douglas

I have always said to you - and you have not objected - that when we make love you are at your softest and gentlest, and the hard edges to which you often refer - fall away. This apparently happens to many men when making love. In the book *What do Women Really Want,* which I have mentioned to you, it is said women want to see the men they love show their vulnerability - because at other times - closeness is reduced proportionally.

Dear Puss

Yesterday was indeed wonderful. My thinking self is inclined to wonder why it was so. But it may be an experience one should not try to analyse. Much love – Douglas

Wimsey

Watched the film *War and Peace* last night – not inspiring. Your point about the film not portraying the book well - is taken. Missing you dreadfully, but it is too late to phone. You need your sleep. So much love – Puss

Dear Douglas

Miss you so. My friend, with whom I was researching material for a book on *Boadicea,* wants to write his political utopian treatise first - so the book is on hold. In the meantime, I am going to edit my multifarious articles on 'love' and put them in a format for publication. Would love to hear your voice and long to see you. Enjoy your beloved son (who is visiting), whatever and however he is. Much love – Puss

Dearest Wim

For some reason that I cannot determine, in recent months, we have fallen into a pattern of not meeting, but rather conversing on the phone. As you know, we both appreciate the quality of our phone conversations which at times has been profound, and at other times very intimate, but it concerns me that this mode of interaction might be preferred by you, to actual eyeball-to-eyeball contact. Much love – Puss

My darling

Last night I watched the film of the French lovers Heloise and Abelard (*Stealing Heaven)* and was very moved by it. Yet though Abelard is supposed to be a famed and revolutionary philosopher, it is Heloise who shines as having the courage to 'do without god' and Abelard who sees his castration as divine retribution and subsequently dedicates himself to the church and encourages Heloise to do the same. Foolishly to my mind, she agrees to become a nun to please Abelard, not because she is interested in religion, but because that is the way to be closest to him.

Surprisingly, what are supposedly erotic scenes in the film, are for me, the most natural and sacred of all - and reminded me somewhat of us. Perhaps others don't make love as we do? They were a beautiful combination of minds, bodies and souls (as we are). All my love – Puss

> ** The love story of *Heloise D'Argenteuil* and *Peter Abelard* from the 12th century is one of history's most passionate and romantic tales (refer to the painting in Chapter 3 – *Abelard and his pupil Heloise*).
>
> Abelard was a medieval philosopher at the Sorbonne university in Paris and a theologian and Heloise - a brilliant scholar of Latin, Greek and Hebrew and a pupil of Abelard. She was also the ward of Canon Fulbert of the Catholic church, who was also in love with Heloise, and was responsible for the castration of Abelard, following his secret marriage to her.

Douglas

We talked of 'mischief' recently and how that was a desirable quality. It would be lovely if we were free to be our mischievous selves together.

I enclose a review of Melvyn Bragg's** novel *Credo* which you gave to me. The book concerns the conflict between the Celtic and Catholic churches on the west coast of England during the 'dark' ages.

I also read the article on Germaine Greer**. *The Female Eunuch* (1970) was stimulating because her ideas were new, though I have never felt any great affinity with them.

For me, a woman worthy of emulation would be one who has tenderness, wisdom, brilliance of expression, humour, vitality, beauty of spirit and a sharpness of perception and response, who also can deal with men or women who attack, in such a way as to bring them to their knees. For me, a woman should be warm and loving, but if preyed upon, be able to defend herself absolutely against any opposition.

Women must strengthen themselves inside so that no-one, male or female, can ever harm them. Likewise of course, a man must make himself invulnerable to attack, so that he too can allow himself to show his tender side without fear. Much love – Pusskins

> ** *Melvyn Bragg (Baron Bragg)* - author, broadcaster and interviewer, whose programme 'The South Bank' ran for many years on British television. The interviews were conducted in the BBC studio on the south bank of the Thames river.
>
> ** *Germaine Greer* : Australian author and scholar, who pioneered the second wave of the feminist movement in the seventies.

My dear Puss

My heart goes out to you for having to return to your office in such a rushed way so soon after our hour together. I keep thinking of your face and laughing, happy eyes. At such times, I find my own eyes drawn very much towards your lips. With you, your lips, as much as your eyes, are the windows of your soul.

My son (who had so many grievances in the recent past), seems to have loosened up today and is talking more freely. *Au revoir*, my darling. Shall drop in for a while tomorrow.

Dear Puss

You know full well that, whatever our problems, making love has never been one of them. No-one could be sweeter, combining as you marvellously do - passion, gentleness and a seraphic joy which still almost frightens me. Was it not I who coined the phrase 'nature's glove' ? The mountain you climb is no common one.

Dearest Wimsey

I am all yours. Whatever you wish to do this evening, I will be happy. Just to be with you is enough. Love – Puss

Dear Puss

My mind is still in a whirl from what happened this morning. I am reminded of those two occasions, some years ago now, when events followed roughly the same course when we were walking at eight in the morning among the shrubs near the Pelican Point bird sanctuary.

I hope you believe me when I say I had no designs in my mind – consciously at least. My initial attitude towards you was inclined to be unresponsive. But then, how quickly, naturally and wonderfully, we were swept away, almost as if some higher power had set us free of constraining fetters, though in saying this, perhaps I am speaking more for myself than for you, since you are not afflicted as I am, by conflicting pulls.

By way of illustration, when I got back to the house, N. was on the point of setting off for the beach, fearing I might have drowned unnoticed, while swimming alone out to the buoy. You can imagine my feelings when greeted in this way. Is it (therefore) so certain that your situation is more distressing than mine?

Dear Douglas

It is very late tonight and I yearn for my pillow. One day perhaps, your head will also rest upon it. As Robert Browning writes :

> Where my heart lies - let my brain lie also.

Will think of you snug and warm in your cot. Goodnight, sweet prince

From what you have said to me, you were brought up by an excessively affectionate mother. Perhaps having had such a background and then being faced with years alone in boarding school, you are simply defending yourself against potential hurt. As you know, we have different values. For instance, I accept reincarnation. You think this is not important but it underlies my attitude to life. You do not consider that we may 'have been together before' - as I mention in my song *The Wheel of Karma (Chapter 18)*.

It seems to me, that you have not been with N. 'before' - though we can't be sure of that. The type of *relationship* you have with her is largely functional - not inspirational. You had children together, studied together, had the same profession, enjoyed gardening, television, swimming, animals etc. but to my mind, have never 'met' at the deeper level we have enjoyed. Correct me if I am wrong.

I realise that what you have shared with N. over the years was worthwhile at one level, but a new phase began when we met, and to keep a foot in both camps means you are no longer true to yourself, or to either woman. Both women have chosen to remain with you, so we are all equally culpable. You said last night - as Mercutio says in Shakespeare's *Romeo and Juliet* – 'a plague on both their houses' - but of course, that includes your house, as well.

**

Is there a way I can share 'all' with you - even the dark nights of your soul? Surely it is not only roses which we are destined to enjoy together ? Yet there have been many good times – singing under the lamplight outside your house, playing cats for real - inside your house, making love in the park at night and on the bay, in the early morning under my pink shawl. If you would like to go to the park for lunch tomorrow, I will be gentle and put my best paw forward. Love – Puss

**

The careless lifestyle of the English poet and novelist *Vita Sackville-West*, with her mansion and servants and trips to the continent, makes me frustrated with my nine to five office existence and the idiocy of the work that I do.

I want to escape and break out of the confines of the present situation. Seeing you, makes me aware of all that I want to be, and I can't stand the mediocrity of everything else. Please contact me as soon as possible.

Dearest love

I cannot go to bed this evening without writing to you of the indescribable sweetness of our meeting today. It was as if we were thrice blessed. When you left, I was aware of my cup being full - perhaps even overflowing. There is nothing more we can give to each other, than our full attention - and that was given. Whereas at times I have felt restless in your company, ever desiring 'more' - today 'more' was given unasked, and therefore contentment reigned.

Obviously it is not possible to be in a state of perpetual bliss (unless one is 'enlightened' in the eastern sense), but I have transferred some of my longings for this mystical state, onto our love - because we enter such a world now and then - albeit for only a short time. When we are 'in love' - however transiently - we 'are' enlightened.

And perhaps because the joy is great, so is the fall when that state disappears. It is almost as if we are vehicles for each other to enter a realm which is not otherwise easily accessible. For a few moments here and there, we both experience 'glory'. What a lovely word. Goodnight my love. My peace I leave you. Much love – Puss

Dearest Douglas

Being with you today left me with a feeling of excitement on the one hand, and a renewed sense of vigour on the other. Being with you balances all the tension and apprehensiveness of work, with a great feeling of joy. Making love with you is like being in heaven for a little while. Love – Puss

**

The relationship between grandparents and children is more or less of unconditional love, because there is less expectation, less contact, and therefore less heavy emotional content. I have never had grandparents, so this experience is unknown to me. Your soulmate-confidante-lover-friend and Ned-substitute

Dear Puss

A few more erect roses (as the last ones sadly drooped after a few days). You were sweet and very happy last night. I never cease to marvel at the innocence of your joy at such times.

Dear body and soul mate

Feeling a warm glow from last night. I'm not surprised you are tired after swimming rough seas, making love, reading late and then getting up early - plus working on the roof. Please look after your back. Please also keep any little boxes for me which would make a nice nest for my petals, when my roses have shuffled off their floral coils. I am getting quite a collection. Puss.

Dear Wimsey

You know what it was that affected us the other night – playfulness ! From the first moment when you rushed in and knelt at my feet and said 'sorry', and we danced to the music and you kissed me, we were feeling happy. We even descended or ascended to giggling at various points throughout the evening.

So therein lies the secret ! You have also found this with your grandchildren. It is the sheer lightheartedness that makes you feel so warm towards them. They have not yet been corrupted.

Likewise, you used to say the reason the beach was so exciting, was the childlike fun you felt when you were being tossed about by the waves. Joy forever - your Puss

**

Don't laugh (which seems strange to say after what I have just said), but my mother is beginning to see things which aren't physically there. She is not on any medication which would produce hallucinations, and she has always been rather 'psychic'. In the last few days, there has been a man in her house sitting in a chair. He doesn't speak, but whenever she approaches, he disappears. It is always the same face and it doesn't frighten her, but she seems to want to talk about it.

My mother and I believe that when a person exits planet earth, their spirit often appears to someone who has been close. When my father died, it happened to me, though I didn't see him, but felt his presence. When my cousin was blown up in a plane which was hijacked over Singapore, my mother felt his presence. When her father died, she felt the same. All very interesting.

At first, I kept saying to my mother – "Go to a different doctor. It's all your imagination" - but the way she talks make me wonder if she sees things that others don't or can't. The police now ask clairvoyants to help them locate people who have come to grief – with some success.

Years ago, I used to go to various spiritualist groups around Perth to see if there was any sense in them. There was one spiritualist church nearby, that particularly impressed me. This morning, I finally talked to my mother about spiritualism and I think she felt relieved, because she and her mother and brother often went to spiritualist churches in their youth. My family on both sides has a strong religious and psychic streak.

This probably sounds Double-Dutch to you. Are you aware that spiritualism is very, very strong in England? In some countries, hospitals have healers and psychics on their consulting staff.

Because of the auspiciousness of tomorrow (full moon), perhaps the man my mother sees is our friend L. who died recently, and when his ashes are scattered at sea, his soul will find peace? Your ever-loving soulmate – Puss

**

After we have been so intimate, with every cell opened up as it were, I find it difficult to be simply practical and return to earth. Sometimes when we first meet, we are both full of what we want to tell each other, and at other times, we are only thinking of the other. Perhaps that is the secret (of communion). To place the other's welfare ahead of one's own.

Guess what – I have discovered the spiritualist group is just around the corner from my mother's home. Perhaps she might be tempted to go along. Much love – forgive me for wanting to be always in your arms – Pusskins

My darling

Perhaps at heart we are both romantics? Why else would Jane Austen appeal to us? Despite her criticism of the social customs of the time, she extols the virtue of matches born of love - above all else. I wonder if her heart ever fell (or rose) for another. Must go to bed. Take care my love, of your precious body (after the blow to your head) as well as your heart. Goodnight sweet prince – Puss p.s. My diving into the wave today was a bit like finding 'god' unexpectedly !

Dear Puss

Many thanks for your concern for my head. I woke early today and admired the moon in a clear sky, so went to the beach immediately, in order to swim by moonlight. It was only six degrees, but after running to the groyne, the water seemed almost warm. No collisions this morning, though I find my head is slightly swollen. Warned other swimmers to take care.

Dearest Douglas

Our talk tonight was as always - pretty deep. I don't think it matters with whom moments of 'love' are felt. In some ways, they creep upon one unexpectedly, even between lovers - such as we are. I believe it is a case of 'allowing' it to happen. You have been quite gay at times lately, as if your 'happy centre' in the brain was hit, when you collided in the water (joke).

Before I arrive at work each day, I sing a few arias in the local hall, and I am always surprised my voice is there without 'warming up' and capable of so much - without ever practising. We must sing together again some time, as the acoustics in the hall are so wonderful. It is effortless to sing passages which are otherwise very difficult.

My poor, dear mother is having all sorts of dreams and hallucinations. Tonight she thought someone was trying to get into bed with her. Perhaps it is wishful thinking. I suppose I must resign myself to the fact that sooner or later she will need more care than my brother and I can give her. I would love her to remain independent for as long as possible. She has such a tough spirit deep within.

Dear love – when we talk as we did this evening, I wish we could go on and on, and never cease. I remember, when I was in India, becoming so in tune with Bhagwan, that I felt that if he ever left his body, it would make no difference, and when he did - it did not.

Likewise, if we ever have to part, i.e. one of us leaves our body (and it is just as likely that it could be me, despite our age difference) - and because of our daily separations and trials - but also due to our correspondence and daily phone calls - we might well find that each other's essence is still permanently present. In that case, our separateness physically now, may turn out to be a blessing - and there will be no difference.

What a comforting thought. It is certainly true, that at times that you and I almost live on air – in the love sense. This is the meaning of my song *The Wheel of Karma* - which implies we shall be together in spirit, when that day comes (i.e. when one of us leaves earth). Sweet dreams – Puss

Dear Puss

The thought in your last letter is certainly an interesting one - the more so for running counter to conventional thinking. Is it related perhaps to the notion that some fictional characters may 'live' more vividly in one's mind than real people do - after they die?

You should not reproach yourself for not coming down to the beach at this time of year. I would not myself go, if it were not for the prospect of being able to swim. It was bitingly cold this morning, running up to the groyne in the wind - but the swimming was good.

Seven of us converged out to sea on the buoy at the same time from different directions, and six of them were women. How things have changed in the last few years. They were previously men - for the most part.

Dearest Douglas

I had a very vivid dream last night. I was watching a trapeze artist and then decided to 'have a go' myself (which is something I longed to do as a child). The exhilaration was incredible. You cannot imagine the feeling of surrender and power - floating through the air without any attachments, other than the swing.

A parachutist must have similar feelings. Ecstasy ! At one point in the dream, I did a somersault backwards and was amazed at how easy it felt. Symbolically of course - danger and freedom are related to each other. It was another of those 'special' dreams that felt significant.

My poor nuclear family is in the wars due to my mother's hallucinations, so she spent the night with my brother. The doctors feel they will be able to 'control' her hallucinations with medication, so hopefully they will settle soon.

Dearest Wimsey

When we lay on the floor – drifting in and out of sleep, I felt happier than I have ever felt before - with you. It felt so whole – as if for a little while, we were one. Sweet dreams – Puss

**

When you speak of growing older, it makes me sad. *Carpe diem* (seize the day) my love ! All else is futile. I do not think my mother ever imagined what it would be like to be eighty. When she was seventy, she used to protest, saying "I'm not old."

The main feeling I have when you discuss these matters, is not sadness at your 'ageing', but extreme sadness, because I fear not being able to be with you - if you become ill or indisposed.

I wish we could grow old gracefully together and give up the ghost at the same time. Please tell me you will always allow me to be with you - until you leave your body. All my love – Puss

Dearest and loveliest of men

You were so gentle at lunch – somehow we got it right. I do love you so. A lifetime with you would not be enough. Am wading through Jane Austen's novel *Mansfield Park*. Her other novel *Persuasion* was a breeze, by comparison – light and fluffy. Can't relax sufficiently to write sweet nothings right now. Puss

My dear Puss

Life must be very trying for you at the moment, with your mother staying with you. You are bearing up in a way that does you credit. I do hope, both for her sake and yours, that the hallucinations turn out to be simply a phase.

Shobha's mother was admitted to an assessment unit for the elderly, several days later, after a very distressing incident when she became locked in her own home, and could not work out how to open the door to escape. Fortunately at 5 am, feeling intuitively something was wrong, Shobha visited her mother, and rescued her from what was virtually a sauna - as the hot water was running - all the windows were closed and covered with water and the heat in the rooms was extreme.

Dear Douglas

Mum is safely in a transitional hospital at last – a lavish government complex where she has her own room with views to a garden. The staff are incredibly kind. She will be assessed to ascertain what type of care she will need, now that her psychological condition has altered so dramatically. Much love

My dearest Puss

Yes, it was fun yesterday - without qualification. Much love – Douglas

Dear Douglas

Life seems so much better since you called this morning. I can see the colours of the leaves and feel the wind in my hair again. When we are not *en rapport,* I don't see or feel these things.

How odd that you and I both long to be in England and yet we are here. For me it would be a journey of discovery. For you - a simple relaxation amongst known pleasures. But can you be sure those pleasures would be there? Why for instance, did you come to Australia? There must have been something about England which did not appeal. It was such a massive step. With tenderness

Dearest Wimsey

I did not know that even though Winston Churchill affectionately called his wife Clementine 'Puss' - that she had also drawn little pictures of cats when writing to him (as I do), to represent themselves – a large cat and a little one.

Dear Douglas

I think you become affected by my preoccupation with 'passing over' and seem to be reflective recently about your age. I am a little troubled when you start to ponder about such things, though it is one of my preoccupations – but out of interest, not fear.

I was hoping we could go to the hall soon and practise some songs. I find that when I am singing, there is an undercurrent of joy that flows through the rest of the day. Sometimes I sing constantly around the house - even when I would not say I was particularly happy.

But the acoustics in my home are superb and that makes all the difference. That's why 'singing in the shower' is often mentioned - because not only is it a place of relaxation, but often bathroom acoustics are good, so it is an excellent time to soar. God knows what the neighbours think !

I am about to hop into bed with *Middlemarch (*a novel by George Eliot). It is so unlike Jane Austen. Elizabeth (one of the characters) is odd - yet retains her pure femininity. Dorothea (the heroine) is pure intellectual material, and lets the feminine graces lapse - to her detriment.

Darling – I wish Wimsey (my teddy bear) was a little larger. I hug him and kiss his little brown nose - but he is so small. Sometimes when I kiss him - he really feels like you.

My mother is thriving in her new abode, and talking of coming home, which is a healthy sign. We will meet with the doctor and social worker soon to discuss a plan. My brother and I seem to be the only visitors to the hospital where she is staying, which is very sad.

There are so many disadvantages to being institutionalised. My mother always seems to be fighting with one of the nurses, and usually wins. Perhaps that is where I get my wild spirit from, which brings me to your door at times. But I feel I 'must' come – as if life and death depended upon it.

Dear love – until tonight. Swim for me – until I come. You are so dear to me. Please think fondly of all that we share. Much love – sleep well – Puss

Note written by Shobha to herself

It was full moon this morning and Douglas says he draped himself under the moon at the ocean. It must have been splendid. We met by 'accident' in the street and he called at my home in consequence. It was very special and he felt so close, yet we were both playing at being just 'friends'.

At one point he commented that my white Bhagwan dress (which I wear to celebrations at the centre) looked almost bridal. As he said this, he gazed at me in such a naked way - and I saw his heart. He was for one very brief moment totally innocent and I could feel that he wanted me – that we were made for each other.

Yesterday we went to the park and lay in the warm sun and curled up together. Feeling his warm head against me was so delightful. Time stopped and I wished never to rise from such a perfect state. Perhaps life is only a series of such peaceful moments. Dancing at the orange celebration was 'bliss'. So also - it is to 'sing'.

Dear friend and lover

You will always be to me a source of love – a fountain perhaps – maybe even a well – as you once expressed it - and I hope I can be that also for you.

Roamed in the park several times today, on the hill overlooking the river, and meditated for a while. As always, what arose was my love for you with concomitant tears (sweet ones, of course).

You said yesterday it was more important to love than to be loved. Best of all, is to love and be loved in return. Without this, we are but poor creatures.

On the weekend, I missed you terribly and summoned my brother to visit me. This happens but once a year - so it is unusual and therefore sincere. When he left, I realised how much I love him. Being of the same womb must affect this, but it is more than that. In his time, he has truly loved me - and, as you say - love begets love.

The words of Elizabeth Barrett Browning's poem spring to mind -

> I love thee
> to the depth and breadth and height
> my soul can reach

Perhaps we could perfect a love - where we never meet - but commune by pen and phone. In a way, the gross everyday occurrences reduce that which is deepest in us. Far better to touch now and then, and live on an exalted plane for a few moments here and there.

Dear Douglas – these thoughts will keep me warm until we meet. I may take a week's leave soon to reflect a little more. It is such delight.

Dear Shobha - Douglas' birthday

The flowers are beautiful, and are now in a large vase on my study desk. I have not yet opened the parcel or any of the five birthday cards. I must open them in your presence, in which case you must request an 'exceptional' meeting.

Dear Douglas

Have been watching a very sentimental film from 1955 with *Vera Lynn*. I found her songs enthralling for their sheer energy. As a child, it was my dream to 'go to the front' (if there was a war) and sing to the troops, as Vera did. Children are very impressionable.

The theme song *Somewhere over the Rainbow* was sung by my father throughout my life. Keep warm. I envy you your icy swims in the ocean.

Dear Shobha

The water was masochistically fine this morning, and was an ideal preparation for Mozart's *Requiem* during breakfast. Did you know that Jane Austen has been compared with Chaucer and Shakespeare?

**

As you know, I am divided. My general standing disposition is against (making love), for reasons I do not need to explain. But when I am with you and we kiss, my mind begins to play on the natural consummation of what we are doing. Nor do I believe you, when you say you would forever be content, merely to kiss. Your actions belie it.

Dear Puss

You were delightful as ever, in *modo amandi*. The roses ought to survive your weekend at the folk festival. Have taken the plunge and bought a chainsaw – rather late in life. So pray for me.

In some strange way, when I sit alone in your house, with so much evidence of you all about me, I feel more strongly than at other times, that you belong to me and that your concerns ought to be mine. Much love – Douglas

Dearest sweetest creature

You were so exquisite today. When you are in your 'kind' side, you are perfect. I find such joy welling up inside. But due to past experience, I often fear 'the worm will turn' and I believe my fear is justified. Sometimes you do not realise you have 'turned', which causes difficulties.

I love you with all my heart when you are gentle, but if you 'turn', I cannot and must not even speak to you. Perhaps I should find names for your various moods. Would love to talk to you *ad infinitum*. Today was a taste of the divine. Much love – Eve

Dear Douglas

There are moments when the look in your eyes is very revealing. I believe women want most of all for their men to be vulnerable - and show their hidden splendour. Yet of course, all male conditioning is geared to the opposite. It is a dilemma. Perhaps both men and women should develop their male and female sides and be able to use them at will, or as required.

I remember in India feeling for the first time that I had a 'male' side. The sense of power that gave me was immense. Since then I have always felt I could marshal my male energy when needed.

When you lie with me, so often your feminine emerges and I am amazed. In those times, you are the dearest possible soul I could ever hope to share my dreams with. I wish those times would last forever. Yet of their nature - they evaporate.

Our last few talks have been deep and disturbing - yet for all that - of great value. The important ingredient through all our trials, is kindness. We have become quite skilled at slinging barbs at each other. If only we could temper these with consideration.

There are times darling, when you are all that I could ever hope for in an intimate union and you radiate a warmth that is quite overwhelming. I wish we could bask in this glow all our days. Be true to our love, however confused you may be. We are a rare pair of swans. In the east - swans are a symbol of perfection – usually flying alone into the mountains (which is odd since they partner for life). Each time I see you - I fly.

Dearest Wimsey

Today was a rare moment in our history. Much love – Puss

Dear Puss

Some replacements herewith for your faded roses. I would ask you why you keep the (petals of the) old ones, if it were not that my mother was a confirmed keeper of dried flowers. For her, they were memories, of events and places.

Douglas

A comment on reincarnation for you - from the German poet *Johann Goethe*, who was writing to his beloved:

> Tell me, what is destiny preparing ?
> Tell me why we two have drawn so near ?
> Aeons since, you were my sister - sharing kin with me,
> or else my wife most dear.
>
> Everything I am, my every feature,
> you divined - my every nerve could thrill;
> read me at a glance.
>
> No other creature
> knows me as you know,
> nor ever will.

And another from British poet and painter Dante Gabriel Rossetti

> I have been here before
> but when or how I cannot tell
> I know the grass beyond the door
> the sweet keen smell

> The sighing sound
> the lights around the shore
> You have been mine before
>
> How long ago I may not know
> but just when at that swallow's soar
> you neck turned so
> some veil did fall
> I knew it all of yore

My Wimsey

Feeling pleasantly weary after our communion. Would love to fall asleep in your arms. God (good) be with you.

> Thanks to the human heart
> by which we live
>
> Thanks to its tenderness
> its joys and fears
>
> To me the meanest flower that blows
> can give thoughts that do often lie
> too deep for tears
>
> *William Wordsworth – Intimations of Immortality*

Darling Wimsey

Your latest blooms are perfect – each one alone is magnificent. They are at this moment at their peak – as we were yesterday. Pink is such a delicate shade in roses. They come alive for me. I wish they could last forever. *Et nous aussi.* I am so glad you felt at peace for a little while. If you are happy, I am also. Much love - Puss

Dear Puss

Your little note was delightful – as was our brief encounter yesterday. Have wondered a little what made up the magic mix. I feel at peace today and I seem to be emerging from my curious shifting back and neck problems - all symptoms, I suspect, of the same malaise.

How disgraceful of me to have forgotten the provenance of 'thoughts that do often lie too deep for tears'. And how strangely moving those last few words are ! Poetry sometimes defies even the most profound analysis. As Sam Johnson said of the poet *Dryden* – *"he delighted to tread upon the brink of meaning."* I am reminded, for some reason, of Shakespeare's words -

> She sat like patience on a monument
> smiling at grief.
> Was not this love indeed ?
>
> *Twelfth Night*

I am also reminded of a line from the film *Moonstruck* when Loretta (played by the American actress and singer *Cher*) complains of the death of Mimi in Puccini's opera *La Boheme*, saying "We are not here to be happy, but to fall in love with the wrong people."

My dear Puss

Yesterday was fun - though I feel slightly guilty that we did not go out for a walk - as we were about to do - when events took *another course.*

After singing in the hall on the weekend together, I have been pondering on what you said about singing and the importance of breathing - the more so because yesterday, my run at 6 am and swim at 8 am went particularly smoothly, with a sense of having a lot in reserve. It seems almost ridiculous that deep breathing could have the effect we spoke of - since so few people are conscious of it.

Darling Wimsey

We seem to have reached a happy moment in our lives. Singing certainly makes it richer. Much love – Pusskins

Dearest love

Watched the film based on Austen's book *Pride and Prejudice* until 2 am, as I could not sleep. It is excellent as you say - though I believe you have a better bargain in me, than in the beautiful heroine Elisabeth Bennett.

Douglas

Your reading of 'Jane' has made you obsessed with her, as if her books were your bible. The novels are interesting; her insights are deep at times; the language is beautiful to say the least - but the situations are unrealistic and the characters just that. They exist only on paper.

How you can hold up Elisabeth Bennett as a model woman - is simply beyond my comprehension. She is a fictional heroine, and while she may stir you to your very depths, I see no point in recommending to someone living in the twentieth century that they follow the behavior (non-sexual of course) of a woman from an earlier period.

Those who hearken back to bygone eras are not long for this world. We have to evolve a style of living and loving which is in keeping with our times.

Dear Douglas

Watching the film based on Austen's novel *Sense and Sensibility*, has moved me to tears - especially on hearing the last words of Marianne - "I have so many questions to ask him". Perhaps men love to impart knowledge to women and women love to be - if not taught - at least inspired. What a woman has to teach a man, is more a question of a subtle presence - implying many unspoken mysteries, rather than simply bald facts. Together - they balance one another.

I believe that *Sense and Sensibility* as portrayed on screen, has equally as much to offer in character development as *Pride and Prejudice.* In fact, all four characters, change roles as the plot progresses. In view of *Sense and Sensibility,* would you like to meet on the morrow, provided we give respect to both sense and sensibility? Jane has softened my heart.

**

I grieve for you and feel so strongly your concern for your son, but also his pain at your attitude towards him. As an observer and your friend, it seems patently obvious to me why he would be distressed, and because I know you, I realise also how you feel. But I cannot agree with you.

You may have watched the programme on Prince Charles tonight. He did not get on well with his father (Prince Philip) and Lord Mountbatten assumed the paternal role. So - estrangement happens in the so-called 'best' families. In fact, according to my psychologist friends, for many men - their fathers are notoriously absent or hypercritical.

I believe your expectations of your son are the problem - which he may have sensed from childhood - as you say he was hypersensitive in his early life. Although he is not the eldest son, but the youngest - he is the one who has come closest to you in terms of making it to Oxbridge, and therefore the one on whom - as you admitted today, you may have pinned your hopes. But he is not you, and does not have your background, tastes, cultivation, mind or aspirations. He is a scientist. That in itself is a major difference - since you have no interest in science.

I do not believe parents should live vicariously through their children. Your son's destiny is entirely independent of yours. Have you read the novel by Somerset Maugham called *The Razor's Edge* which addresses this issue? Your son does not seem to be the sort of man who could have appreciated (your) All Souls College in Oxford.

When will you realise that you are unique? You have a wonderful mind and are interested in a wide range of disciplines. Scientists are noted (as a rule) but not always (as in the case of your biologist friend J.S. Haldane), for their tunnel vision and introversion.

Dear one, I may deceive myself, but it seems to me that all your son needs in this world is to feel loved by you - and while you continue to attack him for his current lifestyle and his behaviour, his resentment towards you will deepen. Have you ever told him you loved him? Have you ever hugged him as a man? This is what the soul craves - and he is a lost soul at present. And so will you be, until you find a way into his heart. You have often said to me "You have no rights" and "You must have no expectations." I say the same to you as far as your son is concerned. "You have no rights. You must have no expectations." Try to love him as he is - without wanting him to fulfil some plan you have for him. He must follow his own path.

Your distress is mine. *Quel che l'incresce, morte mi dà.* (What grieves you - grieves me.) Goodnight my love

Beloved Wimsey

Perhaps you could stress to N., that as a man of learning, it is vital for you - now that you are no longer teaching, to have fertile minds with whom to share your ideas, and I am one. A man who has been an educator all his life, may miss the teacher-student dynamic. It seems rather proscriptive for you to be allowed (by N.) only to relate to her.

At the beach, it is not possible to engage in really deep and meaningful discussions with others, but I am often surprised that you do not feel the urge to discuss your ideas with minds other than my own.

I am of the opinion - and I believe you also agree - that marriage - or indeed any man-woman relationship, can become stultifying if there are no contacts with other souls from time to time. If I did not exist, I am sure you would feel a natural desire to fraternise with others in a deeper way. Much love, my dearest

Dearest Douglas

This evening's farewell to my director has made me a little pensive. His departure marks the end of an era for me and perhaps even for the university. In the midst of a sea of fools (or rather, those not of my persuasion), the one small comfort has been the odd poetic verse which he sprouted from time to time - and the magazines from England such as *Country Life* - which appeared magically upon my desk now and then - and were put there by him.

In his goodbye speech, the registrar of the university compared my director to the butler Jeeves, as portrayed in the books of the English author, *P.G. Wodehouse*. It was a far from favourable comparison, and to my mind - quite demeaning. My director also made an unforgiveable mistake, by calling the cleaners and other non-academic service staff, the 'little people' of the university, presumably versus those 'at the top'. Fatal. Now that the festivities are over, I feel I have given birth. Arranging the function has engaged so much of my psyche in recent weeks.

The new incumbent is a colonel, who is still in command of an army reserve battalion and I receive daily calls from the army. Horrors! I realise you found the army a rewarding experience at one level and even my director was a conscript - but for myself I have always found the notion of the 'forces' repugnant. To have to come face-to-face with it daily, grates with me, and will be a spur to my finding another occupation.

To lose poetry and wit and to inherit war! A person without poetry in his or her soul is to my mind, not a person at all. So many Australian men are devoid of 'kulcha' (culture) and it is frightening. Perhaps you and I have been born with a propensity to love language and beauty. Some people don't seem to have 'souls' at all. They merely function.

I am so tired of being surrounded by empty vessels. Where are the true free spirits – the dreamers – the mystics? Certainly not at our university. I weep for the beauty there could be, and thank 'god' for the beauty we share together. How vital it is to find kindred spirits and how empty is life when one is surrounded by those who are not. Until we commune – much love - your kindred spirit – Puss

Dear Wimsey

You say you have found a new identity with regard to your son. Is it that you no longer feel you have to play the parental role? If so, I heartily approve, but only because this now paves the way for real friendship with your offspring, based upon common loves and interests.

It is chaotic here at the university with two leaders – the old and the new. They are treading on each other's toes and causing consternation.

My good friend Helen, with whom I travelled around England and Wales, has been appointed as personal assistant to the Vice-Chancellor. I find this kind of role unsatisfactory. I have no wish ever again to be any type of assistant. It is so wonderful to instruct others and make decisions and accept responsibility, without having to refer to a higher authority.

Chapter II

In the dew of little things

28

And let there be no purpose in friendship
save the deepening of the spirit.

In the sweetness of friendship
let there be laughter
and the sharing of pleasures.

For in the dew of little things
the heart finds it morning
and is refreshed.

Gibran

Dear Shobha

We seem to have drifted apart in the last three months. Responsibility for this is chiefly mine. To try to explain why this has happened is not an easy matter, since we are often not conscious of what it is that moves us. But I have no doubt that a general accelerating physical tiredness has, on my side - probably been the most important factor.

Whether there is anything organically wrong with me, I do not know. I imagine many people, especially down at the beach, think me fit for my age, since I run much as I have done for the past twenty years. But I pay an increasingly heavy price for this in terms of subsequent tiredness. It is not a simple matter. Despite its after-effects, I still enjoy running and it puts me on a 'high'. If I am indeed fitter than most men of seventy-one - is it not probable, that this is precisely because I continue to stretch myself in ways that most of my contemporaries do not?

When I first met you, I did not experience this fatigue. At that time I was still running down to the beach on Sundays, which is about seven kilometres - and I had been doing this for about four years. My fastest time, incidentally for this run - over a period of six years - was on Christmas day, when I was sixty-two years old, and had known you for five months. I suspect it was our meeting each other which was the cause.

The relevance of all this to us, is that my growing fatigue seems to be changing my outlook on life. The Douglas you met then, was a different person from what I am now. Whatever one's style of life, a man probably changes as much between the ages of 62 and 71 as he did between the ages of 17 and 26, whereas people do not usually change much between the age you were when we first met (36) and your age now (45).

Dearest Wimsey

Thank you for our lovely swim in the morning. I wonder how long the calm seas will last. It is a pity for me it cannot be a year-round experience. But perhaps I appreciate it more for this reason. One day you must show me what to 'do' with a wave. Much love – Puss

Dear Wimsey

When we first met, I asked you to tell N. that we were lovers and you did so - without hesitation. Why is it so difficult now - to be open about our love - when we are so much further down the road? After our 'kissing' meditation when we lay together today, I felt such peace, but when we started to dissect and analyse – the pain returned. Surely there is a secret here. Perhaps we should simply 'be'. Much love – Puss

Dear one

Let us sing on Sunday if possible. It would be nice to start the year with a song. Much love - Puss

**

Our society seems to be based on people doing what they want when they are young i.e. they fall in love and marry, and then for the rest of their lives, they suffer for it. Why not apply the principle that when you are young you follow your heart, and when you are old, you also follow your heart (as I do). It makes far more sense to me.

Where there is fear and deception, there cannot be peace of mind. How can one drink lemonade happily when one has tasted champagne? The person before and after is not the same person. To look back - having embarked upon a course of action - is fatal. Remember Lot's wife (in the Old Testament) who looked back – and was turned into a pillar of salt.

For my part (as you know), I always advocate being open, because in that way there are no lingering regrets. Everyone knows the true situation and can judge accordingly what is best to do. We are all of us adults, and should live according to our inner light. The pity of marriage (and subsequent children and acquisition of material possessions), is that it snuffs out this light very early, in most cases. Love happens before the light is so 'snuffed'. All my love – Puss

Dear Douglas

Bhagwan left his body three years ago yesterday and there was a celebration last night. I knelt outside your window afterwards in the darkness, feeling very bridal – all dressed in white. I wish you had been awake. You are rarely out of my thoughts.

Dearest Wim

If I do not materialise on the morrow (at the beach), know that *je t'aime* nevertheless. If you do not appear, I shall assume you adore me also ! Much love – Puss

Douglas

I believe you have a number of serious psychological problems, which preclude having an intimate relationship with a woman – which is healthy and whole.

In view of your avoidance of me after moments of intimacy - coupled with your eternal criticism of my behaviour - I can't see any point in any further contact in the flesh, unless you are prepared to work on some of your difficulties viz.

- your dual personality – waxing hot then cold in your moods
- your inability to sustain intimacy – which is often followed by abandonment
- your inability to resolve conflict e.g. it is always me, who has to heal the wounds - admitting error seems to be anathema to you
- your ambivalence towards making love – in healthy relationships, either partner should be able to take the initiative, without being condemned – you seem to exalt love-making one day and condemn it the next as beneath you
- your inability to commit yourself totally to anyone i.e. to surrender
- your judgmental attitude towards others and high level of expectation
- your inability to care for others in times of distress, because of your own fear of weakness - you abandon people in need, where the healthy response is to comfort
- your inability to love yourself
- your disappointment with your children - which is related to your impossible expectations of them

Full moon

Have just been up to your house - walking on the grass and watching you walk up the stairs. Almost tapped on the window. Wish that I had. Threw some bougainvillea flowers onto the landing outside your study. You will find them in the morning. Wondering what on earth you are doing there - when I am here and vice versa. We should be together.

Dearest Douglas

I read the article on cultural blocs and agree absolutely. Each culture is based upon a certain religious ethic and it is this, I believe, that is the most powerful emotive force that separates us from others. The beauty of mysticism for me is that it reflects the essential sameness in each religious tradition and beyond.

The mystical traditions of Islam, Buddhism, Hinduism, Taoism (China), Judaism and Christianity are the same (from an experiential viewpoint). This is the only way individuals will ever be able to relate to those from other blocs - by experiencing an understanding which goes beyond culture and words. Much love

Dearest

You left several minutes ago, and already I can feel my longing for you. Yet it is sweet. We had such fun today. If ever you were to depart from my life, as indeed one of us must depart from the other, I do not think that anything less than 'god' would satisfy.

Without you - all seems without meaning, or rather you give meaning to everything. Perhaps you are 'god' in disguise and one day you will reveal your secret to me?

I wish I could write in French, but it is too soon after the 'event' for such concentration. I prefer to bask in the '*reaction agréable*' (afterglow).

Darling – merci, merci, merci

After you left, I kissed the pillow where we had lain and felt so deeply that whatever transpired between us is so wonderful that I cannot imagine ever being without you or how we could ever live without each other. Sometimes I think it is better that we don't ever recover from our loss (of each other), as the grief could lead to a total transformation. *A bientôt* – Puss

Dear Douglas

Last evening I went to a 'gay' dance with a group of friends. As you know my friend T. organises a show every month to raise funds for victims of AIDS. I enjoyed the occasion greatly.

The dancing was interspersed with two stage shows which were a parody of the members of the English royal family. The gay couples looked very happy, though it took a while to accustom myself to the sight of two women dancing closely together and men likewise - and cuddling in the same way as heterosexual (straight) couples.

What surprised me was that each person I encountered was pleasant and friendly, which does not usually happen in a group of strangers. I think they assumed because I was there, I was accepting of them and we therefore had something in common. In love – Shobha

My dear Puss

A rushed note in reply to the first of your *belles lettres* (beautiful letters). It occurred to me for the first time that the distinguishing feature of artistry in writing, music and painting is that one returns to whatever it is - either Austen's novel *Pride and Prejudice,* Mozart's opera *The Magic Flute* or Constable's painting *Haywain* - with pleasure - despite having read, heard or seen it before.

The appetite grows with what it feeds upon. But it does not explain what it is which causes the pleasure, so that we wish to revisit them.

When I bring this note round to your home, I will smuggle out two of the pink roses I mentioned to you. If I fail, it will be because N. is reading on the terrace.

Don't hesitate to discuss matters with me regarding the university, if it helps to simply ventilate ideas. *Je te sens* - I feel you

Douglas

In the ABC programme '*J'accuse*' (I accuse), which made you angry - author *Fay Weldon's* role was to analyse, dissect, critique and destroy. She tempered her accusations with many ideas that support Jane's work. Did you expect unadulterated praise? Although Jane Austen has become one of our particularly sweet areas of conversation - I do not worship her as a goddess.

I am mortally wounded at times when people criticise Bhagwan, as you have occasionally 'dared' to do. Perhaps it is the same with 'your' Jane? This is one of the indications of love perhaps? If someone criticises 'you' to me, however true and realistic that criticism might be - I would defend you to the end. I found the treatment of Jane interesting and there was nothing abhorrent. A new slant on a well-known author is to me, quite healthy. To see Jane as a more real creature through her letters to her sister Cassandra - does not spoil her novels. It enhances them.

It is ridiculous to expect to agree with an author in all respects. Jane comments on society's foibles. Do we also expect her to care about slavery and the poor etc? How can she - when they are beyond her experience?

I don't find Fay Weldon a particularly attractive personality, but there was much said in favour of Jane, and I found many of the observations were similar to my own, and for this reason, quite reassuring. I do not have to accept Jane hook, line and sinker to enjoy her books. I 'do' have to accept Bhagwan hook, line and sinker, in order to love him.

Weldon remarked at one point that Jane's parents were not necessarily good to her. This may be a sore point with you at present - in view of your difficulties with your son. I hope you are not too upset by the programme. One hates to see the object of one's love dethroned - if only for a moment.

On the subject of heroes being dethroned - before I went to India, I became interested in the writings of the 'enlightened' master *Ramana Maharshi*, who came to me in a dream, and said 'Bhagwan is now going to be your teacher'.

At that time I had not yet heard of Bhagwan - who as you know, was the last step in my exploration of alternative philosophies, and thereafter - no spiritual teachers have had any influence upon my understanding.

Sleep well, my love. Your roses are so wonderful – most of all because they have come from you. I shall wake to the sight of them. When you water your rose bush *chez toi* (at your house) - think of me. Puss

Dearest

I am becoming more like you each day. I walked out of the opera last night, and have just returned home. I'm not sorry I went, as I like to assess the quality of a performance, but I found it rather hard to listen, as the soprano's voice was strident and mediocre, with too much of a waver in it. Her top notes were excellent and powerful, but her lower register was not.

She looked far too old for the part of Madam Butterfly who is supposed to be fifteen or thereabouts, and her head-dress made this more apparent - though she moved lithely enough on stage. If her voice had been adequate, the age would not have mattered.

The tenor (Pinkerton) had a wonderful voice for the most part, except the top notes were a trifle weak, but he looked like an Australian footballer and acted like one. When he approached Butterfly, you felt he was dying to get his greasy paws on her as quickly as possible. He wore white trousers and a shirt with braces, which made him look more like a construction worker or a painter than an American naval officer.

What distressed me was the plot itself. Butterfly renounced her Buddhist faith for the bastard, who later marries another woman in England and returns to Japan to take Butterfly's child back with him. And her Buddhist relatives reject her, because of her 'mock' marriage - so there is double trouble and she is left isolated – hence, her suicide.

Pinkerton (before his marriage to Butterfly) talks of 'playing games' and Butterfly being like a 'doll'. Despite the odd aria where he professes poetic love, he was totally unconvincing as a lover, and every time he touched her, I felt ill - because she was so simple and trusting. I could not detect, except in Suzuki (Butterfly's servant), any fine gestures or meaningful glances. It should had been called *The Rape of the Innocent.* So all in all, my dearest of loves, grand-kisser-in-the-park and light-of-my-existence, it was a rapid and disappointing experience. I am sincerely glad to be home.

Because of my exposure to your opera tapes and videos, I now seem to be capable of making intelligent judgments about the standard of a performance, or perhaps 'those who can't, simply criticise' - but I doubt it. It is more true that those who have tried (such as myself), who find it extremely difficult to sing perfectly, can still appreciate excellence and cannot tolerate mediocrity.

Dear warm creature - you looked so lovely in the park. You are so dear to me. All my love

Light-of-my-loins and love-of-my-life

It almost seems criminal to return to my world of work after lying with you. Such different worlds. When I walked into the garden at the university this evening, I again felt transported, and was so struck by the beauty of the trees and the heavy dew in the atmosphere that I could not move. A little touch of heaven. Being with you today was so heartwarming. We are such lucky children to have each other and be able to curl up together so lovingly.

There was a programme this evening which maintained that seventy percent of Australian women were iron-deficient. Perhaps this is why there has been an improvement in my energy level in the last year or so, as I have been taking iron tablets for that length of time. If so, I am delighted to have hit upon a solution. Are we really just a collection of chemicals? How sad if it were so.

Will dream of you and visit on the astral plane tonight. Please be there, my love – Puss

Dear Puss

Am leaving you four avocados from my tree. Yesterday was delightful in spite of time constraints. Have often wondered how you adjust when you return to your desk and have to apply yourself to matters practical. But in fact, much the same is often true of me.

Dear Douglas

It must be wonderful in life to excel in a sphere one loves, instead of trying to do one's best in a field in which one has only marginal interest - such as administration (in which I am at present engaged). Perhaps then it would not matter if one was loved or not, and one could be simply happy doing what one felt one must (so many 'ones' in this sentence). I hope that joyful day comes - before I leave this planet. You have reached your peak of excellence in so many fields. It ought to make you feel contented. I would like to sing a song perfectly or write the perfect poem, but alas, I must console myself by loving the perfect love, or perhaps I should say the perfect lover (at times). I love you with all my heart.

Ramana Maharshi

Dear Douglas

Could you bring your recording of Verdi's *Requiem* when you next come (even if we don't have the opportunity to listen to it) and the accompaniment for *Star of Eve*** which I made recently, for your song?

Re surfing the waves – I am tired of coming home from the beach crying because I have let you down. It would be best if you assumed I never wanted to swim out to sea, and then if I did, it would be a pleasant surprise. You looked rather courageous in the sea this morning - as you came in.

*** Aria from *Tannhauser* (opera by Richard Wagner) which Douglas was learning.

Dear Puss

The surgeon said it will probably take me a while to recover from the cataract operation. No swimming for two weeks. No running or making love for at least three weeks (joke). You were very 'gay' yesterday and on the phone this morning.

Douglas

I do not for one moment think your physical problems are connected with age. They may however, be connected with stubbornness, obstinacy, obsession with work, refusal to relax, refusal to face your emotional problems, inability to resolve your relationship with your son etc.

I know my words fall on deaf ears. I know you far better than you know yourself. Nothing short of a transformation will help you. You cannot live in fear forever.

I don't believe that age has affected you to the extent you maintain. I do believe our triangular situation may have depleted your energy resources. Your concept of a friend or lover may be different to mine.

For your edification - my concept of a lover is someone :

- who cares for me when I am sick, tired, sad, depressed, tearful or in despair
- who can comfort and hold me and let me cry until the sadness has passed
- who can hold hands, cuddle, kiss and make love as acts of intimacy and sharing
- with whom I can share ideas and make plans for the future
- with whom I can share friends
- with whom I have common interests e.g. opera, poetry, swimming, writing
- with whom I can live and sleep and eat
- with whom I share a spiritual orientation to the world
- with whom I can go to the theatre, films, social activities and travel
- for whom I can long and pine and miss and want to be in constant contact with, and when there is an enforced separation, cannot wait until it is over
- with whom I feel the desire to be together a lot of the time, unless forced apart by circumstances
- with whom there is a desire to be with, through important events
- who wishes to be together - at the end

I am sure your understanding of a lover does not fit with mine. With such disparate views, how could we ever be happy? For me, love is the most important thing in the world - without which we are beggars. Anything less than adoration (for each other) is not enough !

**

Watched a programme this evening on poaching of elephants for ivory in Kenya. It was strangely moving seeing the young, orphaned elephants being cared for by a white woman, and one old female elephant adopting the orphans as her own - year after year.

What a pity one species preys upon another. If only it were possible for animals to co-exist (and humans as well), yet it seems not to be the way.

I am beginning to tire of the battle of the sexes. 'Fight' seems to be at the heart of existence itself. I wish there was no battle to be fought, just differences to be appreciated. You and I are so vastly different in many ways, and that is precisely why it works. We are born equal, but different. Is it so difficult to accept? Must away to my slumbers – see you in the morn.

**

I am mortified. I feel terrible about assailing you in the way I did - my only defence being that you trod on one of my corns, or rather laughed at one of my sacred cows. When one is angry, care for the other evaporates in the moment, because of the emotion and the hurt felt, and one is immune to the pain caused to the other.

I would not deliberately set out to injure you, but having felt attacked - I defended. Have you not heard my slogan that "I never attack – but if attacked, I slaughter."

My sacred cows by the way, are whether god exists or not (a non-question for me), whether there is continuity of life (again a non-issue), whether Bhagwan is enlightened or not (of course he is) and whether the love between a man and woman should be exclusive (yes – for me at least).

I do not believe it is possible to have two 'soulmates' or to be 'in love' with two people at the same time, though there are many types of love. Nor do I feel it appropriate to make 'love' with more than one person at a time. Nor do I feel it appropriate to live with a person if you love another.

You appear to advocate dual allegiances - one to a family of marriage, and another to the 'other woman'. Despite all our talk of advantages (for you) of not living together, you know I would never countenance loving you and your living with someone else. That we try to come to terms with it, does not make it palatable or acceptable to me.

I know deep inside that you care. There is so much in your behaviour to indicate this. What we share is so special that I feel no-one else has ever loved as we love. Every true lover probably feels this way. The thought of sharing you at the deeper level with anyone else, is simply not possible.

We are a kind of unit together - despite the absence of a legal tie and the fact that we do not cohabit. I would support cohabitation, but not marriage, because it is meaningless for lovers. The most precious, ethereal, mystical, fragile nature of love makes a formal contract unthinkable. Where would the mystery lie - if it was neatly packaged and served up every day predictably. There is nothing that grieves me more on this planet than to be out of rapport with you - and to be in harmony with you, makes all other wishes seem trivial.

Dear Douglas

I know this is a hard time for you – waiting and wondering what will happen (with your son). I wish so much that I could help, but know I cannot. I hope you find an opportunity to speak with him alone. Pride in such matters is fatal. I always maintained contact with my parents, even when I knew they were wrong in the way they treated me, but I am not sorry I took this approach.

Dearest

I have found a lovely poem of Robert Browning :

> God be thanked
> The meanest of his creatures
> boasts two soul-sides
>
> One to face the world with (and)
> one to show a woman
> when he loves her

How true.

Darling

I am wondering whether you have yet passed on Anthony Storr's books *Churchill's Black Dog* and *Solitude*** to your son. Given his interest in the Swiss psychoanalyst Carl Jung - he might find them interesting as the basis for some future dialogue with you.

Hamlet is commencing next week on radio with Kenneth Branagh as Hamlet, Judi Dench as Gertrude, John Gielgud as Priam and Reginald Briers as Polonius. It is being hailed by critics as a marvellous performance. I am beginning to feel that Shakespeare should be listened to - as with opera - rather than watched. Much love for the morrow – Puss

> ** *Churchill's Black Dog* is a study of depression by British psychiatrist Anthony Storr, who also stressed the importance of solitude - for children.

Dear Puss

Am genuinely sorry if I offended you by my silly story about a veto on making love. Our phone conversation this morning made me so expectant that I would have brought flowers with me when we met at lunchtime, had I not been rushed for time. Though perhaps it's just as well I didn't, since it might have seemed to you an unseemly show of confidence.

At the moment, my son is out walking with N. In course of time I expect a thaw of some sort will happen (between us). When he called to pick up N., I gave him a few articles from his 'file', which I had collected over the last eight months. I also gave him a copy of Storr's *Solitude*. Much love

Dearest Wimsey

It seems as if your son has seen the 'light'. Any communication at all – no matter what it is - will be good at present. Things seems to be progressing splendidly on their own. I don't think it matters right now whether he talks to you or N. People sometimes circumnavigate before they make their real advance - in this case, towards you.

I am curious however, as to how N. is taking his approaches and what is transpiring between them. I do hope he appreciates Storr. When you visit me in the evening and we lie in the soft light together, there is a kind of magic in the air. Much love – Puss

Dearest Duggles

Have just returned from seeing the film *Enchanted April*. It was pure 'enchantment' with a theme similar in some respects, to E.M. Forster's *Passage to India* viz. English women - bewitched by the effect of being in another culture and climate - are changed forever. I found the same idea in an Agatha Christie novel *Absent in the Spring* written under her pseudonym Mary Westmacott. An English woman went on a journey in the Arabian desert and found her 'other' side i.e. discovered herself, as it were, but then returned to England, but was unable to sustain the change.

The play and film *Shirley Valentine* (of some repute) addressed the same idea – English woman (working class this time) goes to Greece and does not wish to return to her humdrum marriage.

In *Enchanted April*, there were four English women renting a villa in Tuscany, and two eventually asked their husbands to join them. Due to the effect of the Italian sun and idyllic surrounds, they all fall in love with each other once again, which is a nice touch.

It is no wonder the British flock to the continent in the icy season to find their souls. Cold can really chill the heart. Joan Plowright was quite brilliant as the aged, eccentric, unloved English lady who softened in the end. An adult fairytale.

I have often said to friends to "Beware of me, because if you are in an unhappy relationship, it will end, and if you are not in a relationship and wish to be, you will fall in love." And so often, it happens. I can feel it in the wind.

Your son also - as a consequence of his altercation with yourself and N. and his own 'search' - talks of 'falling in love' for the first time.

It has been said that it is not possible to truly 'fall' in love if one did not love one's parents, and the mother - in particular. 'The sins of the fathers are visited on the children'.

All parents seem to suffer tremendously. I know my mother did on my behalf, but that is now past. It will be a great gift for me, to be able to be with my mother, when the time comes for her to leave this planet - with no feelings of bitterness or regret. Must away – may see you on the morrow – Puss

Dear Puss

Have left some carnations on your verandah. Could not find your key. Yesterday was a delightful mix of hymen and hymns. Who would believe us - if told? Much love

Dearest of all possible Wimseys

The trees are greener today. Your blooms gladdened the heart. How easily we come to count upon these treasures. I am not so sure about the hymen – unless by that you mean that you were a 'high' man at the time (joke). I always feel I can't bear to separate from you 'afterwards'. It is so terribly warm and it feels like sacrilege to part. The hymen and hymns are to my mind, inextricably linked in that making love is for me - the peak. I find myself singing the hymns (we have been practising), throughout the week, and sometimes I find myself hoping no-one will hear me.

Years ago I used to feel slightly embarrassed in public carrying a bible on Sunday to church, because it would be thought I was overly religious. My mother was afraid I might suffer from religious mania, which plagued one of her friends. Dearest love, thank you for so very much. Puss

Dear Douglas

Sorry about the tears, though perhaps sorry is not the right word. When I am at work and busy, it is necessary to play a role and to hide feelings. But when I am with you, because you bring out the deeper part of me, I feel I can be myself, and hence the tears. When I returned to work, I was quite desolate, because I felt I had disappointed you in some way. It required two bars of chocolate (my dopamine fix) and three cups of coffee – to feel whole again.

When I don't go swimming in the early morning during the week, a very mild malaise is there. A kind of irritation – a feeling there is more to experience. Being inside all day in my new position (at work), it could be even more important now, to be active first thing in the day.

Forgive me if I annoy you. You are so dear to me, but now and again I cannot give you the riches of my heart because I am not myself. The old adage that 'cleanliness is next to godliness' should be altered to 'breath is next to godliness'. When we aerate our lungs, as at the beach - we aerate our lives as well. This was also Bhagwan's philosophy, (as he was a long-distance athlete and swimmer), hence his very active dynamic meditations. An un-aerated Puss

Wimsey

Have been having the weirdest dreams. Last night you and I were stranded in the middle of the river near the hill, where we sometimes meet. Our craft overturned and we were forced to scramble onto the hull of the boat and remain there all night in the cold. Eventually we swam to shore and I was not sure whether to call an ambulance or find a bed for us somewhere. We went to hospital at one point and I was screaming to the staff 'not to separate us', in view of the ordeal we had been through together.

Could you let me know N.'s birthday and your anniversary so I can avoid these dates on my social calendar? Years ago, I used to feel thwarted if I could not see you on these days. Now, it feels entirely sensible to keep out the way. Is this maturity – common sense – or enlightenment? Must rush – duty calls – a confused and weepy Puss

Shobha

I cannot pretend to understand why you felt as you described yesterday. But then neither can you. You speak as the helpless slave of the fluctuations in your emotions, whereas I was brought up to try to brush them off. It was good to see you at the beach this morning. The water was wonderful. I lay on my back out at sea - somewhere near where the buoy was supposed to be - and gazed up at a very bright Venus in the sky.

Dear Douglas a.k.a. Wimsey

Have just finished watching the film *The Ruling Class* featuring Peter O'Toole (my favourite actor). Terribly moving. A kind of comedy cum tragedy cum musical. The gist of the plot is that O'Toole (Jack) inherits a title from his daddy - who is an earl.

However, as a consequence of his schizophrenia, Jack believes he is Jesus, and attempts to dispense his religion of love to one and all. Quite healthy in a crazy sort of way, except that over time, he is 'cured' by a psychoanalyst and becomes a bitter, twisted psychopath.

Did you ever see *Man of La Mancha* - the musical based on the book *Don Quixote* by Cervantes - which has a similar theme? Don Quixote (O'Toole again) attacks windmills and is generally an abandoned free spirit, but his family attempts to 'cure' him. On his deathbed, he vacillates between sanity and madness, and the vultures (the family) sit by his death bed, hoping they will still benefit from his will, if he remains sane.

In the film O'Toole talks to a village woman above love, saying "Aren't you interested?" and she replies "Of course not, I'm a married woman" which I think is hilarious ! Peter is uniformly magnificent. In fact, I would say in his role as Jesus, he excels - far more than in *Lawrence of Arabia.*

The whole point being, that what we consider sanity or normality is of course, the true disease. It made me feel like going out and saving the world. If only it was possible to live truly in the present and not give a damn what anyone else does or thinks, and just follow the path of the heart and one's inner convictions.

You were very sweet today. Your pinkness (or is it pinkiness) in bed is very appealing. Sometimes it feels like a haven from the world, yet oddly enough we discuss the very same world while we are together. Much love – Puss

Dear Puss - Shobha's birthday

Am so sorry you were upset by my seeming failure this morning to wish you 'many happy returns'. I have yet another reference book for you - as a small present. A trifle dull perhaps ? But I have always tried to give you books that last. If you would really prefer frilly panties or some such, we could go to some appropriate boutique later in the week. Am thinking of your smiling face when you called - after swimming at the beach.

Dear Douglas

Have been watching a film based on William Golding's book - *Lord of the Flies*. A little frightening. To be Ralph (the main character) and find oneself at odds with the rest of the mob of children (in an isolated situation), would be an horrific experience. How sad that he was forced to be aligned with those who were either young or weak and did not know any better - a poor-sighted, simple fellow whom everybody ridiculed.

There are so many situations for children, particularly boys I believe - where they are tortured in so many ways by their schoolmates. I wonder about the differences in the socialisation of boys and girls. I feel it is far easier to be female.

Women are expected to be pretty, lovable, gentle, soft and emotional (albeit compliant), whereas boys are expected to be tough, competitive, aggressive, greedy, mean and unkind to those who are not so strong. How sad. Admittedly there are some not very nice girls and some gentler souls among boys, but these could be the exception - rather than the rule.

I am glad to be female, and able to give full licence to all that is beautiful and good. I am so glad that you are a 'gentle' man and not a typically aggressive, competitive type, though I recognise both elements are present within you to some degree. If women could be assertive and men gentle, all would be well.

Would love to see you tomorrow, body permitting, or even body not permitting. Much love – Puss

Dearest Puss

You always look at your most beautiful when we make love. Today especially. A combination of joy and serenity that never ceases to surprise me, and which makes me feel unworthy of you.

Am off to the university to photocopy my son's review of Golding's *Lord of the Flies,* which was written when he was very, very young. He is at present out walking with N. - the third meeting since he apologised to her for having written two offensive letters. By implication – it was justifiable to 'offend' me. An odd business - in view of all this nonsense about being unloved as a child. Much love – Douglas

Dearest and loveliest of bedmates

Today was such fun. Making love on the run has its own joys. Your flowers startled me when I arrived *a casa* (at my home). Somehow I did not expect them so 'soon'. Your letter gladdened the cockles of my heart yet again. We are wonderful – aren't we?

Dear Puss

A cold, but beautiful, morning. A full moon quite high in the sky down at the beach and a sea congenial for swimming. Like another world. As it was only five degrees Celsius, there were very few people down there and even fewer swimming.

Sweetest Wimsey

Am feeling strangely discontented and missing you very much. Perhaps it is the thought of you going to the other side of Australia with N., though I know it is important to see your eldest son. Somehow I wish it was you and I who were going; that we too could embark upon some major endeavour together and leave the world behind.

Last evening I stopped outside your house and a very yellow moon rose from the horizon on the other side of the river. Quite spell-binding.

Wish we could always be as one, as we were yesterday. I tire so of mediocrity. I am beginning to feel one should live life to the hilt, and not care about the future, or plan for when one is older. Far better to go with a bang – never a whimper. There is nobility in that.

Yet one must pursue one's enthusiasms, otherwise life is without substance or meaning. I wish we were able to pursue our enthusiasms together, without interference. Perhaps one day we shall be free. It is my prayer. Much love – Puss

Douglas

If truth be told - what you are really objecting to - with regard to our behaviour on Sunday, is that love-making occurred as a consequence of what you perceive as my longing, rather than an overflowing in both of us – one being a natural bubbling over, and the other a rather strained endeavour.

I agree with you that this is a great pity, and certainly I would prefer that we overflow rather than that you oblige me (as a gentleman), to prevent wounding me.

It is difficult sometimes to be 'perfect' - as you require me to be. I was not as sensitive to your feelings as I could have been, and in hindsight it is obvious that when we both come to our bed joyfully and light-heartedly, problems do not arise. I stand corrected. Judging from your behaviour after the event, I felt you were also deeply moved, but it seems I was wrong. How very sad.

Dear Puss

Your presents embarrass me by their extravagance, welcome though each of them is. I am touched by the aptness of the book by Afrikaner adventurer and author *Laurens van der Post*, given my current situation with my son. As too with the practical usefulness of the '*chariot pour mécaniciens*' – which sounds so much more impressive than a 'mechanic's creeper' (*which is used to lie on one's back while working underneath a vehicle).*

Yesterday afternoon was very pleasant. I sensed in some way, a Shobha I had not met before, almost as if you had decided after reflection - on a new role. Was this entirely fanciful on my part? In saying this, I take it for granted that roles govern much more of our behaviour than is commonly recognised. Much love

Dear Shobha

Your inveterate opposition of heart and mind is a false antithesis.

If 'mind' is taken to mean the disposition to look for descriptive uniformities or tendencies in the phenomena which surround us, there is no field of which it can be said, the mind has no place.

This is as true of human behaviour as it is of physics or chemistry, and not the less so because - for understandable reasons - we as yet know very little of the 'chemistry' of human behaviour.

As for the 'heart', much human behaviour is governed or influenced by emotions and attitudes, such as – without trying to be exhaustive – affection, lust, sympathy, greed, kindness, envy, pride, jealousy, guilt, hatred and shame. We all differ in the extent to which our behavior is influenced by these various, often conflicting, emotions and attitudes.

But it is generally accepted by psychologists, that the emotional or attitudinal make-up of each individual at any one time is the result of causes - genetic and environmental - even though - in our present state of knowledge - we cannot explain what these causes are - or how they operate.

It is true that strong emotions, such as love and hate, often cloud the detached inquiring faculty of the mind. It may also be that the satisfaction from some forms of emotionally-driven behaviour, such as sexual congress - is like to be greater if the mind is not present.

But this does not support the sweeping view that the inquiring mind is out of place whenever behaviour is being driven by emotion. There is growing scientific support for the view (long recognised by the poets) that the behaviour of women tends to be more emotion-driven than that of men. *Vive la différence.*

Dearest

I would not like you to think that I am not grateful for the myriad ways in which you have extended my 'boundaries' and enriched my life since we first met. It is simply that what we have given to each other over the years is so different. It has - as I said this evening - always been my deepest wish to bring you into the heart and the soul from your dwelling place in the body and the mind - and to some extent - I believe this has happened - though the transformation is not complete.

You still 'teeter on the brink' - not of meaning - but of understanding. What you have been for me, you already know. At one extreme, you have brought me into the twentieth century in a technological sense - through computers, videos, compact discs etc., at a time when I was firmly lodged in a post-hippie Eastern mentality, which discounted the importance of possessions and material success - despite Bhagwan's attempts to move his commune in a modern and technological direction.

At the intellectual level, you have introduced me to the depths of the Western intellectual tradition - of which I was largely unaware.

At the romantic level, you have reawakened and developed my great love for opera and poetry, and this has been our common meeting-ground, far more than any other - because it is a blend of the heart and mind.

At the physical level, you have given me courage to face the deep: the great ocean - and in my limited way, to conquer it, and therefore some of my childhood fears.

Likewise, through running and rising early, you have altered my entire lifestyle, so that where once I was cautious and not adventurous, now at least in my mind, I court the idea of climbing mountains on the other side of the world and actually climbed Mount Snowdon in Wales, as a result of your inspiration.

Through you, I have come to love England deeply and now Europe holds out its promise. And through you, finally, and in the deepest possible way, I (we) have found a communion through making love, for which I always hoped, but had begun to feel would never be possible.

You say at times that you do not share my emotional or spiritual life - yet at rock bottom, I believe that it is precisely this, that binds you to me - because these are the areas in which you still feel at sea, and there is room for learning.

Just as I learn from you in all the areas with which I am unfamiliar, so too are you learning - despite yourself. We are beautifully complementary, my love, and so it should be. Yet I do not feel that you always understand yourself.

If your son advocated the mind utterly, you would probably encourage him to follow his heart. Because he advocates the heart, you encourage him to follow the mind. Talk to your child as if he were your lover. This is the only way for you - to both drop your inhibitions and be prepared to be 'as little children' together.

When two souls really understand each other, they are the same age - or rather no age at all. In order to be a friend, this is how it must be - and to be a friend to one's own child, is a miracle. Sweetest dreams, my darling . Happy birthday for tomorrow – Puss

Dear Puss

I hope the flowers will reassure you. Am reflecting on what made *All Passion Spent* so delightful - as a film. Indeed, engrossing. The lack of rush and action had much to do with it, together with a common philosophy and peace of mind shared by the three leading characters - largely because of their extreme age.

Also, there was an honest and sensible acceptance of death, without you will note, the imagined consolation of a life hereafter.

Death - properly faced (in the film) was no occasion for sorrow, but rather the natural consummation of a long life. Individuals like Scottish philosopher David Hume, who died with a smile on his face - can by example teach people how to die.

What is it but a final sleep? We always slip happily into sleep – something curiously neglected as a biological phenomenon. Much love

Sweetheart

Have just unearthed the manuscript of a 'book' I was writing some years ago called *'Kissing the Joy as it Flies – for Soulmates only'*. Do you remember it? For some reason, I feel inspired to complete it now. It is of course, a comment on the type of relationship which we share. I was surprised on reading through the opening chapter, that it reads rather well. Distance in time often gives a fresh perspective. Much love – your soulmate (Note : The manuscript was written in 1997. It is now 2017 – twenty years later).

Dear Shobha

A small gift to mark the tenth anniversary of the day I first met you and started to get to know the remarkable person you are.

My near horror of anniversaries is rather silly. In your case, it is compounded by a sense of guilt, because our anniversary reminds me, increasingly sharply as each year passes, that I have not offered you what you want and what I owe you.

You came into my life only a few months before I retired, and have enriched enormously what has turned out to be probably the period of my life in which my zest for its pleasures has been at a peak and my mind has been at its most active and free-ranging. Without you, this could not have happened. It would be a solace to think your life has also been enriched - if not in quite the same way.

Dear Douglas

Today was all an anniversary should be. Several things you said however, have made me rather reflective - even though anniversaries are for me, not occasions for reflection. I wonder what it is that you think 'I want'. I am not even sure myself - now.

There was a time when I wished to be with you totally, to travel with you, to live overseas, to write books with you, to socialise with mutual friends of our own persuasion, to dance and sing gaily when the opportunity presented itself, to meditate together etc. but these days, I don't seem to crave for anything in particular - together.

We have established a way of communicating which - while not perfect - is sufficiently nurturing and nourishing for us both to not be unhappy. This does not mean that if life changed for both of us, and we were able to share some of the above, I would object.

But I no longer see the point of desiring what is not likely - in the near future. I also do not understand why you should say that you 'owe' me something. Surely in love, there can be no talk of such things.

To love as best as one is able, given the circumstances, in sincerity and honesty - is all that can be hoped for. Yet I believe I understand what you are trying to say. I am sorry if I occasion guilt in you. I do not think that is good.

Guilt breeds resentment, and I don't wish you to resent me for wanting what you think is 'more' than what we already have. Our lunch was near perfection, though you still seem a little detached. Please stop reading Sam Johnson, as he always affects you adversely - in my opinion.

I have already read much of *A Year in Provence* (your anniversary gift) and it is tremendously entertaining, with a wonderful sense of humour. The author Peter Mayle, portrays the French as an extremely eccentric, dotty breed. I suspect I shall feel more at home with the Italians when I travel to Europe, because of their effusiveness and warmth - but only time will tell. After reading Mayle *(who describes living in France)*, it seems a pity to be a 'tourist' - but there is no alternative on one's first trip. Thereafter - one should simply 'sojourn'.

The Folio Society editions of Thomas Hardy's novels arrived on my doorstep last evening together with Robert Browning's *Pied Piper* poetry - in a miniature edition. They are beautifully bound and presented – you may like to borrow them.

Have now finished the Taylor Caldwell novel on Saint Luke entitled *Dear and Glorious Physician* - and it has moved me in mysterious ways; reminding me of my Christian youth, and my passion and intense devotion for Jesus.

I feel the same intensity of course, with Bhagwan, and miss the constant call - not to 'arms' - but to be an ambassador of 'something'. It is so much easier when one's guru is 'in the mortal coil', because there is always the prospect that one will be asked to 'go here' or 'go there' - just as the early disciples of Jesus were required to spread the gospel.

Yet how to spread Bhagwan's 'gospel' of love, celebration, laughter, dancing, singing and authenticity - except by simply being oneself - wherever one is placed.

There are too many possibilities of becoming egoistic if one sets out to be 'spiritual'. Yet sometimes I yearn for some direct spiritual contacts. I was contemplating my range of associates yesterday, and not one of them has any interest in spiritual matters. You and I discuss many things which touch on the spiritual – thankfully.

After our lunch today, I could feel the sun burning into me, combined with the effect of the champagne. It was quite delightful. You said it would give you solace to know that you had enriched my life, but can you doubt it?

I feel that lovers come together when they need to come together, for some 'higher' purpose, and that they part when that purpose has been served. I am not absolutely certain what it is that you are to teach me. I am sure you will have more idea than myself. But I do believe that I am with you to assist in the softening process, or perhaps we should call it the 'gentling' process.

Do not fear that what you say to me after making love, about my being beautiful etc. is not fully understood. I likewise often say to you before and after lovemaking that you are beautiful - more so than at any other time. We have a transforming effect upon each other, which may to some extent, account for our mutual 'beauty'. Darling - the hours creep on apace. Much love – Puss

Douglas

I shall never agree with you that it is good and desirable to quell all emotions. They are the stuff of life. They account for all the richness of human experience, without which each day would be a morbid and melancholy affair.

Dear friend

Today I met with the friend, with whom I travelled around England and Wales, and her intended husband. My first impression was of a very young man - shy, a little inhibited, who did not maintain eye contact, and was difficult to draw into conversation.

As lunch progressed, I began to wonder whether she had warned him about me, and that he felt on show or under inspection. Perhaps he knows as much about me, as I know about him - which is a great deal.

As time went on, things eased a little, but I felt disappointed because of the Australian accent (what else?), the relatively poor expression (because of you - I am used to a very 'high' standard), and the lack of content in the conversation (i.e. the absence of ideas). Perhaps I was expecting too much.

At one point he spoke 'down' to her in a patronising way which I did not like. There was absolutely no visible affection between them, and very little eye contact (again), and when there was - it did not appear very 'loving'. A pity. She is very dear to me, and I wish her the very best in life.

Perhaps that is what love is – to desire the best for another - even if it causes oneself distress. But I would dread her marrying a man who would not help her to be 'happy'. It is unthinkable that such a flower should be damaged. This man does not seem at all mature in the way I would hope, but perhaps it is too soon for me to judge. First impressions cannot always be trusted, yet intuition in my case, is generally, but not always - correct.

She confided to me yesterday that after two weeks constantly together, they were beginning to irritate each other. They have agreed to live together, but I know she would like to marry and he shows no signs of 'settling down'. I have occasionally said to her that I feel she needs an older man who will really appreciate all that she is - not a young blade, who is careless with affections and feelings.

This man appears to be a do-er i.e. only happy when occupied in activity, and not prone to contemplation. He was surrounded by friends in England, misses Europe, has only one friend in Perth, plus a few relatives, and is already a bit 'itchy'. He is looking for work, but until he finds this, will probably feel very un-homed.

I do not think he will be happy here. It is too quiet, for an outdoor, adventurous, socially-oriented person who is used to the bright lights, and crossing the English Channel to climb each weekend in Europe. From observation, I do not think his love for Helen is strong enough to justify staying here. What a pity (for me) as I will lose her companionship.

Hope you don't mind me sharing my thoughts with you. I guess I would like to see her blossom into womanhood happily, without the 'traumas' I have experienced on the way.

I do hope that you find in your eldest son (at least) something enduring, which you can share. It seems to be rare in families. Your relationship with your brothers puzzles me a little. Are you intimate with them at all in any way, or have you cut them off because they left their wives and thus merited your disapproval? I know my father ceased contact with his two brothers when he married my mother, because they had both divorced their wives.

One wonders what is the purpose of families. Perhaps compatibility is not a matter of shared biology, but shared interests and pursuits. After I returned from India - for several years - my brother, his wife and I went to folk clubs three nights a week together, and we were a happy little team. Since the folk scene has virtually disappeared from our lives, so has the unity of our threesome.

Douglas

You have two voices: two personalities: two sets of attitudes. When you are warm and gentle, you are supreme. When you are cold and acid drips from your tongue, I feel burnt in all the deepest parts of my psyche - and it is ugly.

With all the caring and compassion lavished upon you by N. when you are ill or tired, has it never occurred to you to comfort me, when I am in need of care? I cannot believe you are so heartless that you do not even know when I am ill. You simply believe it is not the case, and say I am pretending. Is there nothing you can do to help me?

You have someone who dotes on you day and night. Cannot you also extend yourself for me occasionally? I am so weary, and tired of fighting. Why is it so natural for women to care, and for men to run away when they are needed? I need you to comfort me.

> Let's contend no more, love
> strive nor weep.
> All be as before, love
> only sleep.
>
> *Robert Browning*

Dear Puss

I attach a copy of your anniversary letter to me. It is one of the finest I've had from you – characteristically generous and in your best flowing style.

Dearest love

I love you with all my heart and soul, and after holding and being held by you today, I love you a thousand times more. You kissed me with such rapture. We live and breathe for each other.

Dearest, I do not myself believe your time on this planet is as limited as you say, but if it was to be so, then every day and minute is precious. Life without you is inconceivable. I only hope my body disappears when yours shuffles off. I have no other dream. Love is all. As Elizabeth Barrett Browning expresses it -

> How do I love thee?
> Let me count the ways.
> I love thee to the depth and breadth and height
> my soul can reach.
> I love thee with the breath, smiles, tears
> of all my life,
> and if god choose,
> I shall but love thee better
> after death.

Douglas

You would be amazed at how contented I become when I know I am seeing you 'on the morrow', rather than facing the eternal void. Perhaps there is a secret in this, and you might find I am more reasonable if we always have times to 'look forward to' in the future.

I agree I was one tornado of discontent last evening, but I cannot agree I should have been otherwise. As you know, it is my firm belief and experience that if anger is felt, but not expressed, it becomes even more poisonous at a later date. Your son's anger is also, despite appearances - a step towards wholeness, for him.

Nevertheless, I was heartened when you rang this morning. Please dearest – let me cry. There is no greater gift you could give than to simply allow my tears when they happen. If I could, and you were able, I would be there for you if you wished to cry - but we both know this will never happen. Much love – Shobha

Dearest dolphin-mate

I love to see you underwater and play with you. Often wish we were alone at sea. Could then take far more liberties than I do at present.

The advent of Christmas (no pun intended), even though it is two months away, always makes me wistful. I long for the impossible, and wish I could make it all happen.

We must do some singing over the Christmas break. I will obtain the music for the musical *Hair*. Some of the songs are great fun e.g. *Good morning Starshine* and *This is the Dawning of the Age of Aquarius*.

Helen is leaving England in November and returning to Australia on Christmas day - after a month in India and several weeks in Thailand. Her mother is troubled about her travelling in India alone. I must say, I would not enjoy the experience - particularly from the health point of view. If she picked up hepatitis, it is impossible to travel, because it is debilitating and contagious, and there would be no-one to care for her.

Shobha's note to 'god'

>Help me to be true to my own light
>Only when I am strong is there any possibility of growth
>Let me not give way to doubt but always be courageous
>If you are with me, I cannot fail
>Whatever happens will be for the best
>Help me to trust in you and my own strength
>Give me energy - for I am weak at present
>I need your guidance
>Care for Douglas

Shobha's prayer

Dear god - please let Douglas come to my door in his pyjamas.

Dear Douglas

It was so good to see you today, albeit for a short time. Your timing was impeccable.

After talking to my brother last evening for about an hour, he told me that I did not like 'confrontation'. By this, he meant confrontation of ideas - rather than emotional confrontation. I found this surprising, as when you and I talk, we are (almost) always on opposite sides of the fence. But we do not usually get emotional about it.

O for the peaceful life - and yet I would not like a day to pass me by, without there being stimulation of some kind, or a little challenge, or something new happening. The possibility of one day succeeding another without any variation or growth is anathema to me. What say you? Much love – Shobha

**

Am itching to clear my house of non-essentials. Do you ever feel such an urge? It is as if - having been through a crisis of some kind, it seems important to reduce one's life to what is absolutely significant, and to ignore the rest. If you were to choose two books to take with you to a desert island, you might take Jane (Austen) and Sam (Johnson).

I would of course take a book of Bhagwan, and probably *The Prophet* of Kahlil Gibran. Sometimes I feel that is enough - and all other literature is worthless by comparison. I would of course, take 'you' with me to the island - in case I became bored with spiritual matters. Sleep well – may see you on the morrow – goddess willing. I will be 'receiving' at noon, if you care to drop by.

Dear Shobha

You were wise not to come down to the beach this morning. A strong southerly made running a trial, and ruled out swimming to the buoy - except for a few brave souls.

Relations are still very strained here, so much so that neither N. or I had anything to eat yesterday. This has happened once or twice before, after an explosive argument. Possibly through lack of food, I am feeling very weary today. Or it may be because of quarrelling with N. She - for her part - becomes much more affected.

Your two little books (on Jane Austen) are delightful. Have read quite a few of the Austen letters, which I have not come across before. They show - as perhaps one would expect - that her letter writing is looser, freer and more colloquial than the prose of her novels.

One interesting point that emerges, is that the facility and apparent ease of James Boswell's** writing style, was often achieved only after much re-drafting and revision, illustrating the maxim 'hard writing makes easy reading' – and the reverse. Shall be in touch. The beach should be more inviting tomorrow.

   **   *James Boswell* : biographer of English writer and moralist Samuel Johnson

Dearest

Have just finished watching a programme on the Australian musical group *The Seekers* and their reunion tour. They sang together as you know, twenty-five years ago, and came together again years later, for a world tour. Their songs are full of joy and exuberance. When I was a folksinger in my youth, they had a profound impact upon my life. I have never since known a group which expressed such happiness.

A poem for you -

>when i ail
>you touch my fevered brow
>all heat expires
>
>when i weep
>you embrace me as my sobs increase
>and then subside
>
>you are the treasure of my heart
>and in your absence
>i am less than whole
>
>but in your presence
>we are one

Douglas

What shall we two do? I am dying from a broken heart and feel as if I am in a vice, and the blood is slowly being squeezed from me. I assume your suffering is equal to mine.

Wimsey - my little teddy bear, is looking rather shabby from being hugged too much. I think that you would rather die, than give an inch. How about a centimetre?

••

I enjoyed our swim this morning - though the heat is difficult to handle. The best way to cope with the heat seems to be to keep active.

Someone said to me several days ago that people become tired when they do not have enough to do. Do you think there could be any truth in this? Perhaps it happens when there is nothing particularly urgent that needs to be done.

I attempted to read the three novels you lent me, but the only one I could continue with was the one by Nevil Shute - and even that is not 'English' enough for me. I have become a purist.

When I mentioned detective novels, I was thinking only of Dorothy Sayers and Agatha Christie. There are very few other authors in the genre whom I can accept.

I believe it is not the detective novel *per se,* but the style of the authors that is appealing i.e. couched in *olde-worlde* English and located in a traditional English setting.

Darling – miss you a little. Wish I had a friend with whom to engage in happy activities. Those who are in 'couples' can do so much more together. I feel a little confined. I would so much like to watch the sunset these hot evenings and it would be pleasant to stroll with you by the sea.

Darling

My soul is restless. Christmas makes me aware how separated I am from my 'spiritual' community and all it represents.

Following upon my letter to you of several days ago, I have decided to focus upon my favourite mystical poets, and imbibe and devour their verse, so my own latent poetic ability might flower once again.

The workaday world does not encourage one to be poetic. It is too rough. There is so much to be done in the workplace - and without delay. It is not conducive to reflection.

Dear love - as you have chosen Jane Austen and Sam Johnson as your inspiration in literature and philosophy, I am also beginning to realise it is better to focus and dive deeply rather than scattering one's energies. Just as it is better to love one woman totally - than to love many superficially (hint?).

My choice of poets would be *Kahlil Gibran, Rabindranath Tagore* and the Indian mystic *Kabir* together with the Sufi poet *Jalaluddin Rumi*. You probably do not know of Rumi and Kabir. Theirs is the ecstatic love poetry of the mystics.

There was also a female mystic (a rarity) called *Meera*** whose bhajans (songs of devotion) are worshipped throughout India. Her songs or prayers were to the 'god' Krishna and are sublime.

When I was in India I obtained translations of her songs and was inspired by them. I also went to a film in Hindi on her life - which included her songs. There are so few women who write and sing in this way.

In her worldly life, Meera was a princess who renounced her husband for 'god' and danced through the forest and in the temples. Crowds followed her and sat at her feet. She is an historic figure.

If I had a dream, that would be it - to sing and dance in such a way - and by so doing, to plant a little love in the hearts of others.

It is very important in order to be creative, to cut oneself off from others by going somewhere, even if only for a short while, so that all one's ties are severed, which enables 'one' to enter a slightly altered state.

For me, dancing, singing and poetry are all capable of producing such ecstasy. I waffle on - my love. Will retire now to my cot - Shobha a.k.a. Meera

Meera (also known as Mirabhai)

Meera by Giri Raj (traditional depiction)
sixteenth century mystic, poet, singer and devotee of Krishna
the principal Hindu deity
who has been worshipped in India since 400 BCE

Chapter 12

Love
knows not
its own depth
until the hour of separation

28

Darling

It was so terribly kind of you to call this morning. Just what the doctor ordered. Thank you from the bottom of my heart. You looked rather nice in your gown. I had the sudden feeling that I wished you were 'mine' - in the sense of seeing you each day at that hour - as you were then.

My sweetest love

Je suis désolé (I am sorry) that I was not home when you called. The roses are the most beautiful shade. The question of 'indulging' your talk should not arise, because as far as I am concerned, I usually have infinite time to speak with you, unless I must return to work. The limitations you feel, may be because 'you' do not have much time because of other constraints.

It is probable we are both terrified of not being able to get our point across in the time available, so the other is waiting in the wings, with the next point to be discussed. On days like yesterday, we both seem to grow an inch or two in understanding, and it is very satisfying. I really do feel that adversity tests the bond between two people such as ourselves. I suppose the secret lies in attempting to understand what the other feels.

Dear Douglas

I was pointing out to my friend M. this evening, that when one enters the research field as she is about to do, it is perfectly reasonable these days, technically speaking, to contact anyone anywhere in the world, who is an expert in one's chosen field. Most students think this is out of the question, but the world is so small these days, it is possible to contact anyone at almost any time. Completing a higher degree gives a kind of standing which should encourage students to liaise with those who have made it to the top. It is time to rub shoulders with the truly great. I wish I could help her in some way. Research can be a lonely exercise.

I have been reading Bhagwan, who reminds me that all desire is futile and brings frustration. This is the basic Buddhist premise, of course. Bhagwan went on to add however, that we *have* to desire - in order to know desire is futile. Changing one's lot in life may not bring happiness - but through it, we learn that changing one's lot does not bring happiness. A bit deep for the midnight hour - is it not?

Sweetheart, you are so kind to me in so many ways. Apart from being your soulmate, there does not seem to be anything practical I can do for you. Is it enough for me to be there for you, as a heart and soul and mind, when you need a friend? Apparently one of the meanings of the Sanskrit name 'Shobha' is 'ornament" (as well as grace, elegance, grandeur and splendour – take your pick!). Can I ornament your life for you? I am getting silly as the hour creeps on apace. May sleep come soon. Perhaps I should go for a jog or dance? *Jusqu'à demain (*until tomorrow*)* - Puss

**

Herewith the film of *Maurice,* which is based on the novel by E.M. Forster, and concerns two boarding school friends who discover they are both gay. One hides the fact and marries to cover his tracks. The other does not. I hope you find it as unsettling as I did. The phrase 'to love and not to count the cost' springs to mind.

The choice seems always to be whether to maintain the status quo or to have the courage to follow our hearts. The body and heart can be so closely intertwined. I follow my heart in loving you, but it is a perilous journey and I often lose the way. The union of our bodies from time to time helps me to bear that journey more easily. *Bon soir – dors-tu bien* (Goodnight – sleep well)

Douglas

Have just watched a programme called *Madness*. It is distressing to realise most psychiatrists know no more now, than they did years ago - about the causes of mental illness. Much of such illness - I believe – is spiritually-based.

Those who marry in our society for example, and have their 2.5 children, two cars, a boat, two-storey homes, go to the best schools, enjoy fine dining and holidays abroad on a regular basis, may not be so distressed. Illness may take place when people don't fit the mould of those around them - by dint of personality or circumstances, or do not have any of these so-called 'advantages' – and may become isolated.

It is, as you have often said - only when one thinks the grass is greener, or has a taste of greener grass - thus giving substance to one's hope - illness might occur.

Illness of a psychological kind, may of course be the precursor to some adaptive, creative and wonderful change. As the psychiatrist *Anthony Storr* has said - creative geniuses suffer at times (which is fairly obvious). I personally feel most mental illness can be cured or helped with love and a sense of belonging and purpose - though where there are genetic factors, brain damage or biochemical disturbance - this would probably not be the case.

Faith in 'god' or something beyond oneself (of a benevolent nature), and the actual human touch of a person who loves you - are in my opinion, the strongest forces that exist to restore a person to equilibrium - but that equilibrium may not be the same for us all.

One can become adjusted to a 'higher' level of appreciation. Imagine being adjusted to the Australian way of life, where crowds can become drunken and unruly after a public event and inflict themselves on others. Yet no-one would dream of saying these people are mentally ill. It is almost accepted as normal Australian behaviour. What an indictment !

Will see you in the morning - goddess willing. I miss you very much. Perhaps it is the moon? Puss

Dear Puss

I hope you will not find my little gift inappropriate. A book of the commonest fish on 'our' reef. As you will see, the main distinguishing features, apart from colour and size, are the location and shape of the tail and fins. One of these days, we must get hold of masks and snorkels.

Ce n'est pas seulement le main que tu veux toucher dans la mer
(It's not just the hand you want to touch in the sea)

> Sweetest Puss, I do not goe
> for wearinesse of thee.
> Nor in hope the world can show
> a fitter Love for mee
>
> *John Donne (adapted)*

Am still bemused by yesterday. It was both perfect and yet surprising that we were able to be together in such a natural and beautiful way. Could it possibly be that reading Donne had a liberating effect? If so, I must read more.

I am in bad odour with N. Witness her removing your phone number from automatic dialling on my study phone. Am surprised she knew how to tinker with it. She realises, I suppose, that the telephone is a special link between us.

Mon bien-aimé (my beloved)

I do hope the atmosphere is not too strained *chez toi*. We were so peaceful together yesterday. It really was as if time stopped for a little while. Bless you, my love – *avec tout mon coeur* (with all my heart) – *Puss*

My dear Puss

Yesterday was much like the previous Sunday, with the same elements of naturalness and surprise. Since Donne wasn't present in our minds, could it be something to do with the study of French?

It's very difficult to know how far to exert oneself at my age. As time passes, I am constantly being reminded in the course of doing things that I am (understandably) losing strength, and I accept that this process is going to accelerate.

Yet I still believe that it is better to err on the side of stretching oneself, rather than surrender to the mode of life which most men of my age accept. But this is more a matter of temperament than of philosophy. Much love

Darling

You are very dear to me, and looked terribly vulnerable and pink lying on my bed this afternoon. Rest seems to heal both of us in a way I find quite surprising. The way we touch each other, when we are relaxed, is quite transforming. All my love – Puss

Dear Puss

The sea again was very pleasant this morning. We have had a delightful week, and I am pleased to notice how relaxed you have become in the water. We seem to have found a new harmony in making love in these past two or three weeks. Could our swimming together account for this?

Perhaps we could spend an hour or so going through a couple of chapters of French or read *Candide*** together? Incidentally, have you noticed Peter O'Toole (*Shobha's favourite actor*) is on television tonight in *My Favourite Year* with Audrey Hepburn (*Douglas' favourite actress*). Much love

> ** Satire of French novelist *Voltaire* (1759), which traces the epic journey of his hero *Candide* - who concludes after coming full circle - that 'tending one's garden' is the path to understanding and enlightenment.

Mon bien-aimé

Quel dommage (what a pity). We missed each other by five minutes. Have just taken my mother back to hospital. Even though I thought I had spent several hours with her in a loving way - on the return journey, she complained that I always take her back early. It seems one can never satisfy one's parents. Much love – Puss

Darling

It was fun going through the French verb tables last evening at your home. You are so thorough and spoil me in a way by caring so much for my accent. Yet I am delighted to be so spoilt. I wish I could have nestled into you a little more on the sofa, but of course, the law of the cosmos seems to be that the moment one is off guard and relaxes totally, one is discovered by N. So it cannot be. All my love – Puss

My darling

A pity we could not 'consummate' yesterday's delightful afternoon by swimming together this morning. In fact, once one got through the breaking waves, it was plain sailing - if you can use such an expression for swimming. As you have said in your inimitably and openly joyous way - we were very good yesterday. Odd that I admire you for saying so, yet could not bring myself to be so outspoken. Much love

Sweetest love

Can still feel you entwined around me. *Je t'adore.* Puss

My darling

Thank you for your charming note. I wonder at your energy, after a full day (at work), in being able to write to me in French – and with so few mistakes. Over Easter perhaps, we might go through your French letters to me - to check on where you have gone astray.

Your new costume looked very becoming this morning (at the beach). Surely I was not the only person to remark upon it? I noticed incidentally, that people have more fun when - as this morning - a roughish sea forces them to play together in the surf.

As so often before, your unalloyed happiness awakens a sense of humility in me, though I won't speculate on why this happens. Almost a sense of unworthiness. How unlike the ordinary character of your Douglas.

Dearest

Sweetheart - we were so lovely today. *Une Puss heureuse* (one happy Puss).

Douglas

I visited my friends in the hills this morning to ease the pain – they are such interesting people. It takes a whole day for us to exhaust all topics of conversation. I never tire of their company. With most people an hour is enough. Perhaps I am fortunate, for I like to believe that we three are changing the world with our ideas. I do so wish to be surrounded by like-minded souls.

For the record, I 'believe' or as least, this is my understanding, based upon my experience - that :

- god or the goddess or 'it', is a force/light/energy/intelligence which permeates everything in the universe

- the universe functions according to cosmic and scientific laws and if we stray from these, there is difficulty, disease, disaster etc.

- it is not always clear what these laws are

- one of the laws is *karma* i.e. if you hurt or help another, you will also be hurt or helped somewhere down the track i.e. you reap what you sow

- reincarnation – when we leave the body at so-called death, there is an intervening period to reassess and learn before being recycled i.e. entering another body, and the process of being born and dying continues, until the cycle is complete i.e. there are no more lessons to be learnt

- there are no more lessons to be learnt when one realises (all the time) that one is divine i.e. god is not pie in the sky when you die, but within one's own heart (and also of course, in everyone else's heart as well)

- it is a question of remembrance - and we are all in various states of remembrance of our 'godness' (goodness). Most of us have glimpses (if we are lucky). I have glimpses when in love, singing, dancing, being dumped by waves etc. You have glimpses at other times e.g. listening to music and surfing the waves, but you presumably don't call them 'god'

- 'evil' to me not a helpful concept. One simply 'forgets' or one 'remembers'. Most people are in a state of forgetfulness that they are divine (i.e. they don't remember), and many also actively and deliberately oppose the law of *karma* (do unto others as you would be done by)

- those who do not believe in god, simply have no memory of their previous births and no experiences sufficiently strong or meaningful to convince them otherwise

- pain is one of the best ways of learning that there is another dimension coexistent with our everyday turmoil

- I have always felt my sole purpose in being with you was to help you to 'remember'

- I do not wish to come back to another body i.e. to be recycled. I wish to remain 'on the other side' (whatever or wherever that is), to assist those in their bodies (who have incarnated yet again) to remember their divine nature

- I do not expect you to accept the above - but I would like you to at least understand the basic ideas

- if there is a religion that represents the essence of these ideas (other than 'mysticism' (where any exalted state of consciousness represents contact with the 'divine energy' or whatever we choose to call it), then it would have to be Buddhism.

- All other religions have lost their way by imposing anthropomorphic deities at the top to frighten the masses into submission, together with a system of beliefs, rituals and prescribed behaviour - though Buddhism also offends grossly in this latter regard, but at least, there is no deity as such

- god does not have arms and legs unless they are yours (i.e. Douglas) and mine

- there is a whole hierarchy of souls who are in varying states of understanding the above. Those who have 'remembered' are assisting those who have not. It is a friendly community. I wish you could join.

Happy remembering, from a remember-ee

Darling

Today I was connected (at work) to 'email', which is a computer system for communicating with persons in other offices, departments and universities all over the world. If you were connected, I would be able to write you notes during the day and vice versa - in private. Is it worth considering? It could be fun. Must away – hopefully to sleep. *Avec amour – Puss*

Dear Puss

This is in part, an overdue allusion to the delights of Sunday afternoon. Please don't take it amiss if I occasionally comment indirectly on your use of a word. It's done in good humour. I admire the way you often search for the right word. Your working vocabulary is wider because of it.

The beach and sea were fun this morning, though N. is very low and talks of 'doing away with herself'. What worries me about this is not its novelty – she has threatened to do so before – but the cool way she speaks of it. I have thought once or twice recently that she was on the verge of consenting to some sort of compromise 'deal' (with regard to us). But this may have been wishful thinking.

Dearest Wimsey

Tell N. (if the occasion arises) that she was so named (by us) after I watched a programme on the endangered numbats at the zoo, and as I have found it difficult or impossible to say her actual name for ten years, because it hurt too much, so I put two and two together - the zoo and N. (because at that time she was working for the zoo as their lawyer). Perhaps she could choose an appropriate animal for me – preferably a horse or something furry. Minette (Puss)

Douglas

Just now I realised what is the problem (between us). You have not surrendered. In all our time together, I have deluded myself you have surrendered to me, when it is not so. Hence I always feel something is missing.

If you had surrendered - you would no longer be with N. It would be impossible. I have never been able to understand how you could love me and not be with me, but the simple truth is that you do not love - in the surrendered sense. What you do feel, I cannot comprehend. I have always wondered why you and I were so unbalanced in our feelings for each other. It is because, though in brief moments, you appear to surrender, it does not last, and the fear returns and you put on your armour or withdraw into your carapace. For me, to love is to surrender - and to live without having done so, is to have wasted one's life. Yet it cannot happen by an act of will. What a paradox ! It must be something that overcomes you. I pray that you will have the courage to lose yourself one day - and metaphorically - die. Anything less, will not do. Puss

Dear Shobha

I have not tried to get in touch with you, since you asked me so summarily 'to go' - though you have been much in my thoughts and I have been hoping to hear from you or see you down at the beach.

Given the sort of woman you are, I understand your being hurt by what I said about your importance in my life. It was I confess, a silly and wounding thing to say, for I have always been scornful of people who profess or ask me to rank pleasures or people, since their variety makes them incommensurable. For example, loving both opera and the beach creates no conflict of choice or preference which needs to be resolved. So also, as a rule - with people. Sensible people do not feel any need to rank their friends. *(Shobha's note : How naive !)*

You will of course, say it is otherwise in the triangular situation of you, N. and me. But even here, I suggest, the need for ranking or preference is not as obvious as you seem to assume - the reason being that you and she complement rather than oppose each other. This was surely implicit in my saying to you, soon after we met, that I was not previously conscious of anything missing from my life.

The very character of our communion has always been the product of its intermittent and sometimes uncertain nature - enabling us to avoid the trivial and the dull. *Byron***, I am sure, would agree with me. As he said, one cannot live a life of perpetual passion.

As my recent behaviour towards you shows, I do not regard what you call ML (making love) as being of any great importance in itself, but rather a bridge of entry to a higher state of communion. Would not *Kahlil Gibran*, the psychoanalyst *Erich Fromm, C.S. Lewis* and even Bhagwan - agree with this?

**   *Lord Byron* : English poet who was known to be cynical about love

Mon bien-aimé

I long for a type of relationship with you which is exclusive and in which we both adore each other, and exist for each other, without any third party - without interruption - and directed towards some elevated goal e.g. writing together or at the very least, meeting with like-minded friends to discuss and share our feelings and ideas. In a better world, perhaps?

And yet you don't seem to feel any desire for such a life at all. You seem quite content *chez toi* (at your home) with what you call your mundane life, and find a bit of intensity with me. You don't believe in the possibility of love enduring. You assume it will fade, and that domestic propinquity will kill it, if nothing else. But if it does kill it, perhaps it was never love? Why should love die on exposure? It seems a fearful way to live.

C.S. Lewis said he missed love as a boy after his mother died, and this cut him off from love again - except perhaps with his housekeeper who seems to have been a mother-substitute. But when he opened up again and was ready to face the hurt - love was there fully and completely - when he married.

Perhaps you are not ready to open up completely and be hurt. Perhaps you are still closed to some extent - because you were left in England by your mother, against her will and your own, at the age of eleven, when she returned to Africa, and thereafter you saw your parents only rarely.

It is easy for me to say, because I did not have the same experience, but I have certainly had the experience of loving and losing and it hurts like hell. That is why I am so afraid at times of losing you.

Because our love is deep, I am even more afraid that I will not survive without you. But who knows, perhaps it would be a kind of release - a kind of euphoria and an end to the pain. Hopefully I will exit first - for both our sakes. Puss

Dear Douglas

If it has been your experience that love 'dies at the altar' as you say (though you were married in a registry office) - then I should understand, because it was also so for me, after my marriage day. But I prefer to believe two persons who are 'in love' such as we are - can live together harmoniously and love can grow and need not die. Because we are not in a situation which will allow us to experiment, to see whether your view or mine is correct - we will never know.

**

So sorry we were sprung (upon by N.). I had a sense before she arrived, that I should depart. Hope you are still in one piece. A pity - because we were just beginning to 'go a little deeper'.

Perhaps - after meetings of this nature, we should both repair to our respective rooms to jot down a few things here and there, otherwise our ideas will be lost forever. It is a mistake in our work-a-day world to rush from one activity to another. The spaces in between are probably *the* spaces which we should cultivate.

Will probably not go to the beach tomorrow morning for diplomatic reasons. No doubt the atmosphere *chez toi* will be a little frosty for a while. Come and make love with me soon. *Bonne nuit* (goodnight) - *Minette*

Dear Puss

For some reason N. blew up, in a particularly explosive way, after I rang you this morning to thank you for giving me C.S. Lewis' books. What hurt her - and not for the first time (on hearing one side of our conversation), may have been the lightness and laughter and impression of intimacy this conveyed to her.

By 'intimacy' I don't mean physical closeness, but a kind of bantering rapport which has never existed between me and her. When I put this to her later, she came near to accepting my suggestion and conceded that this disposition to banter** is part of my nature - evidenced by my treatment of my children when they were young and my grandchildren now.

I may leave *Surprised by Joy*** at your house after I have extracted a few notes. It is a mind-expanding book in many ways. You were very sweet yesterday. I have said this before - but it bears repeating again and again. Much love

** Banter - A mélange of playfulness, word-play and seriousness - indulged in only when the other 'party' responds appropriately.

** Surprised by Joy : partial autobiography of British author C.S. Lewis (including an account of his conversion to Christianity).

Wimsey

Have been reading more of C.S. Lewis and yes, there is definitely something in it. When I first met you, you tried to convey to me the moments when you experienced 'stabs' of joy e.g. listening to Wagner, swimming out to sea in the morning etc., and that is precisely why I paid attention to you - rather than to the other roughly two (now 3.5) billion men on this planet. You were, unbeknown to yourself, sharing with me your experiences of – dare I say it – god (or goodness).

Needless to say, these are the only moments, I believe or rather 'know', which are worth living and dying for. I remember, a few days after our first meeting, or rather 'getting to know you better', that I said to you, in response to your statement that what we were experiencing was 'unreal', that *au contraire* (to the contrary), these were the only moments which *were* real.

Yet Lewis states the longing for such moments – which become one's life's obsession in the early stages of an apprenticeship in 'joy', must ultimately be replaced by surrender and acceptance.

In Lewis' book *A Grief Observed,* you will note that he states his suffering abated when he let go of his desire to see and feel Joy (his wife, who had died) and abandoned his suffering and mourning. In that very 'letting go', she was 'there' - instantly, vividly and totally.

What a paradox ! Do you remember the Leunig cartoon in *The Common Man's Book of Prayer* which I gave you for Christmas :

Lord, give me the strength to hold on – *and* to let go?

The mark of a man or woman is knowing when to do what. And it keeps changing. Hence the need for constant vigilance.

On a more worldly note, I lay out in the sun this afternoon beside my Buddha-lady statue under the guava tree, as we used to do in the early days, and the 'stab' was there i.e. looking through the leaves to the sky, listening to the birds, thinking of you, thinking of Lewis or perhaps not thinking at all.

Yesterday I played Pavarotti before you arrived, and tears flowed because of the sheer beauty of his voice. The man holds nothing back. That quality is 'divine' - is 'god'.

And it is to be found in countless things, but we are often not sufficiently alert enough to notice. We are so busy running here and there. My reason for taking three weeks leave was to simply slow down, so I could regain my capacity to 'listen' – and it is slowly returning.

Consider on what occasions you have felt a leap inside – on finding a letter from me in your mail box or under the door, or when I return home and find roses inside the door, or find you unexpectedly on my doorstep in the morning (at dawn), or when we suddenly touch each other under the sea, or being tossed over by a wave, or a passage of Lewis which is uplifting.

All these and many other ways in which we mortal creatures experience 'it' ! What more do you need? To put this into a doctrine - give it a building (church, temple etc) and a hierarchy of male administrators, is to profane it utterly. O – I forgot. Also moments when making love.

So – one can only hope without hoping that more and more of these moments descend – the mystics call it 'grace or transcendence'.

Christian mystics call it the *holy spirit*, the *'peace that passeth understanding',* the *'still small voice within'* and the *'cloud of unknowing.'* The ways of describing (or alluding to) it, are infinite.

Such insights convey with them a kind of knowledge which cannot be put into words. Provided we do not analyse them away after the event and thus destroy their effect, they transform our lives. Puss

There is a famous prayer of the American theologian *Reinhold Niebuhr* –

> God, grant me the serenity
> to accept the things I cannot change,
> courage to change the things I can,
> and wisdom to know the difference.

Dearest of friends

So – the holiday is almost over, and it has worked, in the sense that it has taken three weeks to slow down, to get out of the nine-to-five routine and find another way much sweeter.

How I wish it could continue indefinitely – rising late when one wishes - reading the paper at leisure - enjoying the first cup of coffee – swimming out to sea with you unhurriedly - wondering what the day will bring and then setting about making something happen from one moment to the next; the little pleasures of which you have sometimes spoken, and to which C.S. Lewis refers, and especially the delights of nature – lying under a tree pondering the meaning of it all.

This break from work, has thrown me from one side of my personality to the other. At first - collapsing in exhaustion, then having to weather feelings of ill-health and a total lack of energy; railing against god and Bhagwan and yourself and the university, and wanting desperately to find a way out and a new way in.

Finally - surrendering and realising it is really very simple - this moment is this moment is this moment. I love kissing the pillows after you have left and feeling you still being there. Sometimes I wonder what it would be like if you were truly there. Perhaps we would both become frightened. Today has been a feast and the bed is still warm.

Have almost finished Lewis and am sorry to put the book down. I have taken to jotting down page numbers - à la Payne - in order to talk to you about them. I find Lewis' reference to the occult as 'dark' – very surprising.

For myself, it has always been anything but: rather an attempt to apprehend in a non-scientific way, the actual nature of things. I have encountered many people who are afraid of the psychic - even those who have direct experience of visions and communications from the 'other' side. Instead of befriending these visions - they resist and close them off.

Christians of course, have been taught the occult is 'evil' - whereas in fact, it is simply a deeper layer of existing consciousness. Yet many of the so-called saints were canonised because of their 'visions' (or other-worldly experiences). How hypocritical it all is !

When you and I make love, we move a layer deeper. We say things we could not say at other times. We are to an extent transported. Likewise - with the psychic realm - one enters a different state and sees things differently. That is all.

I liked what Lewis said about not being able to produce a state of joy - on demand. It is also true that if one meditates (for example), the likelihood of a 'state' occurring is increased, as it is when swimming out to sea or walking for hours alone, or making love, or listening to music. What is important is to do all these things - but drop the longing. With this - I agree absolutely. I am rambling. Must get back to reading Lewis.

My mother absconded yet again this afternoon and was found by my brother's wife, several blocks away from the nursing home near their home. I was very shocked. I keep hoping the problem (her mental state) will go away and she will settle down and become happy, but it seems to be a pipe dream. At rock bottom, I do not want to be responsible for her pain (as I don't know how to help her), yet I want her to be happy.

Dearest, I love it so when you are nestled against me. It seems a pity to ever part. *Bonne nuit - mon amant* (goodnight, my love) - your Puss

**	English writer C.S. Lewis is also noted for his *Chronicles of Narnia* (for children) and his comments on the human condition in *A Grief Observed*.

**	Douglas made dozens of notes for each book he read, for his own use, and also talked to Shobha about them, when time permitted. Shobha has kept these together - as they indicate the turn of Douglas' mind on many matters.

My dear Puss

Our talk this morning was genuinely illuminating. Forgive me for tending to hog rather more than my share. Is it too much to ask you to 'indulge me' (as the Irish statesman, Edmund Burke was happy to indulge Samuel Johnson), notwithstanding that Sam often said that Burke was 'the first man everywhere' and had 'one of the most luminous minds of his age, and was ready to discourse on all subjects'? If yesterday lunchtime did contribute a mite to my tiredness later, I cannot think of a happier way of expending my strength. Much love and gratitude.

My sweetest love

I agree with you about spacing out your exercise. Some fitness experts say it is necessary to exercise for three sessions per week, i.e. not every day. When you 'do' exercise, it is important to extend yourself - but that does not mean you should push your body beyond its limits. Wish you were here. Would love to hold you, as we held each other yesterday. I truly believe in 'forever'. Puss

Dear Douglas

I was hurt on Sunday when you said to me 'you don't seem to realise I am married to N.' It occurred to me at the time, as you lay with your arms around me, that perhaps *you* did not realise that you were married to N. ! Marriage is a commitment to love another to the exclusion of all others. Technically, you are no longer married.

I also do not wish to continue with an arrangement where you are permitted to contact me when you wish, but I am 'punished' with your disapproval, when 'I' make contact with you. This is unforgiveable.

**

You will probably recall that in my article *When it's time to say Goodbye,* which was written just before I met you, that I suggested that if a person could not find all that he or she wanted in one person – he or she should find it elsewhere.

I know that for you - affection is not so important - but it is very important to me, and now I feel I should try to satisfy this side of my nature with other people. You are not available to go out to social events, and it is obviously ridiculous that I should stay at home because of this - so again I will make every effort to go out with friends when possible. You do not share my interest in matters spiritual or mystical, and this is the most important aspect of my life - so rather than getting frustrated because you cannot share these things with me, I shall develop these interests with others of like mind (or rather soul).

I see that I have not seen things rightly, because I have been wishing for you to be a certain way when it is not in your nature, while at the same time depriving myself of all that I truly love (at times). We must each go our own way, and if we meet now and then and find something we can both share, that will be beautiful.

But at present, what I am seeking is warmth, affection, tenderness and understanding, and this is more likely to be found amongst those with whom I have a spiritual affinity.

Darling - full moon

What has always surprised me about 'us' is that the physical side has not been as important as the binding quality which emerges during and after making love. Yet perhaps they are inextricably entwined. I believe that you and I commune, as in all other aspects of our lives together, in a most unusual way, and that is why, despite a few hiccups now and then, it is so special. *Dal suo pace, il mio dipende* (on your peace – mine depends), Much love - *ta Minette un peu triste* (a little sad)

My dearest love

How wonderful it would be if every marriage was a meeting of souls. But my beloved Bhagwan says - and you say - and I know - that it is a rare phenomenon.

Am off to finish J.R.R. Tolkien's *book The Hobbit.* The end fast approacheth. Having countless books to read certainly makes life rich and worthwhile, especially with winter on the way.

The frustration I complained to you about last weekend – of not having companionship, is so much lessened when there are books calling out to be read. What a blessing for those people in the world who are in some way confined. Bhagwan did little else but give a discourse each day, and read, once he moved to Pune in the seventies.

I am not necessarily arguing for reading as a way of life, but as a way to joyfully endure situations which are not palatable. The secret seems to lie in always having several books or authors in reserve, so that there is little room for too much reflection upon one's state.

I hope I am not becoming an advocate of 'an empty mind is the devil's workshop', 'nature abhors a vacuum' etc. I don't think so. Given happier circumstances e.g. the presence of yours truly in and around my home, I would happily support the notion of an empty mind. It is so easy to have an empty mind - when one is happy.

I wish that you had not mentioned N.'s unhappiness in the same breath as I confessed to you my happiness. It had a way of dampening my spirits. It is so rarely that I feel such contentment. I would prefer *not* to have it contaminated.

I hope you can rest after your exertions. There is nothing more wearying than tiredness – is that tautological? Much love – Puss

Douglas

After you excused yourself, I rang Father B. (from the beach swimming group), because I realised that he is probably the only person I know with whom I could discuss 'god'. Most people can at least cope with 'love'. I am not even sure that he has any experience of god - but at least he knows the jargon.

This made me wonder. Despite the fact that these two words are my favourites (god and love), there is no-one at present with whom I can share my understanding and experience. If I talk to Christians about god, they immediately show they have not really understood, because they are judgmental about others and talk of 'sin' etc. Not at all what I mean.

You say I am 'singular', but only in this society. In the East, men and women live and breathe 'god'.

When I was in India, the only people I could bear to be with were the Indians - because their language was the language of devotion (*bhakti)*, and we would sit for hours in the evening talking of the 'love of god' and knowing what it meant, because it was happening right then (as we spoke). In the West, there is a great sterility around these words. No-one talks or knows about it - few feel it and even fewer can express it.

I wonder that you and I - having known each other so long - still cannot even begin to understand each other. I wish it was possible to sit with you, hold you and look into your eyes - without constantly analysing what is meant by a certain word. Don't you know there is another language - without words?

Dear Douglas

When we make love happily, we are like children again, and the future seems far away. I am for my own reasons - sad - because of a lack of a cause. I want everything I do to be meaningful, even if you say one should not be so serious about life. I find the odd social encounter rewarding, but deep down I like to believe what I am doing is 'significant'. This gives a passion to existence. Much love – Shobha

Shobha's first poem for Douglas in French (two versions)

la chaleur, le baiser, l'etreinte affectueuse
nous deux et tout le monde effacons

the warmth, the kiss, the fond embrace,
we two - and all the world efface

and also

le baiser, le toucher, l'entreinte affectueuse
nous deux, sommes baigné, dans joie douce

the kiss, the touch, the fond embrace
we two are bathed in sweet joy

Dear Puss

Your French poem - though simple - moves me very much. The roses I left for you are yellow, only because they seemed to be the best of a not very good Monday morning collection.

There was an unusual air of gaiety at the beach this morning. It came, I think, from there being so many people playing in the waves at the same time. In the old days a group of us, on such a winter morning, would literally get in line, with much exhortation and laughter.

Would you like to have lunch with me tomorrow – your birthday? You were very sweet and happy yesterday. As I said, in some way I enter your world. Am on my way into the university, where I will make a copy of my poem. It was written by me in Ceylon during the war - for a young woman in the British army. *Ton amant*

Dear Douglas

It was good to talk with you. Bear with my silence and sobs if you can. They usually precede an attempt to communicate with you deeply. As the French scientist and philosopher *Pascal* (1623-62) said – 'The heart has its reasons that reason does not know'.

Your parting statements about 'consideration' and giving a little on each side, moved me very much. I don't think anyone could have put it better. It seemed to make things much clearer than before.

Perhaps I should come to interpret a touch of your finger (after a dispute), as the hand of god herself? Until tomorrow - my love

Dear Puss

You were strangely happy yesterday, almost as if you had undergone some sort of conversion. Recollections of India ?

Fax sent by Shobha to the Imperial Hotel in London where Douglas was staying

Urgent – Could you please put the attached note in the box for Professor Douglas Payne who will be arriving on 23 August. Shobha Cameron.

Beloved Wimsey – heart - Puss cartoon

Sent to Shobha from Uppingham, Rutland (United Kingdom)

Dear Puss

How clever and naughty of you to find out where I was staying in London. I am reminded, of course, of your finding out my son's unlisted phone number last year when I was staying with him in Canberra.

Your fax was first seen by N. However, she took it without much objection, though she was provoked by it to tell me that just before I sealed the large carton of our letters the day before we left Perth, she could not help noticing a letter from you lying at the very top, in which, so she tells me, you asked me to come and make love to you soon.

I often think of you fondly. Separation, I suspect, will make me more conscious of your importance in my life, even if it falls short of the impetuous, consuming, exclusive (romantic) love you sometimes demand of me.

Letter from Douglas to Shobha from Wales

Dear Puss

Holidays are very wearing in the sense of forever being rushed. I buy *The Times* every day - but it is rarely read. In order to write to you, I got up before 6 am this morning and am sitting in the Plas Hall Hotel about four miles from Betwy-s-Coed, on the winding road to Ffestiniog. It is listed as one of the best hotels (for value) in Britain (modest, excellent food, relaxed atmosphere and friendly).

As the crow flies, it is only eight miles from (Mount) Snowdon. N. and I reached the summit in 3.5 hours. I could not have wished for a finer day for climbing. Sunny with a light cooling breeze. I found it easy going, apart from raising blisters on each heel with my new boots, resulting from losing two earlier pairs. I now realise the new ones had never been broken in.

Have been out today, climbing the southern slopes of *Cader Idris* (a mountain in Wales) for two and a half hours in pouring rain, and managed quite well - despite being completely soaked.

Spent a couple of hours in Jane Austen's house at Chawton and would have stayed longer but was due at Heathrow to take delivery of a new Renault - which had been driven across from Paris.

I was moved almost to tears by some of the exhibits in the house - such as the pages of the Scottish novelist Sir Walter Scott's diary - in which he praises Jane so highly and justly. Also Jane's letter to her nephew Henry, about working on a piece of ivory only two inches wide (which was her desk at the time).

I have been interrupted again – by dinner. This is far from being an easy-flowing letter, partly because of N's undisguised objection to what I am doing.

On a narrow road this afternoon, I met a modern shepherdess, wearing jeans, but quite pretty, who asked me to stop the car to allow a flock of sheep to pass. I mention this because she was using, not a crook, but a mobile phone, to keep in touch with her fellow shepherd - who was driving the sheep.

Early tomorrow, I am leaving for Dover, in order to cross to France the following morning. Then down to N's sister at Villecroze in Provence. Having just consumed three-quarters of a bottle of Medoc, I am prepared to say I miss you. Not just because you are my confidante, but physically. When I get back (to Perth) and have recovered from my five-week 'holiday', we must go somewhere for a few days. Much love

Dear Puss – after Douglas' return from Europe

I shall not this time add flowers to flowers, since it would smack of gilding the lily. It was a strange and disturbing day. We are indeed an unusual couple – no pun intended. *Con amore*

Dear Wimsey

I found the Morris** film was a little disturbing. Though supposedly on love, it focused far more on the physiological than the emotional - to my mind. What seems so terrible is that after such an intense experience as love-making, couples can become distant from each other and even hostile - perhaps because the intensity cannot be sustained indefinitely. This is not always the case - but as Morris says, love-making does not guarantee lifelong happiness, yet in cultures where the man and woman are not long apart, there is more likelihood of happiness. There goes your theory. Proximity breeds closeness, not separation !

His comments that ninety-nine percent of humanity lives in paired relationships hit home for me. I am aware at some depth of my being, that I am not happy unless I am in such a close communion, and whatever you say or believe for yourself - for me, it is the case that peace and joy and contentment come when I am surrounded by the love of another human being. *Avec amour* – Shobha

** A film based on the book *The Naked Ape* by zoologist Desmond Morris.

Dearest Douglas

This is difficult to say yet it must be said. My entire purpose for being on this planet at this time is a spiritual one. This is becoming clearer to me each day, and the time may soon come when I will become even more involved in this purpose, and this will affect our relationship greatly. You have not been able to understand this side of my life, and I now understand why this is so.

I have endeavoured in every possible way to demonstrate the truth as I see it to you, but I have not succeeded in imparting or transmitting it to you. I fear it may only be in my absence someday, that you will begin to understand.

Know that I will never leave you. You will always be in my heart, and your spiritual welfare will always be of utmost concern to me. I believe this is the only reason we have been together.

You have given me so much. You have shown me how to love totally (yet) I speak a different language from you. Know always that we cannot be parted. Souls of like kind and affinity are always one. Remember this - whatever happens. Even thinking of me, I will be there and so too, will you be there for me.

We have learnt over the years, that despite constant separations, we can still be in tune at a deeper and more 'esoteric' level. We have reached a plane where we can in a sense, communicate without seeing each other. It is as if you pervade my being - and I yours. This is the ultimate. To be together in spirit - not in body.

As far as spiritual purpose is concerned, I know it is my task to remind others that there is 'more' - that there is another dimension which is inherent in all that we do and see in this very moment. This has always been my conviction, but because of the 'traumas' of our relationship, it has at times become obscured.

Because we come from different worlds, it may be that I must go on alone in the future. You may join me whenever you wish, but I cannot linger with you as completely as before, because you do not hear me or listen to me or wish to come with me.

Therefore there must be some change in our pattern. We have both loved each other excessively in our own ways, though I have declared my love, and you have reservedly admitted yours - only on occasion. Yet we both know that what has happened to us has been magnificent and deep, and that we are no longer the same in consequence.

Dearest – trust that there is a process at work of which you are not aware right now, yet which nevertheless has you in its hand, and will someday reveal itself to you.

Time will show all that needs to be shown. The gradual opening of the heart and finally the opening of the soul - are inevitable. It is simply a question of time and readiness. There is no time in this dimension.

When you decide to embark upon this great adventure is entirely up to you. Heaven does not coerce, even if Shobha has attempted to do so. When you long for other realms and are no longer content with the simple round of daily existence, it will happen.

There is a saying in the East which I have always held dear – 'When the disciple is ready, the master appears'. And not until then. When you are ready - god will happen to you. There is no other word for it. But it will only happen when it has become the most important quest, when all else has become meaningless, tawdry, dull and empty. Only the empty heart can receive the unknown. While there are thoughts and ideas, imaginings and fantasies - god cannot enter in. The empty mind is god's workshop. May the day come soon. Until we meet – my dear, dear love

Dear Douglas

Has it ever occurred to you, as it has just occurred to me, that our lives are one large exemplification of the romantic plot as expounded in literature and art and music down the ages?

The entire undercurrent of all our actions and thoughts is the thwarting of romantic love, just as this is the eternal theme of Jane Austen's novels. Her heroes and heroines only come together on the last page.

It is as if we devote all our waking and even sleeping hours to achieving a resolution between what we desire and what we feel we must not (in your case) and cannot (in my case) have.

Although you are engaged in other diversions, as I myself am engaged in work for most of each day, nevertheless, I believe our conflict provides us both with the primary motivation for our lives. The attempt to bring some greater harmony or understanding, dominates our existence.

Should we ever resolve the conflict, I wonder what would transpire. Perhaps it would be the end. Perhaps the beginning. We shall never know, because you will never have the courage, yes courage, to be with me, and therefore I by default, will never be able to experience life with you.

Mon ami

The songs my new singing teacher intends me to sing, are a little beyond me at present – love songs of the French composer Gabriel Fauré for example. I find them a little tuneless. Also an aria of Lui (the queen's servant) from Puccini's opera *Turandot*. I would rather sing the arias of Turandot herself i.e. the queen.

Still, I will trust M. for the time being. She has produced some of the best singers in Australia, so she must have some insight. She is quite outrageous. We gossiped for half an hour about other teachers at the Conservatorium, their quirks and foibles etc. It is fascinating stuff, and we still had time for the real lesson.

She could almost become a friend. Her language use is so colourful and quite arresting. She is very critical of others, but in a theatrical way - which almost makes it excusable. *Avec amour – ton amie – Minette*

Dear Douglas

Do you remember when you were in England you sent me a card saying 'It's the nights I miss you most' with a teddy bear dragging another teddy up the stairs. In my case, it's the weekdays, weeknights, weekend days and weekend nights – I miss you most. *À tout à l'heure - Minette*

**

What a pity you can't live here a day a week? Then you could become tired of me and then crave me alternately. In a better world ? Happy moon – Puss

Beloved

I firmly believe, that the task of a parent is to make his or her children independent, so that the parent is no longer needed.

One of the advantages of my living alone, is that when we speak on the phone, at least from my end, there is no possibility of interruption. When you phone me and N. is out - you are quite a different person.

I am beginning to realise that we are really fortunate because we have an affinity of the mind as well as in other areas. Many people have an affinity with their beloveds, but not of the mind. Perhaps it is not possible to find all four levels fulfilled in one person as I suggest in my article *When it's Time to say Goodbye.*

Yet I feel I relate to you at all four levels to some extent i.e. physically, emotionally, intellectually and spiritually (even if you don't believe you have a soul). Do I deceive myself ? If you were more spiritually-oriented, perhaps our dilemma would not exist - because we would be truly one.

This may account for your inability to be with me fully. Our missing link ? Enough of this. Must away my love, because my body craves my pillow - not to sleep, but to rest and read and reflect. Much lovingness – *ton cherie*

Douglas

I wish for once in my life (at work), that I was fully and absolutely appreciated for all that I do (which is usually achieved with a fair degree of grace and intelligence). Yet I seem to land in situations where I have to fight for mere existence. I wish someone other than you, would 'discover' me. Perhaps it is too much to hope for ?

My cousin from London is staying with me, but I want to be alone. I am tired of her company and would like to retreat to my hermit-like existence again. How I have grown to love solitude - at least some of the time. I feel like a prisoner with her nearby. *Jusqu'à la plage – ton ami* (Until the beach - my friend)

Dear Douglas

The film of *The Lion in* Winter is fantastic. The best I have seen of actors Katharine Hepburn and Peter O'Toole. It has many messages for parents – rather opportune in view of your many sons. Makes one feel families are not really a good thing overall. Must run – love – Puss

Dearest of men - mon cherie

We are all parts of the universe, bits of the cosmos, wondering and struggling - and if we are very lucky – creating - which brings a sense of unity to it all.

My sister-in-law is becoming almost a friend – and you may say, why 'almost' – but because of her severe illness, for many years I kept my distance because I simply did not know how to behave around her. I do feel that even within families, the only worthwhile relationships are based upon affinity. She is interested in art and literature and beautiful things - so there is some common ground.

At a dinner party last evening, I was placed next to a young couple who are marrying in two weeks' time. She works at the university and he is completing a Masters degree in maths and wants to go to Oxford. They both play violin and have singing lessons and drive along in the car singing two-part harmonies of their violin pieces – it sounds idyllic. Even we (you and I) have shared such moments.

If only all relationships were based upon such common joys. I can think of no better way to spend an evening (apart from making love with you), than listening to friends performing music and performing oneself - and the talk that would necessarily surround such activities.

Wish it was possible to work in a field where one respected one's workmates. We are a friendly bunch, but there is not much content. Would love to be carrying out research on something deep and meaningful, or writing in an area where what I wrote 'mattered'.

Arthur Koestler's role** of 'provocateur' is to me, one of the most important - even though he was not necessarily loved for it. I find his work inspirational. I miss you – *Minette*

** *Arthur Koestler* : Hungarian-British author and journalist

Douglas

A day or so ago you alluded to 'loving me' and I poured cold water on your protestations. In this I was wrong, because upon reflection, there are many benefits of loving *in absentia*, though perhaps there are even more in loving '*in presentia*' -

- to love another (in absentia) can be a tremendous joy. As you know, when alone, feelings simply well up and overflow, or catch one by surprise, with a tremendously enhancing effect

- according to mysticism and other fringe schools of thought and experience, love cannot help but benefit the cosmos in general and humanity, in particular. Every positive thought or feeling entertained seeps out into the cosmos and merges with all other positive thoughts and feelings to contribute to the well-being of the planet

- according to 'esoteric' theory, any thought or feeling is transmitted, regardless of physical presence, to the object of one's thoughts or feelings. This afternoon at precisely the moment I began this letter, you rang, and this has happened on many occasions. When I think of you - you appear. When you phone me at the office, I know - just before I pick up the phone, that it is you calling.

- successive feelings of love may be cumulative in their effect, and although one instance of feeling love may not in itself be sufficient to lead to action - in time, the combined force of those feelings may precipitate movement in the direction of the beloved

With these words of 'wisdom' I shall leave you.

**

The Verdi opera *Rigoletto* was rewarding. The Perth-born baritone was supposed to be one of the best in the world but was disappointing. However, the local soprano was perfect as Gilda - with thrilling cadenzas.

My friend K. loved it – surprisingly - because opera is not her 'thing', though her mother started an opera company in Western Australia. We both looked rather sweet in our long gowns (my opinion). I had lent her a black dress for the occasion. Several of the arias tore my heart, and I realised (yet again) that opera definitely triggers some of the deepest emotions I feel - as it does for you. The tenor, also from Australia, was inspiring, with a little of the Italian flair. So, despite being merely a concert version, it was quite a success. Listening to opera reminds me how long it has been since we communed together in this way. Must sleep - Puss

Darling

Have decided to devote my life to poetry, opera, you and god in the reverse order. I was transported at *Rigoletto* last evening, and realised yet again, that opera is sublime in its effect. Poetry of course, being the language of love - simply complements the above.

During the memorial service yesterday for one of my friends, there was a short prayer, with the response 'god is compassionate to all 'his' creatures' and my first thought was that god is anything but compassionate.

Most human beings are reeling under one form of atrocity or another in their lives, either from their spouse or children, or parents, or society or injury or circumstance. It is not that I think 'god' has erred, but simply that the nature of things is such that one can certainly not say that the universe is unfailingly compassionate. There is so much suffering, so many horrid deaths, so much emotional 'trauma'. For some of us that trauma is subtle, e.g. the absence or too much presence of one's parents. For others, there is simply naked violence.

The mystics speak of good and evil both being necessary in order for the other to exist, which at least makes more intellectual sense, but Christianity I am afraid, is simply a band-aid for tortured souls.

I said as much to K. who has had no exposure to Christian thought, being a product of a Jewish mother and a Buddhist father – both lapsed. It is interesting to be in the presence of someone who does not have the background of Christianity. You and I take it for granted, even if we don't accept it. Much love – Puss

My dear Puss

Hope your Bali holiday went well. It has been strange to be out of touch with you for a week. Your absence leaves a large hole in my life. Am writing this note in your kitchen with all the windows open - to let the sea breeze blow through the house.

Have put a few items of food in your fridge, most supplied, willingly and surprisingly - by N. I am shocked that I do not know whether you ordinarily eat eggs. That I don't, is an index of the nature of our relationship and the level at which we communicate. Incidentally - why was the book of Alexander Pope's poetry open on your table ?

Sorry to be so practical, but it follows from your going away. As I have said before, when I come into your house in your absence, your distinctive self emerges very strongly from all the material evidences of you: books, music, scores, pictures, photos, notices, clothes etc. It makes me feel at the same time both an intruder and a special tenderness towards you. Much love

Darling

I feel more sympathy with popular books on science in recent times, and being a person without any background in science at all - this is surprising. Yet perhaps it is the total absence of science in my life which now makes it appealing.

Did you watch the news recently, where some local researchers have found that, far from DNA containing all the material which makes a human being 'unchangeable' through generations - learning and other socialising influences 'change' the DNA, so there can be progress from one generation to the next? Must away - goodnight, my prince – Puss

**

Thank you for your gift of a bed. After twenty-five years on the floor as a result of my hippie lifestyle and years in India, it is a blessing not to be attacked by insects, now that I have risen in the world. Bhagwan 'used to say' that to sleep on one's chest was the position of a child at rest, and the way to be closest to god. That explains why I am (obviously) more enlightened than other persons. Must rush – Puss

Chapter 13

You shall be free indeed

30

You shall be free indeed
when your days are not without a care,
nor your nights without a want and a grief
but rather
when these things girdle your life
and yet you rise above them
naked and unbound

Gibran

Dearest soulmate

When I return to work, would it help if you could take N. out once a week to something she would like to see or do, to try to ease her grief, or is this a ridiculous suggestion ?

Somehow, because you and I are not actively unhappy (today at least), it is easier to want to reduce any pain N. may be suffering - though obviously the entire situation is fraught with tragedy - and realistically, it will never be possible for N. to be happy unless I die. And even then, there is no guarantee.

Hope to see you *à la plage demain* (at the beach tomorrow). I may swim out to meet you as you come in, though I will reserve my decision until the time. In this way, you could have a longer swim yourself. Much love - *ton chaud petit poisson* (your hot little fish).

My darling love

It is such a joy, as you yourself once remarked - to be able to go for a walk (as we do) and find we are able to quote the same lines (of poetry). We are fortunate indeed. Send me your energy. I am almost asleep. Please see your doctor - I care about your body. Much love - *ton fatigué petit poisson* (your tired little fish)

Douglas

It grieves me that you do not understand me and that you ridicule me and laugh at me because I am not like you. I find it incomprehensible that when I am distressed or afraid, you do not care - but are scathing in your criticism of me, for not performing as you wish.

You chose me many years ago, presumably because there were some qualities I possessed which you loved. You did not choose me because I could climb mountains or ford streams. Currently our relationship seems to rise or fall depending upon how well I survive in the surf each morning. This is ridiculous.

I do not expect you to meditate or dance or sing or become a sannyasin. I do not expect you to mix with my friends, or sleep the night with me, or go on holidays with me - because there is no point. You are unwilling to change in any way to suit me. I have made many concessions for you – learning to swim - climbing Mount Snowdon in Wales, and taking an interest in so many of your activities - but it is not reciprocated to the same degree.

I am not interested in becoming a fearless Amazon. You already have N., who can ride the waves and horses and is no doubt the sort of woman you admire and want. But she obviously falls short in many respects, otherwise you would not have needed me.

Do not now try to make me like her. That is simply futile. We are different types. I don't want to be a tough, masculine, hardy creature. I want to be myself. If you don't like me as I am - perhaps you should seek your pleasures elsewhere.

I wish you could learn to love your real women the way you admire your fictional characters. It is so easy to appreciate a person in a novel, but that person bears little resemblance to any woman in the flesh.

If you want to know how to behave (towards a woman), read Dorothy Sayers** on Lord Peter Wimsey**. He is stimulating, vital, intelligent and cares in every way for the woman in his life as if she were his own heart. You would do well to master his skills (even though, he too, is fictional).

You have been quite a loving companion in the past week or so, and it has surprised me how you have managed for so long to be in good humour and gentle and tender. It is *not* surprising that now I am returning to work, some tensions should develop and that we should return to form. Thank you for your gentleness - while it lasted.

** *Dorothy Sayers* – English novelist, educated in Oxford at a time when women were a rarity in those hallowed halls of learning.

** As has been mentioned - *Lord Peter Wimsey* is the hero of Dorothy Sayers' novels, in particular - *Gaudy Night* - which is set in Oxford. Lord Peter and Harriet Vane (his lover) epitomise the intellectual type of relationship enjoyed by Douglas and Shobha - with the difference being that Lord Peter and Harriet went on to marry, live together and bear children.

Dear Puss

Yesterday was a delightful surprise – for me and perhaps for you too. Sorry I had to rush away. Swimming (back) from the far buoy (out at sea) this morning was a bit of a slog. Not as rough and adverse as yesterday, but enough to disrupt any kind of rhythm in stroking and breathing. Am leaving the Oscar Wilde biography by Richard Ellman for you, together with a compact disc of Di Stefano**. Much love

**   *Guiseppe Di Stefano – celebrated Italian opera singer*

Dearest

In the early morning at the ocean, Douglas fell at the shoreline on a bank of sharp shells, which scraped a layer of skin from his face, so that it was totally red from the bleeding.

Hope the head is coming along well – do take it easy. I was quite shocked to see you coming out of the water looking disoriented and damaged. Much love until we commune by phone or in the flesh. You were rather nice today in spite of - or perhaps because of - your wounds. Puss

My darling

I feel as if I have failed god - failed myself and failed you. One who purports to be spiritual, as I do - should have no place for concern about the future in her heart. To be worried about old age, ill-health, loneliness and poverty should not be the preoccupation of a spiritual person.

I was watching a programme tonight on 'miracles' and the life of *Francis of Assisi*, and felt so humbled by the beauty of a life which is not dependent upon material possessions - which is also the way of the sannyasin. How stupid I have become. To trust absolutely that whatever is needed will be provided - is the way. It is better to be true to one's path, than to live in fear of all that 'might' happen.

Please forgive me for wanting anything from you, when you have already given me so much of your heart and your life. It has simply been the fear of losing you, that brought me so low that I wondered about my own welfare - when you are gone. But you are here, and each day is precious. It is so futile to waste even a moment. If you want me - I will come.

Darling

Sometimes I worry a little about my status (or lack of it), because everyone at the wedding, was either single, separated, married, living de facto or….. and I was the only one of uncertain origins.

It is a little disturbing. I would like to belong to 'someone'. I don't seem to fit anywhere. There was no-one there who had been divorced (as I was - many eons ago). Perhaps I should not have married when I was young, but waited until I met my soulmate (you)? Because I left my marriage, I discovered Bhagwan, and because I love Bhagwan (as my teacher), I met you, and because……so many ifs (and because-es).

I still wish we could be together properly instead of this piecemeal relationship. But perhaps you could not sustain a 'living with' intimate situation. How I wish you could declare your love for me publicly as they did today at the wedding. It was so inspiring. That is how I believe love should be – shouted from the rooftops with no shame or inhibition. A celebration. Goodnight, my dear one – shall see you in the morning perhaps (at the ocean).

Dear Shobha

It may indeed be that there is something cool and exceptional in my make-up, setting me apart from others - the effect perhaps of my unusual upbringing. Though I get on well with people, I always retain a certain detachment, which no doubt explains why my critical faculties apply to everyone. Nor do I think I am to be pitied for this, for it carries with it a freedom I value. For me the measure of affection is, not kissing, caressing and professions of love, but the degree of concern and sense of responsibility one person feels for another. Your very much concerned Douglas

Dearest Puss

Love's mysteries in souls do grow
but yet the body is his book
•
John Donne

How true and apt. Donne is much of the same mind as you - though he may get there by another path. Odd that he was a realist and not a romantic. Yet he was with us yesterday (while making love). I must get you a copy of *The Soul of Wit*** from the library. Your roving Douglas

> **   From the poem *'To his mistress on going to bed'*. Donne married a sixteen-year-old girl against her parents' wishes, and thereafter his 'career' was virtually ruined.
>
> **   *The Soul of Wit* : A study of the English poet John Donne by Murray Roston

Dear Shobha

Sorry to have upset you at the beach. Allow for the fact that I simply do not understand how you *cannot* wish to swim out on such a morning. You are quite a strong swimmer and would almost certainly benefit from the exercise - especially if your Achilles tendon prevents you from running. However, I promise to press you no further.

I believe it is important for you, at your present age - to be able to exercise your legs and lungs. For myself, I did not start running until I was forty-seven. In course of time, it became easier and less taxing so that I did not reach my best performance until I was sixty-two - not long after first meeting you. If I am fitter than most men of my age, it is because of my running. So too, I suspect, that running also increases mental alertness.

I persist with my Donne browsing. Have you come across –

> 'Tis true, 'tis day; what though it be.
> O wilt thou therefore rise from me ?
>
> Why should we rise, because 'tis light ?
> Did we lie down, because 'twas night ?
>
> Love, which in spite of darkness brought us hither
> should in despite of light, keep us together
>
> **
> I must confess,
> it could not choose but be profane,
> to think thee anything but thee

Dear Wimsey

Your Donne is marvellous. How I wish it was possible to lie with you in both darkness and light.

I am nearing the end of the *Wilde* biography and finding it very disturbing. The prison experience to which he was condemned for his homosexuality, is so demoralising. As he says "One can understand the person who commits an offence, but how can one understand the punishment metered out by those considered to be good?" It is abominable that the treatment of prisoners often seems so much worse than the crimes committed.   I quail at the thought of him returning to his young lover *Bosie*.** I hope he does not do so (I have not yet finished the book), but I fear he will. When a soul is so deprived - any hope of love, is better than none.

I am sorry I was such a pain in the neck this morning. A typical 'hormonal' day - a bit weepy, niggly etc. At those moments I simply cannot be cool and observant. Please love me anyway.

Dearest – forgive me for my moods which are so characteristic and predictable, but taxing for you. I do try to love you in an even manner, but now and then my emotions erupt. I hope you can accept me even then. Much love – Puss

> **   *Bosie a.k.a. Lord Alfred Douglas* : lover of Oscar Wilde, for whom Wilde was imprisoned, having been charged with an act of gross indecency with another male person. Wilde was pardoned by the British Crown in January 2017 - along with 50,000 other gay men !

Dearest

Life is a strange mix at present – just enough frustration, joy, sadness, conflict, peace and harmony not to be able to relax and take things for granted, but not sufficient to be too disruptive.   Absence makes *this* heart grow fonder.   Love – Puss

My darling - full moon

Forgive me if I did (or did not do) anything today which I should (or should not have) done. I hope that covers all possibilities. Perhaps it was the effect of the moon that led us bedwards. Remember me fondly - as I remember you.

How amazing it is for two people who care for each other to actually *be* together. There are so many other forces which might threaten to tear them apart. In our own case, we live in an uneasy state, never knowing when our precarious balance will be disturbed. But for others, it can be even more so.

Perhaps every moment we are free to be with each other, we should count ourselves blessed - even though there 'appear' to be others who are even more free than ourselves - and more blissful.

It seems to me, as the English philosopher *Bertrand Russell*** maintains, that to love a man (or woman) is the supreme experience of being human, and without it, life has not been fully lived. I suspect it only happens once in a lifetime. By its very nature, I cannot imagine it being repeated.

So my dearest, despite our ups and downs - or perhaps because of them - let us celebrate the sweetest of those times when we are untrammelled by worldly cares and can be at peace together. I kiss the pillow where you lay. *Ta Minette*

> I believe myself
> that romantic love
> is the source of the most intense delights
> that life has to offer
>
> In the relation of a man and a woman
> who love each other
> with passion and imagination and tenderness
> there is something of inestimable value -
> to be ignorant of which is a great misfortune
> to any human being
>
> *Bertrand Russell****

Douglas

Your behaviour today when I was upset makes me wonder what type of person really lurks beneath your cool exterior. Whenever I show any emotion - you reject me. What a marvellous way to control a woman. What a marvellous way to protect yourself against life. Far better for you to read your beloved Jane Austen, and shut yourself away from the world in your mansion, than to have to deal with a person with real conflicts and concerns. Whenever you read Austen or your muse – Samuel Johnson, you become severe and insufferable. When you read Wilde, you disappear for all practical purposes. Amazingly when you were reading Donne - you became loving. It is a pity that phase has ended. It seems our 'love' is dependent upon which book you are reading. How truly sad.

Since you do not understand my love for Bhagwan - who of course is my spiritual guide and teacher - there is little to say to you. Since you find me an object of ridicule at the beach, because I don't swim out to sea as you do, there is no point in speaking to you at the beach and embarrassing you further.

Since you also appear to find me deceptive towards you and also deceptive towards myself (remembering always of course, that a person cannot be deceptive if they are unconscious of the deception), I am surprised you court my company at all. I find your behaviour unacceptable. Your addiction to Jane Austen and other authors, does not make you a very inviting companion.

Reflect upon your deeds. If you recover your sense of humour and are penitent, you may phone me. Do not on any account write. Otherwise, please go and share your brilliance with someone else.

Douglas

I find your letters in your present mood too painful. If you wish, you may ring me, but do not do so, unless there is real affection in your heart. For the record -

* affection means 'goodwill, fond or kindly feeling'
* love means 'an intense feeling of deep affection or fondness'
* warm means 'sympathetic, cordial, friendly, loving'

The definitions are from the *Shorter Oxford Dictionary*, which you gave to me in a moment of 'kindness'.

Whenever we create distance between each other as we have now done, there is a sense of relief at first, as if there is some degree of resolution. I find it easy to love you from afar, because there is just me loving you and no response from you is possible or anticipated. You used to say the same - when writing to me.

I was reading Bhagwan last evening and he stated that in 'relationship', there is always tension and conflict, because the other is not performing as expected. Love is only possible when there is no relationship. Love is a state of being. One simply feels loving towards all - not one person in particular.

I feel that sense of loving when I know that I will *not* be seeing you and when I am not requiring anything from you. But to see you fleetingly at the beach is a kind of torture. To be with you and feel you resisting me - likewise. To love you as I do now (i.e. not seeing you) means that I can love you totally and not be disappointed. It hurts so much to hug you and feel you are not also totally there with me.

You also said yesterday that we are different people now from what we were twelve years ago. On one hand, that is obvious. On the other, you seem to imply that one of us has changed.

I do not think I have altered in my feelings for you, but I am more aware of your multi-faceted personality and less idealistic than at first - because experience has taught me that my longing for the moon is unlikely to be fulfilled.

On another matter - far from accepting that sex is of no real importance, I believe it is of the utmost importance and that the way couples make love determines absolutely, the quality of their relationship and you are living evidence of this.

When we are in harmony, the roses appear, the love letters flow and the glow persists for days. When we are not, we pretend all is well, but you do not touch me, you say you just want to be friends and you do not make love again - sometimes for months.

I am sad without you, but not as sad as I would be if I was with you and felt you withholding yourself from me. Love between such as ourselves is only worthwhile when it is total. I do hope you come to understand in time. In the meantime, know that I love you from afar and yearn for the day when you will delight in entering my world - once again.

Dearest

It is important for us to never deny the strength or depth of love which we feel for each other, though how we find a *modus operandi* is another matter. What are the possibilities ? To be lovers and suffer as we do ? To be friends and not meet (but phone and write) ? To be neither lovers or friends and cease contact (help) ? *Jusqu'à demain* (until tomorrow)

Dear Douglas

If I was to wish for a better outcome, I would hope that N. would die one day, so that we could spend a little time together unencumbered, before you yourself shuffle off your mortal coil. But then you would feel guilty, and not be able to enjoy being in love with me - so there is no way to win. How pleasant it would be to not live in the shadow of her presence – to not feel hurried because of her impending return. Yet we are so used to living on crumbs, we would probably be unable to digest a full meal.

**

Last evening was…. rather lovely. It brought home to me the difficulty in parting from you and the wish in myself at least, to be with you longer. I cannot bear such partings. I want to linger and to share more fully. Since you appear to have no desire of a similar nature - we are at odds.

Coupled with our brief and hurried meetings is the matter of inconstancy. Your feelings for me seem to waver, and I find that I cannot any longer be at the mercy of your waverings. I believe it is possible to love a person with kindness most of the time, and I no longer want to be on the receiving end of your moods. I hope that in time I will be able to find someone who can love me.

Since you are not particularly dissatisfied with your style of life, these words will have little impact upon you. Since you can live quite easily without me for days on end, what I am saying will not affect you very deeply. I am tired of being loved as an abstract idea. I need something more tangible.

··
Our meetings at the beach are quite ridiculous and serve only to whet our appetites. Our lunchtime meetings are almost sacrilegious since my mind is still work-oriented, and your feet are almost out the door. Our Sunday meeting is not adequate. A few tired hours later in the afternoon do not do justice to a love such as ours. Admittedly our letters and phone calls have filled the gap somewhat - but they are not enough on their own.

I do not accept your so-called marriage (*Douglas and N. ceased to be lovers when the relationship with Shobha began*). I do not accept your so-called feelings for N. At times you have spoken of your love-less marriage. I feel, as Bhagwan does, that a new love eclipses the old.

If you choose to let your body remain in the same house that is another matter, but I do not feel that you love N. in the sense that I understand the word. Of course, we all have gradients of affection, and no doubt you can put her somewhere on your continuum - just as I place my mother and brother somewhere on mine.

**
Today I am sitting on the stone bench overlooking the moat at the university. A few ducks and seagulls and many students swotting for exams. Full moon has just passed. The sun is magnificent. Perhaps we could take a bottle of champagne to the river at lunch and lie in the sun. I might visit the beach now and then to keep up my body immunity.

Everyone here is dropping like flies with influenza. I have been reading Bhagwan who says the words 'yes' and 'no' should be eliminated from an intelligent person's vocabulary and substituted with the psychologist *Edward de Bono's* word 'po' - meaning 'perhaps'. Life changes so much every moment that only 'perhaps' can be true. I must return to my labours (my work) - though in truth, they are so enjoyable - the element of labour is absent.**

> **   For fifteen years at the university, Shobha was given absolute freedom to create, and carry out various projects of her own devising – in the areas of publications, public relations, event management, heritage and conservation.

I was speaking to your former secretary at the university this morning. It is so difficult talking to Christians, because they are so convinced they are right. They always allude to hell, implying that you are going there and they are not. They deserve to go, because of their arrogance.

You must find me painful also when I talk (to you) about a possible 'life to come'. Yet at least I don't say it IS so - just that *'I'* accept myself that is so - and *others* say it is so. The lady in question at the university has just been to Borneo as a Christian missionary to convert the 'natives'. As an anthropologist who respects cultures in their own context - I find that hilarious.

I do hope you were not stung again today by jellyfish. I don't like to think of you in the icy darkness out at sea – suffering from your stings. I prefer to think of you warm in my arms - emitting tender noises having climbed the peak(s) with me. Much love – Puss

Dear Puss
For some reason I was expecting you to be at the beach this morning. Perhaps because the just-after-full moon shining on the calm water, made it a wonderland. Everyone this morning remarked on the greater coldness of the water. There are very few of us who persist in swimming out to the buoy, or to where each of us *thinks* the buoy was, before it was removed.

My love
'Twas so nice snuggling into you this morning. I could almost have fallen asleep beside you. Those moments of almost drifting, are the most pleasant and the most reassuring - almost as if you and I are part of each other. It would be lovely to fall asleep and wake together. Since leaving you, I meditated for a while and fell into a deep sleep – so rare for me - after seeing you. It seems to me that sleep during the day is probably of far more benefit than sleep in the evening, because it is out of the ordinary. Do you find it so?

I hope you are now feeling stronger – no doubt your malaise was brought on by your conflict *chez toi*. What a pity that our meeting was sullied by your having to engage in open combat on your return to your 'house'. Perhaps N. has a seventh sense and knows when there has been a 'change' of some kind, however small - in your behaviour ?

Your article on the childhood of Sir James Barrie** was very interesting. We all of course, live our lives through others, and there are unresolved parts of ourselves - and more so for some, depending on their experiences. Perhaps when we no longer have any childhood matters to resolve, we may no longer need the 'other' - but are content simply to be with ourselves.

Must away my love - it has been a stimulating weekend. I reiterate that if at all possible, I hope we can be gentle with each other. Despite appearances at times, I believe we are both very sensitive and easily hurt, though you deny the latter. Much love - Puss

**   *Sir James Barrie* : Scottish novelist and playwright

Dear Douglas

When you spoke in your letter of the division in your mind, it concerned me. It is not surprising, and is inbuilt into our situation, but I also feel that it is not desirable for you to be always split in the way that you are.

'Love divideth - loveth none' is one way of looking at it, but also *'a house divided against itself - must fall'*. How biblical I am today. Though it seems your house has not fallen, despite your dividedness, it might be important to ask - how do you manage to live with yourself in a divided statec? I could not do it.

I am simply amazed at how it is possible for you to survive such a predicament. I am not split. When I admit my love for you - it is so. But whenever I try to give you up, I become split - because it is against my nature and what seems to be to me 'right' (for me).

What is your nature? Once you used to say "If it was simply a matter of the heart, there would be no problem." Is that still the case ? As you know - for me, the way of the heart, is 'the' way. For you, it is otherwise. Yet if your way worked - why do you not sleep ? There is an underlying tension because you know all is not as it should be. I firmly believe that harmony reigns when right action is taken, and vice versa. It is a great dilemma. I wish I could help you more. Please talk to me further.

We are a strange couple. We seem to live most of the time on the promise of love rather than love itself. Perhaps that 'is' love? Perhaps it is not necessary to 'be together' as romantic myths tell us. I know Bhagwan felt his sannyasins would take him for granted, if he was freely available, and that his influence would be greater for being more removed - as he was. Perhaps it is also so for us - as you so often attest. Must away, my love - until the morrow. Much love – Puss

Dearest Puss

I am finding *The Last Chronicle of Barset*** pure joy - so much so that it is slightly saddening to be saying so on the eve of my seventy-fourth birthday. However, it is some comfort to bear in mind that Douglas at seventy-four is not the same person as Douglas at twenty-five – or even, for that matter - Douglas at sixty-two – when we met.

Yesterday was also pure joy - and for me – some reassurance too. I was beginning to think I had run my course and to wonder what it would mean for us. Much love.

**   Novel of English author *Anthony Trollope*

Darling

There is much to say. You are spoiling me again. Your letter was one of the most tender I have received from you. Perhaps the blue light** truly makes us both humble towards each other. There are certainly different levels of love, and the most ennobling seems to be that which puts the other before oneself. If only we rose to such heights more often - or even better - lived in that state.

**   Whenever Shobha was deep in meditation or love, a blue light appeared in the centre of her forehead when her eyes were closed. When Bhagwan left India (temporarily as it transpired) for the United States, Shobha asked him (silently), how she would know he was with her - and the blue light appeared, and has appeared ever since - in profound moments.

This morning I came across C. in the refectory at the university (*who was a mutual acquaintance of Douglas and Shobha*). She said some very nice things about your daughter – that she was honest and sincere, which she felt was very rare in her profession. We had the most wonderful discussion over coffee about theology, Christianity, the 'orange people', you, her philosopher husband, life after death etc. and I did not want to leave.

Her husband is not a Christian and she finds this refreshing because he does not use spiritual language. I remarked that I also found you refreshing for the same reason. She is the first devoted 'religionist' that I know, whose spouse is not like-minded in that area. She really understands our dilemma, though it was only mentioned in passing. All my love – your Puss

Dearest love

I am so sorry not to have realised that you were not feeling well. I am all remorse. Do not feel that we must necessarily 'do' something together this week. I am happy just to be with you, in a relaxed way. The world places too much importance on activity. *Á la prochaine fois – ta Minette* (*see you next time – your Puss*)

Dear Douglas

As a sannyasin of Bhagwan, I accept materialism, in that I don't reject the good things of life, but as a spiritual person in the traditional sense, I am not attached to material things.

As an ordinary member of society, surrounded by those who are embroiled in the mortgage game, I am an outcast because I have made no provision for myself in a material way, and I consort with a man like yourself, which prevents me from jointly embarking upon a materialistic venture with another partner and thus securing my financial future. At the idealistic level, you have no responsibility for me and I have none for you, since I am supposed to be liberated and not need a man or depend upon anyone else for anything.

Realistically - even if I contribute towards superannuation in the near future, thus tying myself down to university employment, this will not guarantee me a worthwhile income when I 'retire', nor will I be able to afford to rent a dwelling on a pension.

So - since there is no-one who wants to look after me now, and you will not be available 'then' (having died), I seem to have no alternative but to investigate purchasing some kind of property and committing myself to mortgage payments which will (unless my mother leaves her house to my brother and myself), be far in excess of what I currently pay for rent.

You have always been surprisingly unwilling to offer any suggestions about what course I should take, other than to say I should not pay such an exorbitant rent - presumably meaning that I should move back into a university flat (or share with others). Surely, even if you are not prepared to take me on as a full-time proposition, you could offer some advice as to what I should do for my future. You are supposed to have some expertise in these matters. Could you not share a little of this with me now - instead of waiting until you die to consider my welfare - and perhaps not even then?

**

I have been very depressed since your recent outburst, and still feel very hurt from what I deem to be your false accusations. You attribute to me the meanest of motives and I think you are entirely unjust. Can you honestly say you are always sensitive to my feelings and that you put my welfare first and only consider 'giving' to me and not 'taking' anything for yourself. I doubt it.

What hurts me most of all, is when you cast me in such a light that you imply I deliberately set out to deceive you, or hurt you or lie to you. This outrages me more than anything. Far from your cutting comments hurting me because they are true as you suggest; they hurt me because they are false. It shows me that you have very little understanding of the kind of person I am, and I wonder how I could love someone who thinks so ill of me.

You demand so much of me, though I am sure you would deny you ask anything at all. You say I must speak in a certain way, use certain vocabulary, not be affectionate, not walk fast, not use flowery language, not make advances, never ask for anything, wait to be approached or contacted, not show any human frailty such as tears, not show any anger or strong emotion, yet be prepared to listen to you when you do not listen to me. It is hard to bear. Between two persons who are in harmony, all question of giving and receiving is irrelevant. Both should take place naturally. Only inferior minds talk of such things.

Dearest

Apropos your comment that "it is better to love than be loved" - is this not an underlying tenet of Christianity and also of Buddhism? The pity of it is that to 'deny oneself' as both religions encourage - and love others - as a practice, rather than a natural inclination - brings out the worst in people. Rather - love, for me, is a welling up, an overflowing - which cares for the other naturally – not as a matter of choice. It has no virtue, but is simply the case. To love with intent - consciously - is to my way of thinking – false and unworthy.

The love that denies oneself - as so many Christians understand it - is not desirable. To love - implies that the issue of oneself is irrelevant. One simply loves or does not love. But the situation is clarified somewhat by the understanding (which was first made clear to me by the German psychologist *Erich Fromm*), that only a person who loves himself or herself can love another. Perhaps you should read his book *The Art of Loving.* It has become a classic.

Love is the overflowing of a full cup. An empty cup has nothing to give. Austerity in one's own life rarely leads to sharing. I have tried the Christian way and the austere way, and neither are conducive to love. I prefer not to think of giving and receiving and who is loved and who loves, but merely to feel the joy that comes when there is a response. I heard Bhagwan say the other day (on tape), that if one's behaviour does not evoke love in the other - be sure it is not love.

I am sitting in the park at the top of your hill surrounded by eager magpies. Forgive therefore, my stilted prose. All my 'love' – Puss

Darling

Miss you awfully. Thank god you only have one wedding anniversary a year, so I don't have to keep away from you. Trollope is so good – he has a touch of Bhagwan in him, in that he 'calls a spade a spade' and does not dither with his words. I wish we could read him side by side in bed and laugh at him together. In a better world, we would be free to crawl into each other's arms at will. It is so unnatural to be apart. *Avec amour – ta Minette*

Dear Douglas

If talking of Wills and Testaments has upset you, I refer you to Trollope's novels, where this is a constant topic of conversation. Perhaps I am unduly influenced by these stories. I have also found in the telling of jokes, that while 'you' seem to think it is fair for a man to tell a (c)rude joke, you do not like it if a woman does so. This is unfair.

Dear Shobha

I am becoming increasingly conscious that advancing years at my stage of life affect not only strength, stamina and the common outward signs of ill-health and aging, but also, and perhaps more importantly - one's temper and attitudes.

Subjectively, this is certainly not all a loss - so long as one's mind is clear. Speaking for myself, I believe the detachment which results from loss of physical drive may enhance some pleasures. When I am inclined to deplore all those wasted years before I really discovered Jane Austen and Trollope, I console myself with the thought that I may not have been ripe enough for them when I was younger.

..
Though I do not want to upset you by urging you to stand up to the waves down at the beach, I nevertheless think it important that you should make some progress in this direction this year, when you return to the beach on a daily basis. You certainly have the necessary strength in your legs.

Rather than expecting someone to teach you how to deal with waves, I believe you would make quicker progress by watching someone and then by practising on your own with small waves. Since I seem to have a distinctive and unyielding way of dealing with them, you should watch someone else and see what they do when the waves approach.

Dear Douglas

Please forgive me if I disappoint you. We are so different you and I, and yet so similar in some respects. I find some consolation in knowing that Trollope, at least, understands me, and perhaps he even understands you (god forbid). His characters are so diverse, especially his women, yet he accepts them all with minimal judgment, unless they are outright rogues. Can you do less? Love me still - even if I choose not to brave the waves. Puss

Dearest

It has been an incredible week. Great passion on the weekend with you. Great love with you and for you on Sunday. Great trauma at work for me with my manager G.** Great distress for you with your prodigal son. Great relief at the thought of the holidays to come, giving time to re-assess and move in a new direction. The possibility of my moving house soon. Feeling weary at the pressure of work and hoping above hope, that it will all turn out well in the end, and I will be free from the shackles of G. and able to find a new vocation.

If only I had tunnel vision it would be easy. There would be no choice, and therefore no anxiety. I know you believe that I am suited to administration, and I admit I do it well - but it is not what I want to do - and yet I don't know what it is that I want to do (apart from sing, dance and write).

Please do not laugh at me. My years in India gave me such a taste of joy and bliss, yes bliss - that I am restless and discontented at times. It is a little like losing one's love and yet remembering the beauty and the sweetness and the grandeur of it all, and wondering if it will ever come again.

Perhaps if I win my union case, I should go to India for a little while, just to reconnect. I am surrounded twenty-four hours a day by those who do not share my attitude to life, and I yearn for contact with something higher.

Perhaps I should come back to the beach, though it is not necessary for me to swim out as you do, in order to feel alive and fulfilled. It is not the challenge of the waves that appeals to me in the ocean, it is the relaxation and play and abandon. Puss

G. (*Shobha's manager*) attempted to demote her – because he felt she wanted his job, as she had acted in his place for three months when his marriage was going through difficulties. Shobha presented her case to the Industrial Commission - requesting a promotion rather than a demotion - and after two years, was restored to her former level. G. was later asked to leave the university.

Darling

I have decided to be more careful in future with whom I speak at the beach. Unless there is a particular shared interest, I prefer the company of women for coffee, dinner, the theatre - or perhaps a mixed group. Then there can be no misunderstanding, as happens with the male of the species. New experiences have a way of making me appreciate what I already have. At times like this, I feel the most fortunate of women. Much love - Puss

Douglas

I feel that we may have discovered a few truths this afternoon, even though they may not be very palatable. You were so understanding and yet as you say, I flogged an issue to its death. Perhaps that is why I feel we have made some progress, though I do not feel at all happy or at peace. Rather - consumed by a kind of rage.

If, as you say, you are feeling more compassionate and sympathetic to N. in recent weeks, this might, as you suggest, explain why you feel guilty when you enjoy yourself with me. If you move closer towards one person with whom you are intimate, it follows that you will become more distant from another person with whom you are, or were - intimate.

There is only so much energy to go around. It seems that you and I are only likely to make love if you are at that time angry or disenchanted with N. If so, this is very disturbing. I do not wish our closeness to be dependent upon N's moods and your attitude to her.

I agree with you that this is probably unconscious, and no-one is to blame. Nevertheless, it follows that I cannot be happy if you put your consideration for N. before yourself and myself. It seems someone must always suffer. One will have a full cup and the other empty, or all will have cups with a few drops in them and no-one will experience any exaltation, only dull mediocrity – the level plain as you would call it.

You said some very hurtful things today, but I am aware that I said many things also which were not kind, though I was seeking a resolution, and not a widening of our conflict.

Dear Douglas

Have just finished watching the television program on *Tolkien's*** life. I am so glad you were able to record it - despite some of his family members uttering nonsense. Tolkien's son Christopher, though rather eccentric - spoke well. I am often amazed at the capacity of some English men to produce beautiful speech without preparation – faultlessly. It is a great art. Every word counts. Women do not seem to have this facility to the same degree. Perhaps oratory is encouraged more amongst the male of the species in English schools.

*C.S.Lewis*** and *Tolkien* certainly have much in common, viz. faith, a brooding melancholy almost, though not severe - playful fun and fantasy and as the tape states, and a strong sense of good and evil. Since we have both enjoyed Lewis, it is easy now to see that they both emerged from the same time and place.

I do not think you have ever read Tolkien. I am not sure it is your cup of tea. Interestingly, *The Silmarillion* by Tolkien, is mentioned in the videotape. You remember of course, that you bought me a first edition. I have not yet delved into it, as its content is quite different and more difficult than *The Lord of the Rings*.

I do hope we are able to be at peace with each other again soon, after our distressing interlude yesterday. Talking to you of the poets Keats and Shelley this morning, lifted me a great deal. They are both up with the gods - especially Shelley. Much love to you – Puss

** *Tolkien, J.R R.* : English writer, poet, philologist, and academic, most noted for the trilogy *The Lord of the Rings* and *The Hobbit*

** *C.S. Lewis* : as mentioned before : British novelist, poet, academic, medievalist, literary critic, essayist, lay theologian, broadcaster, lecturer and latterly – a Christian.

Dear Shobha - full moon

October is the month when I have to immerse myself in the mind-numbing business of income tax returns. Glad to hear you found the Tolkien tape rewarding. The few glimpses of him we were shown, reminded me of *Haldane***, whom I knew reasonably well at University College, London, when I was studying law after the war. As for the English male and what you describe as beautiful speech - this comes more from reading and taking care in the choice of words, than from oratory. It is fostered, of course, by those you mix with.

** *J.B.S. Haldane* : British-Indian biologist and bio-statistician

Dear Puss

In haste. I believe I told you I've been immersed in Trollope for four months now. Maybe I should surface for a while - otherwise I shall become a single-writer bore. Much love

Dear Douglas

The film *(not specified)* was definitely of the tear-jerker variety - at least in the last stages. Very little worthwhile dialogue, as is the case with many American films. Looks and gestures are supposed to be enough.

Usual problem – boy meets girl (who is already married) while husband is away. Girl realises how unhappy she has been in her married state, and contemplates fleeing with boy, but decides she cannot abandon her children or husband because they need her. Pines all her life for the other man and receives mementos of their brief time of loving – after his death. A bit reminiscent of the railway station film '*Brief Encounter* which you so admire - though I'm not sure why.

Perhaps that is all you have ever required from me? A brief encounter? The question of whether to stay or leave - is one which many people have experienced - yet the fear of leaving and the unknown future - prevents them.

In some small way, the film touched a spot with which we can all identify. Do we sacrifice the mundane, and even boring present, with someone we know well, and to whom we are accustomed, for the passion and joy and fear of the new - and the possibility that it may not last.

You have answered it for yourself by staying put, and yet continuing to experience moments of passion and joy with me. You have your cake and eat it? I have also chosen the passion and joy for different reasons. It may be that passion diminishes upon exposure, but because we have not been able to indulge our passion fully and regularly - it has remained.

It seems to me that whatever path one chooses, there is difficulty - whether one stays (having never known the joy), or stays – (having known the joy), or leaves (after experiencing the joy and risking its loss). Much love

Dearest of all possible Douglases

Every time we engage in some kind of activity together, there seems to be difficulty, whether it be swimming out to sea or planning a trip to the country or borrowing your vehicle. Perhaps we should confine ourselves to sweet nothings and cuddling up together and sharing our hearts and thoughts. Everything else seems to end in distress.

Ours is an odd 'relationship'. The most practical of enterprises comes to grief. It is as if we can only co-exist when 'relating' about things of the mind - or in my case - the heart and soul - and perhaps with a bit of body thrown in (to keep us happy). But actually 'doing' things together seems fatal.

If this is so, and I believe it is, perhaps we should not attempt to gain the assistance of the other for practical purposes. Ours may indeed me a marriage 'made in heaven' but not upon this earth. Puss

Dear Puss

A book of letters** for you, in place of a bunch of flowers. A pity the introduction is so brief. On the relevance of privacy - someone, like myself, may keep copies of intimate letters, not (necessarily) with a view to publication, but in the expectation that they will no longer hurt - if they are seen by others at some future time.

It was so pleasant to meet you in the water this morning. But I am mystified by what you said about yesterday. It seems almost to be true that we are better – to put it rather lamely – if we take ourselves by surprise. Yesterday, you were 'nature's glove' indeed. I find it difficult to write to you in easy vein with N. only a few feet away in the next room. Much love

** *The Oxford Book of Letters* (published in 1995)

Letter from Douglas to his daughter

So that you are not taken by surprise, perhaps you should know beforehand that I too shall be at His Majesty's Theatre this evening as the guest of Shobha Cameron. Shobha and I have spent many, sometimes, hilarious, Sunday afternoons exercising our vocal cords in the Masonic Hall, and three of the arias I have often attempted, happen to come from Verdi's opera *Don Giovanni*.**

Shobha long ago convinced me that singing can be rewarding, no matter how indifferent one's performance may be, by professional standards. N. knows about the Masonic Hall, my special interest in Don Giovanni and also where I shall be this evening.

** *La ci darem la mano* (Don Giovanni and Zerlina)

Dalla sua pace (Don Ottavio)

Il mio tesoro intanto (Don Ottavio)

Dear Douglas

It seems we are not *en rapport* at present. You seem to be preoccupied with Christmas and all that it 'does not' represent for you. I am still recovering from the slings and arrows of outrageous fortune of last week - hence the tiredness in the mornings which has precluded my beach attendance.

I do hope that you do not become morose about Christmas as the time approaches, as usually happens. For myself, I prefer to enjoy the few simple delights which are incorporated in what remains of the rituals of this time e.g. the Messiah oratorio, carols by candlelight, a few gifts, an office party, the beach party and the Christmas day gathering at the beach. Surely celebration is a wonderful thing for its own sake - regardless of whether Christmas is the reason.

It was such a pity this morning that I did not make it on time to the beach, because it would have been the ideal day for me to swim out if you had been willing. I am beginning to feel that you and I get on better when we swim together, and don't get on, when we don't. Puss

My darling

Have just returned from my friends in the hills. They are a bundle of laughs as usual. They both have an outrageous sense of humour. P. is preoccupied with his stomach ulcer problems, so I gave him a book of seriously rude jokes, and he and his wife and myself spent the afternoon in rollicking mirth. It was my theory that if he laughed, he would get better. Their daughter (with whom I travelled around England and Wales) had sent me a lovely book on the country of novelist *Thomas Hardy*.

As you know, we tramped across Dorset some years ago, and the pictures of *Hardy's cottage, Maiden Castle,** Maumbury Rings**, Stinsford church* (where Hardy is buried)** and various other spots - bring back the joy of that holiday. So do not think that gifts are not good. Sometimes, if chosen with care - they can bring much joy.

A pity there were no baguettes for N. at the French patisserie, so you were not able to visit me today (with your kisses). These are the most delightful moments in the entire week. Could you not fabricate some other excuse so that our tête-à-têtes can continue? Mornings are so right for love. *Jusqu' à demain* – Puss

   **   *Maiden Castle* : iron age hill fort in Dorchester
   **   *Maumbury rings* : Neolithic henge in Dorchester
   **   *Stinsford church* : St Michael's church, Dorchester

My darling
Thank you for today. *Le vin ouvre le coeur* (wine opens the heart). Much love – Puss

Dearest Darling - Christmas day
You were quite sweet today in the water, and have no idea how much delight it gives me when we play around like fish together. The last two days have been heaven (on earth) above and below the water. Wish you were here at the moment – I am so tired, and would so love to curl up in your arms and go to sleep.

Chapter 14
A moving sea between the shores of your souls

31

2 Tango (2012 - Reproduced with the permission of Vicente Romero Redondo

I must go down to the seas again,
to the lonely sea and the sky,
and all I ask is a tall ship
and a star to steer her by.

I must go down to the seas again,
for the call of the running tide
is a wild call and a clear call
that may not be denied.

And all I ask is a windy day
with the white clouds flying,
and the flung spray and the blown spume
and the sea-gulls crying.

John Masefield – Sea Fever

Many waters cannot quench love
Nor the floods drown it

Song of Solomon

My darling
a.k.a. mon grand poisson (my big fish) - New Year's day

It might be kind to give N. some respite from me - by my *not* appearing at the beach tomorrow. It must be galling, despite what you say - for N. to have had to encounter me at close quarters throughout the Christmas period, though it has been delightful for me, and also for you - to be able to liaise underwater.

Christmas is a time of great tension for people with troubles, and if you and I are not currently distressed with other, that is a great blessing. But it is not so for everyone, and N. is vulnerable at this time - perhaps more so than at any other. Christmas is for happy families. We have not always been *en rapport* at Christmas (as you know). We can thank the sea and making love for keeping us relatively happy this silly season. Much love – our kiss under the water this morning was superb. *Ton petit poisson*

My love

You are the treasure of my body and I yours. I am so glad we did *not* make love today, in view of my odd state. You are so right – that it is only when it creeps upon one, that it should be allowed. You are the light of my life. I am surprised and gratified of late to find you so understanding and aware. Your observations today astounded me. You were definitely three steps ahead.

Did you find the programme (on television) on Trollope splendid? It seems odd that since *we* discovered him, the world has followed suit. Who next shall we prophesy for greatness?

Dear Douglas

I have just returned from T. and F. *(friends of Shobha)* and was presented with a list of their troubles. It is gratifying, though a little disappointing, to realise that my hero and heroine, too have their difficulties. One of the points at issue was that T. wishes to have deep and detailed discussions, and is constantly being interrupted by F. diverting him with trivialities, or in some way unconsciously sabotaging his arguments by refusing to continue them beyond a certain point.

No doubt you will appreciate his viewpoint, since you have also at times, found it annoying when you are interrupted - or not encouraged to continue what you are saying.

I found it so easy, because of my knowledge of you, to understand both points of view, and I believe I contributed something worthwhile to the unravelling of the causes of their discontent. There is probably a deeper reason of course. F. wants to be spontaneous, and finds T.'s logical, analytical approach to everything e.g. the analysis of words - rather stultifying at times. It was amazing listening to their complaints, to realise you and I have been through these waters ourselves.

T. refuses to believe there are gender differences, but I am not so sure. Women are, to my mind (at least those with whom I am intimate), quite tangential in their thinking and utterances, and find it difficult to keep to the point.

Dearest Douglas

I realised this morning while dancing to a tape of Bhagwan songs, that there have been two glories in my life – loving him and loving you - and these are in many ways inseparable. To know god on the one hand is only half the story. To translate that love, however awkwardly, into love for a beloved such as you have been to me, is quite another matter.

I miss you so at times and do not really enjoy our current rather low-key way of relating. I would rather be ecstatically over the moon with you, and able to express myself in this fashion - without feeling it is out of place. Must rush, my dear – am full of the spirit. I hope you can understand.

Dearest Puss

Sorry to have left you rather abruptly yesterday, after such a delightful commingling of bodies, minds and souls. When I got back (home), I was suddenly overwhelmed by tiredness and later fell to wondering if our being together in such a way, may not be demanding - and so possibly exhausting.

Please do not misunderstand me. If what I suggest is true, it would not in any way detract from the joy and stimulation we experience. On the contrary, it is naturally to be expected, as when a person is emotionally exhausted after listening say, to *Parsifal*. My reflection for the day.

> **   *Parsifal* : Douglas' favourite Wagnerian opera, which he listened to daily, while carrying out his yoga exercises. The opera is based upon a 13th-century epic poem of the knight Parsifal - and his quest for the Holy Grail. The music made Douglas weep.

I sometimes wish my mind was not so active. An intellectual St Vitus dance - probably not healthy and becoming more pronounced as I get older. It stems in part, from a growing impatience with much commonly-accepted thought. Though I tend to regard myself as rather selfish, I find nevertheless that I *do* think of doing things for people when other *kind* souls do not.

Mon bien-aimé

I am engaged in a most peculiar exercise. I have been revising my *Song of Love* (which I now *call Journey of a Sannyasin to differentiate it from the poems),* for the twentieth time - and yet surprisingly, it still admits of revision. But try as I might, I do not come to the end of my editing. It has a life of its own, and I enjoy the process tremendously.

Each time I read it through, I feel as if I am again in India. I am amazed that I was fortunate enough to record my feelings - however simple they may be. That is its magical effect. It feels miraculous – and can be so transporting. It elevates me to the state I describe in the text - and I find myself believing what I have written - so much so, that for a short while - I am actually an enlightened soul. Such deception - or perhaps - a moment of truth. I do hope you will cast your eye over it when I am finished - if indeed that day comes - though you will no doubt only prune it further, until there is nothing left - as is your wont.

Yet all that is really true and magnificent cannot be reduced to mere words on a page. Perhaps there is another secret in language - that has little to do with sophistication of language, but the harmony brought about by the juxtaposition of a few elementary words, in the right manner. When you first became acquainted with my poems, I believe you commented in a similar vein.

My dearest one - how odd that you of all people, should be the one and the only one, ever to have read or appreciated my little book - when we are so far apart in our expressed understanding of the world and its purpose. Perhaps because of your knowledge of me, you were able to sense for a brief second, what it is that I have experienced.

I would love to write to you a *billet-doux (love letter)* in French - but the hours creep on apace, as Gilbert** said in *H.M.S. Pinafore* - and so I must fly.

By the way – did you realise that you said the *word* in your letter of today. You spoke of commingling of bodies, minds and *souls. Wonder of wonders - a miracle, a miracle.***. I notice however, that you omitted '*hearts,,* so presumably you linked hearts and souls together under the one umbrella.

> **   *W.S. Gilbert* – librettist for the Gilbert and Sullivan operas
> **   Song from the musical *Fiddler on the Roof*

Despite the exhaustion, which I believe may have been brought on by anticipation, fear and apprehension on both our parts about whether our making love, would or would not happen, we were a great team in a very subtle fashion. The sleep I felt when you left me, was not just exhaustion. It was a languid and sweet bolt from the blue, as if I was drugged in a very lovely way. How nice it would have been to fall into sleep with you. For most of the populace of course, that is just what they do. *Ta minette avec tout mon amour*

Dearest Puss

I seem in the last few days to be leading a full and exciting, but exhausting life. My enjoyment of Jane Austen's noval *Persuasion*, against my expectations - was perhaps a flow-on from our union earlier in the day. I was in a daze and still am - compounded by tiredness, drug-deficiency and the pulse-quickening near-shave of Friday morning when we were almost caught in the act.   Much love

Darling

You spoil me excessively and I love it so. What else are lovers for but to heal, through acts of kindness and joy, all those incidents in the past which have caused us to see life as less than perfect.

It has been a time of fun and surprise these last few days. Wouldn't it be marvellous if it was related to you giving up your old drug, and the new drug was allowing you to be your outrageous self? Your letters do not astonish me, because there has always been a part of you that lets go occasionally. What is amazing to me, is the persistence of your openness over longer periods.

The Austenian-Trollopian** world is almost complete in itself. It would be possible, if one did not have to venture out nine to five, to live in its aura most of the time, provided one's friends were of a similar 'persuasion' *(pun on Jane Austen's novel Persuasion)*.

For myself, I embrace both the Victorian and the *orange* (mystical) way of life. The first has beauty, wit, delicacy, grace, refinement, gentleness, romance and even love, of the devoted kind. The second has humour, joy, fun, abandon, sensuality, passion, song, dance, ecstasy and the silence of meditation. I want them all.

**

The problem with Calvinist** theory is that work is exalted, and respect is not given to so-called idleness. For me, idleness is the way to enlightenment. To be unoccupied allows time for reflection at worst and meditation at best. To work totally – to be absorbed - is desirable, if the work be good. To relax utterly – as when having communed as we have done with our bodies (and souls) is to me - the greatest state of all. There are pleasures to be found in both.

Dearest – we are so fortunate. Yesterday was a delight. Surprise seems to be the key. And it cannot be managed. Nor indeed can the sea (in the early morning) ! One day - we may try the waves together. But again, it cannot - for a creature such as myself – be arranged in advance.

I shall watch the video of *Four Weddings and a Funeral* then go to bed with Jane Austen and in the words of Gibran – *to sleep with a prayer for the beloved in my heart and a song of praise upon my lips*. Until tomorrow - your Puss

- **   *Jane Austen and Anthony Trollope* : 19th century British authors.
- **   *The Protestant Calvinists* - who extolled the virtues of hard work and industry, broke away from the Catholic church in the 16th century during the Reformation.

Darling

I love you for a great many things – not least, your arrival this morning in the wee small hours on my doorstep - having cycled several miles from your home. In the words of my poem :

> this life is just surprise
> and more surprise
> and so my eyes are wet
> with tears of joy
> and wordless wonder

Sleep well, my love – Puss

My dear melting-mate

Being together this afternoon was like a trial (ordeal) by fire, but I am not complaining. We covered a lot of ground and although there was no absolute conclusion or resolution, we did at least agree that love is *melting* - and that is not insignificant. What we mean by melting is another subject. Do we melt when we listen to music ? I believe we do. Therefore, melting is not only when two egos melt - as this afternoon (for short moments), but also when one's own ego melts and lets an outside force in.

Perhaps it would be fair to describe the state of being influenced by music, as being *in love.* Certainly that is the mystical way of using the term. The highest state - being a kind of *in-loveness* with all things, and not focused upon an object or person. This idea would surely appeal to you.

On returning from visiting my brother, a quote came to mind related to my mentioning to you the book by Janet Frame entitled *Angel at my Table*. The title derives from a saying in Hebrews in the Old Testament -

> Let brotherly love continue
> Be not forgetful
> to entertain strangers,
> for thereby
> some have entertained angels
> unawares

Isn't the language of the Bible magnificent - despite its theological limitations? I would not have believed that these words were in my unconscious, but they were hidden deep down.

You are quite right about the *Book of Common Prayer* in its impact on one's later appreciation of literature (though it was you, in the Anglican tradition, and not myself - who was exposed to it). It is a pity that so many children are not introduced to the best of all spiritual literature at an early age - which at rock bottom, supports the same values and sentiments – caring for one another.

So, my dearest darling, perhaps we should both be careful with each other, because it may be that we are *ourselves* those very angels. The words of course are symbolic. I do not expect to sprout wings (yet).

I did not feel today that there was any trace of real criticism in what we were saying about each other - and therefore no bitterness. I hoped and certainly intended that we were discussing our situation in an objective way, and that neither of us was hurt by the process.

As you said, it was disturbing - and I do not mind that at all. If we were unaffected, that would be a waste. Which is precisely why creatures such as you and I do indeed *change*. If we do not change - what is the point of it all ? To live our daily lives without variation would to me, be pointless. At least this way, we can engage in endless discussion and observation and pretend we are getting somewhere. The exercise itself is satisfying - though we always agree to differ when we part.

Darling – we will never be able to sew up our discussions to our mutual satisfaction. That is why I am writing to you, and that is why we will need to meet again. If all was resolved, we would be at an end. All my love – *ton ange* (your angel)

Douglas - full moon

I am not ungrateful, but I am very slightly on edge in the last few days due to perhaps not being at the peak of physical fitness. Exercise is next to godliness (perhaps).

It is true that my only desire in life is to melt - whether it be in love (*avec toi),* in meditation, in music, dancing .... but (as we have agreed), it is equally true that it is not possible to make melting happen. Melting simply happens, or does not. I weep inside sometimes when I long for a melting moment with you, but I do understand that it cannot be managed. Forgive me.

32
Robert Burns
Scottish poet, composer and collector of traditional songs

Dearest

My love is like a red, red rose
that's newly sprung in June.
My love is like a melody
that's sweetly played in tune.

As fair thou art, my bonnie lad
so deep in love am I,
and I will love thee still, my dear
'til all the seas gang dry.

'Til all the seas gang dry, my dear
and the rocks melt with the sun.
O, I will love thee still, my dear,
when the sands of time have run.

**

Had we never loved sae kindly
Had we never lov'd sae blindly
Never met – or never parted
We had ne'er been broken-hearted

Ae Fond Kiss

The song is of Burns of course – songs I used to sing very much in my folk-singing days (and still do). The sight of your blood-red roses by my bed made me run this evening to my *Oxford Book of Quotations* in the hope of finding many verses which I could send you in response.

I imagined there would be much that was appropriate, but in fact there is no verse which does justice to my sentiments. I was then inclined to rush to my Italian dictionary and to practice that language upon you, but I remembered you asking me not to use another tongue to speak to you of love (due to my linguistic inadequacies). So you are left with my own unadulterated prose for better or worse.

Our lunch today was very, very pleasant. Perhaps we are becoming used to each other ? Sometimes it seems that when we are in a café - all that is around us disappears or is meaningless – almost as if we are in a kind of trance.

When I return to work after seeing you, I would be quite happy to sit and dream for a while before returning to my labours. I am beginning to feel that the creative urge (to write, at least, and possibly to sing), will only return when we *have world enough and time* as Marvell says** - to dwell on some of the ideas that you and I share when we are together.

** *Christopher Marvell* : English metaphysical poet

I do hope you are beginning to absorb the new medication and that there are not too many (side) effects. Let me know if you have any further signs or symptoms. Goodnight my love, and as Gibran would say - may you and I '*sleep and wake at dawn with a wingéd heart and give thanks for another day of loving'*.

Dear Puss

Am on the way back from photocopying in the library. A couple of pieces for you when I've sorted all of them. *The Economist* (from which some of the articles are taken) has been one of the important intellectual stimulants of my life for fifty years. How young this must make you feel.

My back aches a bit from yesterday's extraction of the root of your tree. But nothing serious, I hope. *Ex abundante candela.* A lawyer's phrase - probably not in the Concise Oxford Dictionary, meaning 'from an excess of care' (for you, or at least - your tree).

Darling

Wish you were still in my arms ! How nice it would be to drift into sleep with you... You have a beautiful face and look so lovely in bed – so pink and perfect. We are very fortunate to have each other. Sleep well – my love – your Puss

My Darling

Forgive the choice of vase and the poor flower arrangement. I looked for red roses, but drew a blank. I feel slightly light-headed today. Probably the combined effect of making love yesterday and my five kilometre run this morning. On each occasion, I rather surprised myself, though I must confess that I had been thinking of you for some days. *La Traviata*** with** all its associations for us, must have stirred something. Until then, your superannuated Alfredo.

Shobha performed in the chorus of the Verdi's opera *La Traviata* at the Regal Theatre. Alfredo is the hero of the opera and in love with Violetta.

Darling, darling, darling

What a chilly night to be out and about (at the rehearsal of Traviata). My tootsies are aching from the new high-heeled shoes (for the role). I feel as if I am on stilts.

A little camaraderie is developing amongst the chorus as the staging gets under way and we begin to know our positions and the expectations upon us. No-one seems to know the words perfectly. Being thrown in at the deep end (as I joined the cast late in the rehearsal schedule), has been an advantage for me. I have been forced to learn the entire score - in a short space of time. Our principal understudy for Violetta's role has the flu and another chorus member has injured herself. The four directors need coordinating. Wish I could help them out.

It is fascinating to watch the show evolve. So much simply comes together at a certain point, but great faith is needed. It is a lot of fun. Having a cast of all ages is also a great advantage. The young lend a lightness and the older ones give a kind of stability and assurance. Will see you tomorrow, my love. Keep warm – your Puss

My darling

Am feeling strangely, but pleasantly, languorous. Almost as if drugged. After speaking to you this morning (on the phone), I decided on the spur of the moment to run as far as the boat-house, following a slightly longer course than my usual one, in order to keep off the busy streets. I was expecting to get drenched, but the rain held off.

It is almost three years since I gave up (as I thought - for good) my weekly five kilometre run. I may go back to it. If I resign myself to a slower pace – as I do now down at the beach – I find it does not exhaust me unduly. It's true I breathe hard while running and for some time afterwards. But I've always regarded this as the main object and benefit. So too, with climbing.

I hope you have room – in your house and your heart – for the flowers. Recently, we seem to have discovered a slightly different blend of gentleness and physical warmth. Not very well put, but I'm sure you know what I'm trying to say. Much love

Darling

You must think me the most conceited of creatures to be troubled about a costume (for my role in *La Traviata),* but that is the reality. Now it seems it has been resolved to my satisfaction. The costume I was allotted yesterday has now been discarded and I have acquired a new and beautiful gown – a very rich and bright blue satin - covered with imitation pearls – lots of flesh visible (shoulders) and even a hint of the desired cleavage. Our director insists on cleavage.

So, I can now sleep again. I may have to pay for my costume hire and it is rather expensive (by my standards), but it is worth it for the peace of mind and fortunately, it matches all my other gear i.e. gloves, flowers and jewellery. Enough of all this girlish nonsense ! You are very patient with me. What <u>is</u> nice is the way the girls in the cast help each other. They genuinely seem to empathise and care. Quite surprising. No element of competition.

You are quite right about our kisses (being so stirring) this morning. I was also worried that we would be heard by N. (who was) upstairs. Much love – your very *blue* Violetta

Dearest

I hope you are enjoying the vitality of your small guests *(very young grandson and granddaughter).* Play them some opera – they are never too young. We were raised on Gilbert and Sullivan and other operatic excerpts as children. It is uncanny how much infiltrates a child's brain and heart. Until tomorrow. I love your early morning visits (on the bike). Your Puss

Darling

It is not that I do not wish to meet you. I am simply exhausted (from rehearsals) and must keep body and soul together. Please keep in touch. *Je t'adore.*

Sweetheart - Alfredo

The most terrible disaster happened this evening at the opera. I am still a little stunned. The curtain opened on a card-playing scene, closely followed by the gypsy/matador dance sequence. Half the women were offstage when the curtain rose, but they were supposed to be onstage. The call to the dressing room had not been heard. I'm still not sure why. Faulty equipment, we believe. Anyway, I was talking upstairs to several female chorus members and suddenly became aware of a deathly silence. All the men had gone.

I rushed downstairs with one other girl and saw the curtain rising. I did not hesitate, but moved onto the stage to centre front, gesticulating in welcome to various people at the ball (scene) and finally came to rest in my proper location at the edge of the stage close to the audience - on Alfredo's knee.

Then I realised other women were filtering in slowly one by one. I am told the musical director did not even know anything was amiss. It was glossed over so effectively - but the fact remains, it was a disaster. You cannot have a cast coming on, in such a fashion. It was unforgivable !

We still do not know what happened, but in future we will all be early. The men were already just offstage shifting furniture - so were ready on time. I am appalled at myself for inattention, but I am not sure what I should have heard as a cue. I usually take your aria *Di provenza*** as my cue, but I did not hear it - over the communication system. We are all very unnerved by the experience.

Our director's wife timed the arrival of their baby for Thursday, so we stayed behind for champagne on stage after the performance, to 'wet the baby's head'. Must away my love – Violetta

**   *Di provenza* – aria sung by Alfredo's father in *La Traviata*, and also sung by Douglas in the Hall when rehearsing with Shobha - so it had great significance.

Douglas

Today was so disappointing, from my mother's point of view. She is now eighty-five. I don't seem to have the inclination or patience to deal with her well, when she is out of the nursing home. I am quite good when she is inside. I do not think I will take her out again alone. It is better when my brother is there. My mother does not know he is in England with his wife, and I have not said.

I hope you enjoy the grandchildren tomorrow. As I said before – play them some opera. I remembered last week that I performed Gilbert and Sullivan when I was eleven years old at primary school – *Three little maids from school* and the *The flowers that bloom in the spring* (in costume!). I also used to recite quotations from scripture at this time with one of my religious girlfriends. We loved the poetry of the words. My love of poetry was well-developed by the age of ten, due of course to my own natural inclination and one very special teacher who loved literature. A teacher can be so important - sufficient to change a child's life.

I watched the programme on *Timothy Rice* (who wrote the libretto for the rock opera *Jesus Christ Superstar*), but it saddened me to see how he had aged. The cleverness and simplicity of his lyrics is almost breathtaking for me. JC Superstar did literally change me, as I discovered it at a time when I was reviewing my commitment to Christianity - around the age of nineteen.

My heart has not been missing so many beats today (as it was), so that is reassuring. I think I am still recovering from the opera. It was like being in survival mode for two months. Today was a weepy day at times (hormones of course). I suppose you gathered that. I momentarily lost control because of my chemistry. How frail we creatures are. Sleeplessness makes *you* irritable. Hormones make *me* cry! Dear Douglas – love me tenderly if you can. Your Puss

Dearest

If you find that your changing moods and body sensations make you uncertain at times about whether to meet me, please let me know. There seems to be nothing I can do to assist you during your process of drug withdrawal, except to try not to tax you in any way.

It might be best now and then for us to phone each other rather than meet, if you are not up to seeing me. We can of course write to each other if all else fails. Sometimes our most tender moments have been on the phone or via letters. It is a gruelling business for you, and I wish I could help you in a practical way.

We complain often about the state of the world, but modern technology can be useful to keep in touch in ways unheard of years ago. I wish you had email. A friend of mine recently went to hospital and happily communicated with his wife by phone during this period - without visits. However, there is a certain type of writing (such as ours) which necessitates the pen - however useful and fast a computer or phone may be. Much love and happy birthday – Puss

Dear Puss

In haste. I soldier on with my protracted drug withdrawal programme. Long though it is, sensations change from day to day. You ask (in your last letter) how you can help. Answer : don't complain, directly or obliquely, of neglect. Even more important, don't ask me silly questions, such as whether I think I shall ever want to make love to you again.

Dearest - full moon

I wonder if you watched on television the programme *ce soir* (this evening) on the *history of the marathon* ? It was strangely stirring and I was in tears more than once. You will say that is not unusual for me. The interview with the woman who pioneered women's marathons was superb.

It makes me realise how much more is possible for all of us, and how marvellous it must be to be truly 'fleet of foot'. I used to run to the shops as a child. My mother sent me because I was so quick to return. I was censured by teachers at school for running along the corridors. At university, I often embarrassed myself by running around the campus (whereas now it would be fashionable to put on state-of-the-art running gear to do so).

How good it would be to be like this again. I have always wanted to run a marathon. Everything at present seems to hark back to Greece. I am looking forward to being there soon. Couriers in the golden days of Athens - where the marathon originated - apparently ran 160 miles in 36 hours. What a feat. It sounds impossible - we must discuss this further. *Je t'aime* – Puss

My darling

Yesterday was strange and wonderful. I was serious when I said you made me feel better, for soon after I got back here, I began to feel rather low again. I tried to get some sleep, but did not manage it. Last night, I woke ridiculously soon after falling asleep, after which it was a fitful affair until 3 am this morning, when I gave up the struggle and resigned myself to being wide awake.

And so, to Trollope. Have finished his book *Ralph the Heir.* It is, in many ways, the most Trollopian of his novels: a weak though likeable hero, a rambling uneventful plot, no heroics or extremes of character with smooth and easy conversational exchanges. Yet it contains a fine and subtle study of the corrupting effect of sustained indecision and unrecognised selfishness.

Trollope thought it one of his worst novels, but it was well received by the *Times, Spectator* and other journals when it first appeared in 1871. An American critic asked rhetorically why it was that American writers living in a classless society, were unable to describe people in the natural and amusing way that Trollope - living in class-ridden England - seemed to find so easy.

Contemporary reviews make the point that Trollope's characters gain much of their persuasiveness from his delineation - invariably charitable - of their weakness and self-deceptions. The American author *Henry James* who was writing shortly after Trollope's death - said Trollope did not attempt to tell you why people in a given situation would conduct themselves in a particular way; it was enough for him that he felt their feelings.

This accords with the English novelist C.P. Snow's view of Trollope having been the finest practical psychologist of the nineteenth century. The wider lesson here is that a truly intelligent person often eschews theory.

This makes me wonder whether it may not be that true artists such as Shakespeare, Austen and Trollope – simply 'do it', without the Procrustean** incubus of theory, and as with the centipede** and his flowing legs - could not continue to move - if driven to explain how it was done.

> the centipede was happy – quite,
> until the toad – in fun,
> said "pray - which leg comes after which"
> which worked his mind to such a pitch,
> he lay distracted in a ditch,
> considering how to run

I suspect that Trollope wrote in a trance-like state, quite inconsistent with cool application of worked-out theories. So too, perhaps with Mozart. It then falls to lesser, nowadays academic, mortals to draw attention to the patterns and uniformities discernible in what the true artist does. We must talk about this some time. Sorry to inflict my musings on you. Your Douglas

**   *Procrustean*: enforcing uniformity at the expense of individuality
**   The centipede effect (above) : poem by Katharine Craster in the 1870s with many later variations.

Darling

Sunday gave us both a taste of closeness which was quite other-worldly to put it lamely. I dared to hope, or at least to express the hope, as I so often expressed it in years gone by - that our happiness would last forever - something I am loathe to allow myself to feel, because of the impossibility of our ever being able to share more than a few hurried moments with each other.

Having opened the floodgates - the feelings poured in and out. I wish I could allow that hope to remain. It is so much more beautiful for me to imagine that one day, somehow, somewhere, we might be free - than to accept that a few moments together are all that there will ever be.

Your idea of living in another country with N., or even visiting that country for a long period would of course, mean the end of us. Although you say it was simply an idea in your mind - hearing your 'idea' naturally shakes me to the core. Surely you can understand how I would feel.

We have only a few days more together before I go to Europe, and although it may be unrealistic to hope that our happiness continues, I would prefer in the short time we have left, to float along dreaming that you and I are one. I do not know whether you and I could live together happily - but I am certain that for myself, I would prefer a situation where we are both available to each other, at any hour of the day or night when we choose to be - without the presence of another person influencing our behaviour. That is not the case - and therefore my happiness is not complete. You do not believe in such completeness. I do.

Shobha

Our first kiss this morning had for me, a freshness and intimacy I find difficult to explain. I recognise, more than I once did, the importance of touching, caressing and kissing in warm relationships. Yet I am tempted to suggest we should not kiss as we did this morning, unless it is open for us to go all the way.

Against this, as this morning shows, a kiss may take on a life of its own, so that what starts as little more than affectionate salutation, may lead to a rapid quickening of the pulse and so to a point of no return. When this happens, it is not a smooth progression, but rather a series of steps, sometimes taken only after hesitation.

I have been reflecting today on how we stand in relation to each other and what the future may hold in store for us. It is reasonable to suppose that my protracted program of withdrawal from my drug, which has hammered me almost beyond belief, has something to do with it - together with your impending departure for Europe.

Darling - written by Shobha to Douglas on her arrival in London

The flight was turbulent, but the company delightful. A young woman of Hindu/Buddhist parents and I, discussed religion for five hours from Perth to Singapore and a university lecturer's psychologist wife and I shared our thoughts from Singapore to London.

I found my tour of the *Bank of England* with my cousin's friend, who works there – fascinating. The staff were attired in pink velvet jackets and top hats. Lunch was of course, silver service standard with a nourishing vegetarian menu. We visited the quarters where the Queen, Prime Minister and ambassadors wait to see the governor, and I availed myself of the loo which Queen Elizabeth uses – when she is there.

Visited your Sam's house and *Ye Olde Cheshire Cheese* tavern, which Sam was supposed to frequent. A very cold and windy day. London is freezing. Visited *Leighton House Museum* and walked from Holland Park to the *Victoria and Albert Museum* via *Kensington Gardens.* The Museum was overwhelming as you know, and a few hours do not do it justice. Circumnavigated *Albert Hall* (as it is circular), and could not enter, but was offered cheap tickets for the Proms outside its portals, which I politely declined.

Today I visited the Polish parents of my brother's wife - in Ealing, and was wined and dined in true Polish fashion. One of their relatives is married to a professor of nuclear physics at the Sorbonne, so I have their address and may contact them when my cousin and I visit Paris in a week or so.

There is so much theatre and music here, and it would be wonderful to visit London purely for that purpose e.g. Wilde's *The Ideal Husband* is on at the Old Vic, Shakespeare's *Two Gentlemen of Verona* at the New Globe and the musical *Les Miserables* at the Palace. We managed to obtain seats for *Les Mis* and sat transfixed - after the closing curtain - for half an hour – it was so moving.

Have booked for an evening river cruise with dinner and orchestra up the Seine, for when my cousin and I reach Paris. I will dream of you when I am *under the bridges of Paris* and send you my love. I wonder often about how you are feeling. May each day be a little easier for you with your reduced medication. All my love – your devoted Puss

Dear Puss

I shall post this letter tomorrow, in good time to reach London before you return from your whirlwind European tour. In following your progress from day to day, I find I visualise sharply and at once, the places I know, like Nice, Florence and Rome. But Barcelona was simply a blank.

Though the ravages of winter are only too obvious on the beach, the action of gentler seas has already restored a lot of sand, but the water is still treacherous, with lots of rips and currents.

Have been reading a commentary on Trollope by Michael Sadlier which refers to Trollope's fascination for Kate Field - as reflected in his letters to her. Trollope was forty-seven and Kate only twenty when they first met in Florence. Kate evoked in Trollope, responses and a side of his nature which he never revealed to anyone else.

Sadlier thought it beyond question that Trollope loved her - and that it was equally clear - though he was physically and emotionally a vigorous man - that he never lusted after her - in the sense of wishing to make love with her. This set me wondering about attitudes and expectations in the mid-nineteenth century, and the place of sex in the love of a man for a younger woman.

If you ask why Trollope never fantasised about making love to the beautiful young Kate, the answer is surely that it was unimaginable that he should do so - as making love to a beautiful sister is outside the imagination of most men. And it would be silly and presumptuous for us to think that Trollope's love for Kate was less than it might have been, because of this, or that we, in modern times, are to be envied for our unbridled imagination.

Though sex adds a new dimension to love, I suspect that in doing so, it tends to exclude or put an end to some of the ennobling effects of a man's love for a woman. Turgenev's *First Love*** (where a young man longs for a woman he will never have) - may be the highest form of love.

I am being knowingly provocative in pursuing this line of reasoning. You can take me to task when we next see each other. Perhaps I should admit, for what it may imply, that while you have been away, my imagination of you has at times been pretty riotous. Yet when I made overtures to you after we first met, I was so free of such imaginings that I kept N. posted about what I was doing.

I shall not tempt providence by saying that I am on the mend physically. I am certainly stronger and more robust than I was when I saw you off. Hence perhaps my aforesaid imaginings. For the past fortnight, I have run up to the groyne (at the ocean) and back every morning. I have also resumed doing yoga in a more testing way. My sleep is still very irregular and patchy, with a lot of dreams. But in total, I am now sleeping about six hours a night. I plod on with my (drug) withdrawal programme, with estimated dosage reductions each week.

I think of you a lot and, rather to my surprise, have found myself counting the days until you come back.

** *First Love* : by the Russian novelist Ivan Turgenev.

Shobha writing to Douglas from Europe

There are eleven days to go of the tour (of Europe), and most of the participants are beginning to feel a little weary. Such close proximity to others and such a pace ! Nevertheless, it has been a great experience in knowing how far you can push yourself, if necessary. We are sometimes given a five, fifteen or thirty-minute break and get out of the bus, and it is surprising how much can be achieved in a short time. I imagine the army is a little like this.

You have a choice of whether to go to the toilet, have something to eat and drink, go shopping or walk around and try to get some exercise. In my case, I sang opera with one of the passengers from Malta in these short interludes (to the *chagrin* of the other tour members - though we chose a location away from the main group).

I wish I could talk to you in privacy, but it is difficult to ring you when my room-mate is always present, though I could search for a public phone. Some of the hotels allow you only to use their reception phone, which is of course, entirely unsuitable. I will ring you when I get back to London and perhaps ask you to ring me from my home. That is the only way to be able to speak freely.

I found some English people yesterday on another tour and it was good to slot into the Anglo mind-frame instead of the American one. So many of the people on the tour bus are from America. I have adjusted to most of them, but still prefer European company. The constant expression of the Americans - whatever they chance to see - is 'O my God' - until my teeth are on edge.

I am in Sorrento and about to leave for Pompeii this morning and Assisi this evening. Forgive the rain spots – it has just started sprinkling. The other evening, we went to a tarantella show and in the last act, I was asked to come on stage and participate. I think they had spies in the audience watching people who looked excessively boisterous in their appreciation. I was told to "just copy what I do" by my escort. I did so in a Gilbert and Sullivan, Chaplain-esque slapstick kind-of-way, which seemed quite natural to me.

The principal tenor was dressed in mafia-godfather gear and the other lead singer was in an admiral's uniform. I just happened to be in a long dress of black and gold. It became very amusing, and the finale ended with the three of us upstaging one other in singing '*O solo mio*' and I was able to use my 'operatic' range to full effect.

What was surprising was how it was possible to improvise without notice. Everyone has been saying how good it was, and a few said they thought I was part of the show, so I suppose I have to believe them. It was certainly a lot of fun. My darling – breakfast in five minutes – must go – the food is appalling. I love you with all my heart. Puss

<u>*My darling – Douglas writing from Australia to Shobha in England*</u>

By chance, when I called into the clinic to see my doctor, I met another doctor instead, who knew of me through the university, and when hearing my story, asked why at my age, I was bothering to get off tranquilisers after a stint of twenty-six years. His own mother was hooked in a similar way, and finally decided it was not worth trying to get off them. He thought current attitudes of general practitioners were too coloured by the fear of being sued.

Which leaves me in a dilemma. Whether to persevere with my withdrawal programme, in which I seem to have hit a wall, or settle on a substitute equivalent to roughly a quarter of my long-time use of the original tranquiliser *(which is where I am in my withdrawal programme)*.

Darling, I do look forward to seeing you and kissing you. Oddly enough, this morning's newspaper has a foolish article on the neglect of kissing in modern movies. It seems that the lingering kisses of former times are now found by moviegoers to be a waste of time and rather a bore. This makes me wonder whether our own experience may not be exceptional. I shall put a few things in the fridge for you before you get back. Until the fourteenth.

<u>*Douglas writing to Shobha in England*</u>

Have fitted adaptor to your front garden pipe so you can attach your hose and wash down your front verandah. I also hosed down front door and its flyscreen. Watered your plants yesterday and cut back your lantana bush where it obstructed your drive. Sharpened, cleaned and oiled your secateurs. Drove and washed your car yesterday and put battery on charger for a couple of hours. Most of the victuals are courtesy of N.

Have cleaned and checked your TV, video and hi-fi equipment and reassembled it so the television sound is piped through your amplifier and speakers, to give a much better sound. Beside the television are two tapes with episodes of *Singing in the Streets* and two blank video tapes. There is a current television guide in your lounge, on your piano stool. I have restored the Mac computer and printer and put an extension cord from the kitchen to your back verandah. There is a recorder concert at the university on Thursday. Shall we go and have a smorgasbord lunch first at University House when you return?

My dearest darling – on Shobha's return from Europe

I am feeling rather philosophical at present about our situation. As I said today, there is only a problem if we make one. There is a saying of the German philosopher Nietzsche that *'Life is not a problem to be solved - it is a mystery to be lived'* and that is how I feel - at least today.

Having returned home after a long absence, I am so aware of all the wonderful aspects of life here in Perth. This evening, I sat on the foreshore near your home, and felt our river was at least as lovely as many I had seen. To look for problems, when we are surrounded by so much beauty, seems unnecessary. It is better to focus upon all that is good, rather than potential difficulties.

We have endured our situation for thirteen years, and there seems little prospect of significant change. You thought an absence would be useful to both of us. I cannot see that it has changed anything at all, except from my point of view – I am conscious of all that I have, and grateful for it.

From my observation of you, I can only see that you have been unsparing in your attention and concern for the various material aspects of my life in my absence, which makes me feel extremely tender towards you in my thoughts, when I am away from you.

I am sorry that there have been a few hitches in your attitude towards me since my return, but I do not think it has been entirely without benefit. Both our altercations have left us feeling warmly towards each other, and have probably brought us closer together.

I do not think you will ever be able to relax fully while you have two women in your life. Relaxation comes when the attention is focused, rather than fragmented. It is not easy for you. In a way, it is easier for me and also for N., because there is no doubt, at least in our feelings for you - though perhaps there is much doubt about what to do about those feelings. Sometimes I wonder if your 'wise' attitude towards dying, which you expressed quite eloquently today, is not in part attributable to a very unconscious wish of yours to escape from a situation which cannot bring you peace.

Dearest – I love being with you, and especially love to 'play' with you when we become like children again. There are so many horrendous things that happen in the world, to many people, that I do not wish to dwell upon possible disasters. I would rather be glad for all that we share, and live each day in the hope that we will continue to share in this way. There is no time for regret. It is important to celebrate, because we do not know whether tomorrow will come, and it is more becoming to be joyous than to be sad. I love you - my body and soulmate. Puss

Darling

A few thankyou blooms for being so sweet yesterday. Much love

Darling

What a happy note. I am always a little shocked when you leave blooms on the table. I feel glued to you since yesterday in the nicest possible place. One of the joys of love-making. is remaining together for as long as is possible. It hurts to tear myself away from you. *Jusqu'à demain - je t'aime.* Puss

**

It is also true that one of the joys of doing pleasant things, is imagining telling you about them – in fact, they are almost part of the same process. When I was touring England with Helen on the first occasion six years ago, I thought constantly of what I would tell you, and likewise with *Le Grand Tour* in Europe - this year. The anticipation of being able to share some of it with you, added spice and delight. It is so good being able to love you.

There is too much work at present at the university. Wish I could get on top of it, but it keeps increasing. I may have to work an extra hour or two some nights, when everyone has gone. It is the only way to get anything done. Saw the light on in your study (in your house upon the hill) as I drove home a few moments ago and wished I could come up the stairs and kiss you. In a better world...as I often say. All my love, my dearest Douglas. Your Puss

Dear heart

Bruno (my large white teddy bear and second Douglas-substitute) and I are having a lovely time cuddled up in bed. Only wishing you were here. I think sometimes I try to cling to beautiful experiences

instead of letting them go. Such a glorious day. Have felt such a deep languor since you left. Could sleep for a week (*avec toi*). Love you with all my heart and the other bits as well. The article on kissing was very apt - considering our discussions.

Dear Shobha

You were quite delightful yesterday. The beach was near perfect this morning. Low tide, firm sand and calm water. I look forward to swimming with you. But please don't feel constrained to breast the breaking waves.

Have started *The Belton Estate* – my twenty-sixth Trollopian novel. It is one of his several 'inheritance' stories. The situation lends itself to the kind of study of internal conflict and self-deception, of which the mature Trollope became a master. Hence *Tolstoy's*** admiration of him.

Trollope shows his genuine maturity by not plumping for good or bad uncomplicated people and by his extraordinary charity. Oddly - he was not like this, but inclined to be choleric, in the *persona* seen by his contemporaries. Your Douglas

** *Leo Tolstoy* – Russian novelist and author of War and Peace

Sweetheart

I visited the parents of Helen in the hills today. A student of yours from years ago was present. He is now a senior government official in Zimbabwe, and was recently shot in the head in an attempted assassination, but he says he is *not* going to flee the country under any circumstances. The army/police called on him three times last week to arrest him, but went away empty-handed. They also raided his home. He is apparently the son of one of the tribal chieftains.

Have developed a sore throat, so sadly will not be at the beach tomorrow. I have been looking forward to it all week. Would love to see you for a moment, but will not be able to kiss you for several days – the ultimate punishment.

This morning I purchased sixty-seven two-dollar gifts for the nursing home staff for Christmas (where mum is living). It was quite enjoyable. I wish you could see them all. Much love – your 'funny face' (à la Audrey Hepburn)

Dear darling

Sorry if I was not very scintillating company yesterday. Ayala (heroine of Trollope's novel *Ayala's Angel*) is engaged to her k-night at last. Girls should be angels – men should be k-nights (i.e. gentlemen in the chivalric sense). I am so fortunate to have you. I have always thought of you as my archetypal, chivalric knight.

** Shobha used to call Douglas her k-night with the accent on the 'k'.

Yesterday was very sweet indeed with our stolen kisses. I yearn to be well again, so we can consummate our love - though in truth, I feel we have already. All yours – funny face

Am wondering whether there is not a lesson for us, and perhaps others too, in what happened this morning. Why is it that we 'took off' as magically as we did. In saying this, I hope I am speaking for you, as well as myself.

Chapter 15

All these things
shall love do unto you
that you may know
the secrets of your heart

34

My precious darling

When I am with you - as today - I heartily wish that time would stop, so that we could dwell a little on our love. I hope you were able to savour our *commingling* with a little more dignity and a lot less haste than I (me).

Since 'the day of the stingray at the ocean' and perhaps also the day of 'the kiss in the garden', I have felt joy again in my heart. How great a mastery you have over me. Only when we are at ease together – like children - is there delight. When we are *en rapport* - all is well. I kiss your brow, your eyes and your lips. Your presence with me is still tangible. Your most adoring Puss

My dearest Puss

Thank you again for your delightful note. As ever, at such moments, I never cease to wonder at your joy of spirit. Given your upbringing - how did you achieve such liberation and innocence?

Reading Hall's** biography of Trollope has for me, been a sobering experience. Though I am not myself a writer, I find Trollope very much a kindred soul. He said more than once in later life, that he did not want to live, if he could no longer write - and he did in fact, write up to the end. We should all cease to be, when we are no longer ourselves – physically or intellectually.

I picked up Thackeray's *Vanity Fair*** yesterday, but found it unreadable. Trollope's pure, simple style and complete absence of *fine* writing, has spoilt me for others. *Dalla sua pace - la mia dipende*. (*On your peace - mine depends*).

**   N. John Hall : *Trollope – A Biography*
**   William Makepeace Thackeray : British satirical author

Darling

Went to the *orange* centre *ce soir* (this evening) and Bhagwan spoke on a subject dear to your heart and body. He was talking about making love (of course) and how to deal with the situation when one lover no longer *felt the need* for lovemaking. He said that this was a testing time of whether it was truly *love* or something else.

But he was speaking of a situation where the desire to make love evaporated as a consequence of meditation - and as therefore a natural process and a *higher state*. He stressed how important it was to be gentle and tender with the lover for whom the desire was still there - in order not to hurt their feelings.

I'm not sure if any of this applies to us or may apply to us in the future. Can you imagine my being in such a meditative state that I would refuse you? Perhaps we should cultivate a way of being tender and intimate without advancing fully towards love-making - though knowing yourself and myself, I'm not sure it's possible. Something to consider. Your loving Puss

Darling

Herewith – apart from the roses – my *nearest equivalent hammer* to the one (of yours) that I broke. Though probably not quite as old as your father's (which was an heirloom of sorts), mine is one of my earliest tools and was bought in London about forty years ago.

Yesterday was in part, a mending-of-fences day, if you will forgive the prosaic figure of speech. You were very sweet and you make me feel guilty for what I said to you a week or so ago. Nowadays my sense of well-being can vary a lot from day to day - because of the belated effect of withdrawal from my drug. Much love

Dearest love

I would love to curl up with you and go to sleep. Yesterday has given me an appetite for your company. I love you with all my heart. Puss

A heartfelt beration of Douglas by Shobha

Dear Mr. Payne

I was horrified by your behaviour this morning on your front doorstep. It seems that you are unable to support the friend of your bosom whenever there is any kind of crisis. Rather, you drive the dagger even deeper home. Where have you honed these skills which are so heartless and cruel ? Have you been treated in such a fashion by those who have purported to love you ?

Where did you experience such unkindness, that you administer it to me - at a time when what I most required was tenderness and consolation ? Who are you to be so censorious when you did not even wait to hear my story, but judged me out of hand from the first moment you saw me ? Perhaps you had no sleep during the night and your temper was already frayed, but I consider this a mean excuse, if it is so - and one which is so readily employed by you, that it wears thin after a while.

I find your lack of feeling repugnant. You read Trollopian novels *ad nauseam* and yet you appear to be untouched by them. Not one of the characters in your novels would treat a woman as you did this morning. What is the point in reading about your little heroes and heroines, if you do not attempt to emulate them to some degree ?

You will be delighted to know that G. *(Shobha's manager at the university)* and I are at peace once more, and he has apologised profusely for his misdeeds. I stood my ground and refused to enter into discussion - and he recognised his error.

Since apologies are the order of the day, I think it would be in order if you were also brought to your knees and asked my forgiveness for the abominable way in which you treated me today.

I had grown to trust you, and imagined that in a difficult situation such as this - when I fled the university momentarily, in order *to not to lose my cool,* as you put it, I thought you would be the one person who could understand me – but I found you completely lacking in gentleness.

I cannot forgive you easily. I find such moods as these most unfitting in a lover, or indeed in any well-bred person. I can only wonder at your own upbringing and again ask myself - where have you learnt such ill-mannered ways of behaving?

Is it any surprise that you seem to feel that most people are afraid of you, including your own offspring? Is it any wonder that they do not divulge their thoughts to you? How could anyone ever trust you, if, when bringing to you some sensitive matter of the heart, you repel them as you repelled me ? Only a fool would come back for more punishment. When will you learn to be kind? How is it possible that you harbour such ill-will towards me?

I had not come to set upon you, only to ask for your help and love. How could you ever be of benefit to one who was seriously ill or disadvantaged? It seems your so-called affection flies out the door when there is a real emergency. That is not love, only pretence. The test of deep feeling is in such moments as these, and you have once again failed.

I suggest you continue to read Trollope as a serious undertaking, and attempt to imbibe some of the values and manners of his heroes – the aristocratic ones of course, not the workers, though judging from your behaviour today, I am more inclined to feel that you may belong in the second category.

Look into your soul - if you have one, and reflect upon whether you have acted in love – or whether you did not prejudge the person whom you once held dear, for some personal reason of your own. I did not come to your door lightly, or to criticise you (though I do now). I came in desperation and you met my desperation with loathing. You are not worthy to touch my feet.

My heart

Your difficulties may - as you yourself suggested - be psychological, at least in part. Your sleep pattern alone, whatever its cause, must leave you feeling so jangled, that this in itself is enough to induce feelings of acute distress, if not depression.

Since there is as yet no real information as to the cause of your malady, my brother's opinion is that no progress can be made until you have seen a doctor.

I felt greatly heartened by speaking with my brother, because in truth neither you nor I nor N. has any idea what ails you. I wish with all my heart that you had seen someone weeks ago, so that your suffering could have been alleviated. With all my love. Puss

Your resistance to seeking medical attention to ascertain a possible reason for your condition, contributes greatly to my dis-ease. We are none of us an island – as Donne attests - and your well-being is inextricably bound up with mine. If you are ill – then I am also disturbed until your condition is relieved - *dalla sua pace* (what grieves you, grieves me).

Dear Shobha

Herewith a copy of the nuclear medicine report on my thyroid scan. What it signifies I do not know. For further enlightenment, I shall wait until I speak to one of the doctors. In the meanwhile, I suggest we do not speculate.

Douglas was subsequently diagnosed with hypothyroidism, which accounted for his recent poor health and was the beginning of a slow deterioration over the next eighteen years.

Darling

Have found an article which supports your stand viz. remaining on (thyroid) medication for some time. It also demystifies the use of radioactive treatment somewhat. Tell N. if she doesn't want to read the articles, to leave them alone. Some people become confused by excessive medical information.

As a one-time medical social worker, I personally find it enlightening. It might be a good idea to keep a diary of your reactions until you stabilise your dosage. Much love - your very tired Puss

My darling heart

Despite our tragic circumstances, we are inextricably linked together in a way that baffles me and astounds me and bewilders me and frightens me, because despite the pain, it always seems as if we must go on. And yet I would love to be free.

I would love to be able to simply be with you when the spirit leads us, and not in a prescribed, planned, programmed way, which is so anathema to me - and probably also to you.

Just imagine if you simply arrived at my door unannounced and fell into my arms, or rather, I fell into yours. It would be so sweet - just as it is sweet on Saturdays when you arrive and I never know when you are coming, or if you are coming at all. It is delicious !

My dream is that we would have two homes and simply turn up or ring each other when we felt the urge to BE together, and then go our separate ways when we needed solitude (which we also both enjoy and crave).

I dream and dream and will always dream about this - even if it never becomes an eventuality. Tonight while in meditation, I imagined our going through a kind of spiritual ceremony as soulmates, with only one or two others present who were very close to us - the purpose being to acknowledge in some way, that despite the non-legal nature of our union - at a far, far deeper level - we are one.

In my fantasy, I have always dreamed of such a moment – a secret moment when we express our longing for each other in an eternal kind of way. I have never been remotely interested in legal unions (despite my marriage eons ago). They are meaningless to me.

What matters is the spiritual dimension – the unspeakable mystery which binds people almost despite themselves. I believe ours is such a union, *despite* our sufferings and torment.

Dear heart, I long for spontaneity between us – where we can simply contact each other at will without restraint and be at peace without the constant reminder that we are eating forbidden fruit. Dusk is a wonderful hour. Sweet dreams

Dear Douglas

It grieves me that we have fallen out. I am much affected by the Trollope novel I am reading, to the extent that I have accepted the characters almost as real people, in the way you are *besotted* with Lily Dale (Trollope's fictional heroine in *The Last Chronicle of Barset).* I am so enmeshed in Trollope, and so angry with the way that some of his men treat their women, that I am probably transferring some of my rage onto you.

Trollope's novel *Is he Popenjoy?* as you know, is about the infidelities of the husband and the supposed infidelities of the wife. It is not that people rise to their own defence because they are guilty. Quite the opposite. Witness Mary (in the novel), who refuses to go back to her husband because he unjustly accuses her. She is furious and lets him know this.

Where is your evidence that people who are unjustly accused sit by and passively allow this to happen? The martyred saints? Jesus? I prefer Mary's reaction myself - as an indication of her innocence - not her guilt. I feel we are imprisoned in a routine in which little variation is allowed, and I fear what might happen if you became even less accessible to me.

My darling

I have many bones to pick with you, after reading our friend (Trollope) on *manliness*. The word is outdated, though I do not feel the same way about the word *gentleman*. I am not so concerned about what it is to be a man, as what it is to be a *person*. I do not distinguish between the qualities I would hope to find in a man or woman whom I felt has arrived at an exalted state. I would define such a person as one who :

- displays compassion to others, but is not afraid of anger in a just cause
- does not lean on others emotionally , except in an emergency
- is not afraid to give full vent to his or her feelings, be they tears or laughter (in sympathetic company)
- is able to empathise with the fortunes and misfortunes of others (a variant of compassion)
- shows evidence of wisdom in not prematurely judging a situation or person
- is capable of seeing many points of view apart from his or her own, though not necessarily agreeing with any of these
- is capable of inspiring others and cajoling them out of their miseries, towards a hopeful state of mind
- can hold and caress and support another, when tears flow, knowing the healing effect of such a release
- is able to enthuse on many subjects and has the capacity to enthuse others
- has energy of spirit if not of action
- always looks for the better path and the better side in others, and
- draws out all that is fine and good, rather than reflecting upon actual or potential sadness

You will be greatly heartened to hear that I agree with our friend Trollope on a few points, such as being faithful to true friends, gentle with women, considerate to inferiors, kindly with servants, frank, of open speech, with springing eager energies (?), and of course - lack of affectation.

I do not agree that it is always possible to be loving to children or indeed, to women. Some children are indeed lovable. But not all. But the bone which I would most like to pick with you, concerns sorrows.

I agree it is often necessary to put a brave face upon it - to wear a *persona*, which conceals the inner life. But when one becomes closer to others - this mask must fall, if intimacy is ever to develop. Perhaps the world should not know of one's sorrows, but those you love and who return the gift – 'should' know of them.

The degree to which sorrows can be revealed, for me - indicates the depth of the intimacy. If you are unable to share your sorrow with me, we cannot be one. I sometimes feel that you cannot cope with some of my sorrows, though this is a rather potent word for what I feel - but nevertheless to the degree that you can allow me to express myself fully to you in all the joy and sadness – to that extent we can be intimate.

If you likewise, are in sorrow and cannot divulge it to me, I cannot be your true friend and lover. Withholding creates a barrier, whereas disclosure brings relief and tenderness and could engender a great and noble love in the one to whom it has been disclosed. In this, I shall never agree with Trollope - except to say – if that is manliness - I want none of it. Your *woman* - much love

Darling

There is so much 'politics' at present at the university, with so many people showing signs of wear and tear. As you know, there has been a restructure; several people have resigned from stress; several more are on the edge of breakdowns (their words) and receiving counselling – and one man even mentioned suicide.

I am in the position, fortunate or otherwise, where people tell me of their troubles. Where I feel I can *make a difference* - I do so - by letting the director or others know what is happening - in a general way.

The managers are in their ivory towers and don't have a clue how the troops in the field are operating, and do not understand what is meant by '*service*', and being out and about amongst students and staff who are keeping the campus functioning.

It is very saddening for me to see those who are not my friends, but at least my colleagues, being broken down, losing heart, longing to leave and yet not able to do so.

Wherever I can, I intercede on their behalf, but there is no guarantee that anyone will listen and act. One senior staff member was today offered a redundancy package he does not want. The real reason for the offer is that the director's best friend is the contractor whose firm cleans half the campus. He submits higher prices for tenders, yet those tenders are accepted in preference to university departments who quote for the same services.

As you know, many people grant favours to their friends. This is how the world operates, and many staff at university employ their relatives or arrange positions for them. I want everyone to be satisfied. A worthwhile redundancy payment can reduce the shame of being *phased out*.

My brother informed me this morning that his wife was not well again, and he spent the evening at the hospital, and could not contact me. There was no real danger but the emergency area was overcrowded and I do worry about both of them - particularly because my brother is so alone, if I am not there.

I wish our society operated differently. In an ethnic group, there would be someone for his wife to spend time with during the day – a mother, aunt, grandmother or children, and she would not feel at such a loose end, which causes her anxiety.

It is not always pleasant to spend a working week at home alone, when everyone else appears to be *out there* and occupied. People with disabilities often can't use their time to advantage - whereas a working person, by contrast - might be glad *not* to be employed for a spell.

On a completely different matter, I find that - although I am aware of men as persons, I am not particularly aware of them as sexual beings. It would be very rare for me to find characteristics in a man which I find attractive. Whether this simply means that I am absorbed in you and therefore there is no 'hunger' - or whether most men simply do not appeal, I do not know.

Yet you seem to find many women interesting for one reason or another - although if you spent time with them, perhaps they might lose some of their attraction?

I used to make a point, years ago, that if I found a person interesting – male or female – I would endeavour to spend a little time with them, and almost always the interest dissipated quite quickly. Forbidden fruit is always far more enticing than a bowl of cherries offered to you on a plate.

I saw a photograph of Helen some time ago in the university magazine, and said to myself "I would like to know that woman" – she had such beautiful eyes. I later completed a training course with her, and as you know, I travelled all around England and Wales with her, in perfect harmony and we later wrote hundreds of letters to each other in the years that followed.

In her case, the 'eyes' were indeed windows of her soul and I found a true friend. But this is not usually the case. Most people don't bear up under closer scrutiny. The stage presence is different from the reality.

When I was rehearsing for the chorus in the opera *La Traviata* - the understudy tenor was I thought, a delightful creature and very attractive throughout all the rehearsals and performances - but at the closing party, he sat joking with the cast. One of the jokes he told was so mundane and Australian in tone, I found myself rethinking his character. That is why I suppose, if you can love a person after living with them, day by day, through all domestic routines - it might indeed be love - or perhaps, resignation?

It has been so cold, that at lunch-time I went up to 'our hill', where it was warmer (but not sufficiently dry) and sat on the wet grass. No wonder the ancients worshipped the sun and fire. I wished I could have cuddled up with you and talked in an unrestricted way for hours.

Sometimes it is only after some time, that we find common ground - and from that point on, there is a sweet and very deep harmony between us. But it takes time to reach that point.

One of my fantasies is to be reading, writing or otherwise engaged, and you come up and kiss my neck. I find that very stirring. For myself, I love to kiss your eyes, because it seems to give you pleasure and reminds you of your redsetter Ned, who used to do something similar. I always said I was just a dog-substitute - since we met only days after he 'passed away'. Sleep well, my love - Puss

My dearest love - full moon

There are many things I want to say to you and they all concern your health. You say this is a taboo topic, but I am tired of being silent. I have been very concerned recently because it seemed that you were simply accepting being unwell and not expecting to get better.

Being the person I am, I always seek solutions - and in recent months, have wanted to find a way for you to feel strong and happy again. Yet it seems that you do not want to get better, or at least do not believe it is possible. You have not seen a doctor and don't wish to see an acupuncturist, though they have a good record of helping people - even more so than practitioners of western medicine (on occasion).

You said to me recently that you have felt for some time that you are *dying*. (*Eighteen years later Douglas did indeed die*). Is this because you have been depressed, or is it a real possibility? Apart from hyperthyroidism and age, there is nothing wrong with you of which we know. So is it that you actually *wish to die* ?

You might have trouble saying so to me, because you feel I am so intent on making you better, but if it were so, I think I could accept this, if you would talk to me about it. I am not happy when you say you do not wish to talk about health. I am not interested in being with you if you are not prepared to discuss with me how you are feeling. That is most important, and if you cannot share that with me, we have nothing to say to each other.

I am of course, unable to look after you in a day-to-day way or sleep with you, so I see very little of how you really are. If you are not even prepared to let me know how you feel, we have a worthless relationship. I am not prepared to play games and pretend nothing is happening, when it is patently obvious that you are in difficulty and not comfortable at times. Please give some thought to what I am saying.

Even if you are dying, and even if you wish to die, I want to share that with you. You will only alienate me if you keep secrets from me. I have loved you with all my heart for so very long, that I want to love you in the best way possible - until the end. And for me, the best way is to share any fear or distress that you suffer, as well as the more joyful moments.

I am not sure what else to say, except that if you do not wish to seek medical attention or any other form of assistance, because you actually want to shuffle off and do not want to live any longer and suffer any further diminution of your strength - then I will honour that - but only if you include me in your plans.

If I had my way, I would escort you even beyond the loss of the body into another dimension, but because we do not share a belief in this area, it will not help us to talk further of such things. But you should know that if it is possible, I will be there for you also at that time - should you need me.

If you ever do die, I will be with you in spirit, and I will work in every esoteric way I know (and there are many), to ensure that your spirit has a bright and joyful journey.

Enough of this. I will always be there for you if you share your soul with me. If you do not, then there will always be a separation. Do not worry about how I will cope when you are gone. I will cope. And if I do not cope, then I will simply join you the sooner - so where is the loss?

My darling, I wish there was something I could give to you. I will never stop asking how you are. Please try to trust me and do not become annoyed when I speak to you in this way. If you love me, talk to me about how you feel - for every little detail brings me closer to you, (even though you are conditioned to think that it is not appropriate to talk about your ills).

That is why I am here. If I cannot listen to you when you are ill or down or distressed - then where is the love? It is in these little things, that love is contained.

Dear one, I miss knowing what is in your heart. Do not be afraid of me. Whatever you wish for, I will respect, even if it means that you will have to leave me sooner than expected. If you require my help in any way – in ways we have discussed before, please ask.

My greatest pleasure is to make you happy, or at least to lessen anything that stops you from being so. I wish we had more time, so that we could be around each other, so that as thoughts arise, we could talk about them, without always fearing the pressure of time, or the presence of others. I pray for such peace. Your Puss

Dear Douglas

There is a great deal I wish to say to you but I am not sure where to begin. We do not seem to be on the same wavelength at present. There does not seem to be a way for us to be intimate. You seem to feel that talking breeds intimacy. I do not.

Sometimes it is true that our words bring us closer together. At other times, they create a barrier between us. At present, I feel that whatever I say will not be well received. You seem to be in a state of mind where you do not want to agree, and I meet resistance from you.

I am looking for harmony. It seems you are looking for disagreement. Are you aware that you have become rather critical of society, children, television, films, education and many other things? Perhaps you are too much on your own with your thoughts. Since you stopped going to the beach, you have not mixed and mingled with anyone for any length of time except myself and N.

It is healthy to rub shoulders with others, whoever they are - simply to remind yourself that you are part of humanity. I do not think it is good (for you) to be so removed from others. It is making you very inward-looking and restricted in your interests.

As far as we are concerned, I find it very difficult to be in your company without being affectionate, and you don't seem to be making any overtures in that direction at present. Perhaps therefore, it would be better to keep in touch by phone for a while, although that is still *talking,* and I would rather move away from language for a time.

Darling

Life is very rich. Even the changes that are taking place in you and also in my work are grist for the mill - and we are learning to manage new situations. Life would be a dull affair if it always remained the same. When I truly relax with you, and have no expectations, we are of course, most happy. But now and then I become aware that I yearn for us to be closer, and then the cycle starts of 'wanting' rather than accepting.

There is a wonderful poem of the English poet William Blake, which runs –

> Never seek to tell thy love.
> Love that never told can be;
> for the gentle wind does move silently, invisibly.
> I told my love, I told my love,
> I told her all my heart.
> Trembling, cold in ghastly fears -
> ah, she doth depart.

Dear Shobha

Did you see the Melvyn Bragg** programme on the Welsh baritone *Bryn Terfel* last night? A large part of the pleasure is watching his face while he sings. It is simply a cheat to offer people the spectacle of dubbed singers, even if the dubbing is by the singer himself.

I see that the Welsh village that Terfel comes from, is only a few miles from Harlech (where I stayed recently and where you sent the policeman to get me to the phone - on the road to Caenarfon).

I hope our exchange did not upset you unduly. As tends to happen on such occasions, each of us said some pretty harsh things. Emotionally crippled though I may be, it distressed me to think of you being unhappy.

I also hope you will not attach too much importance to my saying that I sometimes have in mind the need for give and take when talking to you? A degree of self-consciousness in such matters is more likely to lead to good manners - than unreflecting spontaneity.

I believe it was wise of you to suggest breaking away from the routine we have settled into. I already think of you more warmly. Your Douglas

** *Melvyn Bragg* : English broadcaster and author

Dear Douglas

It was a pleasant shock to receive such a warmish letter from you. It has been good, as you said, for our routine to be disrupted. It is so easy to fall into a pattern which at first is fulfilling, but through repetition, becomes much less so.

I do not think that someone who is emotionally crippled is able to confess to being so – there is a contradiction in there somewhere. But it does seem that in recent times we have become rather stilted, and therefore our absence from each other may serve some purpose. I am not very concerned about good manners right now, rather how to find the best way for us to become attuned to each other through our feelings, as well as our thoughts.

Yes, I did watch Bryn Terfel and enjoyed the programme immensely. He is quite impressive in his country Welsh fashion. It is heartwarming to find such a voice with a personality to match.

I am also watching *The House* at the moment, which tells backstage stories from Covent Garden Opera House. You might not be interested, but as a wanna-be performer, the laryngitis of the singers and the bleeding feet of the ballerinas have some meaning for me.

The day of the university staff Olympics (which I am organising) fast approaches, so you will soon not have to endure my obsession with these proceedings, which I have greatly enjoyed, but I will be heartily thankful when they are over. Much love - your Puss.

Shobha visited Olympia in Greece on her 'Grand Tour' of Europe the year previously, and was inspired to create an 'Olympic Games' on the university campus - with traditional events.

Puss

The first day of Spring – have only just noticed it. The roses are the nearest to red I could find. I am still feeling rather under the weather - drifting from chill to mild fever to chill again. I sigh for a few warm and still days. Your Douglas

My Douglas - first day of Spring

I am a little concerned about the variation in your temperature – especially your reference to a slight fever. It is a pity that after such a delightful time spent together, there should be an after-effect which is not so pleasant. I hope that it is still possible to retain some remembrance of what was such a deeply tender interlude.

Your roses are humbly received. I feel a little ashamed of my recent reference to the absence of same from you - for some time. I somehow omitted to remind you of the first day of spring today, but you remembered - in any event.

On the subject of Princess Diana, as we are probably poles apart in our reactions to the media hype, it may be wiser not to discuss the topic at length, as I am rather affected at the 'heart' level, and it is not rational or reasonable or sensible or valid, but nevertheless I am responding in a similar fashion to the rest of the population, which seems to love her because she cared about people in difficulties - particularly the homeless. I find it rather moving, and believe it will inspire a lot of people to take up causes of their own, because of her example.

People like Diana remind me of characters in novels – unlucky people, but who nevertheless stir one by their circumstances. For whatever reason, she had a degree of charisma, and as you know, possessing charisma has the effect of changing people's lives, for better or worse. Much love my dearest - Puss

**

With regard to using the lower case when writing to you - I recall that the author D.H. Lawrence in his pithy sayings called *Pansies*, used lower case - not capitals. The American poet E. E. Cummings in his poem '*anyone lived in a pretty how town, with up so floating many bells down*' also was deficient by your standards - in this regard.

As I sit here, I have a voluminous book of Bhagwan - which is totally in lower case and presented in a poetic format - so I am in good company and acting according to my taste. I shall not change.

Darling

I have not been a very sympathetic or empathetic lover of late. I have been so preoccupied with my various activities, that I have not been fully in tune with what is happening in your world. Perhaps that is why we have come to grief in recent weeks. The last few months have been so busy at work, and I have been caught up in one project after another. It has not been a pleasant time for either of us, and my lack of humility and determination not to give in to you, has not been helpful. I have not been willing to compromise of late, and have been reacting to your criticism of me, instead of wondering why you have become so.

My dearest, please be gentle and I will be kind. Life is not really worth living when we are not at-one-ment. I long for you and for the serenity which we have often known, yet because of your changing health, it might be a little while before it returns. Suffice to say, that I am penitent, at least in the sense that I am feeling fondly for you, and anxious to make amends if I have been insensitive to your feelings. Puss

My darling

There have been a few moments of real joy since seeing you yesterday. Perhaps love has to die to be reborn. Puss

Dear Douglas

I am very upset at not hearing from you today. I feel quite abandoned and it is not pleasant. I will be in court tomorrow for my mother's hearing, so my brother and I can obtain Guardianship, because she has dementia and cannot look after her affairs. I will ring you when it is over. I am not looking forward to it - though it will probably be straightforward.

**

I realise I do have the habit of personalising most things, and this is irritating for you. On the other hand, I am always wary of generalisations which cannot be supported by personal experience - so we are at odds.

Chapter 16

The wind bids me leave you

35

My love

I felt a little stunned today after our commingling. I did not wish to disturb the beauty. While we are wrapped up in each other, the words flow - but when we separate, I find that anything I say falls far short of what I wish in my heart to express, and the words that do form are not adequate, or even intelligent. I suspect you feel something similar - in some measure.

Perhaps nature knows that talk after such an event is not enough - and for many people, they fall naturally and deeply into sleep. For us, it cannot be so - yet whatever we decide to do after we separate, I find myself longing to be linked with you in the deepest way, and it seems to me that if we *go public* at such a time (e.g. go the park for coffee or for a walk), some of the wonder and splendour and mystery and magic is at risk.

It was very disturbing to have been with you today. We change. We are not the same as we were before. It is unnerving. Yet I would not have it any other way. You touch me in a way that leaves me unsettled - yet glad.

I hope you are feeling tolerably at peace since our meeting - but if not, then may any disturbance be profitable, in that it leads to reflection on the nature of affection and the wonder of these temples we call bodies. I discovered a secret today, but I cannot divulge it to you at this time. I will wait for an appropriate moment. Until then – I remember you with all fondness, and thankfulness for our excursion into dangerous territory. I cherish you. Puss

Shobha's attempt to communicate in the Scots vernacular

(Shobha and Douglas were going through a phase of listening to recordings of Robert Burns' songs.)

Ma ain darlin' jo

ah hae bin a' the day wi' scott, burns an' ma dictionary,
wile restin' in ma bed, an' trying' tae git ma mind aroun' the scots tongue,
th' task being mad mair troublesome
as th' scots of burns an' scott
is nae th' same as th' scots in ma dictionary.

wi' a' ma luve for aye.
may our sauls be as ane.
fidgin' fain (quivering ecstatically)
your ain dearie

Darling

I have just watched a programme which has left me feeling very moved - as if I have lived through a momentous historical period. It was an historical treatment of the Australian gay and lesbian Mardi Gras costume parade through the streets - which is held each year in Sydney.

The first march was forty years ago (1978) when I was in India, and began quietly with the main participants drawing bystanders into the parade - so that the throng increased very rapidly.

The police must have become frightened and attacked the marchers - throwing them into wagons and taking them to the police station, where they were bashed and refused access to doctors or hospital. Those marchers from the first event who are still alive, were interviewed forty years on - and they led the march again this year. The difference is that now the police march *with* them, in a strong contingent under the banner *We're here because we care'* - and hundreds of police are on duty to ensure the march goes without any hitches.

I was not very aware in those early days of what it was to be *gay*, let alone aware of the Mardi Gras - but I feel the last forty years have seen so many changes in attitude, and there is so much tolerance now - of what was frowned upon in the past.

AIDS has brought gays (men) and lesbians together (because they felt threatened as a group) - which might not have happened otherwise - as there was often animosity between them. In 2017, Australians voted to allow same-sex marriage after forty years of non-recognition of the rights of the gay community.

I spent many of my university days on the streets marching against Vietnam, and presenting motions to political parties on various matters, and I find it heartwarming to see some changes have taken place, which were absolutely taboo in the seventies, and are now accepted or being considered for legalisation (e.g. twelve months separation to obtain a divorce, where previously fault had to be established, abortion on request and voluntary euthanasia).

In some small way, I feel I have contributed to that change, as I was involved in all three issues at the political level. I am so happy to have been one of the baby-boomers who lived through those tumultuous times. We exploded many myths and took risks in a way that we are not often called upon to do - today.

You have been through an actual war with all its attendant experiences. I have been through an emotional war - in which attitudes have been revised and freedoms made possible - of which we could never have dreamt. Oscar Wilde's imprisonment with hard labour, could not happen today. There would be a public outcry in his defence.

Why do people interfere in others' lives (so that choice is limited)? It ought to be possible to enjoy oneself and help others to enjoy their lives - without hurting oneself or others. It seems so easy and obvious - but it is possible of course, to hurt others unintentionally - if you please yourself - as is the case with you and me and N. Should you hurt yourself in order not to hurt others, and reign oneself in? A person deciding to marry against a parent's wishes for example - does not wish to hurt the parents, but needs to follow their own heart.

Perhaps the *intention* is the only thing that matters (as the law acknowledges). We did not intend to fall in love - nor to hurt N., and it would be foolish to deny we are in love and hurt ourselves further, in order to protect N. from being hurt.

Between the two of us, we span a wealth of history and experience (one hundred and twenty-eight years), and I am so glad to have been alive in this time. I wish I could convey my delight to you - that we are so much more free than we have ever been in the past - and have so many more choices available (even if we do not make them). I kiss your lips. Puss

Dear god - a.k.a. Douglas

Hope all is well and the body is OK after our commingling? Yearned for you at the beach. Wanted to play *God and Adam*** in the water. There was a rainbow right over the beach in perfect symmetry – just for you. I feel lost for words re our encounter, so will not endeavor to find them (the words). Perhaps when things go really deep, one is simply mute. All my love – your Puss

**   Michelangelo painting of *God and Adam* - almost touching fingers

Dear Douglas

It was heart-warming to receive your letter, despite your comment that it is not the flowers-and-roses type of letter that I like to receive. We seem to get on better on paper (at present). Perhaps your original proposition when we met - that we conduct a *pen relationship* – was a sensible one (as it has come to fruition - though it is not limited to simply the *pen*). I did not realise you had given up yoga - though I am not surprised - given your fluctuating state of health.

Last evening I watched the film *Tom Brown's Schooldays*** and wondered at your experience (in boarding school) and if there were any parallels. It also recalled to mind my own experience of *cliques* in the ashram in India, when I felt at times that everyone in a particular group was against me, and how difficult that was - and absolutely terrifying. I wish you would talk about your days in boarding school. They probably had a formative effect upon you.

**   *Tom Brown's Schooldays* – an 1857 novel by Thomas Hughes set in the English public school – Rugby.

My mother is progressing (after her fall), but still very bruised. The nurses say she has nine lives. I find it pleasant nuzzling up to her when I visit and I enjoy feeding her - though the nurses are much better at it than me. She is a difficult customer. But she murmurs and kisses at all the right times - even though there is almost no conversation. It doesn't seem to matter at all - because her smiles and sounds convey so much. It is as if she is my *child*.

Do you remember how you used to say I put my lips together like a little bird waiting to be kissed. My mother does the same. Could it be inherited or learnt behaviour (joke)? I find it rather appealing. If she did not respond in this way, I would be disappointed.

Because her decline has been gradual, I have never really felt she is *not the same mother*. A friend said to remember her as she was - but I have never felt a need to do this. To me - she is essentially the same person - despite her dementia.

I am looking for a new author to read, but am still pursuing *Dickens* - though not with such a vengeance. I do not like to skim - yet with Dickens I find I must do so, as he alternates between the two classes (high and low) in each chapter, and the alternate one is often in the vernacular - which I can't stand.

Nevertheless, there is something about his principal characters (usually the more savoury ones) – which is memorable (e.g. Little Nell in *Old Curiosity Shop*, Nicholas Nickleby in the book of the same name and Mr. Jarndyce in *Bleak House*). Mr. Jarndyce is the *good guy* – philanthropic and never puts a foot wrong – falls in love with his ward – proposes marriage – she accepts out of filial affection, and then he belatedly realises she is in love with and loved by, another man – though the love has not been expressed.

It reminds me of Trollope's novel – *An Old Man's Love* – which is very moving. And also the situation of King Mark in the romance of *Tristan and Isolde***.

Isolde is betrothed to King Mark - but Isolde and Tristan drink a love potion and fall totally in love with each other and Mark is in despair. In *Bleak House*, Mr. Jarndyce surrenders his ward to the lover - befriends them both and lives out his life in an avuncular role. Very poignant.

** *Tristan and Isolde* : the medieval love story, based upon a Celtic legend

Will cease now as dusk has fallen - and I must go about my worldly chores. There is no sense of obligation in my writing to you – rather your words (when received) set me off, *and there it is* (as Eeyore would say in *Winnie the Pooh*). Goodnight – sleep well. Your ever-hopeful Puss

Dear Shobha

Your letter to me was fluent and well put together. This comes, I suspect, from writing quickly - which I can rarely do. Books on *style* e.g. F.L. Lucas - often say that easy writing means hard reading. But not in your case. It's strange that no study, to my knowledge - has been made of the mental process which occurs when a person writes, and the relation of this process to what occurs when we talk.

The vocabulary and sentence construction of writing and talking are clearly not the same. Writing is more formal than talk - if for no other reason than that most of us take more care (and time) in writing, than we do in speech.

Dear Douglas

Today I watched films of both The *Old Curiosity Shop* and *David Copperfield*, so I am all Dickensed-out. There is a time for all things, and his style still appeals, though I sense that, with a little more exposure, it might pall. But there are still a few of his novels to digest. viz. *Barnaby Rudge, Edwin Drood, Hard Times* and *Little Dorrit* plus *Pickwick Papers* - so it might be a while before I am free of his influence.. *A pity we cannot share Charles (Dickens), but I fully understand* he is not your type of author. There is quite a lot of comedy in Dickens that does not exist in Trollope, though Trollope's proper-names are also ridiculous, and can hardly be taken seriously.

I am so sorry we were at odds today. There seems to be no limit to the depths of human sensitivity. Sometimes I deceive myself that I am in control - but a look askance from you, reduces me to a quivering fool. Your Puss

Winter is upon us. It is so much easier to be indoors when it is drizzling with rain outside. Wish you were here so we could cuddle up together in front of a fire. I may as well dream - since there is no possibility of ever actually being together. It is rather quiet at work so I have taken to going over to other departments for morning tea, so there is some conversation during the day above the basic level of chit chat.

I am slowly discovering those with a literary bent. One staff member has taken to reciting a complete poem each evening before he departs. I am being made aware that although I know a few lines of many poems by heart - there are many that are missing. I feel remiss. The art of memorisation is almost lost. Needless to say, the 'reciter of the poetry' was English, and a boarding school product (like yourself).

This afternoon I discovered that two persons with whom I work, were repeatedly beaten in boarding school – one in New Zealand and another in Sri Lanka. The first - in a boys' school where bullying was rife - and the second, in a convent run by nuns. I am beginning to feel my childhood was blessed.

You said to me you were never beaten or bullied and I find that difficult (but not impossible) to believe, unless you were one of the privileged for some reason. I am becoming more and more opposed to the school system, and increasingly made aware by my friends (who are teachers), that there are parents who fail to give their children elementary discipline - and by that I don't mean cruelty - but simply being firm in a decision and holding to it.

I also hear stories of girls of twelve terrorising their mothers by threatening to damage property in the home if they do not get their way. I fantasise about life in village England where children can be educated with a few others privately - with much exposure to adult company and of course, travel – money permitting. This life seems to have gone. Parents are so keen to go out to work in employment, they place their children (who are raw material waiting to be nourished and moulded) into the hands of strangers in child-care centres. It makes me sad.

When I was in India, I was aware, to my chagrin, that I was not always in my 'heart' i.e. in touch with my finer emotions. I described it as being in my 'head' a.k.a. my mind, where I worried about many things. When I 'fell' into my heart, there were no problems. I was at peace and in a kind of rapture. These days, I more or less live in the heart, but when I am with you, I move back into the head at times - and there is misery. What a wonder it would be if both of us remained in our feelings. It would be a heaven on earth. Puss

I have for some time felt the need to be engaged out of hours in some project or other, and have not been able to make it happen. Of course, I have been fortunate in other years in going to Europe, being in the chorus of *La Traviata*, the *Verdi Requiem* and performing with my folk group *Heart and Soul* - which have taken my mind off our situation. We seem to get on so much better when I am using my energy elsewhere, and am not dependent upon you for emotional support.

I am only too aware of your physical condition and your own difficulties and the change in your personality and activity level. In recent times, you seem to talk 'at' me, rather than 'to' me. In my current frame of mind, I am only interested in talking about you, myself and us, and being warm and tender with you.

Recently, I read the book *Eccentrics* (a study of sanity and strangeness) by David Weeks, and found it immensely satisfying and I am currently reading a book entitled *Hermits* (the insights of solitude) by Peter France, which is not quite so inspiring.

I am also reading about the *Cynics* - the school of ancient Greek philosophy, whose principal tenet was that 'ease should be avoided, and true virtue lay in the willing acceptance of avoidable discomfort'. Reminds me of you !

It is educational being on leave, with no commitments. I feel I could slip into a groove where there would be no desire to ever return to the hustle and bustle of the work-a-day world. The leaning of a *hermit* perhaps ? I am going to a lecture this evening on *The Nature of Passion* - so I should be a full bottle if you wish to tax me on this issue – when I return. Remember me - Puss

Darling

I am reading about the Sufi mystic *Hakim Sanai*** and the language is strangely compelling. I have a sense of the familiar - as if I have heard it all before. It resounds in a very deep recess of my being. Perhaps I have been a Sufi in a past existence? It feels odd - but deliciously so. In particular, I have come across the word *adoration.*

Do you remember I used to say *"Je t'adore" (I adore you)* - and you (as usual), asked me not to be so intemperate. But that is exactly the right word. Adoration is an exalted feeling - akin to worship. It implies that the one who adores, feels as if the one who is adored, embodies something far beyond what is merely human. Adoration is recognising the best and highest in the beloved. It is a *transforming* state - as expressed in *The Rubaiyat of Omar Khayyam*** - a divine elixir. And it is not to be deplored.

When you first met with me, you told me you had been feeling ecstatic at the beach that morning - and it was because of me. I have the letter. That is adoration: the effect we have upon each other, which leads us to think and feel the very best about the other: seeing the potential as actual. You may call it seeing with rose-coloured spectacles, but this is one of the effects of love – that one is blind to all that is gross.

I have been feeling very tenderly for you since Sunday. It was a gentle moment, and you yourself said, you are at your softest at such times - which is very heart and soul-warming. You seem to take infinite pains and care in such situations. It is said by some that when the woman submits and the man is active, this is the natural way.

I don't know how it feels for you, but certainly at times there is a kind of rapture (for me) simply because you are in charge. The rest of my life is spent being in control because I live alone (and have done so for many years). And it is a delight to be carried off by you for a short while.

It does seem with us that our unexpected and spontaneous caresses lift us up together in a way that may not happen at other times - and if this is so - because of our limited contact - these moments are likely to be rare.

Because of their rarity they are even more precious. But as we have both perceived, there is an attendant anxiety when we make love - because of the time elapsing between episodes, and the strength of the wish for the commingling to be sweet.

Dearest love – I trust you with my heart, and urge you to reflect upon our love with joy, and anticipate our future encounters, not with apprehension - but with delight. Your Puss

** *Hakim Sanai* : a Sufi mystic and Persian poet of the 12th century.

My glass shall not persuade me I am old
so long as youth and thou are of one date

but when in thee time's furrow I behold
then look I death my days should expiate

for all that beauty that doth cover thee
is but the seemly raiment of my heart

which in thy breast doth live, as thine in me
how can I then, be elder than thou art ?

Shakespeare – Sonnets
(given by Douglas to Shobha)

Chapter 17

Sing to me a deeper song

36

Wellsprings of Joy - Sayings of the Beloved

You are like a well that I drink from
There ought to be a god - so we can thank him

Douglas

When the letters between Douglas and Shobha ceased after sixteen years - the only written evidence of any changes in their relationship in the following seventeen years - were Shobha's jottings of utterances by Douglas - which she felt to be significant - either for their degree of insight or because they were indicative of the depth of his devotion to her (in the absence of any commitment from him in a formal way - which many loving couples enjoy).

The jottings provided a degree of reassurance for Shobha - in uncertain times, and comforted her in Douglas' absence – by enabling her to recollect their earlier intimacy.

This chapter includes the most declaratory of these 'sayings' of Douglas - from both the letter-writing period of sixteen years and the seventeen years thereafter - until he *slipped sideways.*

They were recorded by Shobha because they were - for the most part - offered in the aftermath of love making - and she was aware that Douglas might not recall what he had said, when he had recovered from what was effectively an altered state of consciousness !

There were also occasional quotations of worth from Shobha during this period - but very few were written down. So those given here, are primarily a record by Shobha of intimate expressions of love by Douglas, when he unbuttoned his soul, and laid his feelings bare. Needless to say - the most intimate sayings have been withheld.

By dint of her spiritual (meditative and therapeutic) experiences over many years, Shobha presented herself to Douglas as a relatively peeled onion, in the emotional sense - which was a daunting prospect for an unpeeled onion – as Douglas liked to describe himself.

The reader can assume therefore that much of Shobha's conversation with Douglas was laced with similar declarations of love : expressions of thankfulness for simply being alive and in his arms, and many variations on a similar theme - which Douglas found both overwhelming and reassuring, but also frightening - because of their intensity and frequency..

Douglas was never in doubt about Shobha's feelings towards him - though in the early years - due to their frequent separations - Shobha was critically distressed on many occasions and wondered if she could survive without him. Some of her letters express this torment (though not all have been included - to protect the reader from repetition).

The laboratory experiment in behavioural conditioning (of Russian physiologist *Ivan Pavlov*) comes to mind. Pavlov's unwitting furry subjects (rats) would press a key at will and be rewarded intermittently with cheese. When the cheese was predictably there - say on each tenth press of the key - the rat was happy. When the rat continually pressed the key, but cheese was rarely provided – the rat would die - no longer able to trust that nourishment would be provided on a reliable basis.

Such was Shobha's fate – yet she did not die. Douglas (by contrast) had a fallback position - a wife - if ever Shobha's love should be directed elsewhere - or cease to be directed towards him.

Although hundreds of Douglas' sayings were recorded by Shobha (of a loving nature), they were made over a period of thirty-three years and were not that frequent. Almost always - they were made after making love, which became a sacrament of a kind - which bound them together as one being for a time - and was responsible for their continuing adoration for each other until 'the end' – in spite of their difficulties.

As there was some similarity in the sayings, only one instance of each is included, and many are omitted - so if you multiply all these allusions by Douglas to ecstatic experiences and glorious insights - you will come close to perceiving the changes that occurred in his understanding over time.

Douglas was astounded, when reminded on occasion that these sayings had been written down after their interludes together - and was only apprised by Shobha of their existence, if he later contradicted statements he had made in the intimacy of the bedchamber.

He was suitably chastened when given the exact date, if not time - when such a declaration had been made. They were difficult to refute by the light of day - for the words were indelibly inscribed in Shobha's books of '**Love Sayings – Volumes 1 and 2**'.

The element of relaxation that was present, is far more evident in Douglas' sayings - than in his letters. This can be attributed to the ease with which one can capture the essence of a *live* situation - rather than ponderously pontificating after an event - with pen in hand while composing prose – however beautiful – for Shobha's later digestion.

Douglas regularly sent and gave jokes to Shobha with his letters and in person - together with literally thousands of newspaper cuttings on matters of common interest. Many were, not surprisingly - on relationships and love.

Laughter was a feature of their life together, and they became like little children at times. Douglas was amazed that he was capable of such innocent joy - as the *persona* he presented to the world, was of a serious nature.

One of the many reasons Douglas was enamoured of the ocean and his early morning contacts at the beach, was the effect of the waves - which he believed brought out the *child* in all of the swimmers - as they felt free to be themselves. He experienced a similar measure of joy when attempting - and succeeding - to master difficult operatic arias. These sessions - some of which were recorded by Shobha - are punctuated by peals of delight from both parties.

On the subject of *joy* (while Shobha was exploring the wealth and depth of classical romantic art for this book), she found it concerning, that few classical painters expressed joy and laughter in their work. You would be hard put to even find a smile - apart from *The Laughing Cavalier* of Frans Hal. The smirk of Leonardo da Vinci's *Mona Lisa* is perhaps celebrated - because it is rare. You almost feel she is laughing internally - if not upon her actual visage.

Perhaps joy and laughter are difficult emotions to convey - if not impossible - in a visual way - but the attempt should be made. For the writer of the limerick, and the cartoonist, there is at least the possibility of bringing the reader to the point where laughter erupts spontaneously.

The relevance of joy to the current discussion, is that Douglas and Shobha frequently dissolved in joy and laughter, during their brief but meaningful interludes together - even if this is not always evident in their letters.

As was mentioned earlier, their endearing ways of addressing each other in their letters and concluding their correspondence; the frequent addition of cartoons by Shobha to these missives and the often subtle and witty nature of the many greeting cards they exchanged, bear witness to their elaborate sense of humour and love of jest in both word and speech, and their ability to laugh at themselves and at society.

Douglas greatly admired the cartoons of *Rod Clement* (Australian author and illustrator, cartoonist and caricaturist) who featured in *The Australian* and other newspapers, and Shobha appreciated the work of *Michael Leunig* (Australian cartoonist, poet and cultural commentator) and articles and cartoons from the press were frequently exchanged between them – for further discussion when they met.

Despite the twenty-six-year age difference, Douglas did not encourage Shobha's reliance upon him in any way, perhaps in part due to his existing family commitments. Rather, from the first, it was a relationship of challenge and provocation - of an intellectual and emotional nature. Shobha maintained her own friends, work and living arrangements, so that she could not be drawn into a domestic lifestyle, which she actively eschewed - having consciously ensured in her youth, that she did not bring children into the world.

She wished instead, to dedicate her life to a spiritual purpose, though it was not always clear to her what that would be. She had long since ceased to be concerned with the world's expectations of her, and her meditative and therapeutic experiences meant that there were no limitations on her with regard to Douglas - and it would have been natural for her to enter a relationship based upon freedom - but this was not to be.

Despite the limitations of their access to each other, Shobha's love for Douglas also became her wellspring of joy - from which she drew inspiration – as she was also an inspiration for him. In her love for Douglas - she was true to her own self and did not deviate from that path.

Douglas – though seeking total fulfilment with Shobha in an aesthetic, intellectual, emotional, physical and spiritual way - nevertheless subjugated his personal wish to be with her - for the sake of his family - in which he did not believe - but felt bound by his conditioning - to support.

As he had been abandoned unwillingly in England as a young boy by his parents who lived in Africa, he was not able subsequently to abandon the family he had created (though sorely tempted to do so), in order to be with Shobha in a more complete way.

The Sayings

His quest for the spirit
- I wish I had a soul
- I have learnt a lot from you – in wisdom
- I haven't got it yet - but now and again I get a glimmer of understanding – I need to discover myself
- We are soulmates and I have bared my soul to you today
- You almost convert me to your ideas at times – I have been very influenced by your thoughts
- Tears are the lubricant of the soul

His feelings for Shobha
- You have given me so much happiness
- I feel at peace being with you – I feel at home
- I would be desolate without you and don't know what I would do
- I can't imagine life without you
- I feel so alive I could burst – I am the most fortunate of men
- I feel everything so keenly and feel enlivened by talking to you
- We are the lucky ones
- We are psychological Siamese twins
- Would it surprise you to know, that as I grow older, I find life more exciting - and I find it so because of you - for you share all my enthusiasms
- I have missed you dreadfully – it is unbearable being apart
- I felt a sense of peace descend after seeing you and don't realise how distressed I've been until I see you again
- I regret that I am not younger - so that I could be with you longer

His descriptions of Shobha
- You are my conscience and my heart
- You are a strange creature – woman incarnate
- You are my creature - and I am thine
- You are an enigma
- There is a wholeness and a unity about you

On making love
- Entering you is like entering a new world
- You are nature's glove
- You are at your most beautiful after making love........ radiant
- I am frightened of making love. I feel so vulnerable. I am entering your world
- Why do you cry (after making love) ? A lover must cry (Shobha)
  The tears were usually followed by laughter

- You seem to find such unalloyed pleasure in making love
- You are a happy lover – you become transported
- It is alchemy - making love with you – it is magic
- You cannot talk about two people being separate - when making love
- I can't imagine a more liberated woman
- Let me play upon you – like a harp

On the effect of the relationship
- It only happens once in a lifetime - to love
- When you are in love, you cannot imagine anyone else
- Between us there is the highest intimacy that can exist between a man and a woman
- I am closer to you than I have ever been to anyone
- We are on the same wavelength - we have an affinity
- Weekends without you are like life without salt
- I don't think many people talk together as intimately as we do
- When we are together, we are really together - totally with each other - that is rare
- Sometimes when we are very close - we break new ground and have great insights
- We are foils for each other - a provocation, a challenge, an inspiration
- When I am away from you - I am refreshing myself for you
- You are the most important person in my life
- I believe I love you more than you do
- You are the only one who knows me

S.C.

Chapter 18 – beyond

Then shall you truly dance

For life and death are one
even as the river and the sea are one

For what is it to die

but to stand naked in the wind
and to melt into the sun

Only when you drink from the river of silence
shall you indeed sing

And when the earth shall claim your limbs
then shall you truly dance

Gibran

If you love it is a small death

If you love very deeply it is a great death

If you are really in love
you are no more the same
as you were before

Something has disappeared
and you are reborn

Bhagwan

•

Perhaps on my deathbed
I might come to believe there is something more

Douglas

•

I saw a bright light which was like a revelation and a transformation.

I felt I might die and was surprised to feel that it might be pleasant to do so.

I never realised how pleasant it would be to die.

*After Douglas' near-death experience on the operating table
some months before he slipped sideways*

Douglas

The union of opposites
(unio mystica)

Before Douglas and Shobha met, Douglas had devoted much of his life to excellence of mind and body and was something of an athlete. Shobha by contrast, had focused on her emotional and spiritual life. Together they formed a complete whole and learnt from each other.

Shobha was already intellectually-oriented and was encouraged by Douglas to engage in more rigorous discussion, though it was never mentioned. She also learnt to swim far out to sea and to climb a little, and by so doing, redressed some of her inexperience regarding physical activities - apart from her love of free dance and spontaneous bursts of athleticism.

Over time, Douglas came to appreciate the importance of touch, the primacy of love in life and the possibility of having a soul - which he had not previously entertained seriously - due to an absence of any experience in, or exposure to, this dimension.

In the east and in recent decades in the west – those on the path of *meditation*, have come to view spiritual *enlightenment* as a goal to be experienced or achieved. For those on the path of *love* however - the concept of enlightenment is irrelevant, and *celebration* is the order of the day. That is - celebration of the here and now - of what already exists - without the need to realise any further goal.

Slipping sideways

Although the difference in ages between Douglas and Shobha did not affect them directly for many years, it became apparent to Shobha that Douglas might leave her in the physical sense - due to illness or age.

She had been steeped for fifty years in the tenets of eastern mysticism - which accept that death is an illusion, so it was apparent to Shobha at least - that they were *old souls* i.e. they had known each other before in other lives, and there would be continuity of their spirits beyond the body. Nevertheless, she was still apprehensive - due to Douglas' frequent absences in the present, as well as in the possible future.

However, as time progressed, and particularly during the last years of Douglas' physical life - and given that many of their difficulties together had been resolved. They were at peace with one another, and the prospect of Douglas slipping sideways, became less terrible. Rather an adventure to be embraced. And one which Shobha herself would be facing - in due course.

It was therefore a great surprise to her, to find - that when Douglas did depart for another realm - it was not the shock she had anticipated.

Though it was a blessing for Shobha to be able to spend the last few days of Douglas' life with him exclusively (as N. had been admitted to hospital for treatment), and they were able to spend the last night of his life together, though Shobha was not fully aware that he was *dying*.

Nevertheless, acting intuitively, Shobha –

- removed all trace of her presence from Douglas' home as she felt this might be her last opportunity to do so, and
- requested Douglas' doctor to visit - to reassure Douglas that all that could be done had been done

But unaccountably, she did not consciously realise he was going to die. The doctor gave no intimation to her that death was imminent and did not suggest any course of action. Douglas told the doctor he was *in love* with Shobha and she was a wonderful woman. He remarked to Shobha with tears in his eyes after the doctor had left, that it was amazing that he had finally acknowledged his love for her - to someone.

To this point, it seems Douglas had not declared their love verbally and openly to anyone - unlike Shobha who had let her friends know - from day one. However, Shobha became aware - after Douglas' departure – that most of the legal community of which Douglas was a member, knew of their relationship.

Everything that happened in the last few days seemed to be blessed. They were able to spend their last night together in gentle tenderness. Only once before, when N. was overseas had they been able to spend time together overnight. But of most importance - Shobha's fervent wish (expressed a million times in her heart) was to be with Douglas when he passed over, and this was granted.

For a mystic, the moment of leaving the body is the ultimate moment in life - and all that has gone before has simply been a preparation for that moment. Although Shobha had feared this moment for so long - when it came - she was not afraid. Douglas told her there was a beautiful girl standing beside him, and Shobha later realised that a spirit guide was present - *to take him home.*

Since that time, she has felt his presence with her in an almost constant way, and received many communications from him, which confirm he has adjusted to his new state and will remain in contact with her - whenever she wishes him to be there.

It was only after Douglas 'slipped sideways', that Shobha felt for the first time - she was living simultaneously in the realm of 'spirit' and the material world. So she did not feel Douglas was absent. In fact, he had become more present (to her) than ever before.

Intimations of Immortality

Shobha's dream – 'Peace at last'

Shobha received many intimations of Douglas' presence after his departure.

She consulted a medium on two occasions, and without being permitted to speak, was given detailed accounts by Douglas of what was happening to him, and there were many messages for her, relating to their love, and regrets from Douglas that he had not been able to be with her completely, as they were soulmates. She was also given specific instructions regarding the publication of this book and other projects to honour their love.

Of particular importance to them both, was their love of music - especially the violin, which Douglas had played in his youth. Shobha heard the Paganini Violin Concerto in D major on the car radio on a number of occasions during the weeks following Douglas' physical departure - often when she had consciously asked Douglas to come to her - and usually on the way to the beach at 5 am in the morning.

Douglas had wanted Shobha to purchase a new car as her old one was wearing out. The moment she stepped into the new car and turned on the radio to see how it worked - the Paganini concerto came on full blast.

So many times, he came to her with the violin, playing their favourite music. At first she recorded these instances, but gave up doing so - as they happened so frequently. Until that time, Shobha had rarely listened to the radio, and had not noticed any music for the violin when driving to the beach.

In some ways, it was easier than it had been before, because there was no sense of division or separation or withholding from each other. They were both now in a sense, free - to be all that they could ever be - to each other.

Because they lived apart during their time together, it was now easier to be apart in the bodily sense. They were so used to it. What had changed was *Douglas* - for now he understood Shobha's perception of the world and its purpose. During his earthly existence, he did not - and Shobha longed for a sympathy of minds on spiritual matters - which was not then possible.

For fifty years, Shobha read everything she could obtain, which attempted to describe what happened to the spirit when the body falls away. She also engaged in many meditations and sessions with spiritualists and mystics to explore this dimension.

This was her natural interest, but was also (as an anthropologist), encompassed by her research into eastern mysticism in western countries for her doctoral thesis. She did not complete her research, due to her decision to stay in India.

As a consequence of her practice of meditation for over forty years, it was Shobha's understanding, that leaving the body was an experience upon which we all must embark, and those who have gone before, assure us we will be given every opportunity to understand what is to come, so we do not fear the transition to a non-physical realm - but embrace it as the next stage of the journey.

Now that Douglas has *slipped sideways*, Shobha has become more intimately associated, through spiritualist connections, with what she considers to be a *parallel universe* which co-exists with the material world - but has no physical form.

Communication between the worlds is possible for anyone who is interested, but many are not - and therefore the spiritual world will remain closed to them, until they have a similar desire for this type of experience and understanding.

Our birth is but a sleep and a forgetting

The soul that rises with us – our life's star
hath had elsewhere its setting
and cometh from afar

Not in entire forgetfulness
and not in utter nakedness
but trailing clouds of glory do we come

William Wordsworth – Intimations of Immortality

The words of the song *The Wheel of Karma* - which Shobha composed thirty years before (three years after meeting Douglas) – now became a reality.

> Do you ever get the feeling that we've met somewhere before
> in the dim and distant corners of your mind ?
>
> Do you ever wonder why it is our hearts are in rapport
> and the love we feel inside us seems to bind
> and melt our hearts together as if we were as one
> through the ever-changing scenes before our eyes ?
>
> Do you think we've been this way some time ago - my friend ?
> Can you see it written clearly in the skies ?
>
> There's a time and there's a reason
> for the things we choose to do
> There's a meaning in the movement of the wind
>
> Just as you and I stand here today upon this planet green
> so the wheel of karma softly turns and spins
> Yes - the wheel of karma softly turns and spins
>
> We are told that time is running out - make haste - for all is lost
> The bomb will surely end our lives they say
> Yet when I look into your eyes across the distant years
> time means nothing if we live our lives today
>
> When my spirit leaves my body I will still dance gaily on
> and I'll share with you my laughter and my tears
> Do you think our love can end when together we belong
> when we've shared our hopes our sorrows and our fears ………

> There is no tomorrow and there's no yesterday
> just this moment knowing you are near
> Knowing that our love will ever live within our hearts
> even though our bodies disappear

*

Celebration

In the sixties, new age** guru and British philosopher Alan Watts wrote his magnum opus *The Book on the Taboo against Knowing who You Are*. In the time he was alluding to the situation where men and women search here and there for understanding as to the meaning of life, when a remembrance of their own divinity, is all that is required – a realisation that there is nowhere to go and there is nothing to achieve. According to Watts and many mystics - all is already as it should be - despite our desire to make it otherwise - and realising this - is in fact - *enlightenment*. Again - so simple – as all profound truths seem to be.

** *New age* in the sixties, seventies and since that time, refers to a variety of spiritual practices and philosophies adopted in western countries by those who were and are loose members of a counter-culture which questions the dominant and often materialistic values of urbanised society and offers an alternative lifestyle.

Bhagwan - as a spiritual master, conveyed similar insights (based upon his own experience), to his friends from around the world, who gathered in his ashram.

His first words to Shobha when they met were "*You belong to the stars. You are divine – it is only a question of remembrance*". Later he reiterated to her that "*The doubt that you are not already home*" is the only barrier which prevents understanding. This was a pivotal moment for Shobha, and since that time - though the remembrance is occasionally lost for a moment (or two) – it always returns.

In Australia and in the ashram. Shobha pursued the path of meditation for some years - before realising she was by nature attuned to the path of love - not meditation. Finding her path, she discovered, was a question of innate predisposition – not of choice.

On the path of love, the merging of the male and female *on the outside* in *love* - is said by the mystics, to result in the discovery of the male and female elements *within ourselves* i.e. the *anima* and *animus* concepts of the Swiss psychoanalyst *Carl Jung*, and the *Unio Mystica* of the Sufi poet Hakim Sanai. When this process has happened - the journey is complete. The meshing and melding and merging of our male and female within, is the *end of the quest*. Then all that is left – is celebration.

During their thirty-three years together, Shobha and Douglas did not share their time with anyone else. They were always alone. They were always alone. They did not mingle at the ocean in the early morning or speak to one another in the presence of others except on rare occasions. Because they were either exclusively in each other's company or communicated in writing or by phone, their inner world became more real than the outer world.

For this reason, when Douglas decided to leave the planet, it was easier for Shobha to accept his absence, as they had, in many respects, already found joy, in a reality that was not dependent upon physical presence.

Early in their association, Douglas remarked to Shobha "I have always admired those with spiritual conviction. but as I have not had those experiences myself, I cannot pretend to be in the same fold. It is not a matter of my choosing." However - in his latter years, after a near-death-experience on the operating table, he became more receptive to the possibility of something which was beyond the material world.

We are angels
We have forgotten these things

Trailing clouds of glory
Remembering

The words Bhagwan had spoken to Shobha
over forty years earlier
when she became a sannyasin
were now a constant reminder to her
of that other reality.

Your destiny is far beyond
You are divine
It is only a question of remembrance
You belong to the stars

*

And the words of the Sufi poet Hakim Sanai
resounded constantly in her ears

Remember - this is work entrusted

Remember beloved - we shall

meet again

Illustrations

Cover : The Rapture of Psyche – William-Adolphe Bougeureau – 1895

The Meeting
- Douglas and Shobha – the only photo taken of them together
- Meditation in the ashram
- Bhagwan Shree Rajneesh
- Douglas with his beloved red setter Ned

The Letters
1. *The painter's honeymoon* – Lord Frederic Leighton – 1864

The Lovers
    Taj Mahal – Agra, India
2. *In bed* – Henri Toulouse Lautrec – 1892
    The first photo of Douglas by Shobha
    The first and only photo of Shobha by Douglas (in his garden)

Where words fail – music speaks
3. *Tristan and Isolde* (detail with harp) – Edmund Blair Leighton – 1902

Your body is the harp of your soul
- Sacred (tantric) lovers - temple of Khajaraho (Madhya Pradesh – India, circa 1000)
4. *Lovers* – Lucius Rossi (1846-1913)
5. *The Kiss* (marble) Auguste Rodin – 1882
- *Je t'adore* (I adore you) – Artist : Ayad Alqaragholli – bronze sculpture commissioned by Shobha in 2016 to honour the beach community of which Douglas and Shobha were members for fifty and thirty-five years respectively

Chapter 1 – You were born together
6-10   Sketches by Edmund Joseph Sullivan (1913) for the *Rubaiyat of Omar Khayyam* (c. 1100)
11.   *Psyche and Eros* (marble) – Antonio Canova – 1793

Chapter 2 – When love beckons to you
12. *Apollo and Daphne* – John William Waterhouse – 1908
- Mr. Tickle – soft toy given by Shobha to Douglas
13. *Dr Johnson arguing* (Samuel Johnson by Sir Joshua Reynolds) - circa 1770
- Douglas after climbing Bluff Knoll in the Stirling ranges in Western Australia
- Douglas running along the beach in the early morning

Chapter 3 – A song of praise upon your lips
- Shobha with the Ovation guitar given to her by Douglas
14. *Abelard and his pupil Heloise* – Edmund Blair Leighton – 1882

Chapter 4 – A prayer for the beloved in your heart
15. *Beata Beatrix* – Dante Gabriel Rosetti – 1860
- *The Consecration of Parsifal by Gurnemanz (a knight of the Holy Grail)* artist unknown

Chapter 5 – And think not you can direct the course of love
16. *Miranda* – Tempest : John William Waterhouse – 1916
17. *Acrasia* – John Melhuish Strudwick – 1888

Illustrations (continued)

Chapter 6 – To bleed willingly and joyfully
- 18. *Hero awaiting the return of Leander* : she holds her beacon to light the way, in vain, for Leander to swim across the Hellespont – Evelyn de Morgan – 1885
- Musicians in the ashram came from many countries
- (Shobha singing) by the river near the ashram
- Sufi dancing in the ashram
- Sannyasins celebrating in the ashram
- Silent darshan (Shobha) with Bhagwan
- (Shobha in) darshan with Bhagwan
- Pir Vilayat Khan

Chapter 7 – The pain of too much tenderness
- 19. *Paolo and Francesca da Rimini* – Charles Edward Hallé – c. 1888
- Cartoons appended to Shobha's letters to Douglas
- 20. *Harmony* – Sir Francis Dicksee – 1907
- Shobha in the opera) *La Traviata*
- 21. *The Duet* – George Sheridan Knowles (1853=1931)

Chapter 8 – The deeper sorrow carves into your being
- Bhagwan left his body in January 1990
- 22. *Tristan and Isolde* (knight kneeling in embrace) – Herbert James Draper - circa 1920
- The magic of the river (where Douglas and Shobha used to meet at the university)
- The university gardens
- One of the many bouquets given to Shobha by Douglas

Chapter 9 – Let there be spaces in your togetherness
- 23. *Pleading* (detail) – Sir Lawrence Alma-Tadema – 1876
- (Shobha) about to set off on a tour of England
- The Lake District
- The celebrated gates of New College, Oxford, where Douglas regularly dined in the evenings, when he was a Reader at All Souls' College
- 24. *La belle dame sans merci* – John William Waterhouse – 1893
- Boadicea with her two daughters - J. Havard Thomas (1916) – City Hall, Cardiff, Wales
- 25. Alice (in Wonderland) with flamingo - original illustration – John Tenniel – 1865

Chapter 10 – Sing and dance together and be joyous
- 26. *The minstrel's lady* – George Sheridan Knowles (1863-1931)
- 27. *End of the Quest* (Tristan and Isolde) – Sir Francis Dicksee – 1907

Chapter 11 – In the dew of little things
- 28. *Soul of the Rose* – John William Waterhouse – 1908
- Douglas in the park
- Ramana Maharshi - *Wikipedia*
- *Meera (Mirabhai)* by Giriraj – sixteenth century mystic, poet, singer and devotee of Krishna – the principal Hindu deity (who has been worshipped in India since 400 BCE) : Wikimedia

Chapter 12 – Love knows not its own depth until the hour of separation
- 29. *Romeo and Juliet* – Sir Francis Dicksee – 1884

Chapter 13 – You shall be free indeed
- 30. Woman meditating – *Sergey Nivens – Shutterstock 556314274*

Illustrations (continued)

Chapter 14 – A moving sea between the shores of your souls
    31. *2 Tango* – reproduced with the permission of Vicente Romero Rodondo – 2012
    32. *Robert Burns* by Scottish painter Alexander Nasmyth - 1787
    33. *Accolade* – Lady Guinevere knighting Lancelot - Edmund Blair Leighton – 1901

Chapter 15 – All these things shall love do unto you that you may know the secrets of your heart
    34. *Winged figure* – Abbot Handerson Thayer – 1889

Chapter 16 – The wind bids me leave you
    35. *Into the golden sunset* – William Turner – 1775-1851

Chapter 17 – Sing to me a deeper song
    36. Paolo and Francesca da Rimini – Dante Gabriel Rossetti - 1855
- Douglas and Shobha

Chapter 18 – Then shall you truly dance
- Early morning by the ocean (Shobha) photo *Keeper Creative*
- Douglas in the park
- Shobha's dream - peace at last - their last night together
- Doves in flight – *Canstock* 1743033

Publications and Media

shobhacameron.net
angelicuspub@gmail.com

Bhagwan Shree Rajneesh a.k.a. Osho
Discourses on many spiritual traditions and contemporary issues are available in 650 books, e-books, audio books, CDs and videos (DVDs)

onthelipsoftheinfinite.com

•••

Published by ANGELICUS
Paperback

KISSING THE JOY AS IT FLIES – Letters to the Beloved (2021)
Douglas Payne, Shobha Cameron

YOU BELONG TO THE STARS (2021)
Bhagwan Shree Rajneesh a.k.a. Osho
Shobha Cameron
Douglas Payne, Peta Anderson

•

Published by BHAKTI PRESS

JOURNEY OF A SANNYASIN
Shobha Cameron

IF – A MOTHER TO HER DAUGHTER
(à la Kipling)
Shobha Cameron

SONG OF LOVE
poems of devotion - Shobha Cameron

Kissing the Joy as it Flies

I was deeply touched by the poignant outpouring of your love
over thirty spiritually heartfelt years.

•

This is an epic project
which lays bare your openness and vulnerability
in loving each other so deeply
despite the tremendous obstacles on your path.

•

I had decided I might never fall in love again,
but after reading your book, I feel it might be possible.
You have given me hope.

•

I have just fallen in love after many years of distress,
and I find that every word you write resonates within me,
now that I have found love again.

•

I do not feel many people could achieve in a lifetime,
the special love and relationship you have shared.

•

It is a privilege and an honour to read your book
and to allow us into your world
in such a total uninhibited way.

•

I can see from your letters,
that you lived in a tantric relationship,
where love became so spiritual,
you experienced the divine.

•

I believe your book
will become very significant for others,
long after you are gone.
It will take on a life of its own

IF – a mother to her daughter

I lost a child who was several months old,
and reading your poem
brought back the feeling of loss
in a very poignant way.
It meant a lot to me.
I felt you understood what I had been through
and that is the essence of a poet:
being able to stand in someone's else's shoes,
as if it was their own experience.
Jennifer Parsons

Your book is wonderful.
What a gift to all women. It made me cry.
I am going to give a copy to MY mother.
Katherine Dempsey

I enjoyed how, in the poem *IF*,
you covered the multitude of situations
which can be faced in life – in a positive manner.
Michael Manley

Song of Love

I was again reading your poetry last night.
Many thanks to you for the experience
and all the heartfelt projection of love.
Hanka Bosich

It has been a long time since I have read poetry,
and I found the experience of reading yours,
extremely enjoyable and enlightening.
Michael Manley

Journey of a Sannyasin

There is a lot of wisdom from your experience.
I'm so glad you are now sharing your writings
with the world at large.
Shelley Sayers

I am impressed by your gift for expression
and the beautiful flow of your words.
I wish I could write like that.
Frederick Palmer

I started reading *Journey of a Sannyasin* in the evening
and could not put it down until 4.30 in the morning.
Anne Bradfield

I have started reading *Journey of a Sannyasin*
and am looking forward to completing it.
You have a sincere Sufi-like heart,
and I admire your commitment and tenacity
in completing these volumes.
Alice Winterton

I loved the way you put the various stages of your journey
together with your poems.
Pamela Young

How delighftul, how tender and precious
is the relationship with Bhagwan
that you describe in *Journey of a Sannyasin*.
I am reminded of the smells and sounds of India,
the bird calls at night and the ashram garden.
Barbara Hilton